POLITICAL THEORY OF THE DIGITAL AGE

With the rise of far-reaching technological innovation, from artificial intelligence to Big Data, human life is increasingly unfolding in digital lifeworlds. While such developments have made unprecedented changes to the ways we live, our political practices have failed to evolve at pace with these profound changes. In this pathbreaking work, Mathias Risse establishes a foundation for the philosophy of technology, allowing us to investigate how the digital century might alter our most basic political practices and ideas. Risse engages major concepts in political philosophy and extends them to account for problems that arise in digital lifeworlds, including AI and democracy, synthetic media and surveillance capitalism, and how AI might alter our thinking about the meaning of life. Proactive and profound, *Political Theory of the Digital Age* offers a systemic way of evaluating the effect of AI, allowing us to anticipate and understand how technological developments impact our political lives – before it's too late.

MATHIAS RISSE is the Berthold Beitz Professor in Human Rights, Global Affairs, and Philosophy at Harvard University. He is the author of *On Global Justice* (2012), *Global Political Philosophy* (2012), and *On Justice: Philosophy, History, Foundations* (2020), as well as the coauthor of *On Trade Justice* (2019) and *Holding Together: The Hijacking of Rights in America* and *How to Reclaim Them for Everyone* (2022).

T0371259

Political Theory of the Digital Age

WHERE ARTIFICIAL INTELLIGENCE MIGHT TAKE US

MATHIAS RISSE

Harvard University

CAMBRIDGE
UNIVERSITY PRESS

Shaftesbury Road, Cambridge CB2 8EA, United Kingdom

One Liberty Plaza, 20th Floor, New York, NY 10006, USA

477 Williamstown Road, Port Melbourne, VIC 3207, Australia

314–321, 3rd Floor, Plot 3, Splendor Forum, Jasola District Centre, New Delhi – 110025, India

103 Penang Road, #05–06/07, Visioncrest Commercial, Singapore 238467

Cambridge University Press is part of Cambridge University Press & Assessment, a department of the University of Cambridge.

We share the University's mission to contribute to society through the pursuit of education, learning and research at the highest international levels of excellence.

www.cambridge.org
Information on this title: www.cambridge.org/9781009255219

DOI: 10.1017/9781009255189

First published 2023

A catalogue record for this publication is available from the British Library

A Cataloging-in-Publication data record for this book is available from the Library of Congress

ISBN 978-1-009-25521-9 Hardback
ISBN 978-1-009-25519-6 Paperback

For Kozue

Contents

Preface

It seems probable that once the machine thinking method has started, it would not take long to outstrip our feeble powers ... At some stage therefore we should have to expect the machines to take control.

—Alan Turing[1]

The world of the future will be an ever more demanding struggle against the limitations of our intelligence, not a comfortable hammock in which we can lie down to be waited upon by our robot slaves.

—Norbert Wiener[2]

1 THE NEED TO DO POLITICAL THEORY FOR THE DIGITAL AGE

Political thought explores how we should live together. Our lives increasingly unfold in digitally interconnected ways, and so at this stage, political theory must investigate how to inhabit this digital century. Much innovation in the digital domain is driven by machine learning, a set of methods that analyze the myriads of available data ("Big Data") for trends and inferences. Unlike conventional programs, machine-learning algorithms learn by themselves, drawing on their supply of data. These algorithms are based on so-called "neural networks," programs that imitate the ways in which brain cells interact with each other. Typically, such algorithms are what efforts at creating artificial intelligence (AI) amount to today. Owing to their sophistication and sweeping applications, these techniques are poised to alter our

---

[1] Alan Turing, "'Intelligent Machinery: A Heretical Theory,' a Lecture Given to '51 Society' at Manchester," AMT/B/4, The Turing Digital Archive, https://turingarchive.kings.cam.ac.uk/publications-lectures-and-talks-amtb/amt-b-4, last accessed June 27, 2022.

[2] Wiener, *God & Golem*, 69.

world dramatically. In some circles, there is much enthusiasm about what might be possible: "No objective answer is possible to the question of when an 'it' becomes a 'who,'" writes one engineer, "but for many people, neural nets running on computers are likely to cross this threshold in the very near future."[3]

At the time of writing, the production of AI models appears to be moving into its own kind of industrial age, much beyond earlier stages when these models were more artisanal and speculative. These advances have drawn on breakthroughs from around 2010 – in the words of a Google Senior Vice President for Research, "the 2010s were truly a golden decade of deep learning research and progress"[4] – when computers became powerful enough to run enormously large machine-learning models and the Internet started to provide the humungous amount of training data such algorithms require to go through their learning process. Since then, conceptual breakthroughs in programming have led to the creation of ever more complex and sophisticated software – and the supercomputers required to enable the most advanced AI models to unfold their full power have become so expensive that, short of well-funded governmental AI strategies in the wealthiest countries, the field is likely to end up being dominated by the research agendas of private companies with substantial resources.

Regarding *specialized AI*, at the high end, one may think of algorithms winning at chess or Go – where the point is not only that AI beats human players, but the stunning progression of how that has happened: Initially AI drew lessons from the history of human play, then it played against itself, yet later AI taught itself the rules of the games, and eventually it created systems that could learn and win at multifarious games (all of which happened within a few years). Still at the high end, one might also think of speech recognition and natural language processing, including the emergence of large language models capable of generating human-like products. But leaving such high-end technology aside, specialized AI already operates in multifarious everyday devices. In contrast to such distinctly specialized operations, *general AI* approximates human performance across domains. Once there is general AI smarter than us, it might well produce something smarter than itself, and so on, perhaps very fast. That moment is known as the *singularity*, an intelligence explosion that could alter the course of human history in ways nothing else has ever done. In opening his 2021 BBC Reith Lectures ("Living with Artificial Intelligence"), Stuart Russell declares "the eventual emergence of general-purpose Artificial Intelligence [to be] the biggest event in human history" (regardless of whether such emergence is precipitated by an intelligence explosion).[5]

---

[3] Agüera y Arcas, "Do Large Language Models Understand Us?" 183. For the state of the art in AI research and of the discussions of its ethical dimensions and impact on societies as of spring 2022, see Manyika, *AI & Society, Spring 2022 Issue of Daedalus*; Liang and Bommasani, "On the Opportunities and Risks of Foundation Models."

[4] Dean, "A Golden Decade of Deep Learning," 69.

[5] "The Reith Lectures: Living with Artificial Intelligence," BBC, www.bbc.co.uk/programmes/m001216k, last accessed June 27, 2022.

To be sure, the possibility, nature, and likelihood of a singularity remain intensely disputed, and we are nowhere near anything like it. But "nowhere near" might mean in terms of engineering capacities rather than time. A few major break-throughs – and the recent past is certainly full of breakthroughs, and here one might think again of the advances in game-playing and language-processing just mentioned – could radically transform the field. (As a Microsoft Chief Technology Officer wrote in 2022, "I have been surprised so many times over the past two decades by what AI scientists and researchers have been able to accomplish that I have learned to heed the second half of Arthur C. Clarke's first law: When a distinguished but elderly scientist states that something is possible, they are almost certainly right. When they state that something is impossible, they are very probably wrong."[6]) Engagement with these developments from a standpoint of political theory is inevitably constrained by their evolving nature. But while an intelligence explosion would undoubtedly revolutionize politics (to put it mildly), many questions for political thought already arise from the increasing presence of digital technology across domains all around us.

To be sure, often these questions are not fundamentally new but have assumed fresh relevance or need to be rethought. We must do political theory for the digital age. And eventually this age might transform into an entirely new world populated with new kinds of superintelligences. My starting point is the liberal-egalitarian outlook articulated by John Rawls and others. Using this outlook *as a starting point* does not mean that at any moment in this book it would be sensible to ask, "And what would Rawls say about this?" There is too much novelty to the problems we encounter here for that to be sensible. At the same time, every journey into new territory must start from somewhere. Notwithstanding its attractions as an innovative approach to the problems of our time, the liberal-egalitarian outlook has neglected two themes that are becoming increasingly important in our digital century.[7] The first (more general) theme is the distinctive importance of technology for political thought. The second (rather specific) one is the roles of citizens as *knowers* and *knowns* – that is, as both holders and providers of "data" and "information," to use two of the defining terms of our age. And, of course, the possible advent of superintelligences is not on the radar of Rawls's theory at all.

There is nothing to bar liberal-egalitarian thought from paying more attention to technology, to recognize it as a domain that creates philosophical problems all its own, rather than derivative ones. Putting these problems on the agenda of liberal-egalitarian thought ushers in authors from traditions that have made technology

---

[6] Scott, "I Do Not Think It Means What You Think It Means," 83.

[7] That outlook must be supplemented in other ways, especially through the addition of racial themes, which many authors have noticed and on which I have written myself in Risse, *On Justice.*

central: phenomenology and especially Marxism, which has put technology front and center all along in ways that I think all traditions of political thought should now. The Marxist tradition makes frequent appearances in this book. Similarly, nothing in liberal-egalitarian thought sits uneasily with an explicit articulation of matters of epistemic justice and epistemic rights (justice and rights to the extent that they are concerned with what people may know and what may be known of them). But epistemic justice has been theorized largely outside of the liberal-egalitarian tradition, and epistemic rights is a rather new topic anyway. Here too an adequate articulation within liberal-egalitarian thought requires turning to authors who have done relevant work, in this case especially Michel Foucault and writers in the Science, Technology, and Society (STS) tradition. The possible advent of super-intelligences requires new conversations altogether, no matter how speculative they would be for now.

This book means to help set an agenda in a new domain of inquiry where things have been moving fast. Michael Rosen once referred to political theory as "the oasis where the caravans meet."[8] Political *philosophy* differs from political *theory* by focusing on the depth of arguments made in and about the political domain, holding at bay not only much of the societal background but also other kinds of inquiry that might bear on the questions at hand. Political theory is more broadly oriented and manages its trade-offs differently, tending to integrate more breadth at the expense of in-depth investigations of ideas. At this stage, in the process of transferring political thought to the digital domain, it is important to take the more comprehensive view of political theory rather than the narrower one of political philosophy to make sure we transfer the debates in their full richness into this new era. Accordingly, "political theory" is in the title of this book.

This book aims to create a better footing for the philosophy of technology and for discussions around epistemic rights and justice in the liberal-egalitarian outlook, as a way of helping to bring into the digital era – the era of AI and Big Data, and possibly the age of the singularity – the debates that have traditionally preoccupied political thinkers. In this spirit, my focus is on themes rather than authors. Inevitably, the kind of work that needs to be done here creates some strange-bedfellow phenomena that generate questions about the compatibility of these authors. But one feature of the way in which the advent of AI affects political thought – and this is one of the main points I hope to make, by the very manner I approach my topics – is that the relationship among various traditions must be reassessed. Still, the grounding in the Rawlsian approach is the guide to creating coherence and sets the stage for the broader conversations to unfold.

---

[8] Rosen, *Dignity*, xvi.

2 THE RAWLSIAN STARTING POINT (AND THE CONNECTIONS TO MARX)

Let me explain the basics of the Rawlsian starting point, with an eye on the relationship of its central elements to Marxist thinking. Rawls is of historical importance for political theory because he offers a complex account of distributive justice that integrates many ideas about how to organize society from the preceding two centuries or so. During this period, industrialized societies were becoming sufficiently interconnected to generate a new level of questioning about the absolute and relative statuses of different groups in society. "Social justice" emerged as an area for both political mobilization and intellectual inquiry.

Originally developed in his 1971 book *A Theory of Justice*, Rawls's theory of *justice as fairness* envisions a society of free and equal citizens holding equal basic rights and cooperating within an economic system that is egalitarian in certain respects.[9] Citizens are free in that each person feels entitled to make claims on institutions. Citizens are also free in being able to take responsibility for their lives (if provided with suitable opportunities and resources). Citizens are equal by virtue of having no artificial constraints imposed on their capacities to participate in social cooperation over a lifetime. Rawls aims to describe a just arrangement of major political and social institutions of a liberal society: political constitution, legal system, economy, family, and so on. Their arrangement is the *basic structure*. Individuals are supposed to cooperate within its confines. Compliance is enforced, through police, courts, and other agencies.

There are multifarious ways of organizing the basic structure. Different rules favor different groups by increasing that group's chances of seizing larger shares of the social product. Rawls insists that nobody *deserves* to be born with social advantages or disadvantages, or to be more or less gifted than others. For this reason, citizens are not at a deeper level entitled to having rules of cooperation that let them benefit from such assets. To be sure, any social system generates legitimate expectations: If someone performs in accordance with standards within the system, they can legitimately demand the rewards anticipated by those standards. But nobody is entitled to a society arranged in such a way that *their* talents generate large shares of the social product. After all, society's rules should be acceptable to everybody. In light of the characteristics of the basic structure that we just observed, Rawls submits that all social primary goods – cooperatively produced under conditions where compliance is enforced – are to be distributed equally *unless* unequal distribution works to everyone's benefit.

A division of labor occurs within the institutions that make up the basic structure. These institutions distribute the main benefits and burdens of social life, the *social primary goods*. These goods are basic rights and liberties; freedom of movement and free choice among a wide range of occupations; powers of offices and positions of

---

[9]   The 1999 revised edition is now commonly used. See Rawls, *A Theory of Justice*.

responsibility; income and wealth; as well as the social bases of self-respect, the recognition by social institutions that gives citizens a sense of self-worth and confidence to execute their plans.[10] Recognizing social primary goods as the subject (or the *distribuenda*) of a contemporary theory of distributive justice reveals the sheer range of things we provide to each other through joint activities at the level of society as a whole.

For Rawls, distributive justice requires substantially equal political and civil liberties and fair equality of opportunity in education, while economic inequalities within these constraints are permitted only if they are to everybody's benefit, especially to the benefit of the least advantaged. More specifically, Rawls proposes the following principles of distributive justice. The first – which deals with political status – states that each person has the same indefeasible claim to a fully adequate scheme of equal basic liberties, a scheme that is compatible with the same scheme of liberties for all. The second principle – which deals with relative economic standing – falls into two parts. The first part states that social and economic inequalities are to be attached to offices and positions that are open to all under conditions of *fair equality of opportunity*. The second states that remaining social and economic inequalities should be to the greatest benefit of the least-advantaged members of society (*Difference Principle*).[11] Fulfilment of the first principle, on political status, takes priority over the second. Within the second, fair equality of opportunity takes priority over the Difference Principle.

Theorizing social justice in an era of political and economic interdependence means recognizing the extent to which our lives are shared. Rawls's principles combine and rank different ideas. Rawls does not defend one idea as central to social justice but integrates various approaches from the nineteenth and twentieth centuries. Ideas about what people deserve and ideas about what people need are present, but so are liberty and equality. A recognition of the breadth of the domain to which considerations of distributive justice apply comes with a sense that no unitary criterion can guide the distribution. The first principle secures equal citizenship for each person by protecting civil and political liberties, a protection that also goes far in securing for each citizen similarly effective influence on political processes. The first part of the second principle makes sure that one's prospects do not vary given the segment of society one happens to be born into. The second part guarantees that the group that makes the largest concession vis-à-vis a baseline of equality makes as small a concession as feasible. The way of ascertaining whether such an arrangement has been achieved is to identify other feasible arrangements and determine if the respectively least advantaged *in one of those arrangements* would be better off than they are in the current arrangements. If they are, we should switch to that arrangement.

---

[10] Rawls, *Restatement*, 58f.
[11] Rawls, 41–43. It is called the Difference Principle because it regulates differences among citizens.

Rawls uses utilitarianism as a foil. Utilitarianism is associated with authors such as Jeremy Bentham, John Stuart Mill, and now Peter Singer and is influential among economists and policymakers. Utilitarianism identifies right action with maximization of collective well-being. By contrast, Rawls does not think such maximization is the correct response to the task of devising a society that free and equal citizens could respectfully coinhabit. Rawls connects to the Kantian tradition, in which respectful treatment of each person (rather than goals formulated at the collective level) is the driving theme. Social primary goods are goods generated through cooperation. Accordingly, their distribution should be justifiable to all. But no distribution would be so justifiable if any individual could be expected to make enormous sacrifices for the sake of social improvements, as utilitarianism implies.

Rawls distinguishes five types of institutional arrangements:[12] laissez-faire capitalism (a political economy defined around the private ownership of the means of production, with very limited state interference mostly to guarantee public safety and other basic forms of protection); welfare-state capitalism (which differs from laissez-faire capitalism by providing assistance or payments to low-income citizens, and thus includes redistributive elements that could come in a variety of forms); state socialism with command economy (where the state owns and regulates the means of production); democratic socialism (which shares with state socialism this commitment to no private ownership of means of production, but where control over firms is widely dispersed); and property-owning democracy (where it is private ownership of means of production that is widely dispersed). For Rawls, social justice requires either democratic socialism or property-owning democracy. Most tellingly, in addition to laissez-faire capitalism, he rejects welfare-state capitalism, because it condones substantial inequalities in the initial distribution of property and skill endowments, merely *re*-distributing some income ex-post. This undermines the ideal of equal citizenship.

Unlike the Marxist tradition, Rawls does not think capitalism's ills are beyond the reach of reform. The response to tensions within capitalist production is not necessarily to envisage a society that leaves behind capitalism. The response is to offer, and realize, a better ideal of justice based on a sensible understanding of society as an interconnected system in which benefits from cooperation must be assigned fairly. In terms of institutional reform, this might take us to either a property-owning democracy (a reformed capitalist system) or democratic socialism (a version of collective control that is highly emancipatory by distributing control widely). Also, Marx sees class conflict as the driving political theme in society and revolution as the only way of resolving class conflict. Marx has a simplistic notion of conflict in industrial societies. But he also thinks conflict can, and inevitably will, be overcome. As I explain later, Rawls has a more complex understanding of these conflicts that societies face today. And he does not think the conflicts can be, or even

---

[12] Rawls, Part IV.

ought to be, overcome. Instead, they must be handled properly. The notion that does the crucial work in this regard is *public reason*.[13]

Public reason requires citizens to be able to justify decisions on fundamental political issues to each other using publicly available values and standards. In such contexts, the expectation is that citizens seek to find reasons that are compelling to others (whom they acknowledge as equals); in doing so, citizens should be both aware that others have different commitment and equipped with some sense of what those commitments are. The kind of fundamental issues Rawls has in mind here include questions about which religions to tolerate, who has the right to vote, who is eligible to own property, and what are suspect classifications for discrimination in hiring. These are what Rawls calls constitutional essentials and matters of basic justice, including the principles of distributive justice themselves. Public reason functions differently from "comprehensive moral doctrines," which are comprehensive in providing guidance across the whole range of questions that arise in human interactions. The major world religions are examples. The standpoint of public reason only applies to the much more limited context of fundamental issues about which citizens are expected to debate *as* citizens.

The crucial conflicts about such fundamental issues that societies face today are, first, disputes about how the goods of economic production and other advantages from interconnected life in modern societies are shared out, and then also disputes about the degree to which the rules of interaction favor conflicting conceptions of the good. The latter kind of conflict arises because public spaces must be shared among adherents of different doctrines with deep metaphysical and epistemological disagreements. After millennia of intellectual investigations and disputes (and now also with a deeper understanding of moral and evolutionary psychology that teaches much about how values enter people's lives), we realize that people inevitably and enduringly interpret human experiences differently. It is a significant step to think about conflicts that arise in living arrangements the way Rawls does: as clashes among competing ideas about both comprehensive doctrines and the sharing out of societal advantages that are unavoidable but not profoundly problematic if managed correctly, through an appeal to suitable conceptions of public reason and distributive justice.

This Rawlsian view is our starting point. It makes regular appearances throughout and thus brings coherence to the outlook presented here. It provides useful guidance for the digital age. But the subject matter demands that many other authors and viewpoints also enter, including some that normally do not appear in inquiries framed by this Rawlsian outlook. Again, this book deals with questions that could not be on Rawls's radar or on the radar of the generation of scholars after him that expanded the outlook. These questions were not much on my own radar when I took Rawls's theory as a starting point for perspectives on global justice.[14]

[13] Rawls, *Political Liberalism*.
[14] Risse, *On Global Justice*; Risse, *On Justice*.

So, despite offering that starting point again in this book, there are chapters in which Rawlsian theory does not enter at all.

Comparisons to Marx have already made an appearance. And while I use the Marxist tradition sometimes in contrast and often as a corrective to the liberal-egalitarian tradition, all this is instructive only because these traditions share quite a bit. One commonality is the conceptualization of society as an intensely interconnected endeavor with cooperative and coercive elements that must be arranged the right way (and whose proper arrangement can be understood from a suitable theoretical angle). In addition, Marx himself also acknowledges a recognizable public-reason standpoint. We can see this by looking at his important 1843 essay "On the Jewish Question."[15]

That essay responded to contemporary writer Bruno Bauer's claim that it was incoherent for Jews to ask for religious toleration. Bauer argued that, since religious toleration granted equal standing to multiple religions, Jews could demand toleration only if they saw Judaism as one religion among others. (A similar point would then apply to other religious or secular views about the good life, though that was neither Bauer's nor Marx's concern.) Marx replied that asking for toleration only implied accepting that the difference among views of the good life was politically and legally irrelevant. This standpoint involves distinguishing between what Marx calls "the point of view of a man" and "the point of view of a citizen." It is from the former (suitably generalized across genders) that one would make decisions about one's life. The point of view of the citizen should be adopted when making certain decisions in political life, such as, in Rawls's view, decisions about constitutional essentials and questions of basic justice. Marx's point of view of the citizen, accordingly, is a public-reason standpoint.[16]

3 SUMMARY OF THE BOOK, CHAPTER BY CHAPTER

1 *Introduction: Digital Lifeworlds in Human History*

This chapter takes stock of the current situation confronting political theory. I introduce the concept of *digital lifeworlds* and explain its relevance in the narrative of humanity. I use Max Tegmark's distinctions between Life 1.0, 2.0, and 3.0, respectively, for guidance in locating digital lifeworlds in history. We do not know

---

[15] McLellan, *Karl Marx: Selected Writings*, 46–70.

[16] To be sure, the similarities only go so far, since the second main point of Marx's essay is to insist that the political emancipation that comes from the adoption of the standpoint of the citizen is insufficient for genuinely human emancipation. For this standpoint left individuals divided within themselves (between those two outlooks) and separated from each other by differences of religion and class. True human emancipation, for Marx, requires elimination of both forms of alienation. By contrast, Rawls accepts such conflicts as unavoidable features of modern life. Chapter 8 returns to "On the Jewish Question." For discussion of the relationship between Marx and Rawls, see Scanlon, "Some Main Points in Rawls' Theory of Justice."

if Life 3.0 (the kind of life that designs both its culture and physical shape, the physical shape of individuals) will ever arise. But if it does, it will be from within digital lifeworlds – lifeworlds that already fundamentally change our lives and thus require intense scrutiny even if there will never be a Life 3.0. To understand these lifeworlds, we need appropriate notions of "data," "information," and "knowledge" and characterize the connections among them. To that end, we enlist Fred Dretske's understanding of knowledge in terms of flow of information. Such a notion of knowledge allows for a broader range of knowers than humans (to whom classical analyses were limited): It includes both animals and artificially intelligent beings as knowers. I also draw on Luciano Floridi's work on the philosophy of information for a related look at digital lifeworlds from a more detached standpoint ("infospheres populated by inforgs").

2 Learning from the Amish: Political Philosophy As Philosophy of Technology in the Digital Century

The Amish are an unusual case of a community intensely concerned with maintaining control over how technology shapes its future. Though the community's old-fashioned ways strike many people as perplexing, in the age of AI, there are good reasons as to why technology and its regulation should be just about as central to mainstream politics as they are to the way the Amish regulate their affairs. Technology is not neutral, as many still think, but is intensely political. This also means that political philosophy and philosophy of technology should be more closely related than they typically are. In fact, mainstream philosophy of technology has unfolded largely separately from mainstream political philosophy. The primary exception is the Marxist tradition that has long investigated the role of technology in the dialectical unfolding of history as Marx theorizes it (including, in the case of figures such as Herbert Marcuse, an investigation of the use of technology in the thwarting of Marx's own predictions). This chapter uses the Marxist tradition to identify three senses in which technology is political (the foundational, enframing, and interactive senses) and argues that the Rawlsian tradition also has good reason to recognize versions of these senses. In an era of AI and other technological innovation, political philosophy must always also be philosophy of technology.

3 Artificial Intelligence and the Past, Present, and Future of Democracy

Modern democracies involve structures for collective choice that periodically empower relatively few people to steer the social direction for everybody. As in all forms of governance, technology shapes how this unfolds. Political theorists have typically treated democracy as an ideal or an institutional framework, instead of considering its *materiality*, the manner in which democratic possibilities are to some extent shaped by the objects needed to implement them. Specialized AI changes the materiality of democracy, not just in the sense that independently given actors now deploy different tools. AI changes how collective decision-making unfolds and what its human participants are like.

This chapter reflects on the past, present, and future of democracy and embeds into these basic reflections an exploration of the challenges and promises of AI for democracy in this digital century. We explore specifically how to design AI to harness the public sphere, political power, and economic power for democratic purposes. Thereby, this chapter also continues the discussion from Chapter 2 by developing how technology is political in the foundational sense. This chapter also investigates current questions about how AI could threaten or enrich the democratic processes of the present. Only in Chapter 11 do we ask if superintelligences might in due course themselves be part of a democratic process. Nonetheless, many themes of subsequent chapters already make an appearance here.

4 *Truth Will Not Set You Free: Is There a Right to It Anyway? Elaborating on the* Work Public Reason Does *in Life 2.0*

We first explore how damaging untruth can be, especially in digital lifeworlds. Digital lifeworlds generally create possibilities for spreading information at a pace and volume unheard of in analog contexts. But misinformation and disinformation spread the same way, which greatly enhances how individuals can tell stories about themselves or have them substantiated in echo chambers in the company of like-minded people. This set of considerations provides support for a right to truth. However, next we see that untruth is immensely important to people's lives. It is not just that people fail to have a preference for truth, but rather that untruth plays a significant role as an enabler of valued psychological and social dynamics. The considerations that pull into the opposite direction notwithstanding, there can therefore be no comprehensive right to truth.

Contrary to a well-known Bible verse, for most people it is anyway not the truth that sets them free. It is acceptance of worldviews in likeminded company that does so (worldviews, or comprehensive moral doctrines, which tend to contain plenty of untruths), in any event if being set free means having an orientation in the world. But that there can be no such *comprehensive* right is consistent with there being a right to truth *in specific contexts*. And to be sure, protecting the public sphere (as introduced in Chapter 3) for the exercise of citizenship from a public-reason standpoint means the state must protect truth telling and sanction untruth. But typically, as we conclude, the moral concern behind truthfulness is in this context not best captured in terms of an actual right to truth.

5 *Knowing and Being Known: Investigating Epistemic Entitlement in Digital Lifeworlds*

Michel Foucault problematizes the relationship between knowledge and power in ways that more traditional epistemology has not, with power always already shaping what we consider knowledge. To capture the nexus between power and knowledge, he introduces the term "episteme" (for the totality of what is considered knowledge at a given time, how it is obtained, by what rules it is structured, and how all that is shaped by power relations of sorts). The significance of an era's episteme is easiest to see in terms of what it does to possibilities of self-knowledge. Therefore, I pay special attention to this theme by way of introducing the theoretical depth of Foucault's notion. I then develop Foucault's ideas further, specifically for digital lifeworlds.

With this vocabulary in place, I introduce the notion of *epistemic actorhood* that lets us capture the place of an individual in a given episteme. It is in terms of this place that we can turn to the notions of epistemic rights and epistemic justice. Epistemic actorhood comes with the four roles of individual epistemic subject, collective epistemic subject, individual epistemic object, and collective epistemic object. Using this vocabulary, we can then also articulate the notions of an epistemic right and of epistemic justice and develop them in the context of digital lifeworlds. Digital lifeworlds engage individuals both as knowers and knowns in new ways. The framework introduced in this chapter captures this point.

6 *Beyond Porn and Discreditation: Epistemic Promises and Perils of Deepfake Technology*

Deepfakes are a new form of synthetic media that broke upon the world in 2017. Bringing photoshopping to video, deepfakes replace people in existing videos with someone else's likeness. Currently most of their reach is limited to pornography and efforts at discreditation. However, deepfake technology has many epistemic promises and perils, which concern how we fare as knowers and knowns. This chapter seeks to help set an agenda around these matters to make sure that this technology can help realize epistemic rights and epistemic justice and unleash human creativity, rather than inflict epistemic wrongs of any sort. In any event, the relevant philosophical considerations are already in view, even though the technology itself is still very much evolving. This chapter puts to use the framework of epistemic actorhood from Chapter 5.

7 *The Fourth Generation of Human Rights: Epistemic Rights in Life 2.0 and Life 3.0*

British science fiction writer and social activist H. G. Wells was a major advocate for a universal declaration of human rights of the kind that was later passed in 1948.

Wells paid much attention to the importance of knowledge for his era, more than found its way into the actual declaration – though, to be sure, recognizable epistemic rights do play a role in the human rights movement. However, at this stage in history, an enhanced set of epistemic rights that strengthen existing human rights – as part of a *fourth generation* of human rights – is needed to protect epistemic actorhood in those four roles introduced in Chapter 5.

Epistemic rights are already exceedingly important because of the epistemic intrusiveness of digital lifeworlds in Life 2.0, and they should also include a suitably defined right to be forgotten (that is, a right to have certain information removed from easy accessibility through internet searches). If Life 3.0 does emerge, we might also need a right altogether different from what is currently acknowledged as human rights, the right to exercise human intelligence to begin with. This right will become important again in Chapter 11. Human rights must expand beyond protecting "each of us from the rest of us" to protecting "us from them," much as such protection would have to prevail conversely. The required argument for the validity of the right to the exercise of human intelligence can draw on the secular meaning-of-life literature. I paint with a broad brush when it comes to the detailed content of proposed rights, offering them manifesto-style as the Universal Declaration of Human Rights (UDHR) does.

8 *On Surveillance Capitalism, Instrumentarian Power, and Social Physics: Securing the Enlightenment for Digital Lifeworlds*

"Surveillance capitalism" is a term coined by Shoshana Zuboff to draw attention to the fact that data collection has become so important for the functioning of the economy that the current stage of capitalism should be named for it. "Instrumentarian power" is a kind of power that becomes possible in such an economic system, power that deploys technology to obtain ever more knowledge about individuals to make their behavior predictable and thus monetizable. "Social physics" is a term used by computer scientist Alex Pentland to describe the potential of quantitative social science to put Big Data to beneficial use. The primary goal of this chapter is to discuss how surveillance capitalism in digital lifeworlds threatens the Enlightenment ideal of individuality itself (as discussed by Kant and Durkheim) and what it takes to secure the Enlightenment for digital lifeworlds. That is, I draw on democracy and epistemic rights to discuss how Enlightenment ideals can be secured in such lifeworlds.

Since this chapter is the last in a row of chapters concerned with rights, we also discuss (and reject) the position that rights, especially human rights, are enough to articulate a promising normative vision for society. This discussion draws on insights from Max Horkheimer and Theodor W. Adorno's *Dialectic of Enlightenment*, which has synergies with Zuboff's work. It is important to be clear on the scope and limits of a rights-based vision for society since such visions have become prominent in our neoliberal world. But contrary to such a neoliberal understanding, a strong view of democracy, as discussed in Chapter 3, is also required for a promising normative vision for society. And so is a plausible theory of distributive justice, a subject to which we turn in Chapter 9.

9 Data As Social Facts: Distributive Justice Meets Big Data

In the age of Big Data and machine learning, with its ever-expanding possibilities for data mining, the question of who is entitled to control the data and benefit from the insights that can be derived from them matters greatly for the shape of the future economy. Therefore, this topic should be assessed under the heading of distributive justice. There are different views on who is entitled to control data, often driven by analogies between claims to data and claims to other kinds of things that are already better understood. This chapter clarifies the value of approaching the subject of control over data in terms of (a notion of moral, rather than legal) ownership. Next, drawing on the work of seventeenth-century political theorist Hugo Grotius on the freedom of the seas, and thus on possibilities of owning the high seas, I develop an account of collective ownership of collectively generated data patterns and explore several important objections. This chapter also connects to my earlier work on distributive justice in *On Justice* and *On Global Justice*.

That a seventeenth-century figure would appear as we try to throw light on a twenty-first-century problem might startle or even irritate. But Grotius's account of the ownership of the seas formulates basic and immensely plausible ideas about what kind of thing should or should not be privatized. It offers lessons for our current debate. Since control over data matters enormously and is poorly understood, we should treat questions about it as *genuinely open*. This is a good time to bring to bear unorthodox thinking on the matter. Chapter 5 introduced epistemic justice, and Chapter 7 introduced new epistemic human rights. Both themes reenter here.

10 God, Golem, and Gadget Worshippers: Meaning of Life in the Digital Age

The question of the meaning of life is about how a human life is connected to other things and themes of value around it. Meaning of life and technology are not normally theorized together. But once we realize that all human activity is always technologically mediated, we see that any acts in pursuit of personal significance, too, are so mediated. However, this point then opens the possibility that technology enters the human quest for meaning *the wrong way*. This chapter explores what that possibility means and how to respond to it.

I use as my starting point Robert Nozick's proposal for how to think about the meaning of life. Nozick's account makes central the idea of "limited transcendence," essentially folding the kind of transcendence normally involved in interaction with divinity into a finite life. This understanding of meaning receives much plausibility from the fact that finite lives are the only sources of meaning open to humans. Nozick's high-altitude view does not make sufficiently clear how technology enters. But once we bring in additional ideas from Don Ihde and Hannah Arendt, we can see clearly how it does. Next, we turn to Norbert Wiener's classic *God & Golem*. Wiener is concerned with "gadget worshippers," people who surrender control over their lives to machines in ways that are not appropriate to what these machines can do. Working with this notion, we can throw light on how technology can enter into the quest for meaning the wrong way and offer some advice for how to counterbalance that challenge.

11 *Moral Status and Political Membership: Toward a Political Theory for Life 3.0*

I introduce a distinction between "slow and relatively harmonious" and "fast and radical" as far as the integration of AI into human life is concerned. Regarding the "slow and relatively harmonious" scenario, I explore a set of questions about how it would make sense for humans to acknowledge some such status in machines (in a variety of ways). But we must then also ask whether self-conscious artificial intelligences would be fully morally equivalent to humans. I explore that issue by asking what an increase in moral status for machines would mean for the political domain. Chapter 3 already explored why AI would affect the democratic process in the near future. Here our concern is with a scenario further along when questions around political membership of intelligent machines would actually arise. One question is whether there is a cognitive capacity beyond intelligence and self-consciousness that is needed for involvement especially in the political domain. Paying attention to what is appropriate to say about animals in that regard turns out to be useful. I turn to Christine Korsgaard's as well as Sue Donaldson and Will Kymlicka's recent discussions of animals to investigate the matter.

As far as the "fast and radical" scenario is concerned, I first explore why philosophically we are so dramatically unprepared to deal with an intelligence explosion, with a focus on what kind of moral status a superintelligence might acknowledge *in us*. Finally, I attend to Tegmark's discussion of political scenarios that could arise after an intelligence explosion and add a public-reason scenario that, under certain circumstances, could offer a vision for a political context genuinely shared between humans and superintelligent machines.

4 A NOTE ON OMISSIONS

One set of topics I do not cover at length – though the topics do make regular appearances – is how inequality and fairness across groups in society are affected by AI and Big Data. The ways in which algorithms perpetuate patterns of discrimination and exacerbate economic inequality has become the single most covered issue in this field in recent years. Monographs authored by Ruha Benjamin, Safiya Noble,

Cathy O'Neil, Virginia Eubanks, Joshua Simons (whose work is forthcoming), and others and a substantial number of articles have advanced the debates around these topics in ways for which there is no counterpart among the topics that I do cover at length. And to be sure, my Rawlsian outlook (and my own development of it for the global domain in *On Global Justice* and *On Justice*) already comes with views on inequality that carry over into the digital century.

One other omission of sorts that I should note is that this book does not seek to reach a bottom-line judgment about the existential risks posed by the development of AI.[17] We do encounter several large-scale dystopian scenarios throughout that offer dire assessments of the human use of technology, issued by authors such as Martin Heidegger, Lewis Mumford, Jacques Ellul, and Herbert Marcuse. We also occasionally touch on the more recent literature on existential risk. But for one thing, I have not been able to make up my mind about whether it is appropriate to call for a radical stop to or a temporary moratorium on technological advancement. Certainly, the aforementioned dystopian scenarios – while indeed insightful enough to offer warnings – are too bombastic in scope to allow for conclusive validation. At the same time, I take it as a given that technological advancement will continue anyway for the time being, one way or another, if only because of geopolitical rivalry. The task for political theory, then, is to think about the topics that will likely come our way, distinguish among the various timeframes (such as Life 2.0 and Life 3.0) in which they might do so, and make proposals for how a democratic society should prepare itself to deal with the changes in the technology domain that it might eventually have to address.[18]

---

[17] For a call for a moratorium on work that might lead to the creation of artificial consciousness, see Metzinger, "Artificial Suffering."

[18] Note that I capitalize "Chapter" when talking about specific chapters in this book (as in "Chapter 1"), but not when talking about chapters in other books. In some situations, that will help avoid confusion.

Acknowledgments

I am grateful to audiences at the University of Hamburg; the Wharton School of the University of Pennsylvania; the University of Tokyo; Harvard Law School the Universities of Freiburg, Heidelberg, and Cologne; University College London; the University of Alabama at Birmingham; Massachusetts Institute of Technology (MIT); and Northeastern University for discussions of some of this material over the years. I am grateful to my coauthors Catherine Kerner and Steven Livingston for earlier work on some of these issues. I owe thanks to Diana Acosta Navas, John Basl, Elettra Bietti, Gabriella Blum, Matthew Braham, Maria Carnovale, Hamza Chaudhry, Austin Choi-Fitzpatrick, Christoph Durt, Linda Eggert, Sam Gilbert, John Goldberg, Amanda Greene, Wilfried Hinsch, Philip Howard, Sheila Jasanoff, Peter Niesen, Sushma Raman, John Shattuck, Silja Vöneky, and Jim Waldo either for comments on parts of this material or for organizing events at which some of it was discussed (or both). Philosophical interactions with Tim Scanlon over the years have found their way into this project in more ways than might be apparent.

I owe much of my inspiration to the members of the Human Rights and Technology Fellowship at the Carr Center for Human Rights Policy at the Harvard Kennedy School (which I am fortunate enough to direct, alongside the Carr Center's formidable executive director, Sushma Raman) for ongoing discussions of the normative dimensions of technological innovation. I am also indebted to the speakers in our Toward Life 3.0 webinar series, including Nikita Aggarwal; Jay Aronson; Ron Deibert; Teresa Hodge and Laurin Leonard; Sheila Jasanoff; Alexa Koenig; Philip Howard; Sabelo Mhlambi; Safiya Noble; Frank Pasquale; Bruce Schneier; John Tasioulas; Shoshana Zuboff; and others.

I am also very grateful to the members of the Graduate Fellowship Colloquium at the Edmond J. Safra Center for Ethics (which I am fortunate enough to have directed over time jointly with Danielle Allen, Eric Beerbohm, and Meira Levinson, respectively) for discussions of some of my work and for creating often highly insightful cross-connections. And I am grateful to the participants in my course on the philosophy of technology that I have offered in recent years to students at the Harvard Kennedy School, the Harvard Graduate School of Design, and Harvard College for the many insights they have offered, and especially to my teaching fellow Cat Wade for doing such an amazing job twice with this course (as well as to course assistants Grace Stone and Stephen Dwyer for being excellent in their roles). As it has turned out, insights from my course on the meaning of life, which I have taught many times in various versions in different locations, have also been invaluable for this project. I am grateful to all who have contributed to this course over the years.

The penultimate version of the manuscript benefited enormously from Katherine (Kate) Williams's keen eye for grammatical subtleties and from her high standards of clarity of expression. Every chapter became noticeably better after Kate made her way through it. I am much indebted to Matt Gallaway at Cambridge University Press for approaching me several years ago about writing a book on this subject, and for his enduring interest in it over the years. Four anonymous reviewers for the press gave useful advice when the direction of this project needed it most.

In Chapter 6, I use material from "Beyond Porn and Discreditation: Epistemic Promises and Perils of Deepfakes Technology in Digital Lifeworlds" (coauthored with Catherine Kerner), *Moral Philosophy and Politics* 8, no. 1 (2021): 81–108. In Chapter 7, I use material from "The Fourth Generation of Human Rights: Epistemic Rights in Digital Lifeworlds," *Moral Philosophy and Politics* 8, no. 2 (2021): 351–78. I am grateful to De Gruyter publishing company for permission to use this material here. Throughout I use bits and pieces from "Human Rights and Artificial Intelligence: An Urgently Needed Agenda," *Human Rights Quarterly* 41 (2019): 1–16. I am grateful to Johns Hopkins University Press for permission to use this material.

1

Introduction

Digital Lifeworlds in Human History

Can we produce the required adjustments with the necessary speed? . . . To ask in advance for a complete recipe would be unreasonable. We can specify only the human qualities required: patience, flexibility, intelligence.

—John von Neumann[1]

1.1 LIFEWORLDS, ANALOG AND DIGITAL

Phenomenology is a twentieth-century philosophical movement that makes central the investigation and description of appearances (phenomena) as people consciously experience them – rather than making central any causal explanations of the origins of these phenomena. It is from this movement that the term "lifeworld," from German *Lebenswelt*, has become familiar. This term characterizes the immediate impressions, activities, and relationships that make up the world as a person experiences it and as people in shared contexts experience together.[2]

Until the 1940s, our lifeworlds were fully "analog." "Analog" comes from the Greek *ana*, meaning "according to," and *logos*, which means ratio or proportion. Analog lifeworlds involve interactions and technologies driven by tactile, acoustic, or other physical experiences. They are organized around measurements that *represent* what they measure – as a clock's moving hands represent time, making clocks analogous to time. As far as electrical circuits are concerned, the term "analog" refers to the representation of information or signals in a continuous range of voltages or currents. Many innovations that brought electronic computing (computing done by way of controlling the flow of electrons) on its way were analog. But in

---

[1] von Neumann, "Can We Survive Technology?", 519.
[2] On the background of the term in the work of Edmund Husserl, see Smith, *Husserl*. I take the term "digital lifeworld" from Susskind, *Future Politics*. On phenomenology, see Moran, *Introduction to Phenomenology*.

time, we have increasingly come to inhabit digital lifeworlds structured around electronic devices and numerically coded information that use electrical circuits that operate at a number of discrete levels ("digital" information, from the Latin for finger).[3] Digital information allows for reliable transmission and storage. The explosion of computational power generated by the invention and progressive miniaturization of semiconductor circuits has worked well with such information.

Within decades, digitalized computing has become dominant in ever more domains of life. Digital lifeworlds started to connect humans, sophisticated machines, and abundant data in the elaborate ways that now shape our reality. These changes have come far enough along for us to think of the twenty-first century as the digital century. Today's digital lifeworlds are *pervasive* in that ever more devices do their tasks linked to the Internet; *connective* in letting people in far-flung locations interact more or less instantly; *sensitive* in that sensors trace ever more things and information; *constitutive* in that machines are essential to our reality, rather than representing cyber add-ons to a life otherwise focused; and *immersive* by offering more and more augmented or virtual reality to supplement and enrich the physical reality we inhabit with our bodies.[4] In an interview with the German magazine *Der Spiegel* in 1966, Martin Heidegger was asked what replaced philosophy – and he answered that it was cybernetics.[5] It may not be specifically cybernetics (on which I say more later, and which is more on the analog side of technology), and philosophy may not actually have been replaced, but this statement is just one of a myriad of symptoms of how technology has taken over our lives in newly comprehensive and powerful ways.

But not only is the twenty-first century the digital century; digital lifeworlds might well be the last stage in a period of life on earth (Life 2.0) that could eventually be replaced by a new period (Life 3.0). Life 3.0 would differ from what has occurred so far in that at least many of the entities that inhabit it would be able to design both

---

[3] There are complexities to the digital versus analog distinction. See, for example, Lewis, "Analogue and Digital"; Haugeland, "Analog and Analog"; Lesne, "The Discrete vs. Continuous Controversy in Physics." See also Floridi, *The Philosophy of Information*, chapter 14. Sometimes "digital technology" is incorrectly equated with "computers" or "electronics." However, the distinction between "analog" and "digital" captures differences in how information or signals appear. Computation can be done in both formats and can be done using different kinds of energy (in the case of "electronics," a certain kind of control over emission and flow of electrons). Specific electronic devices may well integrate both types of circuits. Still, what has come to be known as the Digital Revolution has seen numerous transitions from fully analog to at least largely digital technology, for example, from analog to digital computers, from telex to fax, Video Home System (VHS) to Digital Versatile Disc (DVD), compact cassette and gramophone record to compact disc, photographic plates to digital photography, analog to digital cinematography, analog to digital mobile phones, and so forth. Talk about "digital lifeworlds" captures the *increasing relevance* of digital devices in our lives, rather than a complete replacement of analog components.

[4] Susskind, *Future Politics*, chapters 1–2.

[5] Quoted in Zimmerman, *Heidegger's Confrontation with Modernity*, 199.

their physical shapes and their cultural context. Entities in Life 2.0 have been able to design their cultural context (could *learn*, that is, both individually and collectively) but not their physical shape. Entities in Life 1.0 can neither engage in learning nor change physical shapes and find themselves with a fixed understanding of the world and a particular physical shape from the beginning. To be sure, there might never be a Life 3.0, or it might differ from what theorists of general AI now ponder. Still, not only is there a distinct possibility that there will be such a Life 3.0, but the changes that unfold all around us and that may or may not lead to Life 3.0 are by themselves momentous. And what is overwhelmingly plausible is that, if there will be Life 3.0, it is going to emerge from the digital lifeworlds of Life 2.0 that we already inhabit.

This chapter introduces some major themes and concepts that help us comprehend digital lifeworlds and their place in human history. In a manner loosely organized around the year 1948, Section 1.2 explores some defining aspects of the twenty-first century that have emerged from developments in the middle of the twentieth century. Among these developments is the beginning of AI research; Section 1.3 discusses that topic in more depth. Also central to digital lifeworlds (and to AI) are the notions of data and information. Assessing how talk about data and information became prominent, as we do in Section 1.4, further illuminates the place of digital lifeworlds in history. Once the notion of information is on our radar, we need to explore its relationship with knowledge. Section 1.5 does so, and in the process connects to Luciano Floridi's philosophy of information. Floridi sees the world as a place filled with interconnected informational organisms (*inforgs*). One question about the inforgs of the future is what kind of moral status they might have. Section 1.6 aims to show how open-ended a question this is for now by exploring whether machines might eventually be conscious. Section 1.7 draws on the various themes developed across the previous sections and embeds digital lifeworlds into the sweep of history by elaborating on the distinctions between Life 1.0, 2.0, and 3.0.[6]

1.2 THE YEAR 1948 AND BEYOND

There is a danger in singling out particular years as a form of coming to terms with large-scale change. Nonetheless, as far as the transition into a world shaped by electronic computation is concerned, 1948 is noteworthy. To begin with, that year MIT mathematician Norbert Wiener published *Cybernetics or Control and Communication in the Animal and the Machine*, and Claude Shannon, a researcher at Bell Labs, published "A Mathematical Theory of Communication." Wiener's piece presents the concept and theory of cybernetics to a broader audience. Drawing on the Greek word for helmsman, cybernetics deals with the behavior of dynamic systems and explores how this behavior

---

[6] These distinctions I take from Tegmark, *Life 3.0*. For reflections on how communication is affected by the digital age, see O'Neill, *A Philosopher Looks at Digital Communication*.

is modified by feedback. Shannon's article formulates a mathematical theory of communication. He provides a formal model of what it means to convey information from senders to receivers, quantitatively analyzing transmission to measure the amount of information conveyed. Both pieces were seminal for the multidisciplinary efforts to master both an increasing abundance of information and rapidly developing capacities for computation.[7]

By then British mathematician Alan Turing had developed the Turing machine, a model of computation that defines an abstract machine that manipulates symbols on a strip of tape following a list of rules. For any computer algorithm, a Turing machine capable of simulating that algorithm can be constructed. In 1943, cybernetician Warren McCulloch and logician Walter Pitts proposed that something resembling the Turing machine might provide a good model for the mind, a theory that came to be known as the "computational theory of the mind." In time, Alan Turing would come to represent the scientific revolution triggered by innovations in computation, much as Copernicus, Darwin, and Freud had stood for earlier revolutions and the accompanying changes in human self-understanding.[8]

In 1950, Turing published "Computing Machinery and Intelligence," which proposed an experiment that would become known as the Turing Test, an attempt to define standards for machines to count as "intelligent."[9] The field of "artificial intelligence" was inaugurated (and the term coined) just a few years later, in 1956, when it was launched by a small but now-famous summer school at Dartmouth.[10] In Princeton, in the 1940s and early 1950s, John von Neumann advanced the theoretical design of digital electronic computers and built machines that accelerated the development of hardware. He also provided an analysis of the structure of self-replication that preceded the discovery of DNA and constructed the first self-replicating automata. George Dyson succinctly captured the contributions of these pioneers:

---

[7] Wiener, *Cybernetics or Control and Communication in the Animal and the Machine*; Shannon, "A Mathematical Theory of Communication." For the context, see Kline, *The Cybernetics Moment*; Gleick, *The Information*, chapters 8–9; Conway, *Dark Hero of the Information Age*. For the postwar impact of cybernetics and the communication sciences on social and human sciences, design, art, and urban planning, see Halpern, *Beautiful Data*. For the mathematical theory of information, see Cover and Thomas, *Elements of Information Theory*. For Shannon's and related efforts, see Losee, *The Science of Information*; Devlin, *Logic and Information*. See also Adriaans, "Information." Wiener's cybernetics was analog in nature, and much of the work to speed up digitalization was often done in contrast with cybernetic approaches. Still, Wiener's ideas reentered discussions about the increasing presence of computational devices in human life; for recent assessments, see Brockman, *Possible Minds*.

[8] Floridi, *The Fourth Revolution*. See also Kittler, "The Artificial Intelligence of World War: Alan Turing."

[9] Turing, "Computing Machinery and Intelligence"; Bernhardt, *Turing's Vision*. On Turing, see Agar, *Turing and the Universal Machine*.

[10] Nilsson, *Quest for Artificial Intelligence*, chapter 3.

Alan Turing wondered what it would take for machines to become intelligent. John von Neumann wondered what it would take for machines to self-reproduce. Claude Shannon wondered what it would take for machines to communicate reliably, no matter how much noise intervened. Norbert Wiener wondered how long it would take for machines to assume control.[11]

On the other side of the Atlantic, German engineer Konrad Zuse had worked on similar projects since the midthirties. Zuse labored in near-total intellectual isolation from an apartment in Berlin and thus fails to make an appearance in Dyson's summary of the pioneers' main projects. While aerial bombings in 1945 disrupted Zuse's efforts, he apparently built the world's first functioning programmable digital computer. The computational age that would increasingly turn digital was on its way, with the publication of those two pieces by Wiener and Shannon in 1948 among the stepping stones into it.[12]

Von Neumann was deeply involved with governmental efforts to harness science for military purposes (a cause from which Wiener had become alienated[13]). Shortly before his death in 1957, von Neumann published "Can We Survive Technology?" in his capacity as a member of the US Atomic Energy Commission. In the article, he reflects on the world that technology (to whose relentless advance he had added so much) was creating.[14] He starts by observing that our planet is now too small to absorb much of what might go wrong with the deployment of technology and too politically decentralized to manage technology well. After walking readers through some challenges that arise from these conditions, von Neumann concludes by stating that all we know for sure is that we need "patience, flexibility, intelligence" to persevere (a passage that is also in the epigraph of this chapter).[15] Readers are left uncertain as to how much this is a counsel of despair or a call to action from someone who knew better than anyone about technology's destructive potential.

That potential has also been a topic for a slew of techno-skeptical philosophers. One way or another, these thinkers have tried to alert humanity to the dangers of letting technology run its course without critical investigations as to how it has changed humanity and who stands to benefit. Lewis Mumford, a leading, American

---

[11] Dyson, "The Third Law," 35.

[12] Dyson, *Darwin among the Machines*; Dyson, *Turing's Cathedral*; Nilsson, *Quest for Artificial Intelligence*; Ceruzzi, *A History of Modern Computing*. See also Buchanan, "A (Very) Brief History of Artificial Intelligence." On Zuse and attempts to come to an appreciation of his work, see Bruderer, *Konrad Zuse und die Schweiz*; Rojas, *Die Rechenmaschinen von Konrad Zuse*; Böttiger, *Konrad Zuse*. Unsurprisingly, there is ongoing disagreement about the relative importance of the work of the various pioneers.

[13] During World War II, Wiener worked on weapons technology, which he came to regret after Hiroshima and Nagasaki. He refused to contribute further to any research that would help the military; Wiener, "A Scientist Rebels." On Wiener's postwar pacifism in contrast with John von Neumann, see also Heims, *John von Neumann and Norbert Wiener*.

[14] von Neumann, "Can We Survive Technology?"

[15] All quotes are from the last two paragraphs of the article; see von Neumann, 519. For a virtue-ethics-based proposal for what we need to get through, see Vallor, *Technology and the Virtues*.

critic of the machine age, is among these writers. Already in his first book on the subject, the 1934 *Technics and Civilization*, Mumford traces a veritable cult of the machine through Western history that frequently devastated creativity and independence of mind.[16] Our willingness to make machines central to human life resulted from a particular mindset, a commitment to societal organization that would make people receptive to the introduction of physical machines. The cultivation of such a mindset reflects plain power interests.

Decades later, Mumford's two-volume *Myth of the Machine* elaborates on themes from his earlier work, characterizing modern doctrines of progress as scientifically upgraded justifications for practices that the powerful had deployed since pharaonic times to maintain power.[17] The essence of the various *megamachines* that ruled humanity over time was the domination of technical knowledge by elites; this domination had benefitted them greatly while relegating the masses to a "megatechnical wasteland."[18] To Mumford, the digital age – of whose initial stages he was a keen observer – again harbors the dangers of streamlining human capacities; these dangers have been at work since the dawn of civilization. Like others in this tradition of grand techno-skeptical thinking – one might think of Heidegger, Jacques Ellul, or Herbert Marcuse, who all make appearances later in this book – Mumford offers a theory whose sweep and scope make it hard to assess conclusively. At the same time, like those other authors, Mumford employs an analytical lens that issues a warning we should heed. That warning is that our world *just might* be something like the world these skeptics describe.

Worries about what technology might bring have also created the genre of *dystopian science fiction*. As it happens, it was in December 1948 that George Orwell sent to his publisher the manuscript of *Nineteen Eighty-Four*, a novel that captures some of the great fears of the twentieth century.[19] Set in an imagined future in 1984, the book explores the realities of mass surveillance and repressive regimentation. Orwell's imagination was limited by the analog realities of his time. But it is striking that *Nineteen Eighty-Four* would appear at the dawn of the digital age. After all, it would be the *digital* age, with its awesome possibilities, that eventually made Orwell's dystopian fears come alive in ways beyond what he could imagine. His dystopian worries set the stage for the digital era as much as the pioneering work in computer science did that made the technology possible, and as much as the political choices did that shaped the postwar order in which all this unfolded.

As far as such political choices are concerned, 1948 also saw significant movements in the efforts to create a global governance system. The United Nations (UN) itself was founded in 1945, emerging from the calamities of World War II, which had

---

[16] Mumford, *Technics and Civilization*.
[17] Mumford, *Myth of the Machine*; Mumford, *Pentagon of Power*.
[18] The title of chapter 11 of Mumford, *Pentagon of Power*.
[19] Orwell, *1984*. Bowker, *Inside George Orwell*, chapter 18.

also done a lot to drive foundational research on computer science. About three years after the UN's founding, on December 10, 1948 (the week Orwell submitted his manuscript), the UN General Assembly took a historic vote. There was a growing sense that, repeatedly and dramatically, human affairs were being derailed in the twentieth century. This awareness made the late 1940s a period when the project of institutionalizing human rights briefly flourished before the world plunged into the Cold War. To be sure, the Universal Declaration of Human Rights that was passed by the General Assembly on that day was nonbinding. Only in time would it give rise to international conventions that were binding on signatories. Nonetheless, the UN thereby adopted as one core value the momentous idea that each person deserves a certain level of protections and provisions that assumes the form of rights.[20]

As it happens, it also was in 1948 that the General Agreement on Tariffs and Trade (GATT) came into effect, a legal arrangement to promote and structure international trade. The GATT, too, was part of the post–World War II governance system. It substituted for a more ambitious International Trade Organization (ITO) that ultimately failed to pass over US resistance.[21] So on the one hand, the creation of the UN system distilled efforts at global coordination beyond anything previously seen. On the other hand, the nonbinding character of the Universal Declaration and the foundering of the ITO indicated the limitation of the willingness of the powerful to collaborate on the creation of a postwar world that would soon (and against resistance from imperial powers) also become a postcolonial world. Nonetheless, it is within this newly devised global political and economic system, with its built-in (if stunted) moral ambitions, that digital lifeworlds would grow over the decades (with all the accompanying change across many domains of life). Eventually, this system would also be the one in which the Internet of things, with its boundless and boundary-dispensing possibilities for interconnectedness, would arise and unfold.

1.3 ALGORITHMS, MACHINE LEARNING, AND AI

To describe the changes from analog to digital lifeworlds, we need to talk about algorithms, machine learning, and AI. *Algorithms* are finite sequences of well-defined instructions. Computer-implementable algorithms can do anything that can be coded as long as they can access the data they need, at the required speed, and operate in frames that allow for execution of the tasks thus determined. Progress over the decades has been colossal in all domains that make computer-implementable algorithms effective. Their effectiveness is enhanced through enormous increases in computational

---

[20] On the Universal Declaration, see Morsink, *The Universal Declaration of Human Rights*; Lauren, *The Evolution of International Human Rights*.

[21] On ITO and GATT, see Risse and Wollner, *On Trade Justice*, chapter 2.

power in conjunction with Big Data, the availability of vast amounts of data on everything in the world. Ever more data are gathered as we increasingly shift activities into digital formats, storage is becoming ever cheaper, and replication and transmission of digital information are easy. Algorithms outperform humans wherever tested and are noise-free: They reach the same decision when encountering a problem twice. Still, human-designed systems reflect human bias. They rely on data that capture our past, automating the status quo unless we prevent them from doing so.[22]

Unlike conventional programs, *machine-learning algorithms* learn by themselves. Programmers provide data, which a set of methods ("machine learning") analyzes for trends and inferences. Owing to their sophistication and sweeping applications, these technologies are poised to alter our world dramatically. Such algorithms are typically what we mean by "artificial intelligence," even though conceptually this term captures all design efforts at approximating natural intelligence.

The proposal for that now-famous 1956 Dartmouth summer school (by John McCarthy, Marvin Minsky, Nathaniel Rochester, and Claude Shannon) begins as follows:[23]

> We propose that a 2-month, 10-man study of artificial intelligence be carried out during the summer of 1956 at Dartmouth College in Hanover, New Hampshire. The study is to proceed on the basis of the conjecture that every aspect of learning or any other feature of intelligence can in principle be so precisely described that a machine can be made to simulate it. An attempt will be made to find how to make machines, use language, form abstractions and concepts, solve kinds of problems now reserved for humans, and improve themselves. We think that a significant advance can be made in one or more of these problems if a carefully selected group of scientists work on it together for a summer.

It is with these in-hindsight overambitious lines that the phrase "artificial intelligence" entered the world of science. "Intelligence" itself is not further analyzed but spelled out in terms of several problem areas. To this day, details of intelligence research are mostly circumnavigated in AI research by taking as a hallmark whatever is considered intelligence in humans. Accordingly, "general" intelligence in machines typically means performance that approximates human success in problem-solving.

---

[22] On this subject, see also Julia Angwin, "Machine Bias." On fairness in machine learning, see Binns, "Fairness in Machine Learning: Lessons from Political Philosophy"; Mittelstadt et al., "The Ethics of Algorithms"; Osoba and Welser, *An Intelligence in Our Image*. On Big Data, see Mayer-Schönberger and Cukier, *Big Data*. On machine learning, see Domingos, *The Master Algorithm*. On how algorithms can be used in greedy ways, see O'Neil, *Weapons of Math Destruction*. That algorithms can do a lot of good is also behind much of the potential of social science for improving the lives of individuals and societies; see, for example, Trout, *The Empathy Gap*.

[23] The proposal is dated August 31, 1955, and is partly reprinted in McCarthy et al., "A Proposal for the Dartmouth Summer Research Project on Artificial Intelligence."

Intelligence has come up for much debate, especially among psychologists, in recent decades. Generically, intelligence is understood as the ability to make effective and efficient use of information to make predictions and solve problems. One major disagreement is about whether there is one general intelligence (called "g" among those eager to measure it) or whether instead intelligence is multifaceted. Prominent among versions of the latter view is the theory of multiple intelligences proposed by Howard Gardner; these intelligences represent relatively discrete intellectual capacities that are sufficiently independent of each other to make the plural appropriate. Gardner distinguishes visual-spatial, linguistic-verbal, logical-mathematical, bodily-kinesthetic, musical, interpersonal (social), intrapersonal (understanding of self), and naturalistic intelligence (the capacity to make consequential distinctions in the domain of nature). He has entertained the possibility of there also being an existential intelligence (pertaining to "big questions"), and a pedagogical intelligence (allowing people to convey knowledge or skills to others).[24]

In varying degrees, research into *specialized* AI has intersected with some of Gardner's intelligences (least of all, it seems, with existential, intrapersonal, and pedagogical intelligences). Regarding specialized AI, at the high end one may think of AI mastering chess or Go. We encounter it more commonly in smartphones (Siri, Google Translate, curated newsfeeds, etc.), home devices (Alexa, Google Home, Nest, etc.), personalized customer services, and GPS systems. Specialized AI is used by law enforcement, the military, browser searching, advertising and entertainment (e.g., recommender systems), medical diagnostics, logistics, finance (from assessing credit to flagging transactions), speech recognition, trade bots, and also in music creation or article drafting (e.g., GPT-3's text generator writing posts or code).[25] Governments track people using AI in facial, voice, and gait recognition. Smart cities analyze traffic data in real time to design and adjust public transportation. COVID-19 has accelerated the use of AI in drug discovery. Natural language processing – normally used for texts – interprets genetic changes in viruses. Amazon Web Services, Microsoft Azure, and Google Cloud's low- and no-code offerings could soon let people create AI applications as easily as they can design websites.[26]

[24] Gardner, *Frames of Mind*; Gardner, *Intelligence Reframed*; Gardner, *Multiple Intelligences*. For broader discussions, see Hunt, *Human Intelligence*; Sternberg and Kaufman, *The Cambridge Handbook of Intelligence*. On "g," see Mackintosh, *IQ and Human Intelligence*.
[25] For the connection between intelligence and the ongoing work on natural language processing, see, for example, Manning, "Human Language Understanding & Reasoning"; Rees, "Non-Human Words."
[26] For current trends, see Chojecki, *Artificial Intelligence Business*. For the state of the art, see Mitchell, *Artificial Intelligence*; Taulli, *Artificial Intelligence Basics*; Russell, *Human Compatible*. See also Future Today Institute, "Tech Trends Report 2021." For musings on the future of AI, see Brockman, *Possible Minds*.

General AI, as we noted, is typically taken to approximate human performance across domains. If Gardner is correct, this presumably means that general AI would approximate human performance across most or at least many of his multiple intelligences. But were we capable of producing anything like such AI, the resulting AI might not relate to human intelligence on what Steven Pinker calls a "boundless continuum of potency."[27] That is, we should not think of AI as trumping human intelligence but as something different. However, if there ever were to be an AI that in some recognizable sense is broadly "smarter" than us, it could presumably produce something smarter than itself, and so on, possibly very fast. That moment is the singularity, an intelligence explosion with conceivably grave consequences. We are nowhere near anything like that; however, "nowhere near" means in terms of engineering capacities. Imitating mundane human tasks that combine agility, reflection, and interaction has proven challenging. But a few breakthroughs might accelerate things enormously.[28]

While we do not know when or even if there will be general AI, the direction of research gives observers reason to assign nontrivial probabilities to the possibility that there will be general AI *at some point*. Computer scientists and engineers increasingly discover the power of the brain's architecture. Inspired by what millions of years of evolution did to generate the brain, neural nets have been deployed in pathbreaking ways in machine learning. Apparently, a promising passageway into the future has been revealed. Once imitations of carbon-based evolution generate general AI, that AI has permanent advantages over natural intelligence. In the design process, there will be manifold opportunities to remove human fragility and boundedness and expand on all the capacities evolution has brought about. In terms of materials, silicon is superior to organic brain tissue in information processing. Uploading would allow creatures near-immortality, enabling them to survive even under circumstances lethal even to the most resilient carbon-based life.

Our brain shares an evolutionary-comparative framework with the rest of life: All nervous systems on earth are governed by the same electrochemical principles of information processing that emerged over a billion years ago. There is an astounding degree of shared cognition across vertebrates and invertebrates. By comparison, general AI – even though built by humans – is alien intelligence in that it will not *evolve* from that framework. It also has vastly superior abilities for computation, storage, and access to stored data. Much in the way that human cognition relates to the world – and the kind of science we have built over centuries – is driven by limitations in precisely those domains. So even while inspiration from the brain

---

[27] Pinker, "Tech Prophecy," 109.
[28] For optimism about the occurrence of a singularity, see Kurzweil, *The Singularity Is Near*. For pessimism, see Larson, *The Myth of Artificial Intelligence*. See also Bostrom, *Superintelligence*; Tegmark, *Life 3.0*; Eden et al., *Singularity Hypotheses*; Chalmers, "The Singularity: A Philosophical Analysis." For considerations against strong AI drawing on the work of John Sear and Kurt Gödel, see Bringsjord and Govindarajulu, "Artificial Intelligence," section 8.

might advance AI research, such differences in limitations and abilities could lead to the development of a type of intelligence whose primary feature is that it is *very different from* rather than *distinctly superior to* human intelligence across domains.[29]

1.4 DATA AND INFORMATION

Shoshana Zuboff's term "surveillance capitalism" (discussed at length in Chapter 8) captures the relevance of data collection for how companies prevail or fail today. Bruce Schneier calls data the "exhaust" of the information age, comparable in harmfulness to what air pollution was to the industrial age.[30] In a facetiously reverential spirit, Yuval Noah Harari and others talk about "dataism" to express that information flow now is of supreme importance.[31] And indeed, one cannot comprehend digital lifeworlds without talking about data and information. Conversely, understanding how talk about data and information became so prominent helps us understand the place of digital lifeworlds in human history.

The term "data" (Latin for "given") came into English in the early eighteenth century, mostly through mathematics and theology.[32] It was used to describe principles or passages from scripture that served as starting points of arguments and remained unquestioned. "Fact" is an ontological term: It refers to what is in the world. "Evidence" is epistemological: It addresses how something supports the credibility of certain claims. "Data" originally was neither of those but a rhetorical term specifying a role in discussion: "Data" was what is presently beyond reproach, regardless of whether it could be questioned on other occasions.

By the end of the eighteenth century, a shift had occurred within this rhetorical use, driven by the empiricism of the age. Vocabulary that guided the life of the mind was reinterpreted as empirical inquiry became increasingly central to intellectual advances. Accordingly, "data" came to denote results of investigations rather than premises, something "given" in the sense of "found through investigation." By the twentieth century, "data" was a well-established concept still largely without ontological or epistemological connotations. Computation and information theory gave it new relevance. The term was used to denote quantities or symbols (stored, transmitted, or recorded) on which computers perform operations. Only in a next step did the notion of "information" appear, data syntactically arranged in ways that meet certain standards and thereby convey meaning (have a semantic function).

---

[29] On these themes, see Schneider, "Alien Minds"; Marino, "The Landscape of Intelligence." See also Schneider, *Artificial You*.
[30] Schneier, *Data and Goliath*, 17.
[31] Harari, *Homo Deus*. The term "dataism" seems to go back to Brooks, "The Philosophy of Data." See also Lohr, *Data-Ism*; Mayer-Schönberger and Cukier, *Big Data*.
[32] I follow Rosenberg, "Data before the Fact." For a philosophical exploration of the notion of data, see also Lyon, "Data."

"Information," too, entered English in a pre-empiricist stage and was subsequently transformed through empiricism.[33] In the Latin original, to be "in-formed" is to be put into a certain form. Metaphysically, for X to be in-formed by Y meant for X to be shaped (given form) by Y. Basic cosmological or theological principles would do the shaping (put form into matter). Subsequently, in a more empiricist world, for X to be informed by Y meant for X to receive a report from Y. There were no longer "forms" in the world that were embodied by matter, but there were observations absorbed by minds. Form-giving shifted from cosmology and theology to observation. What was preserved, however, is the focus on recipients rather than content, the connotations of novelty, usefulness, or impact to someone. It sounds peculiar to refer to basic mathematical insights (e.g., Euler's identity, $e^{i\pi} + 1 = 0$) as information. That Euler's identity is novel for someone is normally overshadowed by its profundity. Still, there is nothing untoward about students of mathematics finding it useful to have a proof that indeed $e^{i\pi} + 1$ equals 0.

For the longest time, the X being informed, the recipient, was a person's mind. Nothing else *could* be a knower. But then, as John Durham Peters writes, "between the middle of the 18th and the middle of the 19th century, there arose a new kind of empiricism, no longer bound by the scale of the human body. The state became a knower; bureaucracy its sense; statistics its information."[34] So the meaning of "information" changed alongside the emergence of statistics, a discipline bound up with the changing nature of the state and even etymologically derived from "state." Implicit in statistics is a knower not subject to the limits of individuality. Statistical data are "gathered by mortals," but their analysis "creates an implied-I that is disembodied and all-seeing."[35]

Once computers emerge, they do what states have done for a while, though more efficiently and elegantly: "They make vast invisible aggregates intelligible and

---

[33] I follow Peters, "Information: Notes toward a Critical History." For the concept of information, see Capurro, *Information*; Capurro and Hjørland, "The Concept of Information"; Seiffert, *Information über die Information*; Lenski, "Information: A Conceptual Investigation"; Clarke, "Information." See also Kornwachs and Jacoby, *Information*; Rapoport, "What Is Information?"; Peterfreund and Schwartz, "The Concept of Information"; Adriaans, "Information"; Gleick, *The Information*. For various ways of defining information, see Braman, "Defining Information." For recent philosophical reflection, see Janich, *What Is Information?* See also Adriaans and Benthem, *Philosophy of Information*; Floridi, *Information*. In the Adriaans/van Bentham volume, the editors' introduction is especially of interest, Adriaans and Benthem, "Introduction: Information is What Information Does."

[34] Peters, "Information: Notes toward a Critical History," 14.

[35] Peters, 15. See also Hacking, *The Taming of Chance*; Headrick, *When Information Came of Age*. Hacking discusses the story of statistics; Headrick talks about improvements in the organization of information between 1700 and 1850, from the Linnean classification system in biology and the origins of statistics to maps, graphs, encyclopedias but then also postal and telegraph systems. For the argument that changing capacities of government have depended on the implementation of new technologies, and that the adoption of new technologies has depended on a certain vision of government, see Agar, *The Government Machine*.

manipulable."[36] Information is classified as such from the standpoint of a more abstract recipient and as possibly unavailable to human recipients altogether. Kafka's novel *The Trial* provides a striking illustration: In the story, all relevant information eludes the protagonist.[37] Philosopher Ivan Illich, a skeptic of the use of technology out of fear of its dehumanizing tendencies, considered the word "information" itself dehumanizing.[38]

"'Data! Data! Data!' he cried impatiently. 'I can't make bricks without clay.'" This statement, exclaimed by Sherlock Holmes in one of his adventures from the late 1800s, has occasionally been used by data scientists to explain what data are.[39] In computer science, information became the brick to the data's clay. But the fact that "data" and "information" would be combined in the now-standard sense that information is well-structured, interpretable data stems from a convergence of two developments: one that made it natural to think of what is "given" in a specific context as deliverables from empirical inquiry, and one that created a certain mind-independent knower. As Mumford says, the computer existed as a practice long before it existed as a machine.[40] In the 1940s, when Shannon wrote, people were therefore receptive to theorizing communication in terms of information, a manner of understanding communication that amounted to a "relentless encouragement of further communications."[41]

1.5 INFORMATION AND KNOWLEDGE

One might wonder how the notion of information relates to more traditional epistemological debates, especially to knowledge. "Knowledge" has been associated with individual agency in ways "information" has not. Knowledge, many would say, is something only humans have. If so, one needs to explore what this implies for

[36] Peters, "Information: Notes Toward a Critical History," 15.
[37] Kafka, *The Trial*. For the role of information and lack thereof in "modernisms," see also Purdon, *Modernist Informatics*. See also Solove, *The Digital Person*. The themes of this paragraph are also captured in a famous passage from T. S. Eliot often used as epigraph for projects related to digital information: "Where is the life we have lost in living? Where is the wisdom we have lost in knowledge? Where is the knowledge we have lost in information?," from the Opening Stanza of *Choruses from the Rock*, 1934; Eliot, *Complete Poems and Plays*, 96. A similar thought appears in Walter Benjamin's *Arcades Project*: "Just as the industrial process separates off from handicraft, so the form of communication corresponding to this labor process – information – separates off from the form of communication corresponding to the artisanal process of labor, which is storytelling. (. . .) This connection must be kept in mind if one is to form an idea of the explosive force contained within information. This force is liberated in sensation. With the sensation, whatever still resembles wisdom, oral tradition, or the epic side of truth is razed to the ground;" Benjamin, *The Arcades Project*, 804.
[38] This draws on speeches by Illich as reported in Hartch, *The Prophet of Cuernavaca*, 111.
[39] This exclamation appears in the story of "The Copper Beeches"; see Doyle *The Adventures of Sherlock Holmes, and Other Stories*, 321–40.
[40] Mumford, *Pentagon of Power*, 273–75.
[41] Halpern, *Beautiful Data*, 74.

possible nonhuman inhabitants of digital lifeworlds. Alternatively, the notion of knowledge must be reconsidered.

"Knowledge" has been elusive to philosophical analysis. Knowledge goes beyond true belief to exclude cases where people accidentally believe the right thing. Presumably knowledge has something to do with use of the right method, as classically articulated and instantly problematized in Plato's *Theaetetus*.[42] Plato defines knowledge as "true belief with an account (*logos*)."[43] The fact that knowledge is not the same as true belief is easy to see: Somebody might keep saying "it is noon," and eventually they are right. Knowledge involves the possibility of account-giving, no matter how rudimentary (as most people have little to say to substantiate many claims that intuitively pass as knowledge).

Plato explores what that *logos* (the account-giving) could be but finds no solution. Much work in epistemology across the ages has sought to establish what it takes for true belief to be justified. But this endeavor keeps reaching limits with examples that make it a matter of luck that statements turned out true *even though* they constitute true justified belief. Suppose I am dreadfully thirsty on a hot day. I suddenly see water, or so I believe. In fact, I see a mirage. But when I reach the spot, I locate water under a rock.[44] While this seems to be a case of true justified belief ("there is water over there"), it is sheer luck that it turns out that way. Since such examples seem available regardless of what is involved in justification, we cannot equate knowledge with true justified belief.[45]

One prominent effort to come to terms with the notion of knowledge in the face of such challenges – one that enlists the notion of information – is Fred Dretske's 1981 *Knowledge and the Flow of Information*.[46] Information, for Dretske, exists as a mind-independent feature of the world and is quantifiable in ways Shannon captured. Dretske offers this account, which preserves the focus on the recipient that we noted earlier in the history of the word "information":

> A signal r carries the information that s is F = the conditional probability of s's being F, given r (and k), is 1 (but, given k alone, less than 1); where k is the background knowledge of the given actor.[47]

---

[42] Plato, *Theaetetus*. For discussion, see White, *Plato on Knowledge and Reality*.

[43] Plato, *Theaetetus*, 201c–d.

[44] For this example, see Dreyfus, *Recognizing Reality*, 292.

[45] The contemporary debate knows such cases as "Gettier examples." For contemporary epistemology, see Nagel, *Knowledge*; Goldman and McGrath, *Epistemology*; Sosa et al., *Epistemology*. For the historical trajectory of this analysis of knowledge, see also Dutant, "The Legend of the Justified True Belief Analysis." Gettier problems are named after American philosopher Edmund Gettier, who first wrote about them in the 1960s.

[46] Dretske, *Knowledge and the Flow of Information*. See also Dretske, "Précis of Knowledge and the Flow of Information"; Dretske, "Epistemology and Information." For discussion of how the notion of information entered philosophy more broadly, see Adams, "The Informational Turn in Philosophy."

[47] Dretske, *Knowledge and the Flow of Information*, 65.

Dretske then explains what it is for actor K to know something:

> K knows that s is F = K's belief that s is F is caused (or causally sustained) by the information that s is F.

So, knowledge is *information-caused belief*. Dretske's account renders superfluous the search for any account of what it is for true belief to be justified. Ascribing knowledge based on the understanding that knowledge is true justified belief means knowers must be able to hold propositional attitudes (beliefs). It also implies some connection to a justificatory discourse. However, the notion of information presupposes no capacities to hold propositional attitudes or participate in justificatory discourses. This point reconnects to Peters's etymological discussion. His point is that the state can hold, process, and distribute information. But bureaucracies cannot have propositional attitudes or participate in justificatory discourses. Dretske and Peters converge on the point that understanding knowledge in terms of information means that a much broader range of actors can be knowers.

Dretske "wanted a characterization that would at least allow for the possibility that animals (a frog, rat, ape, or my dog) could know things," in ways that would not ask us "to suppose them capable of the more sophisticated intellectual operations involved in traditional analyses of knowledge."[48] As we think about knowledge in digital lifeworlds, such an understanding also opens up a path for AI and other new entities to possess knowledge.

Luciano Floridi has explored where else in philosophy the notion of information is useful. Ethics talks about information to illuminate informed choice and responsible action. Logic has branched out into computer science. Ontology involves study of informational patterns, philosophy of mind needs informational mental states, philosophy of language makes communication central, and so forth. For Floridi, the expansion of information and communication technologies (ICTs) has revolutionized our understanding of the world and humanity's place in it. As Floridi explains by illuminating some of the trends we considered in Section 1.2, our world has increasingly been taken over by ICTs since the 1950s, making clear that we are not standalone entities but interconnected informational organisms (inforgs, as he says). As inforgs, we share with biological agents and artifacts a global environment composed of information, the *infosphere*. The notion of information itself, Floridi submits, has become as fundamental as those of being, knowledge, life, intelligence, meaning, and good and evil. "Information" is a sufficiently thin idea that other notions can be expressed in its terms. Philosophy of information is a comprehensive approach to philosophical investigations.[49]

---

[48] Dretske, "Précis of Knowledge and the Flow of Information," 58.

[49] Floridi, *The Fourth Revolution*; Floridi, *The Philosophy of Information*; Floridi, *The Ethics of Information*; Floridi, *The Logic of Information*. For an introduction, see Floridi, *Information*. For an overview of Floridi's work up to 2010, see Allo, "Putting Information First." See also Bynum, "Philosophy in the Information Age."

Parallel to environmental ethics, Floridi proposes an *e-vironmental ethics*, organized around the idea that any part of the infosphere has intrinsic worth. All informational entities are due some recognition. But since environmental ethics focuses on organic nature, it fails to encapsulate the whole domain where recognition is due. Floridi sees information ethics as a "patient-based" non-anthropocentric approach to be used in addition to traditional "agent-based" anthropocentric theories like utilitarianism, deontology, or virtue theory. Objects and processes in the infosphere can be damaged or destroyed by altering their characteristic data structures. Floridi calls such damage or destruction "entropy." An evil impoverishing the infosphere, *entropy ought to be minimized. Recasting large areas of philosophy from an informational angle might well turn out to be highly prescient when it comes to the transition to Life 3.0.*[50]

1.6 CONSCIOUSNESS AND MORAL STATUS

One question about the inforgs of the future (to stay with Floridi's terminology) is what moral status they would have. The point of this section is to make clear how open-ended a question that is at this stage. For X to have moral status is for X to matter on its own terms and for its own sake, and for others to have to give X consideration along such lines.[51] One common view is that *consciousness* is required for moral status, that machines could never be conscious and therefore could not have moral status. But (even granting that much) how would it be plausible for humans to be conscious while machines could *not ever* be?[52]

One traditional answer is that humans have *souls*. The general stance is metaphysical *substance dualism*, a family of views committed to the existence of nonphysical, mental phenomena. This view is prominent in several religions. In philosophy it is famously associated with René Descartes. Not many philosophers defend such a view today because it is difficult to accommodate mental substances within the worldview that the natural sciences offer. Still, versions of this view do have their defenders, and not merely among the religious. Some contemporary philosophers argue that consciousness is a primitive component of nature. Thomas Nagel, for one, thinks "mind" cannot arise from physical substances and must exist independently in nature in ways we do not yet understand. "In attempting to

---

[50] Floridi, *The Ethics of Information*, 71.

[51] Chapter 11 has much more to say about moral status and related topics; what I offer here is a preliminary discussion intended to get the connection between moral status and consciousness on our radar.

[52] (1) For the philosophy of mind behind what is to come, see Heil, *Philosophy of Mind*; Jaworski, *Philosophy of Mind*; Braddon-Mitchell and Jackson, *Philosophy of Mind and Cognition*; Carter, *Minds and Computers*. (2) Then there is the question of how much consciousness matters. See Levy, "The Value of Consciousness"; Siewert, *The Significance of Consciousness*.

understand consciousness as a biological phenomenon," he insists, "it is too easy to forget how radical is the difference between the subjective and the objective."[53]

To be sure, it is possible that there is what Susan Schneider calls a "consciousness ceiling," which we will reach if it turns out that, unlike brain tissue, microchips and similar technologies fail to support conscious experience.[54] But how could we be certain that sophisticated machines would not also host souls, if indeed souls can be hosted? If God assigns souls, nothing in our experience would tell us whether sophisticated machines could qualify. Or how could we be certain such machines could not host minds if consciousness exists independently in the world? It would be hard to grasp why only entities consisting of carbon that sexually reproduce qualify for possession of mental substances. We have no conclusive reason to think either way at this stage.[55]

In addition to substance dualism, there is *property dualism*, the view that the world consists of one kind of substance – the physical kind – but there exist two distinct kinds of properties, physical and mental ones. Mental properties are neither identical with nor reducible to physical properties but may be instantiated by the same things that instantiate physical properties. Such views steer a middle course between substance dualism and physicalism. One version of such views is *emergentism*, which holds that when matter is organized appropriately (the way, say, living human bodies are organized), mental properties emerge in a way not accounted for

---

[53] Nagel, *Mind & Cosmos*. The quote is from Nagel, 128. The emphasis on differences between the subjective and the objective standpoint permeates Nagel's work. In the philosophy of mind, he made the formulation of "what it's like to be something" central; see Nagel, "What Is It Like to Be a Bat?" (For the view that there could indeed be something, it is like to be a robot and thus that robots can have a subjective point of view, see Kiverstein, "Could a Robot Have a Subjective Point of View?".) For the political dimensions, see Nagel, *Equality and Partiality*. On the question whether machines can be conscious, see also Harnad, "Can a Machine Be Conscious? How?"

[54] Schneider, *Artificial You*. For a critical discussion of Schneider's ideas, see Chalmers, *Reality+*, chapter 15.

[55] This point is strengthened by noting that consciousness comes in a variety of forms that could admit of degrees – and this variety helps the plausibility of the view that machines might eventually be conscious in some way. To begin with, there is sentience, the capability of sensing and responding to the world. A more demanding sense is wakefulness, which requires actual exercise of that capacity of sensing and responding rather than merely having it. One would then count as conscious only while *awake and normally alert*. Self-consciousness is a yet more demanding sense that understands conscious creatures as not only aware but also as aware that they are aware. If it is taken to involve explicit conceptual self-awareness, many nonhuman animals and even young children might fail to qualify. But if only more rudimentary implicit forms of self-awareness are required, a wide range of nonlinguistic creatures might count as self-conscious. Somewhat outside of this classification we find the understanding of consciousness as "something it is like to be *that*," developed in Nagel, "What Is It Like to Be a Bat?" On this view, the essence of consciousness is for there to be a subjective way the world appears from a creature's experiential viewpoint. Bats are conscious because there is something it is like for a bat to experience its world through echo-locatory senses, even though humans cannot emphatically understand what that is like for a bat. Also see Van Gulick, "Consciousness."

by physical laws alone. In contemporary debates, such a view is espoused by David Chalmers.[56] Mental properties are basic constituents of reality on a par with fundamental physical properties such as electromagnetic charge. They may interact causally with other properties, but their existence does not depend on any other properties. Here again we have no reason to think noncarbon material could not be organized in ways that give rise to the same properties.

While Chalmers draws on a priori reasoning, neuroscientist Christof Koch has arrived at a similar view via empirical inquiry. Koch thinks consciousness can be explained as properties of living matter, in ways different from how physics normally explains things. He appeals to Integrated Information theory (IIT), which uses a measure of integrated information as a measure of consciousness. Koch does not think machines can have consciousness as he explains it. To him, intelligence and consciousness come apart: No matter how *intelligent* machines become, they cannot be *conscious*.[57] Koch might well turn out to be right, but for now we should consider it an open question on balance, according to both versions of dualism, whether eventually machines can have "minds" in whatever form humans do.

As opposed to metaphysical dualists, who believe there are two kinds of things in the world (material/physical and immaterial/mental ones), *physicalists* believe there is only one: the kind that physics describes. Based on physicalist views, it is immediately plausible that eventually machines could have moral status. After all, it is the categorical distinction between two kinds of things at the ontological level that dualists espouse and that seems to make it easiest to resist such a view. By definition, physicalists do not endorse that distinction.

One of the best-known contemporary philosophers and public intellectuals, Daniel Dennett, is thoroughly physicalist in his outlook. Dennett argues that our understanding of ourselves includes not only the body and nervous system but also our consciousness, with its elaborate sensory, emotional, and cognitive features, as well as a consciousness of other humans and nonhuman species. However, to him, consciousness is a *user-illusion* indispensable for dealings with others and for self-management. It is our conception of conscious creatures with subjective inner lives that allows us to predict how those creatures will behave. *Human* consciousness is largely a product of cultural evolution. Dennett coined the term "heterophenomenology" to describe the (scientifically false) attribution each of us makes to others of an inner representation of the world.[58] That is, each of us attributes an inner representation of the world to others. Creating general AI, Dennett holds, is possible *in principle*. But doing so would "cost too much and not give us anything we really

---

[56] Chalmers, *The Conscious Mind*.
[57] Koch, *Consciousness*; Koch, *The Feeling of Life Itself*. IIT draws on the work of Giulio Tononi. See Massimini and Tononi, *Sizing Up Consciousness*. See also Seth, *Being You*.
[58] Dennett, *From Bacteria to Bach and Back*, chapter 14.

needed."[59] It also comes with risks: We would overestimate our abilities to construct such machines and cede authority to them rashly.

Arguably the most common understanding of what a mind is among philosophers nowadays is *functionalism*. The mind/brain identity theory, a once-prominent but now-defunct view in the physicalist camp, holds that states and processes of the mind are identical to states and processes of the brain. Functionalism is a successor to that view, according to which what makes something a thought, desire, pain, or other mental state depends not on its internal constitution but on what function or role it plays in the cognitive system to which it belongs. Functionalism abstracts from details of physical implementation by characterizing mental states in terms of nonmental functional properties. For example, kidneys are characterized scientific-ally by their role in maintaining chemical balances. It is immaterial if kidneys consist of organic tissue or silicon chips: It is the role they play and their relations to other organs that make them kidneys.[60]

Functionalism's characterization of mental states in terms of their roles in produc-ing behavior grants them causal efficacy. Functionalism permits mental states to be *realized in multiple ways*. It thereby offers an account of mental states compatible with physicalism without identifying brains with minds and thus without implaus-ibly limiting the class of beings with minds to creatures with brains like ours. This theory is inspired by computer science: The mind relates to the brain as software relates to hardware. Software can run on different types of hardware. Similarly, very different types of physical entities can have minds.

Opponents object that a mind is too easy to come by this way. In particular, there is John Searle's famous *Chinese room argument*. Searle imagines himself in a room following a computer program for responding to Chinese characters slipped under the door. He understands no Chinese but can follow the program for manipulating symbols just as a computer does. Thereby, he produces appropriate strings of characters that fool others into thinking a Chinese speaker is inside. A narrow lesson of the argument is supposed to be that programming a computer may make it appear to comprehend language but fails to produce real understanding. The broader lesson is supposed to be a refutation of the theory that human minds are computer-like computational or information-processing systems.[61]

---

[59] Dennett, 400. See also Dennett, *Consciousness Explained*; Dennett, *Kinds of Minds*. For a short introduction to Dennett's work, see Heil, *Philosophy of Mind*, chapter 8. For more extensive discussion, see Brook and Ross, *Daniel Dennett*; Thompson, *Daniel Dennett*.

[60] Dennett is notoriously averse to using vocabulary other philosophers use, but he classifies his view as a kind of functionalism; see Dennett, *Consciousness Explained*, 460f.

[61] For functionalism, see Heil, *Philosophy of Mind*, chapter 6. For an early formulation of functionalism, see Putnam, "Minds and Machines." The Turing test was influential for this development; see Turing, "Computing Machinery and Intelligence." For discussion, see Block, "Troubles with Functionalism." For Searle's argument, see Searle, "Minds, Brains and Programs." For an exchange among Searle, Chalmers and Dennett, see Searle, *The*

The ensuing rich debate in the philosophy of mind does not concern us. What matters is that, for physicalists, functionalism is the most prominent view of the mind. Based on its terms, the expectation that machines can have moral status is straightforward. This much follows from the point that minds are realizable in multiple ways. That this view involves a broad understanding of what it is to have a mind might also make it possible to offer a differential understanding of moral status. In virtue of having a mind, machines would have a moral status of sorts. But it might be a status different from that of minds that are also conscious.[62]

1.7 DIGITAL LIFEWORLDS AND THE STAGES OF LIFE

We have now assembled the concepts and themes needed to understand the place of digital lifeworlds in human history. Embedding digital lifeworlds into the larger narrative of humanity as Tegmark does in terms of his distinctions among three stages of life is immensely instructive.[63] Life is a process that can retain its complexity by replicating. What is replicated is not primarily matter ("hardware," consisting of atoms) but information ("software," bits). Life is a "self-replicating, information-processing system whose information (software) determines both its behavior and the blueprints for its hardware."[64] Some forms of life are intelligent: They collect information about their environment through sensors and process this information to act back on their environment. "To live effectively is to live with adequate information," Norbert Wiener once wrote.[65]

Such gathering and processing occur in a broad range of ways and at multiple levels of complexity, from stimulus-response mechanisms in bacteria to the complex interpretation of our environment that the human eye enables our brains to perform to the development of languages that let us pass insights and observations into shared pools. Once scripts are available, such shared pools can be preserved with great accuracy and grow over generations. Historian David Christian calls us "networking creatures," emphasizing that collective learning characterizes our species.[66]

Mystery of Consciousness. See also Schneider, *Artificial You,* chapter 2. For functionalists, these principles proposed by Bostrom and Yudkowsky are natural: (1) Principle of Substrate Non-Discrimination: If two beings have the same functionality and the same conscious experience, and differ only in the substrate of their implementation, then they have the same moral status; (2) Principle of Ontogeny Non-Discrimination: If two beings have the same functionality and the same consciousness experience, and differ only in how they came into existence, then they have the same moral status. See Bostrom and Yudkowsky, "The Ethics of Artificial Intelligence," 322–23.

[62] For machine consciousness and ethical treatment of sophisticated machines in combination with a discussion of animals on the same issues, see Tye, *Tense Bees and Shell-Shocked Crabs,* especially chapter 10.

[63] Tegmark, *Life 3.0.*

[64] Tegmark, 25.

[65] Wiener, *The Human Use of Human Beings,* 18.

[66] Christian, *Maps of Time,* part III.

Initially, in Life 1.0, both hardware and software evolve through mutation and adaptation across generations. Design by individuals is not a feature of Life 1.0. Bacteria are a clear example. They cannot individually learn anything beyond what their DNA contains. The transition to Life 2.0 is gradual; a major difference between the initial stages of Life 1.0 and its later stages is the development of consciousness.[67] In Life 2.0, hardware still evolves, but software is designed. Human life prior to the digital age is an example of such life. The "software" now consists of the algorithms and knowledge we use to process information from our senses and decide what to do. As individual humans, we acquire much software first through the learning prescribed by our environment and subsequently through learning under our own direction. Only some of our hardware (body size) and some of our software (ability to process information) are available at birth. That our bodies continue to grow outside of the womb means the potential for growth is not limited by womb size. That our brains do most learning in ways beyond activating what is transmitted through DNA means our learning is not limited by what is encoded in DNA.

What is striking about our current stage of Life 2.0 is that the information in our DNA has not evolved dramatically in the last several thousand years – but during that time the information we have gathered and stored collectively has exploded. In time, this information has generated sophisticated technology that provides the scaffolding for each generation to use and enhance that information. Information is now easier to come by than ever. The Internet allows users to access the world's public knowledge through a few clicks. In 1937, science fiction writer and social critic H. G. Wells, whose work we encounter in Chapter 7, wrote articles about the World Brain. Wells calls for the universal organization and clarification of knowledge, a synthesis of widely scattered educational activities around the world. Such a synthesis would be the eponymous World Brain, "operating by an enhanced educational system through the whole body of mankind."[68] Part of that brain is a *World Encyclopedia*, "an undogmatic guide to a world culture" intended to "hold the world together mentally."[69] Unless humankind pools its intellectual resources, Wells believes, we cannot solve the problems we face. For better or worse, the Internet is the closest thing to a World Brain we have yet seen (though a recent publication on the state of the Internet has the striking title *World Without Mind*).[70]

The possibilities of the human body – our hardware constraints – have been pushed more and more in recent centuries, through better understanding of

---

[67] The renewed interest in panpsychism indicates that one debatable position here is that consciousness is widespread in nature and so might, in certain versions, already be present in Life 1.0. See, for example, Strawson et al., *Consciousness and Its Place in Nature*; Goff, *Galileo's Error*; Goff, *Consciousness and Fundamental Reality*; Bruntrup and Jaskolla, *Panpsychism*.

[68] Wells, *World Brain*, 16.

[69] Wells, 30.

[70] Foer, *World Without Mind*.

nutrition, hygiene, social parameters of health, and causes and courses of diseases. Nonetheless, our bodies constrain what we can do with all this information and the resulting technological capacities. By contrast, in Life 3.0, both software and hardware are designed, and so limitations from the frailty of the body are lifted.[71]

Currently, digitalization mostly serves to advance the software available at this phase of Life 2.0 and the way it can be accessed. Nonetheless, lifeworlds as we inhabit them may well already be driving the transition to Life 3.0. This transition might involve not only the development of new kinds of intelligent entities; humanity might change alongside these developments. The idea that there would or should eventually be a new type of human beyond the biological or cultural and historical limitations of *Homo sapiens* is not new and has perhaps most famously been expressed in Friedrich Nietzsche's idea of the *Übermensch*, the super-human (literally, what is beyond the human).[72] In recent decades that idea has been most commonly pursued under the headings of *transhumanism* and *posthumanism*. In both cases, the point is that the current limitations that characterize the human conditions are overcome through use of technology. Transhumanists put the focus on actual enhancements of individual humans. Posthumanists emphasize possibilities for using technology to renegotiate boundaries between humans and other species.[73]

Whatever the future ends up being will emerge from our current digital lifeworlds, barring a catastrophic collapse.[74] Eventually these lifeworlds might merge into a full-fledged Life 3.0 populated by genetically enhanced humans, cyborgs, and uploaded brains, as well as specialized and general AI embedded into any manner of physical device. We need to take seriously the possibility that these entities *know* things and are *conscious* in ways similar to or different from our own. They also might have a moral status of sorts, either because of similarities to us or because of their inherent features. It might or might not come to that. But we cannot afford to start taking this possibility seriously only once it is upon us. In any event, this phase of Life 2.0 brings changes that are profound all by themselves, even if they do not take us to Life 3.0.

---

[71] The distinctions among these stages are not neat. But one could add more fine-tuning and talk about Life 2.1, 2.15, etc. For reflection on the role of AI in the trajectory of humanity, see also Kissinger, Schmidt, and Huttenlocher, *The Age of AI*. They emphasize the ways AI will affect human security.

[72] See for instance Nietzsche, *Thus Spoke Zarathustra*.

[73] On transhumanism, see Livingstone, *Transhumanism*; More and Vita-More, *The Transhumanist Reader*. A classic piece of posthumanism is Donna Haraway's "Cyborg Manifesto"; see Haraway, *Manifestly Haraway*. Bruno Latour has many affinities with Haraway's posthumanism; see Latour, *We Have Never Been Modern*; Latour, *Reassembling the Social*. For discussion, see Coeckelbergh, *Introduction to Philosophy of Technology*, chapter 9. On the moral challenges from efforts at human enhancement, see e.g., Habermas, *The Future of Human Nature*; Sandel, *The Case against Perfection*. On human enhancement from a virtue-ethics standpoint, see Vallor, *Technology and the Virtues*, chapter 10.

[74] On the possible paths to a superintelligence, see Bostrom, *Superintelligence*, chapters 2–3.

2

Learning from the Amish

Political Philosophy as Philosophy of Technology in the Digital Century

'T is the day of the chattel
Web to weave, and corn to grind;
Things are in the saddle,
And ride mankind.

> —Ralph Waldo Emerson, "Ode, Inscribed to William H. Channing"[1]

We live invested in an electric information environment that is quite as imperceptible to us as water is to fish.

> —Marshall McLuhan[2]

2.1 WORRYING ABOUT TECHNOLOGY

It might come as a surprise that John von Neumann, one of the twentieth century's greatest promoters of technology, and the techno-skeptical Amish would share concerns about technology. But for just that reason, there could be no better starting point than such concerns for a chapter on the need for political thought to make technology more central than some of its traditions have done.

Often looked upon with bemusement but known to large parts of the American public, the Amish are committed to maintaining close control over how technology shapes their affairs. Descending from radical sixteenth-century European Protestants and named for influential leader Jakob Ammann, the Amish are pacifist Christians who fully separate church and state. To Amish communities, technology is never neutral. They do not embrace innovations for sheer efficiency or entertainment value. Though some communities are more open than others, all bar technologies that they suspect of weakening community ties, strengthening dependence on

---

[1] Emerson, *Emerson's Complete Works*, IX (Poems), 73.
[2] McLuhan, *Counterblast*, 5.

government or surrounding communities of nonbelievers, or threatening their pursuit of virtuous lives. The Amish inhabit houses disconnected from the electric grid, cultivate land with horse-drawn machinery and get around in buggies, renounce insurance schemes – including social security – do without TV and radio, and limit the use of phones. If for something to be "political" means that it pertains to how institutions, practices, or actions shape human living arrangements, use of technology is one of the most central political issues for the Amish.[3]

John von Neumann, a giant of modern mathematics, held views on life generally and on technology specifically that share little with those of the Amish.[4] As noted in Chapter 1, his work helped inaugurate the digital age. During World War II, von Neumann – a Hungarian émigré – helped develop atomic weapons. Afterwards he served on the US Atomic Energy Commission, consulting on military research. It was in this capacity that, in 1955, he published "Can We Survive Technology?" which we already encountered.[5] With the need to interfere with the climate already on his radar, von Neumann worries that "once such possibilities become actual, they will be exploited." It takes novel political mechanisms to prevent this exploitation. "Experience shows," he adds, inadvertently echoing the worries of the Amish, "that even smaller technological changes than those now in the cards profoundly transform political and social relationships"; such transformations "are not a priori predictable." Accordingly, "one should take neither present difficulties nor presently proposed reforms too seriously."[6]

All we know, as the article concludes, is that we need "patience, flexibility, intelligence" to get through. But these and other virtues might not be enough for us to survive technology. The *Fermi Paradox*, named after physicist Enrico Fermi, is the apparent contradiction between the plausibly high probabilities for the existence of extraterrestrial life, on the one hand, and the complete absence of credible evidence for such life, on the other.[7] Possibly the constellation of conditions needed for life to emerge is so extraordinary that, the vast size of the universe notwithstanding, either we are alone after all or occurrences of life are so rare that such lack of evidence is expected. But according to another resolution of the paradox, this lack of evidence stems from the fact that intelligent life tends to perish after a while

[3] Kraybill, *What the Amish Teach Us*; Kraybill, Johnson-Weiner, and Nolt, *The Amish*. For a work of political theory that acknowledges how the Amish might serve as a model for what it means to pay attention to use of technology, see Sclove, *Democracy and Technology*.

[4] Macrae, *John von Neumann*; Heims, *John von Neumann and Norbert Wiener*.

[5] von Neumann, "Can We Survive Technology?" For more recent discussions of existential risk, see Ord, *The Precipice*; Bostrom, *Superintelligence*. Specifically on how vulnerable our world currently is with regard to the technological developments von Neumann had in mind, see Bostrom, "The Vulnerable World Hypothesis."

[6] Quotes are from the last two paragraphs of his article; see von Neumann, "Can We Survive Technology?" 519.

[7] See Ćirković, *The Great Silence*; Forgan, *Solving Fermi's Paradox*. For an accessible discussion, see Bostrom, "Where Are They?"

(by cosmic standards). Sometimes this happens accidentally: Asteroids might hit, the nearest sun expires, and other such things. But typically, perdition comes about as self-destruction in the very exercise of intelligence – regardless of any virtues this life might possess. Intelligent life, that is, tends to create technology that eventually brings destruction, and does so *before* this intelligent life manages to connect to intelligent life on other planets (which is why we find no evidence of intelligent life elsewhere even though it is likely that there is such life).

von Neumann's article could consequently be a milestone in diagnosing that it is now our turn to enter this dangerous stage of destruction by the very technology we have created. Still, the great mathematician might well have erred by ending with identifying the human abilities necessary to revert this process. Instead, as one might argue, now should be the time to learn from the Amish and advocate vigorously for a *profoundly different* approach to innovation, one that involves a systematic political process to make sure a high burden of proof is met that technological innovations can sustain (and not destroy) the life humans have built.[8]

However, we do not even need to engage in any cosmic pondering of what to infer about humanity's prospects from the lack of evidence for the existence of intelligent life elsewhere in the universe. Climate change, the possibilities of gene-editing and geo-engineering, the potential for human enhancement from pharmaceuticals and bioelectronics, the potential of nanotechnology, synthetic biology, robotics, and, of course, AI: Reflection on these themes reveals that the use of technology is intensely political and should require broad-based community approval, nationally and internationally. So, at this stage of history, the Amish attitude to make control over technology a central political matter has much to recommend it. A common view is that the Amish are trapped in old-fashioned ways. But it might be the rest of us who are trapped in a technological maelstrom that we are powerless to stop and have little share in shaping – and that might eventually doom us. Considering von Neumann's contributions to technology, the fact that he, too, saw the intensely political nature of technology and worried about how to manage it only strengthens this point. It might already be too late to avoid the destruction. But then again, it might not be.[9]

---

[8] To be sure, if this resolution of Fermi's Paradox is correct, movements like the Amish, in the operations of intelligence across the universe, would generally lose out. Maybe that is because temptations to create technology transcend the ability of intelligent life to sustain complex social arrangements.

[9] In an influential discussion of ethics in an era of technological innovation, philosopher Hans Jonas has argued that use of advanced technology involves collective actions, whose consequences and possibly damaging effects on nature and future people we often cannot know. Both nature and future generations are subject to our collective actions; therefore, we have obligations toward them. The "imperative of responsibility" that Jonas formulates states, "Act so that the effects of your action are compatible with the permanence of genuine human life." Or phrased another way, "Act not destructively for future generations and the totality of their life conditions." To ensure "genuine human life" is to protect future humanity's autonomy, dignity, integrity, and vulnerability. See Jonas, *The Imperative of Responsibility*. In recent work

To be sure, technology is often treated as political. And yet, it is peculiar that specific technologies and their impacts and the pace at which technology changes how we do things are not *much more broadly* discussed. It is peculiar that regulation of technology is not generally considered one of the most essential responsibilities of governments (including and especially the US government) or that differences in how to handle technology are not major election issues. Typically, the private sector – engaging people as consumers rather than citizens – takes the lead in technological innovation and thus in shaping what communities are possible.

What is also peculiar is that, as far as philosophical reflection is concerned, *political philosophy* and *philosophy of technology* in their typical separateness mirror the relative separateness of the political and the technological domains. What is needed is a reorientation of political philosophy, as a field that should be understood *also as* philosophy of technology, to reflect the political nature of technology.[10] Some traditions have incorporated this perspective all along, prominently Marxism and phenomenology, especially the branch centered on Heidegger. My main goal here is to make this case for the Rawlsian understanding of political philosophy organized around the notion of public reason.

Section 2.2 offers clarifications around the political and technological domains to give an initial sense of how they might overlap and how different views of the political domain assign different roles to technology. Sections 2.3–2.5 identify three ways – what I call a foundational, an enframing, and an interactive sense – for technology to be political. I ground these senses in the Marxist tradition, but the second also brings in Heidegger. Making the Marxist tradition central here serves two purposes. To begin with, it is a way of paying homage to how right that tradition has been to give such importance to technology, whereas the lack of emphasis on this topic, especially in the liberal tradition, is now an obstacle to drawing attention to the political relevance of technology when it matters most. Secondly, in the course of this book, we encounter multiple authors from the Marxist tradition broadly conceived. So it will be useful to pay close attention to the Marxist background right away.

Section 2.3 explores the *foundational* role that technology plays in Marx's view of the unfolding of history (which delivers his understanding of the political domain). Historical materialism – Marx's theory that history unfolds in response to changes in the underlying economic base – is a disputed view, to say the least. But it continues to be of great interest for the measure of intellectual plausibility it does have. Section

on AI in human security, Henry Kissinger, Eric Schmidt, and Daniel Huttenlocher echo this theme: "In an era of artificial intelligence, the enduring quest for national advantage must be informed by an ethic of human preservation"; Kissinger, Schmidt, and Huttenlocher, *The Age of AI*, 176.

[10] This view is also taken in Coeckelbergh, *The Political Philosophy of AI*. Coeckelbergh writes correctly that bringing political philosophy and philosophy of technology closer "is an academic gap, but also a societal need"; Coeckelbergh, 4.

2.4 looks at Marcuse's mid-twentieth-century assessment of capitalism as so thoroughly manipulated by technological means that all revolutionary action (the anticipation of which is central to Marxism) is suffocated. Marcuse combines Heideggerian and Marxist insights. Based on this account, technology is political in the sense that it *enframes* all human activity in ways that typically escape notice. Section 2.5 introduces an *interactive* sense of how technology is political, with technology shaping relations pertinent to the political domain. This sense focuses on the role of particular technologies in society.

Section 2.6 turns to Rawls's account of public reason, a plausible conception of the political that nonetheless, on the face of it, ignores technology. However, as I argue in Sections 2.7 and 2.8, the foundational, enframing, and interactive senses in which technology is political are recognizable from the standpoint of the Rawlsian view. In light of the formidable amount of technological innovation in the twenty-first century, with all the risks such innovation entails, it is vital for any conception of the political to make room for these three senses that the Marxist tradition so naturally delivers. Any political philosophy that speaks to the political problems of this century must also be a philosophy of technology.[11]

2.2 SOME INITIAL CONCEPTUAL CLARIFICATION

The concept of technology is used at different levels. At a basic level, "technology" refers to sets of *artifacts* like cars, computers, or voting machines. At the next level, it also includes human *activities*, as in "the technology of e-voting." Thereby, the term also refers to the making and handling of such artifacts. In that spirit, Amartya Sen's finding that famines do not tend to occur in functioning democracies can be captured by saying that democracy is a technology for eliminating famines (putting to work the many artifacts that make democracy work; see Chapter 3). Finally, and closest to its Greek origin, "technology" refers to *knowledge*: It is about the theory behind machines and production processes.[12]

To approach the concept of the political, let us say *power* is the ability to affect people's interests or incentive structures to get them to do things they otherwise would not do, to do things differently than they would otherwise, or to do things for different reasons than they would otherwise.[13] By *order*, I mean a reasonably enduring and stable arrangement of how power is exercised in given contexts. Colloquially, "politics" is the

---

[11] For an effort to connect Rawlsian theory to contemporary information technology, see also Hoffmann, "Rawls, Information Technology, and the Sociotechnical Bases of Self-Respect." Also see Duff, *A Normative Theory of the Information Society.*

[12] I follow Bijker, "Why and How Technology Matters." On democracy being a technology for eliminating famines, see Reich, Sahami, and Weinstein, *System Error*, 74. For Sen on famines, see, for example, Sen, *Development as Freedom*, chapter 7.

[13] See Dahl, "The Concept of Power"; Dowding, *Rational Choice and Political Power*; Lukes, *Power*. Overall, this section follows Risse, *On Justice*, chapter 14.

set of institutions and the practices and activities within them through which order is created. To call *X* "political" is to say *X* pertains to how institutions, practices, or actions shape an order. Normally we use the term when people who are typically not related in kinship try to find reasonably enduring and stable arrangements of how power is exercised (and thus maintain order). But slogans such as "the personal is political" (popularized by feminist writers) indicate that more intimate relationships also fall within the scope of what generates order. In any event, this is a broad notion of the political that also includes the social domain (though one could tease out a separate domain of the social and limit the political to institutions). The *concept* of the political, or of politics, then, concerns ways in which order is created. A *political value* is any value pertaining to that setting.

For the concept of technology, it makes sense to distinguish different levels of concreteness to capture the complexities that come with that concept (as we did earlier). As far as the political is concerned, a good way of capturing pertinent complexities is to distinguish various *conceptions* of the political from the *concept* of the political. Such conceptions offer answers to questions about what kinds of agency and structure will normally or should bear on how order is created. The more plausible conceptions will be responsive to some mix of anthropological considerations connecting political possibilities to human nature, historical inquiries drawing on experiences with methods of creating order, and normative considerations about what kind of order is worth having.

Conceptions of the political often draw on Aristotle's *Politics*, where some seminal claims appear.[14] For Aristotle, humans naturally live in *poleis*. In section 1253a8 of *Politics*, he calls us *politikón zoon*, beings that live in such places. Justice, too, is characterized as bound to the *polis*: The virtue or practice of justice (*dikaiosunē*) is political, and justice (*dikē*) is the basis on which political associations are ordered (1253a33–35). The political usually involves "alternation in ruling and being ruled" (1259b2), as well as rule among those who "tend by their nature to be on an equal footing and to differ in nothing" (1259b5). Conceptions that draw on Aristotle look at processes of creating order by way of emphasizing the transformation of humans through activities of ruling and being ruled. They can also characterize the kind of activity that becomes possible in such a setting and/or the features that essentially matter to shared life in *poleis*.[15]

---

[14] Aristotle, *Politics*. The citations are by way of reference to the standard edition of the works of Aristotle, issued by the Prussian Academy of Science (the so-called Bekker numbering).

[15] Among more recent thinkers, Hannah Arendt and Michael Oakeshott offer such theorizing. For Arendt, life within a *polis* enabled humans to interact in ways unavailable before. Prospects of solving conflicts by reasoned argument made it possible for ruling and being ruled to become temporary states for citizens; Arendt, *The Human Condition*, 26f. Oakeshott defines politics as activity by which rulers and ruled (but not in those capacities) deliberate on how both the *polis* as a whole and the individuals within it are ruled; see Oakeshott, *On Human Conduct*, 159. For discussion of these various accounts of the political, see Alexander, "Notes Towards a Definition of Politics." See also Miller, "What Does 'Political' Mean?"

A very different conception originates with Carl Schmitt, who defines the political in terms of a friend–enemy distinction. For Schmitt, maintaining order inevitably occurs antagonistically.[16] Decisions matter more than deliberation. Accordingly, to him, a properly functioning state is a homogeneous entity with internal competition and dissent largely dissolved.[17] Schmitt seeks to capture an allegedly basic truth, that we live together in communities willing to fight others to the death.[18]

What should be visible already from this brief excursion into the range of conceptions of the political that have been favored by influential thinkers is that different conceptions might have more or less use for explicit articulations of the role of technology, depending on how central technology is deemed to be for the relevant anthropological considerations, historical inquiries, and normative considerations that inform that conception. As we will see, Marx and Rawls deploy different conceptions and vary especially in terms of how much visibility they give to technology.

2.3 TECHNOLOGY IS POLITICAL IN A FOUNDATIONAL SENSE: KARL MARX

For Marx, technology plays a distinctive and explicit role in his understanding of the political, which is part of his theory of history: historical materialism. A sketch of that view appears in Marx's 1847 *Poverty of Philosophy*. "In acquiring new productive forces men change their mode of production," he says, "and in changing their mode of production, in changing the way of earning their living, they change all their social relations." Marx adds the memorable illustration that "the hand-mill gives you society with the feudal lord; the steam-mill, society with the industrial capitalist."[19]

It is, however, the dense preface to Marx's 1859 *Critique of Political Economy* that contains the canonical statement of historical materialism.[20] Marx presents a

---

[16] Schmitt, *Begriff des Politischen*.
[17] Schmitt, *Verfassungslehre*, chapter 17.
[18] For these themes in the American context, see Kahn, "Sacrificial Nation"; Kahn, *Political Theology*. See also Mouffe, *On the Political*. What Schmitt calls the "concept" of the political, I see as one conception.
[19] McLellan, *Karl Marx: Selected Writings*, 219f.
[20] McLellan, 424–27. The manuscripts collected as *The German Ideology*, jointly written with Friedrich Engels in 1845–46, are another much-used earlier source; see McLellan, 176–84. My interpretation follows the influential elaboration by G. A. Cohen. See Cohen, *Karl Marx's Theory of History*; Cohen, "Forces and Relations of Production." See also Shaw, "The Handmill Gives You the Feudal Lord." For an introduction that draws on Cohen, see Wolff, *Why Read Marx Today?*, 52–66. For discussion critical of Cohen, see Elster, *Making Sense of Marx*, chapter 5. In what now is the standard reading, Cohen ascribes to Marx a technological determinism of sorts, an interpretation rejected by Miller, *Analyzing Marx*. Miller's reading, in turn, informs Andrew Feenberg's critical-theory development of Marx's historical materialism. See, for example, Feenberg, *Transforming Technology*, 44–48. For the argument that Miller's rejection of Cohen's interpretation depends on a misunderstanding of what Cohen attributes to Marx, see Buchanan, "Marx as Kierkegaard: Review of Richard W. Miller, 'Analyzing Marx.'"

three-tiered distinction between *productive forces* (or forces of production), *productive relations* (or relations of production, constituting the *economic structure* or *base* of society), and the legal and political *superstructure*. Productive forces are all facilities, devices, or resources used for production. This includes means of production (physical productive resources ranging from land; natural sources of power such as steam, water, or coal; animals; and raw materials to instruments, tools, and machines) and human labor power (strength, skill, and knowledge). Productive forces tend to develop, becoming more powerful over time. Humanity gets better at producing things. For Marx, history largely is a process of growth in productive forces, with more productive social structures replacing less productive ones.

"In the social production of their life," Marx says in the preface, "men inevitably enter into definite relations that are indispensable and independent of their will, relations of production which correspond to a definite stage of the development of their material productive forces."[21] Productive relations, that is, are the human relationships that shape production. This includes all organized relations that contribute to how productive forces are deployed, namely both work and ownership relations, with all their differentiations and division of labor. "The sum total of these relations of production constitutes the economic structure of society," Marx continues, "the real foundation, on which rises a legal and political superstructure and to which correspond definite forms of social consciousness."[22] The gist is that the level of development of society's productive forces explains the nature of its productive relations (its economic structure or base). Meanwhile, those productive relations explain the superstructure – the legal and political institutions – as well as society's *ideology*, its religious, artistic, moral, and philosophical beliefs.[23]

"At a certain stage of development," Marx continues, "the material productive forces of society come into conflict with the existing relations of production."[24] Revolution and epochal change come about when an economic structure no longer develops the productive forces (at which point their development is "fettered") and eventually makes room for a new economic structure better suited to the continued development of productive forces.[25] This transition cannot happen by itself but instead depends on actions of the working class. For Marx, capitalism is marred by

---

Interpreting historical materialism is a central topic in the history of Marxism; for the bigger picture, see, for example, Kolakowski, *Main Currents of Marxism*; McLellan, *Marxism After Marx*.

[21] McLellan, *Karl Marx: Selected Writings*, 425.

[22] McLellan, 425.

[23] As Marx explains in the *Communist Manifesto*, "the ruling ideas of each age have ever been the ideas of its ruling class," McLellan, 260.

[24] McLellan, 425.

[25] What has long marred this account is how productive forces could *explain* the economic structure, while it is the economic structure that *develops* productive forces. There seemed to be a circularity at the heart of Marx's theory of history, rendering it implausible before questions of accuracy would even arise. It is G. A. Cohen's contribution to articulate a notion of *functional explanation* to show how this is possible; see Cohen, *Karl Marx's Theory of*

a class struggle between those who depend on wages and those who own the economy. That this basic conflict exists and that its resolution lies in a revolution are key components of his conception of the political.

In short, what shapes production shapes society across the board, as a result of people responding to what is possible or necessary under the circumstances. In any area, it is available technology (as part of the productive forces) that primarily sets the limits of what is possible and necessary. In that sense, Marx proposes a kind of technological determinism, a *productive-force determinism* (which involves more than machines or technology narrowly conceived).[26] Later thinkers capture technology as a separate, substantive phenomenon. But, for Marx, to see technology as part of the productive forces is to see it as something thoroughly human. Another way that human agency enters (consistent with productive-force determinism) is the emphasis on class struggle and revolutionary strategy. Progress in productive ability inspires people to bring about a new order.

Socialism emerges because under capitalism, the productive relations – focused on private ownership of means of production – can no longer develop the productive forces. But those forces themselves, especially technology, remain unchanged after the revolution that puts an end to capitalism. They would grow in reinvigorated fashion because socialism, abandoning that type of private property, is better suited to enhance productive capacities. Marx condemns capitalism for its economic (and resulting legal and political) arrangements, *not* for its material accomplishments.[27]

History, 249–96. While indeed elements of the economic structure (or the superstructure) change *because* such change is needed to sustain growth of productive forces, change in productive forces does not *cause* those changes in the economic structure or the superstructure. While, say, capitalism does develop the productive forces, its ability to do so is *why* capitalism could emerge (when it did). It could not have arisen otherwise, and it disappears once it fails to develop the productive forces. The kind of challenge such a theory must address to sustain its plausibility becomes clear in Joshua Cohen's review of G. A. Cohen; see Cohen, "Review of 'Karl Marx's Theory of History,' by G. A. Cohen." Joshua Cohen argues that interactions of individuals may or may not in the aggregate sustain growth of productive forces. Whether they do depends on the nature of the superstructure. There is no a priori reason that pursuit of individual interests *generally* creates productive growth. Technological determinists must either acknowledge this coordination problem and renounce the thesis that productive forces by and large develop in history, or explain why that problem normally is solved, for which the theory seems to offer no noncircular resources.

[26] For the term "productive-force determinism," see Shaw, "The Handmill Gives You the Feudal Lord." A challenge is to understand this theory in ways that avoid crude economic reductionism by permitting enough complexity without endorsing vacuous explanatory pluralism.

[27] One question is to what extent all this is social science or (at least also) moral argument, see, for example, Lukes, *Marxism and Morality*; Geras, "The Controversy about Marx and Justice." We can now see, though, that the slogan "the hand-mill gives you society with the feudal lord; the steam-mill, society with the industrial capitalist" must be understood appropriately. Capitalist technology can still be used under socialism. The point is not that particular devices fix a political order but that social structures in a specific sense accompany the growth of productive forces. So, the illustration does not contest the neutrality of technology that makes it available to both capitalism and socialism, as Marcuse thought it did, Marcuse, *One-Dimensional Man*, 154.

Industry and technology are part of the solution to rather than among the sources of capitalism's social problems. Marx does not advocate a romantic critique of capitalism, which bemoans the devastation of allegedly virtuous pre-capitalist relations.

2.4 TECHNOLOGY IS POLITICAL IN AN ENFRAMING SENSE: HERBERT MARCUSE

Marx's conception of the political makes central the basic conflict between the working class and capitalists. This conflict is resolvable, but only through a revolution. To spell out this view of the political, Marx *must* talk about technology, which is *foundational* in the sense that technology is part of the productive forces, which in turn largely explain the operations of power in society.

Twentieth-century social thought had to explain why the revolution as Marx predicted it never occurred. A typical answer was that capitalism persevered not merely by dominating culture (which made the economic structure hold up better than Marx had anticipated), but also by deploying technology to develop a pervasive entertainment sector. The working class got mired in consumption habits that annihilated their political instincts. But Marxist thought sustains the prospect that, if the right path were found, a revolution would occur. In the 1930s, Walter Benjamin thought the emerging movie industry could help unite the masses in struggle, capitalism's efforts notwithstanding to obtain cultural domination. Shared exposure to movies could create experiences that would allow people to engage the vast capitalist apparatus that had intruded upon their lives. Deployed the right way, this new type of art could help finish capitalism after all.[28]

By the time Marcuse published *One-Dimensional Man* in 1964, such optimism about entertainment had vanished. To be sure, Marcuse was appealing to students on both sides of the Atlantic who were yearning for change during the 1960s and beyond precisely because he did *not* share the profound pessimism of other prominent intellectuals in the Marxist tradition. To Max Horkheimer and Theodor W. Adorno especially, ever-expanding capitalism (deploying scientific research and latest technology) was only the latest instantiation of overt patterns of blind domination, with no way out.[29] Adorno's work was so bleak that yet another major thinker in the Marxist tradition, Georg Lukács, described him as having "taken up residence in the 'Grand Hotel Abyss.'"[30]

By contrast, Marcuse did not abandon the Marxist commitment to the possibility of a revolution. But he did regard contemporary culture as authoritarian because entertainment represents a central part of it. Capitalism, technology, and entertainment

---

[28] Benjamin, *The Work of Art in the Age of Its Technological Reproducibility.*
[29] Horkheimer, *Dialectic of Enlightenment.* For Adorno's political thought, see also Hammer, *Adorno and the Political*; Gordon, Hammer, and Pensky, *A Companion to Adorno*, Part VII.
[30] Lukacs, *The Theory of the Novel*, 22.

culture create new forms of social control, false needs, and false consciousness around consumption. Their combined force locks one-dimensional man into one-dimensional society, producing the need for people to recognize themselves in commodities. Powers of critical reflection decline, as people become focused on owning things and lose themselves in entertainment. The working class can no longer operate as a subversive force capable of revolutionary change. Technological rationality has become political rationality: What makes sense for consumers of commercially pro-vided technology makes sense for citizens.

"A comfortable, smooth, reasonable, democratic unfreedom prevails in advanced civilization," Marcuse starts off in *One-Dimensional Man*.[31] Technology immedi-ately enters his reckoning. It is "by virtue of the way it has organized its technological base, [that] contemporary industrial society tends to be totalitarian."[32] He elaborates, "The people recognize themselves in their commodities; they find their soul in their automobile, hi-fi set, split-level home, kitchen equipment."[33]

Marx clearly delineates technology's place in historical materialism: It is part of the productive forces. Its impact on society and the way it is political are founda-tional in that sense. Superstructure (legal and political institutions) and ideology are explained by their role in growing productive forces. That is, if the question arises as to why a certain superstructure and ideology are in place at a particular location and a particular time, that question is fully answered by an account of how they help with the growth of the productive forces. But that also means that superstructure and ideology are to some extent explained by technology, which is part of the productive forces. Within that explanation, however, technology's role is also *curtailed* by its being embedded into the productive forces. By contrast, Marcuse states that when technology assumes a role much larger than that of a subset of the forces of production (that is, "when technics becomes the universal form of material production"), then "it circumscribes an entire culture; it projects a historical totality – a 'world.'"[34]

Strikingly, that discussion occurs right after Marcuse approvingly quotes from Heidegger as follows:

> Modern man takes the entirety of Being as raw material for production and subjects the entirety of the object-world to the sweep and order of production . . . The use of

[31] Marcuse, *One-Dimensional Man*, 1.
[32] Marcuse, 3.
[33] Marcuse, 9.
[34] Marcuse, 154. Marcuse distinguishes "technics" from "technology," beginning in Marcuse, "Some Social Implications of Modern Technology." "Technics" is the apparatus of industry, transportation, and communication, the instruments of human labor. "Technology" is the organization of technical resources, which manifests itself in prevalent thought and behavioral patterns. This understanding makes it easy to create a link between technology and ideology.

machinery and the production of machines is not technics itself but merely an adequate instrument for the realization . . . of the essence of technics in its objective raw material.[35]

It might be surprising that a member of the Frankfurt School would quote Heidegger to make a point: Heidegger was discredited within the school for his affiliation with National Socialism. (After all, the Frankfurt School was a philosophical movement with Marxist roots that came out of a research institute in Frankfurt, the Institute for Social Research, that had to be moved out of Germany under the Nazis at about the same time when Heidegger's affiliation with them was strongest.[36]) However, Marcuse studied under Heidegger, and Marcuse's philosophy of technology in *One-Dimensional Man* integrates both Marxist and Heideggerian themes.[37]

Heidegger's main work on technology is his 1953 *The Question Concerning Technology*.[38] Modern technology is the contemporary mode of understanding things. Technology makes things show up as mattering one way or another. As Heidegger says, the *mode of revealing* characteristic of modern technology sees everything around us as a *standing-reserve* (*Bestand*), resources to be exploited as means.[39] This includes the whole natural world, even humans. In 1966, Heidegger even predicted that "someday factories will be built for the artificial breeding of human material."[40] That theme is present in the excerpt from his work that Marcuse quotes. Heidegger famously offers the example of a hydroelectric plant converting the Rhine into a supplier of waterpower.[41] By contrast, a wooden bridge that has spanned it for centuries reveals the river as an environment that permits natural phenomena to appear as objects of wonder.

Heidegger uses the term *Gestell* (enframing) to capture the relevance of technology in our lives.[42] The prefix *Ge* is about the linking together of elements, as in *Gebirge* (mountain range). *Gestell* literally is a linking together of things. For Heidegger, the *Gestell* is a horizon of disclosure according to which everything registers only as a resource. *Gestell* deprives us of any ability to stand in caring relations to things. Heidegger points out that "the earth now reveals itself as a coal mining district, the soil as a material deposit."[43] Elsewhere he says that the modern

---

[35] Marcuse quotes (and translates) this from Heidegger, *Holzwege*, 266ff. He also refers to Heidegger, "Die Frage nach der Technik," 22, 29.
[36] On the Frankfurt School and the Institute for Social Research, see Wiggershaus, *The Frankfurt School*.
[37] Feenberg, *Heidegger and Marcuse*; Marcuse, *Heideggerian Marxism*; Habermas, "Zum Geleit."
[38] Heidegger, *The Question Concerning Technology, and Other Essays*, 3–35. On Heidegger, see Richardson, *Heidegger*; Zimmerman, *Heidegger's Confrontation with Modernity*.
[39] Heidegger, *The Question Concerning Technology, and Other Essays*, 17.
[40] Quoted in Young, *Heidegger's Later Philosophy*, 46.
[41] Heidegger, *The Question Concerning Technology, and Other Essays*, 16.
[42] Heidegger, 19.
[43] Heidegger, 14.

world reveals itself as a "gigantic petrol station."[44] Technology lets us relate to the world only in impoverished ways. Everything is interconnected and exchangeable. Efficiency and optimization set the stage, demanding standardization, and repetition. Technology saves us from having to develop skills while turning us into people satisfied with lives that involve few skills.[45]

Marcuse took his cues from Heidegger, arguing that the one-dimensional technological universe of advanced industrial society was a (nearly) closed system where opposition was (nearly) impossible. It is because of this connection to Heidegger that I call this way for technology to be political the *enframing* sense. The point is that technology permeates and thereby defines culture as a whole. What a proper understanding of these tendencies makes clear, however, is the loss to human possibilities thus incurred. Like the foundational sense, the enframing sense assigns an essential role to technology in how the political is understood to begin with. Like Marx, Marcuse cannot account for the political domain without talking about technology. But Marcuse looks at this domain when capitalism is some decades further along.

2.5 TECHNOLOGY IS POLITICAL IN AN INTERACTIVE SENSE: ANDREW FEENBERG

According to Marx's 1859 preface, the change to socialism is revolutionary, but only as far as ownership relations are concerned (with accompanying implications for the superstructure). Friedrich Engels famously insisted that the revolution would leave intact the hierarchical nature of work relations.[46] He drew lessons from cotton-spinning mills, railroads, and seafaring: Such workplaces require chains of command. This view collides with certain other statements that Marx also makes, namely, about how communism dissolves the capitalist division of labor. More generally, this position raises concerns around the Marxist treatment of *alienation*.

After all, among the evils of capitalism that preoccupy Marx (especially early on) is rampant alienation. Capitalism condemns people to live in societies whose workings they cannot comprehend and that do not even aim to meet their needs or values.[47] One question is whether alienation flows entirely from capitalist

---

[44] Quoted in Young, *Heidegger's Later Philosophy*, 50.
[45] A few years before Heidegger wrote his piece on technology, in 1947, Stanford mathematician George Dantzig published a seminal piece on linear optimization, introducing his celebrated Simplex algorithm. Decades later, Dantzig would comment that what characterized the pre-1947 era was a lack of interest in optimization; see Dantzig, "Linear Programming." In the post-1947 era, there definitely was a lot of interest in optimization, and it found a stern critic in Heidegger.
[46] Engels, "On Authority."
[47] In Marx's writings alienation is especially prominent in the early *Economic and Philosophical Manuscripts*, McLellan, *Karl Marx: Selected Writings*, 83–121. See also Schacht, *Alienation*; Jaeggi, *Alienation*.

ownership relations and disappears under socialism or flows partly from work relations, thus persisting beyond revolution. In communist society, industrial production still grows the productive forces previously fettered under capitalism. If alienation *also* emanates from work relations, it would be especially the work relations embedded into industrial production where that flow could happen. Alienation would persevere under communism.[48]

Critical theorist Andrew Feenberg has developed this concern.[49] He explores how mechanisms of domination enter workplaces. This could happen, for instance, if machinery is introduced that can be operated by unskilled laborers, laborers with less bargaining power than skilled ones. Skill in production, then, resides in the system rather than individual workers. The design of tools and organization of production become causes of alienation as such workers become replaceable and their role in production becomes nominal and in fact banal. Workers do their share in production but might comprehend neither the production system as a whole nor the workings of society beyond it. Given the workers' substitutability, there are no guarantees (or reasons) that the system would respond to their needs or values. Owners and managers have operational autonomy. They have no reason to approach workers as competent agents whose comprehension of the system ought to be fostered and whose needs and values ought to be considered. Free also from public scrutiny, they can design workplaces for the sake of profits.[50]

Alternatively, design and organization could aim to minimize alienation. Different designs and ways of organizing production can support a more democratic society, for instance, by bringing more self-organization into the technical sphere. Feenberg believes that wherever work relations – as well as also broader social relations outside of work – are mediated by technology, we should introduce more democratic controls and redesign technology to encourage people to use their skills and show initiative.[51]

Technology here is political in an *interactive* sense: It shapes relations among people. In the Marxist context, where the design of tools and organization of production become causes of alienation, technology shapes *workplace* relations; it might create or reinforce hierarchies, or alternatively it might also dismantle or keep them away. But technology is also political in this same interactive sense in society

---

[48] Interesting responses to such concerns are available, but they have typically come from commentators rather than Marx himself; see Kandiyali, *Reassessing Marx's Social and Political Philosophy*.

[49] I draw on Feenberg, *Critical Theory of Technology*; Feenberg, *Questioning Technology*; Feenberg, *Transforming Technology*. See also Feenberg, "Replies to My Critics."

[50] On these themes, also see Anderson, *Private Government*.

[51] Richard Sclove discussed technology as part of an interpretation of strong democracy. Social processes influence what technologies develop, and those in turn shape social processes. For strong democracies to flourish, democratic processes need to shape technologies, and there needs to be constant vigilance as to what impact technologies will likely have; see Sclove, *Democracy and Technology*.

more widely, to the extent that the relations in question concern how order is created. This sense can easily hold true outside of the Marxist context, a point to which I return below.

2.6 PUBLIC REASON

Marxism's conception of the political makes it inevitable that technology must be discussed. The Marxist tradition delivers (at least) three senses in which technology is political: foundational, enframing, and interactive. Contemporary liberalism does not engage with technology at anything approaching this level. Feenberg correctly notes that Rawls, for one, "abstracts systematically from technology and so overlooks the dystopian potential of advanced society," instead regarding "the technical sphere as a neutral background against which individuals and groups pursue personal and political goals." What is problematic about such neglect – and here Feenberg echoes the most basic message of the philosophy of technology – is that

> what it means to be human is decided not just in our beliefs but in large part in the shape of our tools. And to the extent that we are able to plan and manage technical development through various public processes and private choices, we have some control over our own humanity.[52]

Rawls has a conception of the political that does not immediately ask for clarification about the role of technology. We encountered Rawls's views in the Preface (where I also drew attention to their similarities with the Marxist outlook, which make an engagement between these traditions productive). Here I work some more with Rawls's articulation of public reason, a major innovation in political thought that comes with a highly plausible characterization of societal conflict and offers a response to it.[53]

As part of the complexities of the cultural lives that humans have built in history, we have inevitably interpreted the world very differently. We have developed various epistemologies and metaphysics, which inform various comprehensive moral doctrines, which in turn offer advice across many domains of life. Such pluralism does not reveal underlying irrationalities but rather speaks to the difficulties involved in generating substantive defenses of such doctrines. Public reason offers a standpoint from which certain matters are decided, matters that individuals must assess as citizens and that they need to decide together even though they otherwise return to multifarious doctrines for advice. Public reason offers a political vision in which, in a spirit of mutual respect, adherents of various outlooks can still share social spaces and govern those spaces as citizens.

---

[52] These various quotes are from Feenberg, "Replies to My Critics," 176. Feenberg applies these comments equally to Habermas, who seems less guilty of these accusations than Rawls.

[53] Rawls, *Political Liberalism*.

Public reason, that is, must respond to the crucial conflicts that societies face today – to wit, disputes about how the goods of economic production and other advantages from the interconnected life in modern societies are shared out, and also disputes about the degree to which the rules of interaction favor conflicting conceptions of the good, which have resulted from very different interpretations of human experience over time. Public reason deals with political values and principles. For Rawls, values and principles must be "freestanding" to be relevantly "political"[54]: They must address only the basic structure of society rather than the whole range of moral issues, be presentable independently of comprehensive doctrines, and be worked out from fundamental ideas implicit in the public political culture of a constitutional regime, such as the ideas (which are also ideals) of citizens as free and equal persons and of society as a system of cooperation.[55] Reasons that citizens give in debates about matters that concern the basic structure (rather than those that pertain to the day-to-day lives people lead within such structures) may draw on particular doctrines, but eventually must be formulated as reasons acceptable to citizens as such. Citizens cannot be asked to submit to policies and laws that depend on arguments drawing on epistemological or metaphysical stances that not all reasonable citizens can be expected to accept. Only in oppressive regimes would this be possible.

The public-reason picture is controversial. Some have argued that liberalism does not require, or intellectually benefit from, the separation of public reason from comprehensive doctrines.[56] Advocates of such doctrines typically do not acknowledge that other doctrines are reasonable, too, and would at best tolerate them. It might just be too much to ask of any committed advocate to think that one's doctrine is right while *also* agreeing that others could reasonably reject it.[57] Critics have also argued that there is no detached standpoint that would be less controversial than the comprehensive doctrines themselves.[58] Yet other critics might reconnect to the Marxist understanding of conflict (between working class and capitalists) and argue that the time for resolving that conflict has passed: Capitalism's dominance is insurmountable now, and the only worthwhile inquiries concern previous failure.[59]

All these criticisms deserve to be taken seriously.[60] Suffice it to say here, however, that Rawls's view offers freedom to defenders of comprehensive doctrines

---

[54] Rawls, 374.

[55] Rawls, *Law of Peoples*, 133, 143.

[56] Dworkin, *Sovereign Virtue*; Raz, *The Morality of Freedom*.

[57] Wenar, "Political Liberalism."

[58] Waldron, *Law and Disagreement*, chapter 7; Waldron, "Disagreements about Justice"; Enoch, "The Disorder of Public Reason"; Enoch, *Taking Morality Seriously*. See also Wall, "Is Public Justification Self-Defeating?"

[59] Adorno, *Negative Dialectics*.

[60] Risse, *On Justice*, chapter 16. See also Quong, *Liberalism without Perfection*.

on the assumption that they let others live in peace as well. Rawls refers to the persistence of reasonable disagreement as the "fact of reasonable pluralism."[61] He thinks of this disagreement as reasonable rather than just factual because of the challenges that come with passing the judgments involved if somebody were to decide between comprehensive doctrines. Rawls talks about *burdens of judgment* ("burdens"), "the sources, or causes, of disagreement between reasonable persons"[62] – that is, "the many hazards involved in the correct (and conscientious) exercise of our powers of reason and judgment in the ordinary course of political life."[63] These burdens make it challenging for us to make sense of our social world in ways that generate demands on others: After all, making demands on others presupposes that we can think of them as having compelling reasons to see the world as we do. One aspect of being a reasonable person is the ability and willingness to accept these burdens, and thus the difficulties involved in making demands on each other.[64]

These sources of disagreement are "burdens" because they make passing judgment difficult to begin with and they continue to put pressure on whatever judgment has been reached vis-à-vis alternatives. Profound questions of religion, metaphysics, and morality are hard to answer. People *inevitably* answer such questions differently in light of their experiences. Such disagreement does not necessarily reflect irrationality, selfishness, or prejudice but arises in the normal functioning of reason under regular conditions. Reasonable citizens realize this, thereby accepting the burdens of judgment. Such burdens "weigh lightly" on views or advocates if for whatever reason other advocates, too, can be expected to accept these views. The burdens "bear heavily" if others could not generally be expected to accept them. It is because of the heavy burdens that often accompany

---

[61] Rawls, *Political Liberalism*, xvi.

[62] Rawls, 55.

[63] Rawls, 56.

[64] Rawls, 18f, 48–54; Rawls, 18f, 48–54. Reasonable persons have realized their moral powers (capacities for a sense of justice and a conception of the good) to a sufficient degree to be free and equal citizens and fully cooperating members of constitutional regimes. Rawls provides a list of sources of reasonable disagreement about fundamental matters; see Rawls, 50f.

    a. The evidence – empirical and scientific – bearing on a given case is conflicting and complex, thus hard to assess and evaluate.

    b. Even where we agree about the kinds of considerations that are relevant, we may disagree about their weight, and so arrive at different judgments.

    c. To some extent all concepts, not only moral and political ones, are vague and subject to hard cases; we depend on judgment and interpretation.

    d. To some extent the way we assess evidence and weigh moral and political values is shaped by our total experience, our course of life up to now; and our total experiences always differ.

    e. Often there are different kinds of normative considerations of different force on both sides of an issue, making overall assessments difficult.

    f. Any system of social institutions is limited in the values it can admit. Some selection must be made from the range of moral and political values that might be realized.

comprehensive views that Rawls insists that only by "oppressive use of state power" could any one doctrine dominate.[65]

Rawls's understanding of the conflicts that societies face today does not turn primarily on productive forces or relations. Instead, the conflicts turn on the burdens of judgment and the willingness to appreciate these burdens for what they are as a key to a peaceful future. This does not mean that economic matters are irrelevant in designing a just society. On the contrary, Rawls's principles of justice stem from a standpoint that spells out what it means for citizens to have an appropriate share of what society produces together. This standpoint simultaneously addresses the other kind of conflict that societies face today, that deep tension from the multiplicity in underlying worldviews. After all, it will only be by way of coming to terms with that deeper tension that citizens become open to accepting common principles of justice.

Rawls does not think that such deeper tension can or even should be overcome. What matters is that it is handled properly. Marxist theory tends to hold up the hope that under the right conditions, a revolution can resolve society's underlying conflict.[66] Rawls mostly leaves us with the observation that any pluralist society not organized from a public-reason standpoint will inevitably oppress some of its citizens. So we had better make the public-reason standpoint work.

2.7 PUBLIC REASON AND THE POLITICAL NATURE OF TECHNOLOGY: THE INTERACTIVE SENSE AND THE ENFRAMING SENSE

Feenberg is right that Rawls "abstracts systematically from technology and so overlooks the dystopian potential of advanced society." This is not to say that Rawls erred by making central that conflict among comprehensive doctrines to which public reason offers the solution. But public reason must be developed further in this era of technological innovation. The public-reason conception of the political does not by itself immediately trigger exploration of any of the senses in which technology is political that the Marxist tradition generates. But nothing about it is inconsistent with recognizing each of these senses, suitably adjusted. Let me discuss these senses in reverse order (as the original ordering was driven by the historical development of Marxism). The foundational sense I leave to Section 2.8, which also makes the transition to Chapter 3.

That the public-reason standpoint can recognize the interactive sense is easiest to see. After all, this sense is by no means limited to Marxist thought; many ways for technology to bear on human life register as political in this very sense. For these ways for technology to be political to register as such on the Rawlsian account, one

---

[65] Rawls, *Political Liberalism*, 37.
[66] Recall again the discussion of Marx's "On the Jewish Question" in the Preface.

must show how they engage the exercise of citizenship. Let me record some scenarios that theorists of technology have discussed that show how ubiquitous a phenomenon it is for technology to engage the exercise of citizenship.

Lewis Mumford insisted on the importance of the introduction of clocks for the regularization of life. A passion for order and regularity arose in the late Middle Ages and manifested itself in monasteries, spreading from there to other sectors. The mechanical clock – visible from church towers in western Europe and subsequently elsewhere – literally synchronized behavior and thereby enabled people to live by schedules and enormously increased the accuracy with which instructions could be issued and executed. The later printing press was second only to the mechanical clock in terms of impact. Printing meant information and ideas spread more easily, and the same information and ideas would be available in many places and preserved accurately over generations. All of that would open new possibilities for what kinds of human relations were possible.[67] Some decades after Mumford wrote *Technics and Civilization*, historian Lynn White Jr. argued that the invention of the stirrup made shock combat possible, which in turn enabled the feudal order. This device, then, had an all-encompassing impact on what hierarchies could persevere in societies.[68]

Langdon Winner's iconic 1980 article "Do Artifacts Have Politics?" arguably also develops this interactive sense in which technology is political.[69] Winner distinguishes two ways for artifacts to have "political qualities," and thus for technology to be linked to power. To begin with, certain devices and systems can be strongly, perhaps unavoidably, tied to certain patterns of power. Winner's example is atomic energy, which requires industrial, scientific, and military elites to provide and protect energy sources. Then there is the case of devices and systems that *might* be means for establishing patterns of power or authority, but where the design is flexible: Such patterns can turn out one way or another, and how they do is a choice. Winner's example is traffic infrastructure. Built the right way, it greatly assists many people. But traffic infrastructure can also keep parts of the population in subordination, say, if they cannot reach suitable workplaces.

More recently, Judith Wajcman has addressed the extent to which affinities with technology have been integral to the constitution of the male gender. Limited childhood exposure to technology, lack of role models, and labor market expectations have worked in tandem to construct women as ill-suited to technological

[67] Mumford, *Technics and Civilization*, chapter 1.
[68] White Jr., *Medieval Technology and Social Change*, chapter 1.
[69] Winner, "Do Artifacts Have Politics?" See also Winner, *The Whale and the Reactor*, 19–40. Winner's use of Robert Moses's parkways as an example of exclusionary traffic infrastructure has come up for much discussion, also in terms of its accuracy; see, for example, Woolgar and Cooper, "Do Artifacts Have Ambivalence?" Part of the concern is Winner's reliance on Caro, *The Power Broker*. Winner's understanding of artifacts being political comes from an engagement with philosophical treatments of technology. See Winner, *Autonomous Technology*. For related themes, also see Verbeek, *Moralizing Technology*.

pursuits. By contrast, expertise becomes a source of male power over both things in the world and women. One facet of this pattern has been that, not uncommonly, technological advances enable men to replace women in traditionally female professions. For example, for millennia and across cultures, assistance with child-birth was women's work, a midwife's rather than a surgeon's job. But then, in different European locations between the sixteenth and eighteenth centuries, the obstetrical forceps – a device to pull babies from the womb – was invented. Subsequently, surgeons increasingly took over the midwife's job, as surgery was a profession not traditionally exercised by women.[70]

Yet more recently, several writers have drawn attention to how power is exercised in and through digital technologies to perpetuate and even increase economic and gender- and race-based disadvantage. Ruha Benjamin has warned of digital technology's potential to cover, accelerate, or deepen racial discrimination while appearing neutral and even benevolent when compared to previous forms of racism. She coined the term "New Jim Code" (an allusion to "Jim Crow") to draw attention to the dramatic extent this phenomenon has reached.[71] Cathy O'Neil has argued that mathematical models in finance generate enormous incomes for investors by targeting the economically disadvantaged for additional extraction.[72] Similarly, Virginia Eubanks has investigated the impact of data mining and related tools on the working class, insisting that the automated decision-making borne out of col-lected data hides poverty from middle-class observers.[73]

Shoshana Zuboff has argued that the enormous amount of data collection characteristic of this stage of capitalism entails that our lives within digital lifeworlds are increasingly commodified to grow profits of tech companies.[74] Safiya Noble has written of "technological redlining," which implies, for instance, that people of color tend to pay disproportionately high interest rates and premiums, especially in

[70] (1) Wajcman, *Feminism Confronts Technology*, chapter 3. Wajcman also discusses how the role of the twentieth-century housewife was shaped by technology. Substantial decline in house-hold assistance in the United States (and similarly elsewhere) since the 1920s led to (and was partly caused by) mechanization of households. Standards of cleanliness increased (partly also due to availability of machines – for example, washing machines), as did standards of parenting. Housework was increasingly interpreted as an expression of the housewife's affection for her family. There increasingly was domestic technology designed for use by a lone loving house-wife in single-family households. Far from liberating women by making tasks easier, the overall effect was to ensnare women to the home and create the role of the twentieth-century housewife; see Wajcman, chapter 4. See also Cockburn and Ormrod, *Gender and Technology in the Making*. (2) Occasionally innovation advanced the role of women. Friedrich Kittler tells the story of the typewriter, originally invented in the nineteenth century to help people with vision problems (Nietzsche being an early user). But that innovation also made secretarial work available to women, partly because the traditionally male secretaries did not invest in skills to operate the machines; see Kittler, *Gramophone, Film, Typewriter*.
[71] Benjamin, *Race after Technology*.
[72] O'Neil, *Weapons of Math Destruction*.
[73] Eubanks, *Automating Inequality*.
[74] Zuboff, *The Age of Surveillance Capitalism*.

low-income neighborhoods. She has also shown how what we learn if we "just google" something reflects the priority that Google, the company, assigns to certain bits of information. Google's prioritizing follows a commercial rather than a civic or informational logic.[75]

For these ways in which technology is political to register as such based on the Rawlsian account, one must show how they engage the exercise of citizenship – a straightforward step especially for the more contemporary of these examples. So the interactive sense in which technology is political readily registers in the Rawlsian view and can trigger investigations into how technology enhances, distorts, or undermines the exercise of citizenship.

Let us discuss the enframing sense. The point here, recall, is that technology permeates and thereby defines culture as a whole, in a manner that emphasizes losses to human possibilities thus incurred. Mumford, Heidegger, and Marcuse all characterize technology as political in this way. Now is a good occasion briefly to introduce another author who also thought of technology as political in this sense, Jacques Ellul.

Ellul's main theme regarding technology is the diagnosis of a systemic technological tyranny over humanity. His most celebrated work is *The Technological Society*,[76] published in English in 1964 and previously in French under *La technique: L'enjeu du siècle* (literally, *The Stake of the Century*). Technology shapes aspects of society according to its own logic, ranging from the economic and political setup to the ways people live their lives and develop a sense of individuality to begin with. We may govern individual technologies and exercise agency within the system that technology creates (and maintain a subjective sense of doing so): We operate machines, build roads, and print magazines. But technology overall has outgrown human control. Even as we govern techniques, they increasingly shape our activities, and we adapt to their demands and structures. Ellul asks whether human adaptability to technology is as desirable as our acquiescence suggests.

The word in the French title is "technique," and that term also appears in the English text. "Technique," broadly conceived, includes not merely machines and other devices but the complex of rationally ordered *methods* to make human activity more efficient. Technique included the process of adapting social conditions to the increasing relevance of machines – for instance, how housing developed around factories, or how road patterns accommodated high-volume urban traffic. Still, the *machine* represents a paradigmatic type toward which all of technique strives.[77] Machines have created the modern world.

---

[75] Noble, *Algorithms of Oppression*.
[76] Ellul, *The Technological Society*. For recent discussions, see Greenman, *Understanding Jacques Ellul*; Jerónimo, Garcia, and Mitcham, *Jacques Ellul and the Technological Society in the Twenty-first Century*. See also Demy, *Jacques Ellul on Violence, Resistance, and War*; Gill and Lovekin, *Political Illusion and Reality*; Prior, *Confronting Technology*; Vleet and Rollison, *Jacques Ellul*.
[77] Ellul, *The Technological Society*, 4.

Ellul is famous for his thesis of the *autonomy* of technique: its being a closed system, "a reality in itself ... with its special laws and its own determinations." Technique

> elicits and conditions social, political and economic change. It is the prime mover of all the rest, in spite of any appearances to the contrary and in spite of human pride, which pretends that man's philosophical theories are still determining influences and man's political regimes are decisive factors in technical evolution.[78]

For example, industry and military began to adopt automated technology. One might think that this process resulted from economic or political decisions. But, for Ellul, the sheer technical possibility provided all required impetus for going this way. Ellul is a technological determinist, but only for the modern age: Technology, one way or another, causes all other aspects of today's society and culture. In the past it was not like this. But it is now. Eventually, the state is inextricably intertwined with advancements of technique, as well as with corporations that produce machinery, to such an extent that nothing resembling "the voice of the people" has any serious impact on what actually happens in society. Democracy fails, Ellul insists. (I return to this theme in Chapter 3.) In the foreword to the American edition of his book, Ellul denies to the great surprise of many of his readers that he is pessimistic about technology; nonetheless, his view is relentlessly hopeless.

Marcuse, Heidegger, Mumford, and Ellul all describe technology as political in the enframing sense. They all offer grand techno-skeptical narratives that in virtue of being so grand are hard to assess for their ultimate plausibility. But they do issue warnings regarding the prospect of harnessing technology for a promising human future generally and for the future of citizenship in a flourishing public-reason framework in particular. By contrast, Rawls does not formulate dystopian scenarios that threaten the public-reason standpoint (since he is not interested in technology directly). But public reason could and should readily take these narratives seriously, not for their on-balance or in-detail plausibility, but for the warnings they issue. These views should serve as reference points to make sure that citizenship is not thoroughly undermined in this age of technological innovation by the tendencies identified by these thinkers. Citizenship is in good shape only if we can confidently say that these dystopian scenarios are not coming true. Accordingly, the public-reason standpoint can recognize the political nature of technology in the enframing sense (and also the importance of the debates needed to engage these dystopian scenarios).

2.8 CONCLUSION: PUBLIC REASON AND THE POLITICAL NATURE OF TECHNOLOGY – THE FOUNDATIONAL SENSE

To the Amish, technology is political because whether their communities will survive as such or be absorbed into larger society depends on what devices they

---

[78] Ellul, 133.

adopt and what attitudes toward technology they permit. To be sure, if humanity as a whole adopts the wrong technologies, the worst-case scenario is not absorption but perdition. So, it is not quite in the same sense that von Neumann and the Amish worry about *surviving* technology. Nonetheless, what the Amish teach us is that considering technology to be a thoroughly political matter is merely what its transformational potential calls for – already if the result of the pertinent transformation could be the loss of cultural identity, and much more so if it could be the end of intelligent life on earth.

The Rawlsian standpoint has good reason to recognize the interactive and enframing senses in which technology is political. The same is true for the foundational sense, the sense concerned with how technology shapes the operations of power in society. Merely recalling the worries that von Neumann articulated, as well as the Fermi Paradox, makes clear just how important it is to understand this nexus between technology and the operations of power. The Marxist tradition understands the foundational sense in which technology shapes the operations of power in terms of historical materialism – an approach in which productive forces play a determinative role in the unfolding of history, which might just overstate their role.[79] But there are other ways to inquire about how technology shapes the operations of power in society and thus to recognize the foundational sense in which technology is political.

The public-reason standpoint in particular has good reason to inquire about how the very exercise of public reason, or of any kind of democracy, critically involves artifacts, devices, and systems. This perspective takes the *materiality* of human affairs more seriously than is customary among defenders of either public reason or democracy, and is a good way of spelling out the sense in which technology is political in the foundational sense according to the public-reason framework. Chapter 3 investigates these matters.

At the beginning of Section 2.7, I pointed out that the three senses in which technology is political could be transferred to the Rawlsian framework, "suitably adjusted." Marxism has indeed provided us with three senses in which technology is political that we can distinguish quite neatly. The foundational sense depends on Marx's historical materialism (and embeds technology into the productive forces, which determine everything else); the enframing sense depends on Marcuse's reconsideration of the role of technology in society and the ways that capitalism has enlisted the entertainment sector in its efforts to annihilate the political instincts of the working class; and the interactive sense draws on Feenberg's insistence that there can still be alienation at a socialist workplace.

---

[79] Recall, for example, Cohen, "Review of 'Karl Marx's Theory of History: A Defense,' by G. A. Cohen." Joshua Cohen argues that interactions of individuals may or may not in the aggregate sustain growth of productive forces. Whether they do, depends on the nature of the superstructure.

When we disconnect these senses from their Marxist context, the foundational sense will no longer be embedded into historical materialism, the enframing sense might well be disconnected from the power struggle between working class and capitalists, and the interactive sense will have much broader applicability. In the process, the three senses might lose their crisp delineations. Still, technology – especially in our digital century – bears so overwhelmingly on the future of citizenship and on any future humanity might have that political theory must recognize technology for its distinctive role in the political domain. Political philosophy must always also be philosophy of technology.

3

Artificial Intelligence and the Past, Present, and Future of Democracy

Modern democracy is an ongoing experiment, and in many ways, we should be surprised that it has worked at all.

— David Stasavage[1]

3.1 INTRODUCTION: RULE OF THE PEOPLE

A distinctive feature of recognizably democratic structures – an intrinsic rather than comparative advantage – is that they give each participant at least minimal ownership of social endeavors and thereby also seek to inspire people to recognize each other as responsible agents across domains of life. Arguments for democracy highlight possibilities for emancipation, indispensability for human rights protection, and the promise of unleashing human potential. Concerns that defenses of democracy must overcome include shortsightedness vis-à-vis long-term crises, the twin dangers of manipulability by elites and susceptibility to populists, the potential of competition to generate polarization, and a focus on process rather than results. Winston Churchill, speaking as Leader of the Opposition in the British Parliament in November 1947, commented on democracy as follows:

No one pretends that democracy is perfect or all-wise. Indeed, it has been said that democracy is the worst form of Government except all those other forms that have been tried from time to time; but there is the broad feeling in our country that the people should rule, continuously rule, and that public opinion, expressed by all

---

[1] Stasavage, *The Decline and Rise of Democracy*, 296. For a political-theory idealization of modern democracy in terms of two "tracks," see Habermas, *Between Facts and Norms*, chapters 7 and 8. The first track is formal decision-making (e.g., parliament, courts, agencies). The other is informal public deliberation, where public opinion is formed.

constitutional means, should shape, guide, and control the actions of Ministers who are their servants and not their masters.[2]

Often quoted (in various degrees of accuracy), these lines express the sentiment that arguments for democracy must be balanced against the aforementioned concerns, and this balancing involves comparing democracy with "all those other forms that have been tried from time to time."

Democracy means "rule of the people." While it is broadly praised, there is much disagreement about how to understand democracy as a political ideal and about how best to translate the ideal into collective decision-making. In the contemporary discussion, three ways of understanding "rule of the people" stand out. First of all, *procedural understandings* emphasize possibilities for changing rulers through political competition. What matters about democracy, based on such views, is that there are peaceful ways of which all citizens can avail themselves to change the government. Secondly, there are *populist* views, which stress the value of institutions that capture "the will of people." Popular rule, then, is the ultimate political value. Thirdly, there are *liberal* views, which differ from both of these.

In contrast to procedural views, liberal views emphasize the inherent value of both popular rule and individual participation. But in contrast to populist views, liberal democracy constrains popular rule through basic liberties and other demands of justice often codified in constitutions. Such demands are protected even against the popular will. Thereby, liberal democracy also creates space for separation of power, judicial review, or other checks and balances.[3] Rawls's public-reason conception of the political domain, with its accompanying theory of justice, falls in this camp. After all, one hallmark of the Rawlsian view is a distinctive view of the nature of citizenship (and its importance): Civil and political rights are strongly protected (especially against majoritarian decision-making), and public reason delineates a sphere of interaction among citizens that is set apart from ways in which comprehensive doctrines enter their lives. This liberal view is the contemporary understanding of the ideal of the rule of the people that I endorse and use here.

Democratic theorists typically have not focused much on the *materiality* of human affairs: the ways these affairs critically involve artifacts, devices, and systems. They have seen democracy as a set of ideas and human practices. By contrast, the materiality of human affairs has been a distinctive theme in Science, Technology, and Society Studies (STS), especially in the work of Bruno Latour, one of its most visible exponents. Latour has long insisted that no entity matters in isolation but instead attains meaning through numerous, changeable relations. Human activities tend to depend not only on more people than the protagonists who stand out, but also on nonhuman entities. Latour calls such multitudes of relations *actor-networks*

---

[2]   https://api.parliament.uk/historic-hansard/commons/1947/nov/11/parliament-bill
[3]   On different understandings of democracy, see Gutmann, "Democracy."

and refers to the ways in which these various components of such a system affect each other as *translations*.[4]

Specialized AI has much potential for changing the materiality of democracy by modifying how collective decision-making unfolds and what its human participants are like (how they see themselves, what relationships they have, what forms of human life their interactions bring about, etc.). Paying attention to the materiality of democracy is also a way of developing the point that the public-reason standpoint (which I take to be part of the liberal view of democracy) must acknowledge the *foundational* sense in which technology is political. (In this way the present chapter continues our discussion from Chapter 2.) Technology is political, that is, especially in the sense that the material underpinnings of democracy matter for how the democratic ideal translates into practices and can survive.

This chapter reflects on medium- and long-term prospects and challenges for liberal democracy brought on by AI. It does so in a historical perspective that emphasizes how its materiality – the way it is an actor-network – has always shaped the manner in which "rule of the people" has been implemented, and what ways of being human have opened up thereby. I begin by exploring the materiality of "early" (Section 3.2) and "modern" democracy (Section 3.3). Section 3.4 investigates whether technology and democracy are natural allies: that is, if anything about technological advancement distinctly favors or disfavors democratic governance. I argue that democracy and technology, specifically AI, are by no means natural allies. Instead, we need wise design choices to make sure AI strengthens democracy. Section 3.5 introduces a Grand Democratic AI Utopia, an imagined future in which AI is used at a large scale to make democracy work. Nobody has so far seriously proposed anything like this, but it is a scenario worth considering at a time when AI's possibilities are much discussed. As it turns out, we would be ill advised to be guided by such a utopia.

What, then, are the possibilities and challenges of AI for democracy (in its liberal understanding, which I adopt for contemporary discussions) in our digital century? Specifically, how should AI be designed to harness the *public sphere, political power*, and *economic power* to maintain democracy as a way of life? Sections 3.6–3.8 explore these questions. Not only can technology be harnessed to improve democratic politics, but in fact democracy generates certain problems that can only be solved through technology. Nonetheless, the insight that democracy and technology are not natural allies remains valid: It requires sustained efforts to make sure technology is not used to undermine democracy. This chapter brings in several themes that reappear later. For example, Chapter 11 looks at how superintelligences might eventually enter the political domain with humans, but that is not the perspective

---

[4] Latour, *Reassembling the Social*; Latour, *We Have Never Been Modern*. To be sure, and notwithstanding the name of the theory, Latour speaks of *actants* rather than *actors*, to emphasize the role of nonhuman entities.

we take here. This chapter explores how to combine democracy and technological innovation so that the latter advances the former.[5]

3.2 THE MATERIALITY OF EARLY DEMOCRACY

Contemporary representative democracies – typically located in territorial states rather than limited to individual cities – involve structures for collective choice that periodically empower relatively few people to steer the social direction for everybody. As in all forms of governance, technology shapes how this unfolds. Technology explains how citizens obtain information that delineates their participation (often largely limited to voting) and frees up people's time to engage in collective affairs to begin with. Devices and mechanisms permeate campaigning and voting. Technology shapes how politicians communicate, and how bureaucrats administer decisions.

This relevance of technology for democracy notwithstanding, political theorists typically treat democracy as an ideal without considering its materiality much. By contrast, a social-scientific perspective on democracy developed by David Stasavage makes it easier to focus on its materiality and thus subsequently on the impact of AI.[6] Stasavage distinguishes *early* from *modern democracy*, which differ in terms of how they secure the consent of the governed and thus implement the rule of the people. Both contrast with *autocracy*, governance without the consent of the governed. Once we see how Stasavage defines the two forms of democracy, we can readily capture the materiality of both. In other words, Stasavage provides an understanding of democracy that renders it straightforward to connect insights from Latour with democratic theory.

Early democracy was a system in which rulers governed jointly with either relatively small councils or larger assemblies whose members were independent from rulers and thus not directly subject to their whims. Such councils or assemblies provided information and assisted with governance. Sometimes councils were elite gatherings. Sometimes there was broad participation in assemblies or in procedures to select members. The rulers themselves might have been elected to or have inherited their position. Early democracy normally arose in smaller rather than larger polities, in polities where rulers depended on their subjects for information about what the subjects owned or produced (and so the rulers could not tax without such compliance) and where people had exit options and thus could put themselves

---

[5]   On AI and democracy, also see Reich, Sahami, and Weinstein, *System Error*, chapter 8; Coeckelbergh, *The Political Philosophy of AI*, chapter 4. For possible uses of AI in the delivery of public services, see Margetts, "Rethinking AI for Good Governance." For some recent discussions of the some of the pressures on democracy in the digital age, see Runciman, *How Democracy Ends*; Applebaum, *Twilight of Democracy*; Weale, *The Will of the People*; Susskind, *The Digital Republic*.

[6]   Stasavage, *The Decline and Rise of Democracy*.

and their assets physically beyond reach of their current rulers. Under such conditions, rulers had to involve at least parts of the population in governance. Early democracy as outlined here was common around the globe and not restricted to Greece, as the standard narrative has it.[7]

To be sure, what is special about Athenian and other Greek democracies is the *extent* to which they gave a voice to those not directly controlled by the ruling circles: They were the most extensively participatory among known instances of early democracy. To elaborate on that (and thereby to illuminate the materiality of early democracy), let us discuss Athens some more. In the sixth-century BC, Cleisthenes divided Athens into 139 *demes*, groups of people comprising 150 to 250 men (women playing no political role), which formed ten artificial "tribes." *Demes* in the same tribe inhabited different regions of Attica. Each tribe sent 50 men, randomly selected for a year, to the Council of Five Hundred to administer day-to-day affairs and prepare sessions of the Assembly, which included all citizens. This system fed knowledge and insights from all eligible men into collective decision-making without positioning anyone for takeover.[8]

To be sure, this governance system could work only because it enslaved people (and maintained a military to that effect) to do the labor needed to maintain the economy. Only in such a manner could parts of the population have time freed up to attend to collective affairs. Transport and communication also had to function to let the citizens do their parts in governance. The governance system likewise depended on a steady, high-volume circulation of people in and out of office to make governance impersonal, representative, and transparent at the same time. That flow, in turn, required close bookkeeping to guarantee that people were at the right place at the right time.

Such bookkeeping involved technical devices. These devices represent the material ingredients of democratic governance narrowly conceived (while a broader understanding of the materiality of Athenian democracy also involves topics such as production, transport, and communication). Let me mention some of these devices. The *kleroterion* (allotment machine) was a two-by-three-foot slab of rock with a grid of deep, thin slots gouged into it. Integrating some additional pieces, this

---

[7]   To the extent that rule by as actual *demos* (populace) that is *distinct* from an aristocracy is the hallmark of democracy, many cases covered by Stasavage's definition would not count as democracies. After all, as Stasavage defines it, the hallmark of early democracy was that some of the people who were governed by the rulers needed to be involved in the governance process, but this does not mean that the whole demos was so involved. But while governance in ancient Greece was characterized by *demoi*, thus representing a democracy in this sense, the *demoi* included only subsets of the male population. In this way, they were "the people" *only* in contrast to the aristocracy, not by including anything approaching the totality of even the native adult population. To think of Greek democracy as a unique innovation also contradicts the evolutionary story of early bands of humans who succeeded because they were good at cooperating and had brains that had evolved to serve cooperative purposes; see, for example, Boehm, *Hierarchy in the Forest.*

[8]   Stasavage, *The Decline and Rise of Democracy*, chapter 2; Ober, *The Rise and Fall of Classical Greece*, chapter 6; Thorley, *Athenian Democracy*, chapter 3.

sophisticated device helped select the required number of men from each tribe for the Council or for juries and committees where representation mattered. Officers carried around their allotment tokens, pieces of ceramics inscribed with pertinent information that fit with another piece at a secure location. That other piece could be produced if credentials were questioned. Athens was too large for all citizens to be personally acquainted. With speaking times limited during Council or Assembly meetings, a water clock (*klepsydra*) kept time. Announcement boards at central locations recorded decisions or messages. For voting, the Athenians used flat bronze disks as ballots. Occasionally, the Assembly expelled citizens whose prominence threatened the impersonal character of governance; these notorious *ostracisms* were recorded by citizens carving into potsherds the names of those whom they believed should be expelled.

Aristotle argued that citizens assembled for deliberation could display virtue and wisdom that no individual could muster, an argument for democracy (the "argument from the wisdom of the multitude") that resonated through the ages.[9] It took a particular mode of organizing the life of Athenian society (everyone who lived there, including the enslaved people) and certain material objects to make all of this work. That mode of organization and these objects were at the heart of early democracy in Athens; they served as systems and devices in actor-networks to operationalize consent of (some of) the governed in specific ways. What it meant to be a citizen in democratic Athens – and thus this way of being human – was defined by this actor-network that, accordingly, required a lot of more than a certain group of humans putting their heads together in assembly. While Athenian democracy flourished, the nature of that flourishing consisted in the multitude of actors (or *actants*) in that network translating each other's presence into something new. In particular, the life of specific humans could be translated into the life of citizens only in such ways.[10]

3.3 THE MATERIALITY OF MODERN DEMOCRACY

Let us turn to modern democracy. Modern democracy is representative, with mandates that do not bind representatives to an electorate's will. While early democracy as Stasavage understands it is not an exclusively European phenomenon, modern democracy is a European invention. Representatives have emerged from competitive elections under suffrage that has become increasingly universal over the centuries. Accordingly, participation in modern democracies is broad but typically episodic.

---

[9] Aristotle, *Politics*, 1281a39–b16. Also see Risse, "The Virtuous Group."
[10] For the devices, see Julian Dibbell, "Info Tech of Ancient Democracy," which explores museum literature on artifacts displayed in Athens: www.alamut.com/subj/artiface/deadMedia/agoraMuseum.html#3. See also Dow, "Aristotle, the Kleroteria, and the Courts"; Bishop, "The Cleroterium." For the mechanics of Athenian democracy, see also Hansen, *The Athenian Democracy in the Age of Demosthenes*.

The material conditions for the existence of modern democracies resemble those of early democracy: Such democracies emerge where rulers depend on subjects to volunteer information and where people have exit options. But modern democracy is possible in large territories, as exemplified by the United States, and these territories' large sizes (and populations) generate two legitimacy problems.[11] First, modern democracy generates distrust since "state" and "society" easily remain abstract and distant (the distant-state problem). Second, there is the problem of overbearing executive power (the overbearing-executive problem). Modern democracies require bureaucracies to manage day-to-day-affairs. Bureaucracies generate their own dynamics (especially when not as firmly directed as they would be in tightly organized autocracies). Where heads of state are elected directly, executive power might become personal power, which also unleashes dynamics of its own. Eventually, citizens might no longer see themselves as governing.[12] The distant-state and overbearing-executive problems are so substantial that, for Stasavage, "modern democracy is an ongoing experiment, and in many ways, we should be surprised that it has worked at all."[13]

Modern democracy also depends on material features to function (and, ideally, to solve these problems). Consider the United States in 1787/88, Alexander Hamilton, James Madison, and John Jay – under the collective pseudonym "Publius" – published eighty-five articles and essays known as the "Federalist Papers" to promote the constitution. Hamilton calls the government the country's "center of information."[14] "Information" and "communication" matter greatly to Publius: The former term appears in nineteen essays, the latter in a dozen. For these prominent advocates of this trailblazing system of representational democracy, the challenge is to find structures for disclosure and processing of pertinent information about the country.

Publius thinks members of Congress would bring information to the capital after aggregating it in the states. But at the dawn of the republic, the vastness of the territory posed a formidable challenge to gathering and conveying information.

---

[11] Hélène Landemore has argued that modern democracy erred in focusing on representation. Instead, possibilities of small-scale decision-making with appropriate connections to government should have been favored, which is now more doable through technology. See Landemore, "Open Democracy and Digital Technologies"; Landemore, *Open Democracy*.

[12] Howard Zinn has a negative take specifically on the founding of the United States that would make it unsurprising that these legitimacy problems arose: "Around 1776, certain important people in the English colonies (...) found that by creating a nation, a symbol, a legal unity called the United States, they could take over land, profits, and political power from favorites of the British Empire. In the process, they could hold back a number of potential rebellions and create a consensus of popular support for the rule of a new, privileged leadership;" Zinn, *A People's History of the United States*, 59.

[13] Stasavage, *The Decline and Rise of Democracy*, 296. For a political-theory idealization of modern democracy in terms of two "tracks," see Habermas, *Between Facts and Norms*, chapters 7 and 8. The first track is formal decision-making (e.g., parliament, courts, agencies). The other is informal public deliberation, where public opinion is formed.

[14] Cooke, *Federalist*, 149.

One historian described the government's communication situation as effectively a "quarantine" from society.[15] Improvements in postal services and changes in the newspaper business in the nineteenth century brought relief, creating the central role of media in modern democracies. Only such developments were able to turn modern democracies into actor-networks where representatives no longer labor in de facto isolation.[16]

"The aim of every political constitution is or ought to be first for rulers to obtain men who possess most wisdom to discern, and most virtue to pursue the common good of society," we read in Federalist No. 57.[17] To make this happen, democracy requires voting systems, in addition to a political culture where the right people seek office. In the United States, the design of these systems has been left to states. Typically, the orderliness of what they devised in terms of assigning people barely resembled that of the *kleroterion*.

"Ballot" comes from the Italian word *ballotta* (little ball). In voting systems designed by American states in the early days of the republic (and more locally already before there even was a republic), ballots often were small and round: They included pebbles, peas, beans, and even bullets.[18] Paper ballots gradually spread, partly because they were easier to count. Initially, voters had to bring paper and write down properly spelled names and offices. The rise of paper ballots facilitated that of political parties. Party leaders would print ballots, often in newspapers: long strips listing entire slates or pages to be cut into pieces, one per candidate. Party symbols on ballots meant voters did not need to know how to write or read, an issue unknown when people voted by surrendering small round objects or by voice.

In 1856, on the other side of the world, the Australian state of Victoria passed its Electoral Act, detailing the conduct of elections. Officials had to print ballots and erect booths or hire rooms. Voters marked ballots secretly, and nobody else was allowed in polling places. The "Australian ballot" gradually spread, typically against much resistance. Officially, such resistance arose because secret voting (naturally) eliminated the public character of voting that many considered essential to honorable conduct. But the real issue was that secret voting made it hard for politicians to get people to vote for them in exchange for money. And to be sure, such ballots meant that voters had to be able to read, making voting harder for immigrants, formerly enslaved people, and uneducated poor individuals. In 1888, Massachusetts

---

[15] Young, *The Washington Community 1800–1828*, 32.

[16] Bimber, *Information and American Democracy*, chapter 3. For the argument that, later, postal services were critical to colonizing the American West (and thus have been thoroughly political throughout their existence), see Blevins, *Paper Trails*.

[17] Cooke, *Federalist*, 384.

[18] I follow Lepore, "Rock, Paper, Scissors." Some of those themes also appear in Lepore, *These Truths*, especially chapter 9. See also Saltman, *History and Politics of Voting Technology*. For the right to vote in the United States, see Keyssar, *The Right to Vote*.

passed the first statewide Australian-ballot law in the United States. By 1896, most Americans cast secret, government-printed ballots.

The "Australian ballot" was supposed to help with the creation of conditions under which citizens could cast their vote without interference and manipulation. The introduction of machines for casting and counting votes, which in the United States dates to the 1880s, was intended to serve the same purpose. However, machines too can be manipulated, or fail outright. The mechanics of American elections have remained contested, as of course their mechanisms too have been all along – that is, the ways in which the members of the various branches of government are chosen from among those who are eager or willing to take on the task of steering the social direction. The actor-network constitutive of a large contemporary territorial democracy – with all the systems and devices needed to convey information and maintain communication, produce things, maintain the infrastructure, select members of the government, and so forth – is substantially more complex than that of Ancient Athenian democracy. But here to, if we want to assess how this representative system is faring (e.g., in terms of how well it is dealing with the distant-state and overbearing-executive problems) and ponder what ways of being human it makes possible, we must talk about a very large actor-network. We must talk about how a whole range of actors (actants) translate the life of many human beings into the life of citizens in such a system.

3.4 DEMOCRACY AND TECHNOLOGY: NATURAL ALLIES?

Recall that the alternative to democracy is *autocracy*, governance without consent of the governed. More enduring autocracies typically develop a strong bureaucracy that gives their governance an efficiency and effectiveness with which consent-based systems have difficulties competing. Autocracy benefits from technological advances because these make control more effective. At the same time, modern democracy requires technology to solve its legitimacy problems. Careful design of the materiality of democracy is needed to solve the distant-state and overbearing-executive problems specifically. We should ask then: Does anything about technological advancement distinctly favor or disfavor *democratic* governance?

There is much evidence to dissuade us from the idea that technology and democracy are natural allies in any interesting sense. Often advances in production and communication undermined early democracy where it existed.[19] Technological improvements can easily reduce the advantages in information of subjects over rulers. For instance, once rulers have ways of assessing the fertility of land, they know how to tax it, and competent bureaucrats deploying state-of-the-art technology can facilitate this process. Agricultural improvements lead to people living closer together, which means bureaucrats can monitor them (and assess the value of assets). In the Ancient

---

[19] I continue to draw here on Stasavage, *The Decline and Rise of Democracy*.

world, innovations in writing, mapping, measuring, and agriculture made bureaucracies more effective, rendering autocracies with functioning bureaucracies more viable. Conversely, where progress in science and development was slow, survival of early democracy was favored: The conditions under which early democracy typically arose remained in place then. Deprived of technology and infrastructural background conditions that allow them to deploy bureaucracy to tighten control, rulers depend on cooperation from subjects.

Still, it would be an overstatement to say that "technology favors autocracy rather than democracy." Much depends on sequencing. In China, the democratic alternative to autocratic rule has never gained much traction. In recent decades, beginning with Deng Xiaoping, the country has made enormous economic strides under an autocratic system with a competent bureaucracy. Under Xi Jinping, China now aggressively advertises its system, and AI has started to play a major role in it, especially in surveilling its citizens. Indeed, the impact of technology has been to entrench and enhance autocratic rule, not to bring China to the democratic side.[20] Similarly, and this is the good news, entrenched democracies are unlikely to be undermined by technological advances (parallel to how the entrenched autocracy in China is unlikely to be undermined by such advances).

As far as AI and its impact on contemporary democracies are concerned, these broad historical lessons indicate that, in principle, entrenched democracies today could make good use of AI to enhance their functionality. Thereby, AI could become a key part of the materiality of contemporary democracies, much as China has made it a key part of its autocratic system of rule. But it should also be clear that it will require intense efforts to put technology to work for democracies. The remaining sections of this chapter discuss AI specifically in this regard once we have completed the present discussion.

Yuval Noah Harari has recently looked at the relationship between democracy and technology from a somewhat different perspective.[21] He argues that historically, autocracies have faced handicaps around innovation and growth. After all, since in autocracies power is exercised without the need to obtain their consent, the governed will not typically feel empowered to bring about change. In the late twentieth century especially, democracies outperformed dictatorships because they were better at processing information by leaving that task to a decentralized myriad of actors that did feel empowered to put available information to good use.

---

[20] The success of the Chinese model has prompted some philosophers to defend features of that model, also in light of how democracies have suffered from the two legitimacy problems; see Bell, *The China Model*; Bai, *Against Political Equality*; Chan, *Confucian Perfectionism*. For the view that China's Communist Party will face a crisis that will force it to let China become democratic, see Ci, *Democracy in China*. For the argument that different governance models emerge for good reasons at different times, see Fukuyama, *The Origins of Political Order*; Fukuyama, *Political Order and Political Decay*.

[21] Harari, "Why Technology Favors Tyranny."

Accordingly, Harari thinks the state of technology in the late twentieth century made it inefficient to concentrate information and power. Harari echoes Friedrich August von Hayek's "Knowledge Argument" for laissez-faire capitalism. Hayek argued that centrally planned economies could never match the efficiency of markets. Any single agent, including governments or social planners, could possess only a small fraction of the knowledge held across society.[22]

To be sure, Harari's perspective is consistent with what we took from Stasavage: Harari is concerned with efficiency and economic growth, whereas Stasavage explores the conditions under which different types of rule emerge. Notwithstanding certain differences in outlook, especially in interpreting historical evidence, Stasavage and Harari agree that – as we progress further into the twenty-first century – AI offers possibilities to governments that undermine the conditions that make democracy more viable than autocracy. As far as Hayek's Knowledge Argument is concerned, Harari insists that at this stage AI might altogether alter the relative efficiency of democracy versus autocracy. Nondemocratic government becomes more viable at least as an economic model to the extent that AI would make central planning specifically and autocratic governance generally more viable.

Recall that "modern democracy is an ongoing experiment, and in many ways, we should be surprised that it has worked at all."[23] Existing democracies might not be in imminent danger. But we must ensure that individuals matter to politics in modern democracies in ways that solve the distant-state and overbearing-executive problems, and this can only happen via technology. Only through the right kind of deployment of modern democracy's materiality can consent to governance be meaningful and make sure that democratic governance does not mean quarantining the leadership, as it did in the early days of the American republic. Much as AI helped to move Chinese Communist Party rule into the twenty-first century, so it could help democratic states to update their systems. More concretely, and in ways we discuss in later sections, AI could help twenty-first-century democracy to solve those two legitimacy problems. But given what history teaches about how technology strengthens autocracies, democrats must be vigilant vis-à-vis autocratic tendencies *from within*. Once autocratic government is a live option, its viability could increase through technological means, especially AI.

To highlight technology's dystopian potential for democracy – in the spirit of technology being political in the *enframing* sense – let us revisit Ellul. Chapter 4 of his *Technological Society* ("Technique and State") explores the impact of technology specifically on governance. Ellul mentions Lenin as the inventor of political technique, the ways in which technological thinking has been applied to the political domain.[24] One might have wanted to nominate Machiavelli as an early

---

[22] Hayek, "The Use of Knowledge in Society." See also Hayek, *The Road to Serfdom*.
[23] Stasavage, *The Decline and Rise of Democracy*, 296.
[24] Ellul, *The Technological Society*, 232.

master of manipulation and propaganda. But much beyond Machiavelli's time, possibilities of influencing people were limited – simply because people were hard to reach in ways that would influence their thinking. Only the technique of the modern era enabled Lenin, Hitler, and others to enlist large numbers of people for their causes. In the twentieth century, the possibilities of state propaganda increased enormously.

Eventually, as Ellul continues, the state as a whole is inextricably intertwined with the advancement of technique, and then also with the corporations that produce the machinery and everything else that comes with it. But then the state can no longer represent its citizens when their interests conflict with the development of technique. The state has too much of a vested interest in technique and completely depends on it to function, and so must prioritize it above all else. And in such ways it is then technique that determines what happens in society, and it does so without being influenced by anything else that happens in society (which is Ellul's harrowing thesis of the autonomy of technique). Individuals are no longer even taken seriously *as* individuals, and instead are treated collectively as masses (a phenomenon he calls "massification"). The pursuit of justice does not go anywhere, and in a technocratic system, any normative aspirations for the future generally fall on deaf ears.

In the meantime, we end up with a division of labor between technicians, experts, and bureaucrats – the standard bearers of technique – on the one hand, and politicians who (at least ideally) seek to represent the people and who are ultimately accountable on the other. "When the technician has completed his task," Ellul writes, "he indicates to the politicians the possible solutions and the probable consequences – and retires."[25] The technical class understands the technique but has no accountability. For the technician, Ellul continues,

> the state is not the expression of popular will, or a creation of God, or the essence of humanity, or a modality of the class war. It is an enterprise with certain services which ought to function properly. It is an enterprise which ought to be profitable, yield a maximum of efficiency, and have the nation for its working capital.[26]

In his most chilling metaphor, Ellul submits that the world that technique is in the process of creating is "the universal concentration camp."[27]

In contrast to Ellul, recall from Chapter 2 how Winner distinguishes two ways for artifacts to have "political qualities."[28] First, devices or systems can be strongly, perhaps unavoidably, tied to certain patterns of power. Winner's example is atomic energy, which requires certain elites to provide and protect energy sources. Second, devices or systems might be means for establishing patterns of power or authority,

---

[25] Ellul, 258.
[26] Ellul, 264.
[27] Ellul, 397.
[28] Winner, "Do Artifacts Have Politics?"; Winner, *The Whale and the Reactor.*

but the design is flexible: Such patterns can turn out one way or another. An example is traffic infrastructure, which can assist many people but can also keep parts of the population in subordination, say, if they cannot reach suitable workplaces. Much as in the design of traffic infrastructure, careful attention would have to ensure that technology advances democratic purposes. Along these lines, Joshua Cohen and Archon Fung – in reviewing deterministic viewpoints that see technology as clearly favoring or disfavoring democracy – conclude that

> the democratic exploitation of technological affordances is vastly more contingent, more difficult, and more dependent on ethical conviction, political engagement, and good design choices than the technological determinists appreciated.[29]

This perspective offers hope in ways in which Ellul's rather extreme view does, of course, not. Careful design of the materiality of democracy is needed to solve the distant-state and overbearing-executive problems – and to keep democracy flourishing as a way of life in an era of technological innovation. The historical record does not have to make us pessimistic in this regard. But in light of the technological innovation all around us, the only way for us to rebut Ellul is to put our best efforts into using technology for democratic innovation.

3.5 THE GRAND DEMOCRATIC AI UTOPIA

We have so far looked at the materiality of democracy in historical perspective (Sections 3.2 and 3.3) and asked at a rather abstract level if democracy and technology are natural allies in any interesting sense (Section 3.4). For the remainder of this chapter, our gaze is directed at the future, and we are asking how AI might change the materiality of democracy. That is, we are asking whether AI can help solve the distant-state and overbearing-executive problem and overall maintain democracy as a way of life within the confines of a liberal understanding of democracy as introduced in Section 3.1. In a first step, let us consider a *Grand Democratic AI Utopia* as one way of giving us guidance (at least long-term) to how democracy could benefit from the arrival of AI.

We are nowhere near deploying anything like what I am about to describe, and for all I know, no serious scholar or activist currently asks for it. However, futurists Noah Yuval Harari and Jamie Susskind touch on something like this.[30] Moreover, more assertively James Lovelock thinks cyborgs could guide efforts to deal with

---

[29] Fung and Cohen, "Democracy and the Digital Public Sphere," 25. Or as computer scientist Nigel Shadbolt says, addressing worries that "machines might take over": "the problem is not that machines might wrest control of our lives from the elites. The problem is that most of us might never be able to wrest control of the machines from the people who occupy the command posts"; Shadbolt and Hampson, *The Digital Ape*, 63.
[30] Susskind, *Future Politics*, chapter 13; Harari, *Homo Deus*, chapter 9.

climate change.[31] And in discussing future risks, Toby Ord explores how AI might assist with our existential problems.[32] With technological innovation, our willingness to integrate technology into imageries for the future will only increase.[33] Such thinking is appealing because our brains evolved for the limited circumstances of small groups in earlier stages of *Homo sapiens* rather than the twenty-first century's globally interconnected world. Our brains were able to create this world but might not be able to manage its existential threats. So, it might well only be a question of time until some techno-optimists propose the large-scale involvement of AI in our collective-choice processes. Perhaps they will do so as a way of transferring Aristotle's aforementioned "argument from the wisdom of the multitude" – according to which a group might display virtue that no individual features – into the context of twenty-first-century representative democracies.

One might envisage something like this. AI knows everyone's preferences and views, and provides pertinent information to make people competent participants in governance. AI connects citizens to debate views, bringing together not only like-minded people on occasion but also (or more so) those of dissenting persuasions to make them hear each other. Monitoring everything, AI instantly identifies fraud and corruption. It flags or removes biased reporting and misleading arguments. It gathers votes, which eliminates challenges in people reaching polling stations, vote counting, and the like. AI improves procedural legitimacy through greater participation, while the caliber of decision-making increases because voters are well informed. AI calls for elections if confidence in the government falls below a threshold. Voters no longer merely choose one candidate from a list. They are consulted on multifarious issues, in ways that keep them abreast of relevant complexities, ensure that their views remain consistent, and so forth. More sophisticated aggregation methods than simple majoritarian voting are used.[34]

Perhaps elected politicians are still needed for some purposes. But by and large, AI reproduces certain features of early democracy for the twenty-first century while solving modern democracy's distant-state and overbearing-executive problems. AI resolves relatively unimportant matters itself, consulting representative groups for other matters to ensure that everything gets attention without swallowing too much time. In some countries, citizens can opt out of this AI-driven collective choice system. Others require participation, with penalties for those with privacy settings that prohibit integration into the system. Nudging techniques – to get people to do what is supposed to be in their best interest – are perfected for smooth operations.[35]

---

[31] Lovelock, *Novacene*.

[32] See Ord, *The Precipice*, chapter 5.

[33] So the upcoming discussion treats this Grand Democratic AI Utopia as a *sociotechnical imaginary* of a sort explored in Jasanoff and Kim, *Dreamscapes of Modernity*.

[34] For a discussion of majority rule in the context of competing methods that process information differently, also Risse, "Arguing for Majority Rule."

[35] Thaler and Sunstein, *Nudge*.

AI thereby voids previously prevalent issues around lack of inclusiveness. Privacy settings protect data, within the limits set by what is needed to make this whole collective choice system operational. Bureaucracies are much smaller because AI delivers public services, evaluating experiences from smart cities to create smart countries. Judges are replaced by sophisticated algorithms delivering even-handed rulings.[36] These systems can be arranged such that many concerns that might arise about the functionality and place of AI in human affairs are resolved internally. In such ways, enormous amounts of time are freed up for people to design their lives meaningfully.

Again, it is just possible that something like this might become more prominent in debates about AI and democracy. But right away, we should be wary of letting such scenarios guide our thinking, certainly if our ideal of what rule of the people means is what the liberal approach captures. To be sure, AI might develop in such a way that eventually intelligent machines have moral status, which would also raise the question of whether superintelligences might themselves be part of our political processes. Chapter 11 explores these matters, but they arise for a state of technological development that is not currently in place. In this chapter we focus on the view *from here*.

So here is why we – especially advocates of the liberal understanding of contemporary democracy – should be wary. To begin with, what makes imagining a future along such lines appealing is that it holds out the promise that either there is a *most* intelligent solution to many of the challenges in collective choice that we have so far experienced, or that at least there is a set of improvements across the board that make our collective choices *more* intelligent than what we have managed to implement so far. In other words, what is appealing is the idea that there is a one-dimensional kind of intelligence we can isolate as a kind of *pure* intelligence whose realization would dominate any collective choice system we have created so far and can be handed over to artificial devices. But recall from Chapter 1 that intelligence research does not even accept that there is only one kind of intelligence.[37] So the idea that there could be collective choice mechanisms that in terms of intelligence plainly *dominate* what humans have done so far is likely illusory.

Allowing algorithms to engage judgments and decisions as sketched above also harbors distinctive dangers. One is that, instead of investing in education to improve

---

[36] For the argument that "rule by automation" can enhance ideals of freedom and equality in democracies because it can make decision-making in public affairs more even-handed, see Sparks and Jayaram, "Rule by Automation." For the opposing viewpoint that algorithmic communications can be a threat to democratic participation when persons are operating in environments that are no conducive to political sophistication, see Christiano, "Algorithms, Manipulation, and Democracy." For the argument that "automated Influence" broadly conceived causes a crisis of legitimacy, see Benn and Lazar, "What's Wrong with Automated Influence." For the argument that relying on algorithmic systems is procedurally unjust in contexts involving background conditions of structural injustice, see Zimmermann and Lee-Stronach, "Proceed with Caution."

[37] See, for example, Gardner, *Frames of Mind*.

the practical reasoning of citizens (by making them more knowledgeable and better at reflecting on competing possibilities), we invest in building a system that facilitates collective decision-making.[38] That is, instead of making *people* better (also and especially in their role as citizens), we invest in making *systems* better. Ideally, of course, we would invest in both: The Grand Democratic AI Utopia would presumably work best if it helped us coordinate and aggregate the reasoning of wise, prudent, and knowledgeable individuals. But the danger is that, once such an AI-system is in place, a human tendency to delegate things *to the machine* would likely kick in, to the detriment of furthering human capacities.[39]

A second danger is that designing such a system inevitably involves large-scale efforts at building state capacities, which are subject to hijacking and other abuse. Another theme to recall from Chapter 1 (in addition to the research on intelligence) is that, at the dawn of the digital era, we also find Orwell's *Nineteen Eighty-Four*. Technology empowers people to do things, and the more people can do already, the more technology empowers them. Twenty-first-century governments with their already unprecedented capacities to penetrate the lives of their citizens are given ever more powerful tools through technological innovation. The government of Oceania in Orwell's dystopian novel uses those advancements to control the minds of the people subject to them. We should keep that warning firmly in sight: What would also be illusory here is to think that in the hands of governments, AI tools ostensibly designed to help with collective decision-making would *only* be used to bring out the collective will with greater clarity.

In conclusion, the Grand Democratic AI Utopia should not guide our thinking about how AI might enter our democratic processes. But what then are the possibilities and challenges of AI for democracy in this digital century? Sections 3.6–3.8 explore this question in a more focused way than our investigation of the Grand Democratic AI Utopia has allowed us to do. That is, we continue to ask how AI should be deployed to solve the two legitimacy problems of representative democracy and overall maintain democracy as a way of life within the confines of a liberal understanding of democracy; but we now ask specifically how to harness the *public sphere, political power,* and *economic power* to those ends.

3.6 AI AND DEMOCRACY: PUBLIC SPHERES

Public spheres are actor-networks intended to spread and receive information or opinions about matters of shared concern beyond family and friendship ties.[40] Prior

---

[38] For the argument that human practical rationality will suffer if we deprive ourselves of opportunities to practice decision-making by turning decision-making over to intelligent machines, see Eisikovits and Feldman, "AI and Phronesis."

[39] See also Helbing et al., "Will Democracy Survive Big Data and Artificial Intelligence?"

[40] For a classic study of the emergence of public spheres, see Habermas, *The Structural Transformation of the Public Sphere.* For how information spread in different periods, see

to the invention of writing, public spheres were limited to people talking. The flourishing of that early kind of public sphere depended on the availability of places where people could speak safely. The printing press mechanized exchange networks, dramatically lowering the costs of disseminating information or ideas. Eventually, newspapers became so central to public spheres that the press and later the media collectively were called the "fourth estate."[41] The press understood as private enterprise is the only such business mentioned in the US Constitution, which underscores both its importance for public life and the significance of legal regulation for its functionality in the service of citizenship.[42] After newspapers and other printed media, there was the telegraph, then radio, film production, and television. Eventually, leading twentieth-century media scholars coined certain slogans to capture the importance of media for contemporary life. Most famous among them were Marshall McLuhan in announcing that "the medium is the message" and Friedrich Kittler in stating that "the media determine our situation."[43]

"Fourth estate" is an instructive term. It highlights the relevance of the media and the deference for the more prominent among them, as well as for particular journalists whose voices carry weight with the public. (Walter Cronkite, an American broadcast journalist who served as anchorman for the CBS Evening News for about twenty years, was often referred to as "the most trusted man in America";[44] Cronkite died in 2009, and a dozen years after his death it is hard to imagine that it would ever become customary again to refer to anyone in that fashion.) But the term "fourth estate" also reveals that media have class interests of sorts: Aside from legal regulations, journalists have demographic and educational backgrounds that generate agendas. The ascent of social media, enabled by the internet, profoundly altered this situation, creating a public sphere where availability of information and viewpoints was no longer delineated by the "fourth estate." Big Tech companies have essentially undermined the point of referring to media that way.[45]

In the Western world, Google has become dominant in internet searches. Facebook, Twitter, and YouTube offer platforms for direct exchanges among individuals and associations at a scale previously impossible. Archon Fung refers to the

---

Blair et al., *Information*. For the development of media in recent centuries, see Starr, *The Creation of the Media*. For reflections on how communication is affected by the digital age, see O'Neill, *A Philosopher Looks at Digital Communication*.

[41] This term has been attributed to Edmund Burke; see Schultz, *Reviving the Fourth Estate*, 49.

[42] I take that thought from Minow, *Saving the News*, p. 1, 148. Minow frames her whole discussion in terms of that thought, mentioning at the very beginning and at the very end of her book.

[43] McLuhan, *Understanding Media*; Kittler, *Gramophone, Film, Typewriter*.

[44] See, for instance, this article in *Wired* from July 17, 2009: "TV News Icon Walter Cronkite Dies at 92," www.wired.com/2009/07/tv-news-icon-walter-cronkite-dead-at-92/

[45] For an assessment of social media in the historical context of media in the United States, see Minow, *Saving the News*.

kind of democracy that arose this way as "wide aperture, low deference," in which a much wider range of ideas and policies is explored than before and traditional leaders in politics, media, and culture are no longer treated with deference but ignored or distrusted.[46] And not only did social media generate new possibilities for networking, but they also created an abundance of data to predict trends and target specific people with messages. The 2018 Cambridge Analytica scandal – arising from the British consulting firm obtaining the personal data of millions of Facebook users without their consent, to be used for political advertising – revealed the potential of data mining, especially in locations where elections tend to be won by small margins.[47]

Digital media have generated an online communications infrastructure that forms an important part of the public sphere. The size and importance of this part will only increase. The communications infrastructure consists of systems and paraphernalia that make our digital lives happen, from the hardware of the internet to institutions that control domain names and the software that maintains the functionality of the internet and provides tools to make digital spaces usable (browsers, search engines, app stores, etc.).

Private interests dominate our digital infrastructure. Typically, engineers and entrepreneurs ponder market needs, profiting from the fact that ever more of our lives unfolds on platforms optimized for clicks and virality. News is presented to appeal to certain users, which creates echo chambers and spreads a plethora of deliberate falsehoods (*dis*information, rather than *mis*information) to reinforce the worldviews of those users. Political scientists have long lamented the ignorance of citizens in democracies and the resulting poor quality of public decision-making.[48] Even well-informed, engaged voters choose based on social identities and partisan loyalties.[49] Digital media reinforce these tendencies. Twitter, Facebook, YouTube, and competitors seek growth and revenue. Also, attention-grabbing algorithms of social media platforms (whose operations nonetheless often remain unnoticed or opaque) can sow confusion, ignorance, prejudice, and chaos. Such AI tools represent artificial *un*intelligence.[50]

---

[46] For the emergence of digital media and their role for democracy, see Fung and Cohen, "Democracy and the Digital Public Sphere." For the formulation I attribute to Fung, see, for example, this podcast: www.hks.harvard.edu/more/policycast/post-expert-democracy-why-nobody-trusts-elites-anymore

[47] Jungherr, Rivero, and Gayo-Avello, *Retooling Politics*, chapter 9; Véliz, *Privacy Is Power*, chapter 3.

[48] Brennan, *Against Democracy*; Caplan, *The Myth of the Rational Voter*; Somin, *Democracy and Political Ignorance*.

[49] Achen and Bartels, *Democracy for Realists*.

[50] Broussard, *Artificial Unintelligence*. For critical takes on the role of digital media in democracies, also see Foer, *World Without Mind*; McNamee, *Zucked*; Moore, *Democracy Hacked*; Taplin, *Move Fast and Break Things*; Bartlett, *The People vs. Tech*.

Having a public sphere where viewpoints can be articulated authentically and authoritatively recently became much harder through the emergence of *deepfakes*. Bringing photoshopping to video, deepfakes replace people in existing videos with someone else's likeness. They are named after their usage of deep learning technology, a branch of machine learning that applies neural net simulation to massive data sets. Currently their reach is mostly limited to pornography, but their potential goes considerably beyond that. For decades video has played a distinguished role in inquiry. What was captured on film served as indisputable evidence, in ways photography no longer could after manipulation techniques became widespread. Until the advent of deepfakes, videos offered an "epistemic backstop" in contested testimony.[51] Alongside other synthetic media and fake news, deepfakes might help create no-trust societies where people no longer bother to separate truth from falsehood. Chapter 6 discusses these phenomena in detail.

What is needed to counteract such tendencies is the creation of what Ethan Zuckerman calls "digital public infrastructure."[52] Digital public infrastructure lets us engage in public and civic life in digital spaces with norms and affordances designed around civic values. Designing digital public infrastructure is like creating parks and libraries for the internet. Instead of outsourcing the public sphere to the highest bidder, these spaces are devised to inform us, are structured to connect us to both people we agree with and people we disagree with, and encourage dialogue rather than simply reinforcing perceptions. As part of the design of such infrastructures, synthetic media must be integrated appropriately, in ways that require clear signaling of how they are put together. In addition, people would operate within such infrastructures in ways that protect their entitlements as knowers and knowns, entitlements captured in terms of epistemic rights (which we discuss in Chapters 5 and 7).

One option for putting in place a digital public infrastructure is to create a fleet of localized, community-specific, public-serving institutions to fulfil the functions in digital space that community institutions have fulfilled in physical places for centuries. There must be some governance model for this fleet to serve the public. Wikipedia's system of many editors and authors or Taiwan's digital democracy platform provide inspiring models for decentralized participatory governance.[53] Alternatively, governments could create publicly funded nonprofit corporations to manage and maintain the public's interest in digital life. Specialized AI would be central to such work, regardless of which of these options is chosen. After all, it would be through the use of such AI that such digital public infrastructure would be

---

[51] Rini, "Deepfakes and the Epistemic Backstop." See also Kerner and Risse, "Beyond Porn and Discreditation."

[52] See Zuckerman, "What Is Digital Public Infrastructure?"; Zuckerman, "The Case of Digital Public Infrastructure." See also Pariser and Allen, "To Thrive Our Democracy Needs Digital Public Infrastructure."

[53] Regarding Taiwan, see Leonard, "How Taiwan's Unlikely Digital Minister Hacked the Pandemic."

up to the technological standards to which people have gotten accustomed in other domains.

Properly designed digital public infrastructures (supported by specialized AI) could be like Winner's inclusive traffic infrastructure and help solve the distant-state and overbearing-executive problems. The information and connection provided by these digital spaces would mitigate the notion that society is abstract and distant. And to the extent that these spaces draw citizens into the public realm their increased involvement also means that citizens can see themselves as governing, and thus push back against an overreaching executive branch.

3.7 AI AND DEMOCRACY: POLITICAL POWER

The Chinese social credit system comprehensively gathers information about individuals with the assistance of sophisticated electronic tools and brings that information to bear on what people may do in many domains of life. As far as the use of AI for the maintenance of power is concerned, this system illustrates how autocratic regimes avail themselves of technological advances.[54] In addition, across the world, cyberspace has become a frequent battleground between excessively profit-seeking or outright criminal activities and overly strong state reactions to them, which generate tools that also help authoritarians oppress political activities.[55] While most mass protests in recent years – from Hong Kong to Algeria and Lebanon – were inspired by hashtags, coordinated through social networks, and convened by smart-phones, governments have learned how to respond to such movements. They control online spaces by blocking platforms and disrupting the internet.[56]

In his 1961 farewell speech, US president Dwight D. Eisenhower famously warned against the acquisition of unwarranted influence "by the military-industrial complex" and against public policy becoming "captive of a scientific-technological elite."[57] Those interconnected dangers would be incompatible with a flourishing democracy. Eisenhower spoke only years after the Office of Naval Research had partly funded the first Summer Research Project on AI at Dartmouth in 1956 (discussed in Chapter 1), with the military-industrial complex claiming a stake in this technology developed by the scientific-technological elite.[58]

Decades later, the 2013 Snowden revelations showed what US intelligence could do with tools easily classified as specialized AI. Phones, social media platforms, email, and browsers serve as data sources for the state. Analyzing metadata

---

[54] For a recent take, see Reilly, Lyu, and Robertson, "China's Social Credit System: Speculation vs. Reality." See also Dickson, *The Party and the People*.

[55] Deibert, *Black Code*; Deibert, *Reset*.

[56] Fung and Cohen, "Democracy and the Digital Public Sphere." For the theme of power in the context of digital media, also see Susskind, *The Digital Republic*.

[57] For the speech, see www.ourdocuments.gov/doc.php?flash=false&doc=90&page=transcript

[58] Crawford, *Atlas of AI*, 184. Obviously in 1961, AI is not what Eisenhower had in mind.

(who moved where, connected to whom, read what, etc.) provides insights into operations of groups and individuals. Private-sector partnerships have considerably enhanced the capacities of law enforcement and military to track people (using facial, gait, and voice recognition), from illegal immigrants at risk of deportation to enemies targeted for killing.[59]

Where AI systems are deployed as part of the welfare state, they often surveil people and restrict access to resources rather than providing greater support.[60] Secret databases and little-known AI applications have had harmful effects in finance, business, education, and politics. AI-based decisions on parole, mortgage, and job applications are often biased. Such practices readily perpetuate past injustice. After all, data inevitably reflect how people have been faring so far. Thus, they reflect the biases, including racial biases, that have structured exercises of power.[61] Decades ago, Donna Haraway's "Cyborg Manifesto," a classic at the intersection of feminist thought and the philosophy of technology, warned that the digital age might sustain white capitalist patriarchy with the "informatics of domination."[62] These practices have prompted observers to call societies that make excessive use of algorithms "black-box societies."[63] But democratic ideals require reasons and explanations in some way. If algorithms do things humans find hard to assess, it is unclear what would even count as relevant explanations.[64]

Of course, digital technologies can also strengthen democracy. In 2011, Iceland produced the first-ever "crowdsourced" constitutional proposal in the world. In Taiwan, negotiations among authorities, citizens, and companies like Uber and Airbnb were aided by an innovative digital process for deliberative governance called vTaiwan. France relied on digital technologies for the Great National Debate in early 2019 and the Convention on Climate Change between October 2019 and June 2020, experiments with deliberation at the scale of a large nation.[65] Barcelona has become a global leader in the smart city movement, deploying digital technology for matters of municipal governance.[66] The Smart City Index, created in 2019 to provide a global ranking of smart cities, speaks to how much innovation goes on in this movement across the world.[67]

Let me mention some more examples of how digital technologies have strengthened democracy. An Australian nonprofit eDemocracy project, Open

---

[59] Crawford, chapter 6. See also Véliz, *Privacy Is Power*.
[60] Eubanks, *Automating Inequality*.
[61] Benjamin, *Race After Technology*; Benjamin, *Captivating Technology*; Noble, *Algorithms of Oppression*. See also D'Ignazio and Klein, *Data Feminism*; Costanza-Chock, *Design Justice*.
[62] Haraway, *Manifestly Haraway*, 3–90. For the informatics of domination, see Haraway, 28.
[63] Pasquale, *The Black Box Society*. See also Broussard, *Artificial Unintelligence*; O'Neil, *Weapons of Math Destruction*.
[64] On this, see Vredenburgh, "The Right to Explanation."
[65] Bernholz, Landemore, and Reich, *Digital Technology and Democratic Theory*.
[66] Preville, "How Barcelona Is Leading a New Era of Digital Democracy."
[67] "Smart City Observatory."

Forum, invites politicians, senior administrators, academics, businesspeople, and other stakeholders to engage in policy debates. The California Report Card is a mobile-optimized web application promoting public involvement in state government. As the COVID-19 pandemic ravaged the world, democracies availed themselves of digital technologies to keep people connected and serve as key components of public health surveillance. And while civil society organizations frequently are no match for abusive state power, even investigations limited to open internet sources can harvest the abundance of available data needed to pillory abuse of power. The best-known example is the investigative-journalism group Bellingcat, which specializes in fact-checking and open-source intelligence.[68]

Let us wrap up this discussion about political power. One striking fact about the American version of modern democracy is that, when the preferences of low- or middle-income citizens diverge from those of the affluent, there is no correlation between policy outcomes and preferences of less advantaged groups.[69] In such cases, the policy preferences of such people are either actively de-prioritized, or these people are not seriously represented to begin with because the lawmakers do not have their interests in mind (and certainly not at heart). As far as political power is concerned, the legitimacy of modern democracy is therefore evidently questionable.

To improve upon that status quo, democracy could be strengthened considerably by well-designed AI. The digital public infrastructure discussed in the context of the public sphere can be enriched to include systems that deploy AI for improving citizen services across the board. Analyzing databases can give politicians a more accurate image of what citizens need. The bandwidth of communication between voters and politicians can increase immensely. Some forms of surveillance are necessary, but democratic governance requires appropriate oversight. Presumably it takes broadly based democratic grassroots movements to hold politicians accountable for realizing the democratic potential of such technologies without generating too many new challenges.[70]

3.8 AI AND DEMOCRACY: ECONOMIC POWER

The contemporary ideal of democracy typically includes egalitarian empowerment of sorts. But economic inequality threatens any such empowerment. This threat has implications for contemporary democracies, which frequently have capitalist economies. As Thomas Piketty has argued, capitalism generates inequality over time because, roughly speaking, owners of shares of the economy benefit from economic output and growth more than people living on the wages the owners

---

[68] Higgins, *We Are Bellingcat*. Also see Webb, *Coding Democracy*.
[69] Bartels, *Unequal Democracy*; Gilens, *Affluence and Influence*.
[70] On AI and citizen services, see Mehr, "Artificial Intelligence for Citizen Services and Government."

willingly pay.[71] A worry about democracy across history (and much on the mind of Publius) has been that the masses would expropriate the elites. But in capitalist democracies, we must worry about the opposite. It takes sustained policies around taxation, transportation, design of cities, health care, digital infrastructure, pension and education systems, and macro-economic and monetary policies to curtail economic inequality. The Rawlsian liberal view of democracy, for one, insist that economic inequalities be curtailed: Such inequalities are justifiable only to the extent that they are needed to benefit everyone, including the least-advantaged (and similarly for other liberal views of democracy).

One concern about AI is that, generally, the ability to produce or use technology is one mechanism that drives inequality, enabling those with requisite skills to advance – which in turn enables them not only to become well-off but also to become owners in the economy in ways that resonate across generations. Technology generally and AI specifically are integral parts of the inequality-enhancing tendencies Piketty identifies. One question that arises here is how these tendencies play out for those who are not among the clear winners. AI profoundly transforms jobs, at least because aspects of many jobs will be absorbed by AI or otherwise mechanized. These changes also create new jobs, including at the lower end, in the maintenance of hardware and the basic tasks around data gathering and analysis.[72]

On the optimistic side of predictions about the future of work, we find visions of society with many traditional jobs gradually transformed, some eliminated, and new jobs added – in ways creating much more leisure time for average people owing to increased societal wealth. On the pessimistic side, however, many who are unqualified for meaningful roles in tech economies might be dispensable to the labor force. Their political relevance might eventually amount to little more than that they must be pacified if they cannot be excluded outright. Lest this standpoint be dismissed as Luddite alarmism ("at the end of the tunnel, there have always been more jobs than before"), we should note that economies where data ownership becomes increasingly relevant and where AI absorbs many tasks could differ critically from economies organized around ownership of land or around ownership of factories. In these two earlier scenarios, large numbers of people were needed to provide labor; in the second case, to act as consumers as well. Elites could not risk losing *too many* laborers. But this constraint might vanish in the future, and then it might only be a small step from workers becoming economically redundant to them being politically entirely excluded.

To be sure, a lot does depend on how questions around control over and ownership of data are resolved; the relevance of these questions for our future economy cannot be overstated (a subject we discuss in Chapter 9). As Shoshana

[71] Piketty, *Capital in the Twenty-First Century*.
[72] On these topics, see, for example, Susskind, *A World Without Work*; West, *The Future of Work*.

Zuboff has argued, the importance of data collection for the economy has become so immense that the term "surveillance capitalism" characterizes the current stage of capitalism.[73] Surveillance capitalism as an economic model was developed by Google, which to surveillance capitalism is what Ford was to mass production. Later the model was adopted by Facebook, Amazon, and others. Previously, data were collected largely to improve services. But subsequently, data generated as byproducts of interactions with multifarious devices were deployed to develop predictive products and designed not only to forecast what we will feel, think, or do, but ultimately also to control and change these behaviors, always for the sake of monetization. Marx and Engels identified increasing commodification as a basic mechanism of capitalism (though they did not use that very term). Large-scale data collection is the maximal version of commodification: Such collection commodifies all our lived realities.

In the twentieth century, Hannah Arendt and others diagnosed mechanisms of "totalitarian" power, the state's all-encompassing power.[74] Its central metaphor is Big Brother, capturing the state's omnipresence. Parallel to that, Zuboff talks about "instrumentarian" power, exercised through use of electronic devices in social settings for harvesting profits. The central metaphor here is "Big Other," the ever-present electronic device that knows just what to do. Big Brother aimed for total control, Big Other for predictive certainty (that is, the advice given will always be followed because the needs are accurately anticipated). Chapter 8 has more to say on this subject.

Current technological innovation is disproportionately driven by relatively few large companies, which the futurist Amy Webb calls "the Big Nine": in the United States, Google, Microsoft, Amazon, Facebook, IBM, and Apple; in China, Tencent, Alibaba, and Baidu.[75] The Chinese companies are busy consolidating and mining massive amounts of data to serve the government's ambitions. The American ones implement surveillance capitalism, embedded into a legal and political framework that, as of 2022, shows little interest in developing strategic plans for a democratic future and thus shows little interest in doing for democracy what the Chinese Communist Party did for its system – upgrading it into this century. The EU is much more involved in such efforts. But none of the Big Nine is based there (though, to be sure, increasingly many smaller AI companies are), and economic competition in the tech sector seems to be to a rather disproportionate extent between the United States and China ("disproportionate" – that is, even vis-à-vis the large sizes of these two economies).

---

[73] Zuboff, *The Age of Surveillance Capitalism.* See also Véliz, *Privacy Is Power*; Hoffman, *Your Data, Their Billions*; Ghosh, *Terms of Disservice.*

[74] Arendt, *The Origins of Totalitarianism.*

[75] Webb, *The Big Nine.*

To avert the pessimistic side of the predictions about the future of work in ways that strengthen democracy, both civil society and the state must step up, and the enormous power concentrated in Big Tech companies needs to be harnessed for democratic purposes. It is hard to see how that can be done unless the Big Tech companies are either dismantled entirely (beyond simply breaking each of them into several smaller operations that would still each be humungous by any historical standards) or treated and thus regulated as public utilities alongside enterprises like phone companies. They have too much power and autonomy to be made to reorient their purposes toward democracy simply by means of self-regulation.[76]

3.9 CONCLUSION

As we bring about the future, computer scientists will become ever more important, including as experts in designing specialized AI for democratic purposes. That raises its own challenges. Much as technology and democracy are no natural allies, technologists are no natural champions of or even obviously qualified advisers in democracy. No one has expressed this standpoint as dramatically as Ellul. But one does not have to go to such lengths to see the challenges here. As Arendt stated, any scientific activity,

> since it acts into nature from the standpoint of the universe and not into the web of human relationships, lacks the revelatory character of action as well as the ability to produce stories and become historical, which together form the very source from which meaningfulness springs into and illuminates human existence.[77]

Democracy is a way of life more than anything else, one that greatly benefits from the kind of action Arendt mentions (an understanding of action we revisit in Chapters 10 and 11). And yet modern democracy critically depends on technology (and thus on the scientific activity that produces it) to be the kind of actor-network that solves the distant-state and overbearing-executive problems. Citizens in democracies must not rely on tech experts in hopes that they will make sure technology is used to advance rather than undermine democracy. Technological advancements must be widely debated in democratic politics, and citizens should take an active interest in these matters.

---

[76] On the theme of treating Big Tech companies as public utilities following the model of telephone companies and railroads, see Minow, *Saving the News*, chapter 4. One argument one might make in this regard is that if indeed we think of Big Tech companies parallel to telephone companies, then there should be no serious content moderation (either via company-self-regulation or via state intervention) – parallel to how conversations over the phone are monitored only under exceptional circumstances. But since communication on social media involves different dynamics (which allow some people to build an enormous number of followers), more substantial regulation is called for in the case of social media than it has been for telephone companies.

[77] Arendt, *The Human Condition*, 324.

Technology must be consciously harnessed to become like Winner's inclusive traffic infrastructure. Otherwise, democracy as a way of life – and the manner of being human that comes with leading such a life – is under threat from technological advances. A flourishing democratic culture, along the lines of what we have discussed under the headings of public sphere, political power, and economic power, is not only required to make sure further technological innovation strengthens democracy as time goes by. It is also arguably a prerequisite for humanity to keep technology under control so that we can avoid the more dystopian scenarios we have already encountered. As it has always done, the materiality of democracy both reflects and (over time) determines what kind of democratic citizenship is possible to begin with, and thus ultimately what ways of being human are available in future democracies. So there is a great deal at stake when it comes to the ways in which democratic cultures integrate technology.

As Life 2.0 progresses, our questions will change. As innovation keeps happening, societies will change. Innovation will increase awareness of human limitations and set in motion different ways for people to deal with those limitations. If Life 3.0 emerges, new questions for governance will arise. Will humans still exercise control? If so, will there be democracies, will some people or countries subjugate everybody else, or will there be yet other forms of order? Will it be appropriate to involve new intelligent entities in governance, and what will those entities have to be like for the answer to be affirmative? If humans are not in control, what will governance be like? These are questions we address in Chapter 11. For now, let us turn to other questions that are already very much upon us.

4

Truth Will Not Set You Free: Is There a Right to It Anyway?

Elaborating on the Work Public Reason Does In Life 2.0

When complete agreement could not otherwise be reached, a general massacre of all who have not thought in a certain way has proved a very effective means of settling opinion in a country.

—Charles Sanders Peirce, "The Fixation of Belief"[1]

4.1 INTRODUCTION: THE RIGHT TO TRUTH

The Western tradition (as presumably all others) has long known that truth upends human living arrangements. In Plato's famous allegory of the cave, whoever leaves the cave to bring back the truth about the outside world would be killed by those left behind if only these people could apprehend the returnees.[2] Centuries after Plato, Jesus says to Pilate, "Everyone that is of the truth heareth my voice." Those who bring charges against Jesus accuse him of lying for fear that what he says is in fact true. Formulating a question that has resonated through the ages, Pilate responds, "What is truth?" and declares that "I find in him no fault at all."[3] Nonetheless, Pilate sentences Jesus to death based on testimony he finds worthless. That is, the founder of a religion obsessed with truthfulness (of sorts) is sentenced to die based on made-up charges, on the authority of a man who denounces truth altogether. So, both Greek and Christian wisdom are clear that those who bring truth should expect various forms of resistance, resistance to the manner in which truth would upend the arrangements in which those people have become comfortable on whose verdict the possibility of change would depend.

Today, millennia later, concerns around truth arise in digital lifeworlds. Such lifeworlds create possibilities for spreading information at a pace and volume

---

[1] Peirce, "The Fixation of Belief," 13.
[2] Plato, *Republic*, 517a.
[3] Gospel of John 18:37–38 (King James Version).

unheard of in analog contexts. But misinformation and disinformation spread the same way. So, a *right to truth* has some prima facie moral plausibility simply in light of the technological features of digital lifeworlds. Digitalization has also enormously increased the possibilities for preventing, flagging, or removing content ("content moderation"). So such a right to truth is also in principle implementable in digital lifeworlds. To be sure, questions about such a right also arise for analog lifeworlds, and any discussion of a right to truth will draw on philosophical ideas not related to digitalization generally or AI specifically. But the question of whether there is such a right arises with enormous force for digital lifeworlds, especially because of the possibilities generated by specialized AI tools to magnify or even generate viewpoints on digital platforms. This question also arises before the background of that ancient concern about how truth upends living arrangements.

A "right to truth" is often evoked in the context of gross violations of human rights and humanitarian law. There are other domains where *particular* agents have legal or moral entitlements to receive *particular* information (and we encounter some more examples below). What we want to know, however, is whether there is some general entitlement to truth telling, and if so, whether that entitlement would be defeated in certain situations. Explanations would also have to be given as to when that entitlement is defeated. What is at stake is whether we can demand truth by default, under all circumstances, or instead whether there are such entitlements only under certain circumstances. As it turns out, the latter is the case. As will become clear throughout our discussion, truth still has a way of upending human living arrangements, and it should be handled with care.

This chapter enlists a motley group of thinkers on the subject of truth, so let me explain its argumentative strategy. We first explore how damaging untruth can be, especially in digital lifeworlds (where "untruth" includes outright fabrications, but then also exaggerations, omissions, understatements, suggestions, allusions, distortions, or misleading statements). This set of considerations provides support for a right to truth. But next we see that untruth is immensely important to people's lives. It is not just that people fail to have a preference for truth but also that untruth plays a significant role as an enabler of valued psychological and social dynamics. Contrary to a well-known Bible verse ("The truth will set you free;" Gospel of John 8:32), for most people it is decidedly not the truth that sets them free. It is the acceptance of worldviews in like-minded company that does so (worldviews, or comprehensive moral doctrines, which tend to contain plenty of untruths), in any event if being set free means having an orientation in the world. The set of considerations that pull in the opposite direction notwithstanding, there can therefore be no comprehensive right to truth. But this absence of a comprehensive right is consistent with there being a right to truth *in specific contexts*. And to be sure, protecting the public sphere for the exercise of citizenship from a public-reason standpoint (as discussed in Chapter 3) means the state must protect truth telling and sanction untruth. But as we conclude, as far as the public sphere is concerned, the moral concern behind truthfulness is not best captured in terms of an actual right to truth.[4]

Naturally, "a right to truth" could not without absurdity capture a broad entitlement for everybody to know everything that is true. Accordingly, Section 4.2 offers clarification about our topic (and elaborates on the contexts from which a right to truth is familiar). Section 4.3 explores how damaging untruth can be by focusing on the theme of *repetition*. Digital lifeworlds generally and social media especially enable people to surround themselves with news sources that repeat messages over and over. One scenario that comes on our radar is Donald Trump's Big Lie, his ghastly effort to depict the 2020 presidential election as having been "stolen" from him, which was vastly advanced through ceaseless repetition. To highlight the importance of repetition for the forging of a life – and thereby to reveal the full extent to which endless repetition of untruth does damage – we turn to Søren Kierkegaard. The weight of the importance of repetition in human life combined with the enormous potential for generating repetitions of the pernicious sort offer strong support for a moral right to truth. All of this applies with special force in digital lifeworlds.[5]

Such support notwithstanding, the enormous relevance that untruth also has for life undermines any argument for a *comprehensive* right of that sort. Section 4.4 starts making that case with Friedrich Nietzsche's distinction between *will to truth* and *will to value*. Nietzsche held that people care more about having a meaningful story about their lives than about truth. It is the will to value that drives our efforts to describe our lives in meaningful ways, efforts that stand in a complex relationship to the will to understand the world around us the way it is. Nietzsche's ability to put his finger on these complexities continues to make his distinction strikingly relevant – especially in the digital age, with its enormous possibilities for these wills to diverge. Section 4.5 draws out how Nietzsche's distinction illuminates ways for people to make sense of themselves that give only peripheral roles to truth. Trump's Big Lie, for one, offered many people ways of seeing (or presenting) themselves as cheated by reckless liberals who stop at nothing to gain control. The Big Lie also offered people roles in telling that narrative and in the fight against the alleged steal. Comprehensive doctrines, too, typically abound in storytelling of the sort that gives

---

[4] (1) Some readers might say an investigation of whether there is a comprehensive right to truth is bound to fail. For the answer could not possibly be affirmative at such a general level. In important ways this intuition will be validated. However, the issues we discuss here are by themselves so important that it is better to let such an insight emerge from our investigation rather than be guided by it ex ante. (2) "Truthfulness" is either the personal virtue of being committed to telling the truth, or the value of attaching importance to truth, and sometimes it refers to the fact that something is true. The context should make clear what is meant. I generally talk about "truth" without using the direct article, as an abstract noun. The article is typically used when concrete instances of truth are meant to be invoked at least implicitly.

[5] Trump's Big Lie serves as an example at several points. We could easily find competing examples from other parts of the political spectrum. Nonetheless, the Big Lie and the way it was advanced by so many will likely remain of interest as a phenomenon of political psychology for decades to come.

meaning to lives. Drawing on Sections 4.4 and 4.5, Section 4.6 then formulates an argument as to why there cannot be a *comprehensive* right to truth.

Section 4.7 finally turns to public reason. The limited role truth plays in public reason reflects the unavailability of a comprehensive right to truth. After all, citizens are asked to refrain from judging each other's moral doctrines from a standpoint of truth. At the same time, the role that truth does play raises the question of whether there should be a right to truth in specific contexts, especially regarding the protection of the public sphere. However, as I argue in Section 4.8, the moral relevance that protecting truthfulness in the public sphere has is not typically best captured by insisting on a *right* to truth. What matters is not primarily that individuals have certain claims that require specific actions on occasion, but that the functionality of the public sphere is a significant value that requires state action to protect it. The truth will not set you free (and there is no comprehensive right to it), but a society where truthfulness in the public sphere is regarded as a significant value *and* where people can find an orientation in comprehensive doctrines with the kind of story-telling they entail offers good prospects for doing so. This would be the kind of society that sets people free in enduring ways while making sure that others too can be set free in their own, rather different ways.[6]

4.2 "THE RIGHT TO TRUTH"

Let us seize this occasion to introduce some basic vocabulary about rights. This vocabulary does not play a major role in this chapter. However, this is the first of several chapters that deal with rights, and so this stage-setting section is a good place to cover some basics. According to the standard scheme developed by scholar

---

[6] (1) A "story" (or "narrative") in the broad sense is an account of a sequence of interrelated events or experiences, fictional or nonfictional. The narrower sense denotes a fictional account. But the fact that the broader (more common) use is open to the content being either fictional or nonfictional, so either false or true, also illustrates the fact that true and untrue components often merge in a narrative. As we noted, the untrue components might not be outright fabrications, but exaggerations, omissions, understatements, suggestions, allusions, distortions, or misleading statements. In a review of a book on British Prime Minister Boris Johnson, Rory Stewart brilliantly captures the whole range of what might be meant by "untruth." He writes that Johnson "has mastered the use of error, omission, exaggeration, diminution, equivocation and flat denial. He has perfected casuistry, circumlocution, false equivalence and false analogy. He is equally adept at the ironic jest, the fib and the grand lie; the weasel word and the half-truth; the hyperbolic lie, the obvious lie, and the bullshit lie – which may inadvertently be true. And because he has been so famous for this skill for so long, he can use his reputation to ascend to new levels of playful paradox;" Stewart, "Lord of Misrule." (2) In Orwell's *Nineteen Eighty-Four*, the protagonist Winston Smith writes in his diary that freedom consists in being able to say that two plus two equals four, and that all else follows; see Orwell, 1984. On the view defended here, freedom is more complicated. But one cannot blame Smith for articulating that view under the horrible circumstances he must endure.

Wesley Hohfeld, rights might be privileges, claims, powers, or immunities.[7] I have a *privilege-right* to do something if I have no duty not to do it. (I have such a right to marry someone, which means I am not obligated to refrain from marrying – but there is indeed nothing more to this right; in particular, I can exercise this right only if a specific person accepts me.) I have a *claim-right* to something if somebody else has a duty to make it happen. (If I buy something, the shopkeeper should hand it over.) I have a *power-right* if I am in a position to waive a claim-right. (I tell a recommender that I will not exercise my right to see her letter.) Finally, I have an *immunity-right* if I am in a position to decline alterations of my entitlements. (As a patient, I normally have such a right against healthcare providers unilaterally changing privacy arrangements.)

It is obvious in many cases what kind of right (privilege, claim, power, immunity) is meant when rights-vocabulary is deployed, but the matter might also be up for debate. All such rights can be legal or moral. Legal rights are part of some legal framework. For moral rights, we need an argument as to why an adequate response to a certain situation is to give somebody certain privileges, claims, powers, or immunities, regardless of questions around enforcement of the sort that arise within legal frameworks.[8]

Again, I introduce this general account of rights here to have it in place for the remainder of the book rather than for intensive use in this chapter specifically (tough it does make another appearance in this chapter). Let us turn to the right to truth. Such a right is familiar from the broader context of transitional justice, a range of efforts to outgrow oppressive power arrangements in ways that also aim to make amends.[9] Where grave human rights violations have occurred, it is primarily the victims and their families, but then secondarily also society at large, who have claim-rights against the government or other entities to know who was involved. The UN considers March 24 the International Day for the Right to the Truth Concerning Gross Human Rights Violations and for the Dignity of Victims.[10]

Other human rights efforts around the right to truth draw on the right to "receive and impart information and ideas" in Article 19 of the Universal Declaration of Human Rights. For instance, in addition to some domestic freedom-of-information

---

[7] Hohfeld, *Fundamental Legal Conceptions*. See also Wenar, "Rights."

[8] As for what it takes to make a case for moral rights, I follow Scanlon, "Rights, Goals, and Fairness." In this view, such an argument involves an empirical claim about how individuals behave or how institutions work in the absence of particular assignments of rights; a claim that this result would be unacceptable, based on valuations of consequences in a way that takes into account considerations of fairness and equality (as appropriate); and a further empirical claim about how the envisaged assignment of rights will produce a different outcome. Subsequent discussions are in that spirit, but I do not revisit this scheme explicitly.

[9] See e.g., Klinkner and Davis, *The Right to the Truth in International Law*; Vedaschi, "Globalization of Human Rights and Mutual Influence between Courts"; Park, "Truth as Justice."

[10] On that day in 1980, Óscar Arnulfo Romero, Archbishop of San Salvador, was shot while celebrating mass, in retaliation for pillorying violations.

laws, this right appears in the UN General Assembly's 2030 Agenda for Sustainable Development, with the UN Educational, Scientific and Cultural Organization (UNESCO) assigned as custodian for reporting on public access to information.[11] To mention another example, a "right to know" is discussed in medical ethics. This topic appears in the context of genetic information, but implicitly also in the discussion about informed consent.[12] And, of course, the law in certain contexts insists on truth telling, especially when testimony under oath is required. Certain parties thus also have a right to truth in specific matters.

These scenarios formulate entitlements in specific contexts. Thereby, the ensuing discussions of truth in those contexts become reasonably well-defined. But our more amorphous topic here is if there is something like a comprehensive entitlement to an environment where truth prevails (and where then we need to spell out what that means). If there is, one could normally insist on truthfulness, although countervailing considerations may overrule such insistence: After all, it will be true for just about everyone that most events in the world are none of their business. The alternative to there being a comprehensive entitlement to an environment where truth prevails is there being entitlements to truth only under certain circumstances. And as it turns out, the latter is the case.

4.3 REPETITION IN DIGITAL MEDIA: THE CASE FOR A RIGHT TO TRUTH

One way of supporting a right to truth is to investigate the theme of *repetition* with a special focus on its relevance in digital lifeworlds. Such an investigation gets us into waters that are deeper than might be apparent. But coming to terms with the sheer profundity of this topic is an effective way of making clear how much damage repetition of untruth can cause.

Trump's Big Lie – his ghastly effort at overturning the 2020 presidential election by portraying it as having been "stolen" from him – is a case in point. By Trump's admission, repetition was all along key to his making false or misleading statements credible.[13] One extensive study of his efforts to discredit mail-in voting to such an extent that his false assertions about that type of voting would undermine the

---

[11]　UNESCO, "World Trends in Freedom of Expression and Media Development."

[12]　On genetic information, see Chadwick, Levitt, and Shickle, *The Right to Know and the Right Not to Know*. On informed consent, see Faden, Beauchamp, and King, *A History and Theory of Informed Consent*. For consent to be informed, patients must know certain facts. If *informed* consent is required, patients have a right to know such facts.

[13]　In a speech in Florida on July 3, 2021, Trump said: "If you say it enough and keep saying it, they'll start to believe you;" www.cnn.com/2021/07/05/politics/trump-disinformation-strategy/index.html. For the importance of repetition in Trump's rhetoric, see also Snyder, *On Tyranny*, chapter 10.

legitimacy of the 2020 election also reveals how repetition does its work.[14] For months before the first presidential debate in September 2020, Trump's team waged a disinformation campaign around mail-in voting. This set the stage for subsequent efforts to spread disinformation about vote counting. This was an elite-driven campaign, and its primary mechanism was mass media spreading falsehoods from Trump's team and the Republican National Committee. Social media further echoed those falsehoods. That certain claims came from a sitting president made them newsworthy, and their sensational content rendered them suitable for further repetition.

The precise import of social media in Trump's disinformation machinations and in politics generally is a topic for empirical research beyond what concerns us here.[15] What matters now is, first, that the sheer availability of social media has to some extent changed the channels through which information spreads. Second, increasingly techniques powered by specialized AI create and spread disinformation in ever more sophisticated ways, through fake news reports enriched by deepfake video and audio; automated, highly personalized targeting (of end users or influencers) with disinformation; or denial of access to information through flooding communication channels with fake news.[16] The effects of repetition in the spreading of narratives under such circumstances must make us inquire with renewed urgency about such a right to truth in digital lifeworlds.[17]

While the Big Lie represents a case in point, the importance of repetition in political rhetoric has long been recognized. Let me offer an example. In 1949, Frankfurt School scholars Leo Löwenthal and Norbert Guterman argued that totalitarianism deploys psychological manipulation to make people compliant.[18] One device is overwhelming people with endless repetition, for instance, of racist stereotypes, political invective, and violent fantasies (all of which were reflected in American fascist tendencies Löwenthal and Guterman investigated while living in

---

[14] Benkler et al., "Mail-in Voter Fraud." That piece downplays the importance of social media in originating disinformation. But social media still play an important role in repeating falsehoods, and that point matters primarily here. On misinformation campaigns, see also O'Connor and Weatherall, *The Misinformation Age*; Merlan, *Republic of Lies*; Benkler, Faris, and Roberts, *Network Propaganda*.

[15] For a study finding that environments where people can choose their news sources do not normally generate echo chambers, see Dubois and Blank, "The Echo Chamber Is Overstated." The case for a right to truth arises with great force in digital lifeworlds because of their potential for the distorting type of repetition, regardless of whether things actually go wrong at particular times or places.

[16] For a recent assessment of the impact of social media on politics, see Jungherr, Rivero, and Gayo-Avello, *Retooling Politics*. For the concrete ways AI can threaten security, see Brundage et al., "The Malicious Use of Artificial Intelligence: Forecasting, Prevention, and Mitigation." On that subject, also see Kissinger, Schmidt, and Huttenlocher, *The Age of AI*.

[17] For the idea of technology as amplifier, Toyama, "Technology as Amplifier in International Development." See also Chakrabarti, "Hard Questions: What Effect Does Social Media Have on Democracy?"

[18] Löwenthal and Guterman, *Prophets of Deceit*.

the United States as exile scholars). Repetition of that sort primes people to accept whatever they are told next, to the extent that the new input appeals to their biases and predispositions that have now been successfully groomed to make them accepting of additional information from the same source. (This analysis of totalitarianism was published two years before Hannah Arendt's much more famous *Origins of Totalitarianism*, which contended that totalitarianism dominates its subjects through terror and cruelty and does not make much of repetition.[19])

To be sure, politicians themselves have been aware of the power of repetition long before Trump or digital lifeworlds. As many students of Latin learn in school, Roman statesman Cato the Elder concluded his speeches with a call to destroy Carthage ("Ceterum censeo Carthaginem esse delendam"), hoping that repetition would generate agreement. (And sure enough, the Romans did destroy Carthage eventually.) Hitler wrote in *Mein Kampf* that "slogans should be persistently repeated until the very last individual has come to grasp the idea."[20]

Regarding the kind of campaign advanced by Trump, political theorists Nancy Rosenblum and Russell Muirhead contrast what they call the "new conspiracism" with older conspiracism.[21] The older version – though revisionist by definition – obsessed about evidence, at least on the face of it: It depicted established views as fabrications and even tried to recruit audiences to join the investigations. Often forgeries were involved. A notorious example is the so-called *Protocols of the Elders of Zion*, an antisemitic text from around 1900 purporting to set out a Jewish plan for world domination.[22] Interpretations of alleged evidence for this kind of conspiracy have typically been far-fetched. But the fact that evidence is central to the task has been unquestioned, much as liars present their claims as defensible. To be sure, what is typically meant to make the lies defensible is not just the fabricated evidence, but also background theories designed to show how the lies of the moment fit with larger patterns and thereby increase in credibility. For instance, the *Protocols* were presented and defended by writers who also had many other things to say about how Jews had allegedly tried to undermine the Christian world order all along. By contrast, in the new conspiracism, conspiracies come *without any such theory*. Repetition is all there is.

If claims are repeated numerous times – including by people who "just ask questions," ostensibly (sometimes ostentatiously) on behalf of others who have

---

[19] Arendt, *The Origins of Totalitarianism*.

[20] This is cited in Dreyfuss, "Want to Make a Lie Seem True? Say It Again. And Again. And Again." Psychologists have coined the terms "reiteration effect" and "illusory truth effect" for this phenomenon; see e.g., Hertwig, Gigerenzer, and Hoffrage, "The Reiteration Effect in Hindsight Bias"; Hasher, Goldstein, and Toppino, "Frequency and the Conference of Referential Validity." Repetition is also key to retraining the brain after a stroke, drawing on its ability to reconfigure itself; see e.g., Costandi, *Neuroplasticity*.

[21] Muirhead and Rosenblum, *A Lot of People Are Saying*. On Trump's rhetoric, see also Mercieca, *Demagogue for President*; and Hart, *Trump and Us*.

[22] Ben-Itto, *The Lie That Wouldn't Die*.

already repeated these claims – it becomes true that "a lot of people are saying" something (as in the title of Rosenblum and Muirhead's book). That fact sows doubt among those who are not convinced outright. "People generally see what they look for, and hear what they listen for," says Judge Taylor, a character in Harper Lee's iconic novel *To Kill a Mockingbird*.[23] Sowing doubt by repetition might just convince them of something they hope is true. The older conspiracism would enlist epicyclic explanations if evidence did not bear out, adding layers upon layers of theory. The new conspiracism can address critics only by undermining their credibility (doing so also by repetition). Where repetition is the sole source of authority, substantive engagement is impossible.

Repetition reassures people. Even people who recognize statements as false the first time are more likely to judge them as true after hearing them repeatedly.[24] Sometimes proceeding this way makes sense. Condorcet's celebrated Jury Theorem – a major formal result about group thinking originally proved by an eighteenth-century pioneer of mathematical social science – shows the following, under the assumption that each person is more likely than not to be right about proposition p: The larger the number of people who agree that p is true, the closer p's probability of being true is to 1.[25] But that is so only if people make up their own minds (technically, if the probabilities people assign to p are independent). That is, what "a lot of people are saying" provides evidence of the truth of a statement if all judge reliably and think for themselves. In the uncritical spreading of misinformation, this is not true: If people do not judge reliably and think for themselves, "what a lot of people are saying" provides no evidence at all for the truth of any statement.[26]

Repetition also grounds and orients people in the world. A long-standing Latin slogan about learning is "repetitio est mater studiorum" ("repetition is the mother of studies"). It is through repeated engagement that we master material, and mastering it means making it part of how we approach the world. (For a related reason, good teachers typically do not repeat mistakes students make before correcting them lest such repetition makes the errors more engrained.) But repetition brings about this kind of grounding not just in the domain of learning. What we do regularly and often shapes our lives. In the field of philosophy this theme was developed most influentially by Søren Kierkegaard. To appreciate the magnitude of the problems we

---

[23] Lee, *To Kill a Mockingbird*, 185.
[24] Brashier and Marsh, "Judging Truth." See also Kahneman, *Thinking, Fast and Slow*, chapter 5. For discussion of the psychological literature on confirmation bias, see also Rauch, *The Constitution of Knowledge*, chapter 2.
[25] Grofman, Owen, and Feld, "Thirteen Theorems in Search of the Truth."
[26] Victor Hugo makes the following statement at the beginning of *Les Misérables*: "Whether true or false, what is said about [someone] often has as much influence on their lives, and particularly on their destinies, as what they do;" Hugo, *Les Misérables*, 1. That seems plausible enough, and it makes clear how much damage can be done if "what a lot of people are saying" captures misinformation about a person.

are dealing with as we reflect on repetition, especially in digital lifeworlds, let us finish this section by acknowledging Kierkegaard's thoughts on the matter and how they connect to contemporary work on personal identity.

Kierkegaard's book *Repetition* is about how time relentlessly flows onward. If time is unchecked, it overwhelms us and deprives us of our lives. To check its flow, to stop it for a moment, we must practice repetition. "Repetition and recollection," explains Constantine Constantius, Kierkegaard's protagonist (with a repetitive name), "are the same movement, except in opposite directions, for what is recollected has been, is re-peated backward, whereas genuine repetition is recollected forward."[27] One would "recollect something forward" by making it present again, bringing it back, reenacting it in ever-new contexts where it also needs to connect to new circumstances, and thereby shaping the life one leads. To be sure, that we are talking about something that *can* be reiterated in new contexts matters greatly for the plausibility of what Kierkegaard is saying: After all, the mindless and endless repetition of video games would not do this kind of work since it is literally always the same, without there being a sequence of contexts to which it connects.

More than a century after Kierkegaard, psychologist Daniel Kahneman distinguished the *experiencing* self from the *remembering* self.[28] The experiencing self knows only the present. The remembering self is a storyteller, connecting things that happened in the past to what is occurring now or might take place in the future. To that self, life is in fact a story.[29] We can add the Kierkegaardian point that the remembering self can develop the story of its life only by generating repetitive patterns in order to be identifiable to itself in terms of habits, predilections, or aversions (which, again, are not repetitions of exactly the same things, but ways of redoing things in ever-new contexts). The occasional situation in which we must make a major decision provides us with opportunities to take charge of our lives: Sorting out hard choices gives direction to life at critical junctures when different trajectories present themselves. Other than that, it is what we do regularly and often – and how we do it in changing circumstances – that makes us who we are.[30]

Kierkegaard is right about the essential importance of repeating for the design of one's life. But then, of course, how the repeating is done and what *kind* of thing is repeated also matter greatly. If a lot of what Harry Frankfurt calls *bullshit*

---

[27] Kierkegaard, *Fear and Trembling/Repetition*, 131. There is much intellectual context to Kierkegaard's text. My treatment is superficial. See e.g., Eriksen, *Kierkegaard's Category of Repetition*; Schleifer and Markley, *Kierkegaard and Literature*.

[28] Kahneman, *Thinking, Fast and Slow*, Part 5.

[29] "Lift as a story" is the title of Kahneman, chapter 36. Nietzsche also talks about repetition, in the sense of the eternal recurrence of everything, see Nietzsche, *The Gay Science*, section 341. In that case what is at stake is whether a person would want the *exact* repetition of everything, which is offered as a self-affirmation test.

[30] Among more recent work on the theme of repetition, see Deleuze, *Difference and Repetition*; Pickstock, *Repetition and Identity*.

(utterances without regard to the truth) circulates, not to mention plain lies, it is to a certain measure through repetition of that kind of thing that remembering selves are formed.[31]

This brings us back to digital lifeworlds. This point about remembering selves being formed through repetition matters dramatically in digital lifeworlds, with their abundant possibilities for copying and thus repeating ever the same things. AI devices make sure that repetition is highly targeted. At the individual level, falsehoods and half-truths become parts of the iterations that shape lives and thereby start playing a significant role in those lives. At the collective level, political decisions are influenced by such tactics and their effects (as we already noted). The combined force of the importance of repetition in human life and the enormous potential for generating repetitions of the pernicious sort strongly support a moral right to truth.

4.4 NIETZSCHE ON MEANING AND TRUTH

But even though these considerations in support of a right to truth are available, Sections 4.5–4.7 discuss how untruth is too important in human life for there to be a comprehensive right to truth. To begin with, one of Nietzsche's themes is to question the *value of truth* for most people. *Beyond Good and Evil* – where this theme appears most prominently – is among Nietzsche's most important works.[32] It begins by introducing a tension between two human inclinations, two "wills." On the one hand, there is the will to truth, to understand the world around us for what it is. On the other hand, there is the will to value, to decide which aspects or parts of the world to hold in high or low esteem, and then also to make sense of our existence as part of that view of what one finds valuable.[33]

Both wills are easy to motivate. The will to truth is appealing in an evolutionary perspective. It matters to be able to separate dangerous situations from comfortable ones and to teach one's offspring that distinction. Without a basic grasp of the world,

---

[31] Frankfurt, *On Bullshit*. On why there is a lot of *bullshit* around, see Ball, *Post-Truth*. On those who make sure it spreads, see Wu, *The Attention Merchants*.

[32] Nietzsche, *Beyond Good and Evil*. I follow the interpretation in Clark and Dudrick, *The Soul of Nietzsche's Beyond Good and Evil*.

[33] What Nietzsche offers is philosophical anthropology. Philosophical anthropology investigates conceptually how we think about ourselves: what it means to be human, our relationship with the world and with others, and our theoretical and practical powers. Such inquiry aims for plausible insight vis-à-vis the body of accumulated human self-understanding and the concepts it makes central, as expressed in day-to-day conversation, but also in literature, the humanities, social sciences, and the law. The goal is not empirical findings in accordance with disciplinary methodological canons. Ultimately these types of investigation must come together, but accumulated human self-understanding is worth engaging in its own right. Philosophical anthropology is a respectable form of inquiry and should not be sidelined as merely bad anthropology when understood empirically. See Hacker, *Human Nature*, chapter 1.

Homo sapiens would have perished long ago. But the will to value is also compelling. It matters to have a way of thinking about the world that makes sense of one's place in it, to orient oneself beyond concerns about biological survival. Presumably most people prefer to see themselves as playing roles of some significance. Even more important is to have some sense of how one fits in to begin with.

Those two fundamental attitudes (associated with the two wills) readily conflict. It is one thing to search for truth in matters of everyday life (what is the shortest way from here to there, are those fruits edible, where to find water), but quite another to do so around questions beyond mundane inquiry. "By opening our eyes, we do not necessarily see what confronts us," Iris Murdoch noted. "We are anxiety-ridden animals. Our minds are continually active, fabricating an anxious, usually self-preoccupied, often falsifying *veil* which partially conceals the world."[34] As she later adds, "it is a *task* to come to see the world as it is."[35] In the daily lives of many people, taking on such a task, and thus pursuing truth beyond what is needed to get through the day, might be unnecessary. Perhaps answers to questions that go beyond the mundane lead to unflattering insights about my place in the world, predisposing me to disregard or find fault with these insights.

Similarly, it is one thing to find joy in everyday matters (solving a problem at work, preparing a meal, having an exchange with neighbors) or to merely understand how one is expected to act in a given context. It is another to still see one's existence or contribution as significant or at least intelligible as one asks bigger questions about how things matter and why one fares in life as one does. Here, answers that prove satisfactory or bearable might not be truthful. Nietzsche famously said that "life is no argument," only to add that error might be among the conditions of life.[36] What he means is that arguments are the kind of thing typically made to get us closer to the truth. But beyond the mundane kind of inquiry, getting closer to the truth is not essential to how most people see and live their lives.

Nietzsche is especially interested in Christianity because of its historical role in shaping the world we live in. Christianity offers an intriguing case study of how to *suspend* the entirely natural tensions between the wills to truth and value for centuries. For this reason, Christianity offers enduring lessons about how these two wills enter human life. Christianity suspended this tension by building a sophisticated theoretical edifice (what Nietzsche called the Christian "metaphysical-ethical worldview") that also delivered plenty of advice. That is, the will to truth was satisfied through the postulation of a transcendent world beyond experience, whose comprehension was the proper goal of truthfulness; the will to value was satisfied because the world made by the omnipresent, omniscient, and omnipotent

---

[34] Murdoch, *The Sovereignty of Good*, 82. Emphasis is in the original.
[35] Murdoch, 89. Emphasis is in the original.
[36] Nietzsche, *The Gay Science*, section 121.

creator was not only worth inhabiting, but also assigned each person a well-defined place and offered answers to larger questions.[37]

This edifice was held together by the *ascetic priests*, who had the talent to devise it and (to use Nietzsche's well-known and tolerably self-explanatory phrase) the *will to power* to maintain it. They are "ascetic" priests because they valorize life-denying ideals like chastity and poverty. The ascetic priests advocate abstention from pleasures while pillorying their enjoyment as deviations from divine expectations that in turn – on account of the Christian metaphysics – cause the suffering that is omnipresent in many people's lives. Eventually that edifice collapses because an *unconditional* will to truth (which Christianity's maximal divinity requires) makes increasingly many people see that the Christian metaphysics itself is flawed (and that it was introduced mainly to sustain certain value judgments). But that collapse then also reveals the conflict between the wills that, for reasons explained previously, has lain in the nature of things all along.[38]

In the aftermath, some people nonetheless continue to insist on the overriding importance of truth that came with the Christian metaphysics. They dismiss narratives that provide meaning but that do not satisfy standards of truthfulness. The Enlightenment as a philosophical movement is built around the project of holding up standards of truthfulness. To people with such commitments, life *is* an argument. For Nietzsche, scientifically minded individuals who put truth over meaning have succeeded the ascetic priests. Pursuing truth regardless of what it means to life is a version of self-denial. Also, in the respective cases of both scientifically minded individuals and ascetic priests, pursuit and preaching of self-denial enhance these individuals' standings. But unconditional truth has nothing to offer to people who find no personal significance in its pursuit. Such people now badly need to find significance *elsewhere*. After all, "man would much rather will *nothingness*, than *not* will."[39] That is, only adopting a theory that gives meaning to the suffering all around and within us alleviates the suffering.

---

[37] One such question concerns the prevalence of suffering, for Christianity the result of human failure to live up to divine standards. This answer was unflattering – for Nietzsche, Christianity was the *metaphysics of the hangman* – but it illuminated things and provided guidance: *Twilight of Idols*, "The Four Great Errors;" see Nietzsche, *Twilight, et al*. Nietzsche sees a lot of suffering in the world: the "majority of mortals" count as "physiologically failed and out of sorts" (see Nietzsche, *On the Genealogy of Morality*, Third Essay, section 1). Nietzsche detests those who hold – as Marx did, at least roughly – "that *all* human misery and wrongdoing is caused by traditional social structures: which lands truth happily on its head!"; Nietzsche, *Beyond Good and Evil*, section 44, emphasis in the original.

[38] "You see what it was that really triumphed over the Christian god: Christian morality itself, the concept of truthfulness that was understood ever more rigorously, the father confessor's refinement of the Christian conscience, translated and sublimated into a scientific conscience, into intellectual cleanliness at any price," Nietzsche, *The Gay Science*, section 357. For present purposes I do indeed take it the phrase "will to power" is self-explanatory, though much theory could be added about just what he means by it and what role it plays in his thought.

[39] Nietzsche, *On the Genealogy of Morality*, Third Essay, section 28, his emphasis.

Christianity shaped Nietzsche's world. But the systematic point is that combining the will to value and the will to truth *in any form* – as Christianity did in its worldview – creates enormous tensions, and typically efforts at doing so will be driven by power interests. At the time of Nietzsche's writing, more convincing ways of dealing with the two wills, and thus especially of generating meaning in people's lives in a manner that also created a suitable place for truth and truthfulness, had been unavailable (within the context for which he wrote, that is).[40] With the collapse of metaphysical-ethical worldviews that merge these wills in inevitably distorting ways, the quest for meaning (and the desire to find a suitable place for truth in that quest) start afresh. And for most people who get to make up their minds about these things away from the influence of ascetic priests or their counterparts, the will to value outweighs the will to truth.

Accordingly, what Nietzsche questions is the *value* of truth for most people: Truth in effect matters little to most people, there is no reason it should (other than for everyday matters), and so it is inappropriate for intellectuals (people who make pursuit of truth the purpose of their lives) to try to persuade people otherwise or condemn them. Recall Murdoch's point that it "is a *task* to come to see the world as it is."[41] There is no reason everybody should take on that task, certainly not in any comprehensive form.

In light of what we have said so far, now also recall the famous verse from the Gospel of John 8:32: "The truth will set you free." If "being free" is to be oriented in the world, it is not the truth that sets most people free. It is being in the company of others who create a context and place in the world for them. Still, we live in a world where truthfulness indeed is rewarding in everyday inquiries, and where, in addition, we are all accustomed to paying homage to truthfulness at a broad scale (perhaps under the influence of Christianity). And so people normally claim that their beliefs *are* true. But as far as viewpoints that give meaning to lives are concerned, truthfulness does not explain why people endorse them. Claims about how to ascertain truthfulness – that is, responses to questions such as "how do you know this?" – are in effect often adopted *as needed* to sustain views. Since typically individuals are surrounded by like-minded people who cherish similar beliefs, they will not normally seriously interrogate their own beliefs.[42]

4.5 WHAT NIETZSCHE'S ACCOUNT ILLUMINATES

Nietzsche illuminates important phenomena. People do not merely fail to have a preference for truth: Untruth plays an important role as an enabler of valued

[40] Nietzsche, Third Essay, section 28.
[41] Murdoch, *The Sovereignty of Good*, 89. Emphasis is in the original.
[42] For a recent investigation of the nature, value, and scope of the virtue of truthfulness inspired by Nietzsche, see Williams, *Truth and Truthfulness*.

psychological and social dynamics. To begin with, people do a fair amount of self-interpretation to make sense of themselves in their environment. Self-interpretation typically involves facts. But those facts are embedded into larger narratives where connections are made that are no longer warranted by facts. What matters is that we assert something about ourselves rather than that everything (or most of the narrative) is truthful. To quote Harper Lee's judge again, "people generally see what they look for, and hear what they listen for,"[43] and that is true not only for stories about ourselves but also for stories about our social context (about "people like us," our country, etc.).[44]

In addition to our stories about ourselves and our social context, there are stories that form each person's reputation, "a cloud of opinions that circulates according to its own laws, operating independently of the individual beliefs and intentions of those who hold and communicate the opinions in question."[45] Reputation is an accumulated understanding of a person that merges multifarious people's wills to truth and wills to value – to the extent that those relate to that person – into a peculiar amalgam, one not lightly dismissed. According to Gloria Origgi, *to be* basically *is* to be comparable, "to be assigned a value in a ranking, in a system that makes comparisons possible."[46] As we noted in Section 4.4, the two wills stand in a tension since valuing with the goal of finding a place for oneself in the world and truth-finding readily fall apart. Especially because of this tension, "what people say about us and, indeed, about everything that exists provides the only available window through which we can come to know ourselves and recognize the world."[47] Untruth is a big part of this as well: What "people say about us" typically includes the whole range of untruth from outright fabrications to exaggerations, omissions, understatements, suggestions, allusions, distortions, and misleading claims.

Untruths also factor into stories told in the political sphere. Politicians in systems that depend on the consent of some of the governed must win over those people. This is often done with stories about origins (famous battles, fateful encounters, wise decisions or heroic deeds with enormous ramifications, larger-than-life personalities whose forcefulness, sagacity, or endurance made everything possible, etc.)

---

[43] Lee, *To Kill a Mockingbird*, 185.

[44] (1) It also matters that something is told *as* a good story. Diarmaid MacCulloch's exhaustive biography of Thomas Cromwell sold a respectable 32,000 copies in the UK as of July 2021, whereas Hilary Mantle's "Wolf Hall" trilogy (which also tells Cromwell's life) sold close to 2 million (*The Economist*, July 12, 2021, "Missing Pieces," p. 78). Something resembling a good read also matters for stories we tell about ourselves. (2) Advertisement lives off its ability to connect products to stories would-be customers like to tell of themselves. Cigarette advertisement (a model for contemporary misinformation campaigns) is an example. The tobacco industry deployed (e.g.) the Marlboro Man to appropriate treasured American narratives involving freedom and rugged individualism into which many people projected themselves; see Brandt, *The Cigarette Century*.

[45] Origgi, *Reputation*, 63.

[46] Origgi, 243.

[47] Ibid.

to generate legitimacy.[48] Such stories normally only resonate if they are grounded in *something* factual, but then, much as it happened to the two figures in Philip Larkin's famous poem "An Arundel Tomb," "Time has transfigured them into Untruth."[49] Often facts fall into the background or are distorted. What matters most is not accuracy but the connection between politicians and supporters. Recall from Chapter 3 that modern democracies have a distant-state problem.[50] They have a hard time being able to give citizens a sense that they have something to do with the governing, or even a reason to trust the system. Flags and other symbols do some of that work, as do sports competitions and similar events that elicit patriotic sentiments when one's own country competes internationally. Stories about the country and its alleged culture being under threat also help. But nothing beats good stories about foundings to cast populace and country in a certain light.[51]

"No one has ever doubted that truth and politics are on rather bad terms with each other," Arendt explains, and no one "has ever counted truthfulness among the political virtues. Lies have always been regarded as necessary and justifiable tools not only of the politician's or the demagogue's but also of the statesman's trade."[52] Arendt concludes that "conceptually, we may call truth what we cannot change; metaphorically, it is the ground on which we stand and the sky that stretches above us."[53] Her metaphor suggests that truth somehow delineates a space for action to unfold in ways that then, within that space, does not defer to truth. Nietzsche's questioning of the value of truth agrees with Arendt's opening statement. But his questioning is more radical than the metaphor with which she ends. The will to value tends to outweigh the will to truth *across the board* once we go beyond mundane inquiry rather than only within a certain reasonably well-understood space of action.

Donald Trump's trajectory highlights the limited value that truth in effect has for most people in political matters. With the Democratic Party and the liberal professional class perceived (and arguably operating) as a corporate and cultural elite unconcerned with the well-being of the broader population (especially rural

---

[48] One could give countless examples; a striking one is the way the Kim dynasty has written itself into the history of North Korea; see Martin, *Under the Loving Care of the Fatherly Leader*; Fifield, *The Great Successor*.

[49] Larkin, *Collected Poems*, 116. Larkin's poem is a meditation on a monument to the fourteenth-century earl of Arundel and his wife that showed them lying together, hand in hand. The speaker in the poem suspects that the passage of time has altered the couple in the effigy into something that fails to reflect the truth of their real-life circumstances. The speaker believes the hand holding was of little significance to the couple, but nonetheless it has come to be their lasting mark on the world.

[50] Stasavage, *The Decline and Rise of Democracy*.

[51] For an interpretation of the U.S. in this spirit (as a political-theological project, where popular sovereignty is the mystical corpus, and sacrifice the act of self-transcendence), see Kahn, "Sacrificial Nation"; Kahn, *Putting Liberalism in Its Place*; Kahn, *Political Theology*.

[52] Arendt, "Truth and Politics," 545.

[53] Arendt, 574.

Americans), citizens were ready to connect to somebody who accused that elite of incompetence, duplicity, and selfishness.[54] Anybody who presented herself or himself as a dragon slayer to confront that world found open ears. By one count, Trump accumulated 30,573 false or misleading claims as president.[55] His pronouncements incorporated attacks on the credibility of dissenters, which made his voice a deafeningly loud one in a cacophony that prevented any quest for truth from going anywhere. Trump cultivated a loyal following among certain TV networks, and his preferred medium was Twitter. He often told half-truths, weaving in enough factual elements to make it feasible for many to buy his package. With loyalists limiting their news intake and aligning their social media feeds, questioning the veracity of Trump's communications was sidelined among them. "Outsourcing reality to a society network is humankind's greatest innovation," writes Jonathan Rauch.[56] Commitment to one man shaped this network.[57]

The culmination was the Big Lie. Trying to appropriate that term to vilify those committed to election integrity, Trump persuaded large parts of the Republican Party that the 2020 election was stolen, against all evidence and without any success in courts.[58] His narrative filtered available knowledge (supplemented with falsehoods and misleading statements) to make sure that it pleased those whose alienation from the corporate and cultural elite and the policies that this elite stood for or enacted made them receptive. That the Big Lie has done enormous damage and therefore can be enlisted as an exhibit to argue for a right to truth is something we have already explored. But Trump's storytelling also seems to have given many people a way of making sense of their lives, to such an extent that they readily went along with his lie.

4.6 COMPREHENSIVE DOCTRINES AND THE ARGUMENT AGAINST A GENERAL RIGHT TO TRUTH

We have adopted from Nietzsche the point that sidelining truth enables important psychological and social dynamics. We have developed that point in terms of narratives that people tell themselves to be oriented in the world. This point also applies to comprehensive moral doctrines.

Comprehensive doctrines offer across-the-board understandings of the world and the place of humans in it, as well as advice for the whole range of situations that

---

[54] See e.g., Frank, *Listen, Liberal*; Hochschild, *Strangers in Their Own Land*; Wuthnow, *The Left Behind.*

[55] See *Washington Post*, "Trump's False or Misleading Claims Total 30,573 over 4 Years."

[56] This is the subtitle of Rauch, *The Constitution of Knowledge*, chapter 3.

[57] For a take on this from the standpoint of literary theory, see Gess, *Halbwahrheiten*. For the theoretical background of the theory of narration, see Koschorke, *Fact and Fiction.*

[58] As of July 2021, more than 60% of Republican voters endorsed the statement "Trump really won." Only slightly fewer endorsed "Trump should never concede;" *The Economist*, July 3, 2021, "Raising Arizona," p. 30.

people might encounter. The most straightforward examples are the major religions, but also secular worldviews like comprehensive liberalism. By telling individuals what their place is, these doctrines offer ways of thinking about the world, as, for instance, a world created and supervised by deities (or one that lacks such features), a world that is part of a bigger ontological picture (or one beyond which there is nothing), a world rightly dominated by humans (or one where respect for ecological diversity should dominate), and so on. These doctrines must take stances on how humans grasp metaphysical features (e.g., divine revelation, rational thought, empirical investigation). Comprehensive doctrines respond differently to these challenges, reflecting deep metaphysical and epistemological disagreements.

Worldviews can persevere only if they speak to people, providing comfort, offering guidance, and illuminating experiences. They can do all that only if they reach a substantial level of complexity and sophistication. Individuals often grow up in communities endorsing such worldviews. In institutional arrangements and religious and cultural practices, as well as in morsels of wisdom proffered by community members, people acquire worldviews as resilient doctrines. Individuals do not adopt doctrines because these understandings are truthful. And the work they do for individuals does not depend on truthfulness. Doctrines do not survive across ages *because* they are truthful. (It would be impossible for more than one doctrine to do so since they contradict each other.) They offer storytelling replete with half-truths, storytelling that accordingly speaks to people's will to value much more than to their will to truth. (It is, of course, also true that a good deal of storytelling explores virtue and other more universal and noble ideals and, in that sense, does address the will to truth.) The sense in which such doctrines set individuals free, again, is to a large extent by offering them a place in the world. The importance of untruth for (understandings of) life contradicts any comprehensive right to truth.

The standard philosophical accounts of truth are the *correspondence theory* and the *coherence theory*. According to the former, what we believe is true if it corresponds to the way things *are*. According to the latter, truth is a matter of how beliefs relate to each other.[59] Either way, if truth were applied to comprehensive doctrines, metaphysical and epistemological disagreements would erupt. This would happen if we followed the correspondence theory's admonition to assess what there is in the world, or the coherence theory's admonition to make sure beliefs hang together the right way. Claims about truth are divisive because too much is entailed by making them. If a right to truth were prominently integrated into political thought and broadly followed through with action, the world would drown in mayhem. It has always done just that wherever a right to truth has played such a role (think of religious warfare as an obvious example, and also see again the epigraph to this chapter in which Charles Sanders Peirce captures this same thought).

---

[59] See Horwich, *Truth*; Glanzberg, "Truth."

4.7 PUBLIC REASON AND THE RIGHT TO TRUTH

The upshot of Section 4.3 is that a right to truth appears to be a much-needed moral bulwark, a defense specifically also against the pernicious kind of repetition in digital lifeworlds. This point is especially strong in light of the overall role repetition plays in life. But, indeed, claims about truth are divisive because too much is entailed by making them. This is especially so for efforts to assess comprehensive doctrines in terms of truth. That point was the culmination of our efforts in Sections 4.4–4.6 to articulate how important untruth is for life, thereby precluding a comprehensive right to truth. Still, the reasoning thus far can support such a right *in specific contexts*. We encountered some such contexts in Section 4.2. I argue now that public reason reflects all these insights: It reflects the fact that there can be no comprehensive right to truth but allows for the possibility of there being such a right in specific contexts because of the damage that can come from spreading untruth, especially in digital lifeworlds. Section 4.8 adds that we should nonetheless think of truthfulness in the public sphere as a *significant value* rather than stipulating an *actual right to truth*.

Recall the guiding idea behind public reason: Power in pluralist societies is legitimate only when exercised in terms acceptable to common human reason, rather than in terms of epistemological or metaphysical commitments, not all reasonable persons can be expected to accept.[60] Citizens should realize that competent reasoners invariably embrace multifarious doctrines and that this does not by itself present an existential threat to other comprehensive doctrines.[61] This point limits the usefulness and appropriateness of references to truth for matters of citizenship, vindicating the stance that there is no comprehensive right to truth. Citizens should not evaluate comprehensive doctrines as true or false when matters of constitutional essentials are explored. Doing so inevitably ushers in those epistemological and metaphysical differences that public reason suspends.

Truthfulness is neither necessary nor sufficient for statements to play a role in political argument. Not all truths are relevant for collective choice, nor are all untruths excluded from politics per se. Citizens may take their views to be true. But they are also encouraged to recognize that other views might be reasonable to believe even though they are untrue. Rather than truth, what matters in pluralist democracies is *acceptability among citizens*. Reasonable pluralism is an inevitable result of social orders that offer freedom to all but nonetheless allow citizens who are willing to live with others on fair terms to be able to find such terms.

---

[60] Rawls, *Political Liberalism*, 137.
[61] Regarding truth and public reason, I follow Cohen, "Truth and Public Reason." See also Quong, *Liberalism without Perfection*, chapter 8. Rawls's himself held that public reason "does without the concept of truth;" Rawls, *Political Liberalism*, 94. Cohen is right to resist that standpoint and acknowledge a limited but important role for truth in politics. For theories of truth, see Horwich, *Truth*; Glanzberg, "Truth."

The role of truth is limited in the politics of pluralist democracies. But "our (intellectual) response to those who aim to win the world for the whole truth is not to yield the concept of truth," as Joshua Cohen rightly states.[62] In other words, our response to those who insist that humanity must live up to the one true view of the world is not to give up on the intelligibility of truth as such. Instead, the response is twofold, as follows. First, it is to make sense of reasonable doctrinal disagreement and explain how such disagreement does not per se reflect negatively on any participant. Second, it is to point out that the case for shared grounds among citizens does not draw on a skeptical outlook ("nothing can ever be known to be true") or a relativist stance ("there's only truth from certain standpoints"). Instead, this case for shared grounds draws on a common understanding among citizens that precludes appeals to underlying epistemological and metaphysical doctrines.

The appropriate but limited role of judgments about truth on that shared ground needs to be clarified more. Cohen talks of a *political understanding* of truth, which does regard truth as the norm that governs assertions, regards truth as important for that reason, and insists that true belief presents things as they are.[63] To that extent, a political understanding of truth endorses common-sense commitments regarding truth. At the same time, this understanding acknowledges a contrast between truth and justification. That is, one might be *justified* in believing something regardless of whether it is true. Public reason allows for a distinction between truth *in a mundane sense* and *metaphysical* truth. In the mundane sense, to say a sentence is true means that it describes the world as it is, based on standards of success commonly applied to assertions. The ways to go about vindicating such claims range from instant observations to sophisticated scientific methods. Public reason readily acknowledges sentences as truthful in this way.

By contrast, to speak about truth in a metaphysical sense means to debate what ultimately *makes* claims true or false, and thus about what it means for things to be presented *as they are*. (Is there a mind-independent reality? What would it mean for normative claims to represent anything as it really is?) Such inquiries evoke those larger questions of epistemology and metaphysics that public reason suspends. While public reason can make mundane-truth claims, it cannot theorize them and must stay clear of controversies about the nature of truth (which are useless for political purposes).

So public reason vindicates the standpoint that there can be no comprehensive right to truth. In the political domain, truth plays a limited role. But that does not mean that truth plays no role. Public reason also vindicates the point that, in specific niches, there could in principle be a right to truth. One context for which such a right has prima facie plausibility is that of the *functionality of the public sphere* in

---

[62] Cohen, "Truth and Public Reason," 35. For theories of truth, see Horwich, *Truth*.

[63] This view is related to Cohen's "un-foundational" take on human rights; see Cohen, "Minimalism about Human Rights."

which citizens need to be able to interact from a public-reason standpoint. Where dangers from the repetition of untruth threaten the sheer viability of the public sphere (Trump's Big Lie comes to mind again), a right to truth suggests itself as a bulwark of protection even though there is no comprehensive right to truth.[64]

4.8 CONCLUSION: WHAT ABOUT THE RIGHT TO TRUTH?

A right to truth does indeed *suggest* itself as a bulwark of protection for the functionality of the public sphere (which in turn is rather essential for democracies), and one could readily spell out specific contexts for which such a right could be formulated. "If nothing is true, then no one can criticize power, because there is no basis upon which to do so," Timothy Snyder insists in his powerful study of historical lessons learned from the twentieth century, and adds, "If nothing is true, then all is spectacle."[65] For instance, there needs to be truthful reporting on election results, and there should be legal mechanisms against anyone who uses a position of prominence to spread systematic falsehoods about them. In that spirit, the US law should have provisions to sanction Trump's endless repetition of claims about election fraud. Similarly, citizens must have ready access to a whole range of historical and social-scientific facts to make informed judgments about political matters. They also need a certain level of education to appreciate the pluralist ideas behind public reason and thus to even see themselves as equal citizens. Especially given the potential of digital lifeworlds to enable repetitions of damaging claims, democracies must be watchful and defend their foundations.[66]

Nonetheless, from what we have said, it remains doubtful that the most adequate way of protecting truthful discourse is an actual *right to truth*, either morally or

---

[64] Don Price proposed a theory of four different "estates" (for the U.S., but the approach works for democracies generally); see Price, *The Scientific Estate*. There is the political estate of elected politicians responsible to the public; the administrative estate of managers and administrators in public and private sectors; the professional estate (e.g., medicine or engineering) that applies scientific knowledge to serve clients; and the scientific estate of researchers at universities or elsewhere. These "estates" have diverging interests, expertise, and legitimacy. They create an order of diffuse sovereignty, but what matters here is that Price arranges them on a spectrum from truth to power. Scientists occupy the truth-end, politicians the power-end. The closer an estate is to the truth-end, the more it is entitled to freedom and self-government. The closer a group is to the power-end, the more it is required to submit to electoral approval. What this scheme implies about researchers connects back to our Nietzsche discussion. Researchers often make truth their main concern in life. However, though its representatives could serve as advisors, what is done with scientific truth politically must be decided by others. In the political domain – and here we can connect Price to Rawls – power should be exercised from a public-reason standpoint. What matters then is acceptability among fellow citizens. For discussion also see Winner, *Autonomous Technology*, 152–62.

[65] Snyder, *On Tyranny*, 65.

[66] For an assessment of specifically U.S. democracy as of around 2020 with an emphasis on the changes brought by the Trump administration, see Shattuck, Raman, and Risse, *Holding Together*.

legally, in any of the senses in which there might be such a right (claim, privilege, power, immunity). Recall the right to truth as understood in transitional justice, or the right to "receive and impart information and ideas" in Article 19 of the Universal Declaration. In transitional justice, a concern is formulated that arises *for particular individuals*. It is the victims and their families who primarily have a right to know what happened. Similarly, Article 19 speaks to any person who might want to receive information. In subsequent chapters, we encounter additional contexts for which a right to truth would be appropriate.

However, regarding something like Trump's Big Lie, or falsehoods about a country's history or its current social realities, what is at stake is not normally anything reducible to concerns of particular individuals – which would make a set of rights an appropriate remedy. Reducing Trump's Big Lie or such falsehoods that way also creates complex questions about what violations of such rights look like. For instance, it would be unreasonable to go after each person who repeats the Big Lie – even though the law should have provisions against popular incitement of the sort that could only be instigated by someone with great reach.

Truthfulness does matter greatly for the functionality of the public sphere. Public reason can and must recognize as much. But it seems better to capture this significance by saying that these matters are *of great value* and accordingly require vigorous legal protection, instead of capturing it in terms of rights. The increasing presence of specialized AI in digital lifeworlds makes vigorous legal protection ever more important and should constrain what can be done with such AI. But again, saying *that* does not mean the most appropriate way of providing such protection (or of making sense of what is at stake) is in terms of rights that individuals would hold.

The fealty of Trump supporters to a notorious liar must remind us of the limited value that truth has for many people – and also, to be sure, of the basic respectability of people's limited appreciation of truth in light of the importance of storytelling for human life. Existential comfort can only come from narratives that are at least somewhat connected to facts. But *too little* comfort might come from narratives that stay close to facts all or most of the time. "Science and technology revolutionize our lives, but memory, tradition and myth frame our response," so Arthur Schlesinger once wrote, tying together various themes in this book.[67] Whether we like it or not, untruth plays a rather central role in this response. Shattering such endeavors by insisting on truth will not set most people free but instead condemn them to enormous frustrations, to the point of utter despair. We had better understand this as a part of what humans are like: People need a certain kind of storytelling to sustain themselves in a world that often bears down hard on them. One might want to object here that the sheer fact that people have that kind of need has no normative purchase on anything. It is certainly debatable what kind of human "need" is involved here. However, to the extent that the satisfaction of human needs is tied

---

[67] Schlesinger, "The Challenge of Change."

to people's ability to live a flourishing life of sorts (or to survive in the first place) and to the extent that living such a life itself has normative purchase, even the need for this kind of storytelling does have a certain normative purchase.[68]

It is, however, a reasonable expectation that people break through the blinders of their own storytelling in certain ways, including and especially as far as maintenance of a public-reason-based democracy is concerned. To be sure, reasonable as this expectation may indeed be, this is a tall order if ever there was one. But without it, democracies have little chance of surviving. Nietzsche is right: Life is no argument, and, again, the truth will set few people free. Still, a society where truthfulness in the public sphere is regarded as a significant value *and* where people can find an orientation in comprehensive doctrines with the kind of storytelling they entail offers good prospects for setting us free in enduring ways in all ways that matter. This would also be the kind of society that makes sure that others too can be set free in their own, rather different ways.

Recall from the very beginning of this chapter that Western thought early on offers potent warnings about how truth upends human living arrangements: Plato's truth finders are at risk of being slain by those whom they seek to enlighten, and Jesus is sentenced to death based on the orders of a man who has given up on truth altogether, and at the instigation of city leaders who seek to have Jesus convicted out of fear that he speaks the truth. Finding the *right place* for truth in human living arrangements is a good answer to these warnings, an answer that is needed with great urgency for the digital lifeworlds that now shape our future.

---

[68] On the claims of needs, see e.g., Wiggins, "Claims of Need."

5

Knowing and Being Known

Investigating Epistemic Entitlements in Digital Lifeworlds

You are the sum total of your data.
No man escapes that.

—a technician in Don DeLillo's *White Noise*[1]

5.1 INTRODUCTION

Centuries before Francis Bacon the twentieth-century artist, there was Francis Bacon the philosopher-statesman of early Stuart England. This earlier Bacon rose to be Lord Chancellor under James I. As a philosopher, he is celebrated for his inductive methodology. To him, knowledge is acquaintance with facts and regularities "out there." Getting so acquainted is teachable, and the right methods empower people to do things better than other agents ever could. Bacon's famous dictum "knowledge is power" is a paradigmatic expression of confidence in the human ability to comprehend and control our environment.[2] As a politician Bacon eventually fell from grace, but he certainly would have grasped the usefulness of knowledge for statecraft. In what would become the Baconian tradition, knowledge exists independently of power and can be instrumentalized for its purposes.

This understanding of the relationship between knowledge, humans, power, and world has presuppositions that have become problematic, not only but especially in digital lifeworlds. One is that only humans can be knowers, an assumption that

---

[1] DeLillo, *White Noise*, 141.
[2] That dictum appears in passing in Bacon's 1597 *Meditations Sacrae*, section "On Heresies"; see, for example, Bacon, *Sacred Meditations*, 21f. (The Bacon-entry in the *Stanford Encyclopedia of Philosophy* does not even quote this dictum, Klein and Giglioni, "Francis Bacon.") On Bacon, see Gaukroger, *Francis Bacon and the Transformation of Early-Modern Philosophy*; Innes, *Francis Bacon*; Henry, *Knowledge Is Power*. For Mumford's take on Bacon, see Mumford, *Pentagon of Power*, chapter 5. For Winner's, see Winner, *Autonomous Technology*, chapter 4.

would make sense if knowledge required that Platonic *logos* (account-giving) we discussed in Chapter 1. A related presupposition is a dualistic ontology juxtaposing human knowers with entities very different from them, which on this basis are of lesser value. For this, Bacon is sometimes blamed for helping to create a distorted view of nature.[3] What matters most now is yet another presupposition: that knowledge is acquaintance with matters *outside* of the value-laden domain of politics (where power operates) to which knowledge can then be imported.

Michel Foucault, for one, has questioned this last presupposition. For him, power always already shapes what we consider knowledge. To have that nexus in sight is especially important for digital lifeworlds. After all, such lifeworlds make the collection and flow of information central. It is as countless exercises of control that information (and so knowledge) becomes available in certain ways and that inquirers see themselves in certain ways. It is the harnessing of information through channels thus created that enables some people to exercise power over others. To capture the nexus between knowledge and power, Foucault introduced the term "episteme." With that notion in place, I present a framework organized around four roles of epistemic actorhood to investigate epistemic entitlements in digital lifeworlds, entitlements in the domain of inquiry, for example, to results of scientific investigations, to education, or simply to having a voice.

Looking at epistemic entitlements broadens our horizon beyond what we have so far covered. One way of thinking about that broadened perspective is in terms of the role of the citizen. We have previously encountered the citizen of the digital age through the lens of the public-reason paradigm. In the process we have touched on themes around truth, power, public sphere, democracy, and some others. But we have not yet explored the roles of the citizen as *knower* and as *known*. These roles are essential in the digital age since individuals spend much time using or providing data. These data are digitally processed through a set of devices and in the wake of numerous design decisions. Considerations of power enter instantly as we think about how else these decisions could be made and to whose benefit they are. It is in such ways that we are led to turn to epistemic actorhood, epistemic rights, and epistemic justice, themes at the nexus of knowledge and power.

Other thinkers, too, have worked at that nexus, but Foucault's notion of the episteme is especially useful for the formulation of the aforementioned framework for epistemic actorhood. His episteme is often compared to Thomas Kuhn's *paradigm* (which precedes Foucault's notion).[4] A Kuhnian paradigm is a set of beliefs and assumptions that organize scientific worldviews and practices. Foucault's episteme provides a grounding for a broader range of discourses including but not

---

[3] Writer and activist Naomi Klein, for one, charges Bacon with "convincing Britain's elites to abandon, once and for all, pagan notions of the earth as a life-giving mother to whom we owe respect and reverence (and more than a little fear) and accept the role of her dungeon master," Klein, *This Changes Everything*, 170.

[4] Kuhn, *The Structure of Scientific Revolutions*.

limited to science (subsuming a Kuhnian paradigm). Both Kuhn's and Foucault's works raise questions around their view of truth, especially about the possibility of nonrelativistic truth. I take it that working with either approach does not entail that there can be truth, even of the most elementary sort, that is *only* relative to specific frameworks. In other words, taking seriously the sociological and intellectual-historical dimensions of discourses does not entail a commitment to relativism about truth (nor, for that matter, does it conflict with anything we said about the concept of truth in Chapter 4).

While the introduction of epistemic considerations *broadens* our perspective, it also *deepens* certain themes. Chapter 2 distinguishes a foundational, an enframing, and an interactive sense in which technology is political, arguing that it behooves all approaches to political thought (including the Rawlsian one) to take all three seriously. To the extents that digital lifeworlds are increasingly central to human life and that epistemic roles and entitlements are central to digital lifeworlds, reflection on epistemic themes is another way of expounding how technology is political in the foundational sense. Whenever such debate involves particular technologies, it is also a way of elaborating on how technology is political in the interactive sense.

Section 5.2 begins with Foucault's work on the nexus between knowledge and power and his coinage of the term "episteme." Section 5.3 develops his ideas for digital lifeworlds. With this Foucauldian vocabulary in place, Section 5.4 introduces the notion of epistemic actorhood to capture the place of an individual in an episteme as part of a framework organized around four roles of such actorhood. In terms of that framework, Section 5.5 introduces the notion of an epistemic right, and Section 5.6 discusses epistemic justice. Section 5.7 concludes with reflections on how ideas around epistemic actorhood are endemic to Life 2.0 and might have to be rethought as we approach Life 3.0.[5]

5.2 FOUCAULT ON EPISTEMES, SELF-KNOWLEDGE, AND BIOPOWER

For humans, inquiry – systematic gathering of information through language or otherwise – is an essential pursuit. Much scrutiny is devoted to what constitutes successful inquiry, involving fields like epistemology and scientific methodology. To be sure, knowledge acquisition is not exhaustively understood as a rational matter, the kind of thing theorized through an account of scientific methodology. Inquiry inevitably occurs in contexts where information is channeled and presented

---

[5] The Rawlsian understanding of citizenship as captured by the public-reason standpoint might seem to suggest a level of activeness in the role of citizen that the epistemic roles we distinguish now do not bear out. But any conflict there is only apparent. For indeed, the various roles of epistemic actorhood that for good reason are spelled out here in terms of actorhood *rather than* agency constrain how individuals can operate as citizens.

somehow and where it is more or less difficult for people to acquire knowledge, including self-knowledge. Scrutinizing inquiry therefore also involves history, ethics, sociology, and political science.

The Baconian tradition thinks of knowledge as residing outside of the value-laden domain of politics (where power operates) to which knowledge can be imported. By contrast, the idea of a two-way relationship locking knowledge with power permeates Foucault's work. For Foucault, "there is no power relation without the correlative constitution of a field of knowledge, nor any knowledge that does not presuppose and constitute at the same time, power relations."[6] That is, for him, what passes for knowledge is always already influenced by power relations. Every era has its structure of thought, a worldview, or perhaps several that are parts of various "power-knowledge systems," as Foucault increasingly came to think. Individuals can evade these structures only under strains. After all, inquirers would not normally perceive these structures as limitations since they normally cannot (or in any event, do not) conceive of inquiry outside of such structures (or to the extent that they *can*, other people call them to order). These structures also constrain self-knowledge, views of one's personhood and place in the world: After all, basic models for individual self-understanding (which are models of how persons typically come to think about themselves) are part of the available pool of knowledge that then need to be thought through for any given case.

Foucault coined the term "episteme" – from the Greek for knowledge or under-standing – to denote this kind of grounding in conditions of possibility that always already reflect the power relations of an era. The term characterizes the orderly and typically unproblematized ("unconscious," as Foucault would say) structures under-lying the production of scientific knowledge at a given time and place, its "epistemo-logical field."[7] Systems of thought and knowledge (which he also calls discursive formations, in addition to epistemes) follow rules much beyond those of grammar and logic. Operating outside of the awareness of individual participants, such "unconscious" rules delineate a conceptual system of possibilities that determine

---

[6] Foucault, *Discipline and Punishment*, 27. For accessible discussions of Foucault's work, see Downing, *The Cambridge Introduction to Michel Foucault*; Han, *Foucault's Critical Project*; May, *Philosophy of Foucault*; McNay, *Foucault*; Watkin, *Michel Foucault*; Gutting, *French Philosophy in the Twentieth Century*, chapter 9. On the relevance of Foucault for discussions of AI in political philosophy, see also Coeckelbergh, *The Political Philosophy of AI*, chapter 5.

[7] See, in particular, Foucault, *The Archaeology of Knowledge*; Foucault, *The Order of Things*; Foucault, *Power/Knowledge*. Helen Longino has argued that social and cultural values matter to the structuring of knowledge but that nonetheless science has objectivity as long as we understand objectivity itself in social rather than individual terms, see Longino, *Science as Social Knowledge*. She worries that Foucault sees the relationship between knowledge and power "in a univocal way" that excludes, for example, what she calls oppositional science; Longino, 202–4. But once we notice that Foucault in fact acknowledged complexities in the nexus between knowledge and power, this discrepancy disappears.

the boundaries of thought in given domains and periods. Understanding these possibilities requires what Foucault calls an "archaeological" method to unveil presuppositions that individuals could not themselves articulate.

One difference among epistemes is how knowledge is organized. For instance, in *The Order of Things*, Foucault talks of an episteme associated with the "Classical Age," characterizing Europe and especially France from 1650 to 1800, roughly. That episteme permitted no essential role for change over time in its view of nature. Living things were predetermined regardless of historical developments. By contrast, the modern episteme, dominant from around 1800, regards life forms as historical entities, which means they can be formed through historical causes. This mindset has led to evolutionary theory. A fundamental break had occurred in the conception of what it is to be a living being.

In addition to differences in how knowledge is organized, there are differences in how knowledge and personhood are integrated. Foucault's *Discipline and Punish* begins by observing that in the late eighteenth century, the manner of punishment changes.[8] Instead of corporal punishment, including executions in front of jeering crowds, incarceration became increasingly common. The point of punishment was no longer public cruelty but to instill obedience through discipline and routine. Public, often frenzied practices of punishment changed toward more private and insidious ones. Foucault finds that schools, hospitals, and the military operated similarly. An increasingly diffuse exercise of power instills routine in people in this range of seemingly very different institutions.

Foucault famously uses the example of the prison as a *panopticon*, as envisaged by Jeremy Bentham.[9] A paradigmatic architectural model of disciplinary power, such a prison allows just one officer to watch each cell any time while prisoners do not know when they are being observed. They are always expected to be on their best behavior. Much as these prisoners are expected to discipline *themselves*, so is the rest of society. The routines involved in these processes of self-disciplining encourage conformity, limiting our ability to construct identities that have difficulty conforming. Self-disciplining thereby also constrains self-knowledge. Power creates docile creatures more by getting individuals to make themselves compliant than by imposing heavy constraints or supervision. The less obvious the mechanism, the more powerful the disciplinary function of surveillance. It is families and workplaces, everyday practices, and often informal or sidelined institutions that get individuals to act or see themselves in ways that would not otherwise be natural to them. These diffuse patterns of power also shape the scientific discourse and thus an era's understanding of what counts as knowledge.

[8] Foucault, *Discipline and Punishment*, Part I/II.
[9] Foucault, 195–230. For a comparison between the panopticon and the slave ship as models of surveillance, see Browne, *Dark Matters*, chapter 1.

Although dispersed among interlacing networks across society, power still has its rationality and means of attaining its objectives. Docile routine-followers can be readily controlled, partly through "an explosion of numerous and diverse techniques for achieving the subjugations of bodies and the control of populations," where the "bodies" mentioned here are physical human bodies.[10] Such measures amount to a government's "biopower," its practices of public health, regulation of heredity, urban planning, and risk regulation, among other regulatory mechanisms often linked less directly with physical health. Foucault contrasts biopower with the previously existing (and also still present) "sovereign power," which has been based on violence, especially the right to kill. Far from being ostensibly destructive, biopower "endeavors to administer, optimize, and multiply [life], subjecting it to precise controls and comprehensive regulations."[11] Mechanisms of power and knowledge now take responsibility *for life itself* in ways that sovereign power on its own never has been able to.

Exercising biopower requires scientific insights and thus strengthens the status of scientific expertise, creating a new nexus between power and knowledge that made little sense when sovereign power reigned supreme. Society increasingly made those under its power legible to government, involving intricate administrative systems to track identities. Eventually there would be standardized passports (now biometrical, to verify that the holder is the one named), social security numbers, multifarious identification numbers (for governmental or business purposes), driver's licenses, credit scores, health records, and employment contracts. The birth certificate grounds our belonging in a state. Eventually we see our personhood around such identifiability and make ourselves docile participants in power structures thus erected.[12]

One theme across much of Foucault's work is that there is no true self to be deciphered or liberated: There is only a created self. But his later work goes beyond that, stressing increasingly that individuals are not just docile bodies but have ways of actively engaging with imposed norms. They can consciously refuse, adopt, or alter roles confirmed by society's diffuse power. Foucault discusses the exploration of new fields of experience and pleasures and the development of new relationships, modes of living, and thinking. At least in his late work, an era's episteme is not destiny. Courageous individuals have possibilities for a creative lifestyle.[13]

---

[10] Foucault, *The History of Sexuality, Vol. 1*, 140.

[11] Foucault, 137.

[12] On efforts to make individuals legible, see also Scott, *Seeing Like a State*. On identification, see Groebner, *Who Are You?* For an effort to tell the story of modern America as a story of anxieties about privacy (which arise around all matters mentioned in this paragraph), see Igo, *The Known Citizen*.

[13] Foucault, *The Use of Pleasure*; Foucault, *The Care of the Self*.

5.3 MOVING FOUCAULT INTO DIGITAL LIFEWORLDS: DATA EPISTEME AND INFOPOWER

Foucault died before digital lifeworlds approached their current prevalence. Colin Koopman has expanded Foucault's approach to such lifeworlds, using the term "data episteme" for our current system of knowledge.[14] To the extent that an episteme comprises the orderly but "unconscious" structures that underlie the production of knowledge at certain times and places, it is characteristic of our current episteme that data and information drawn from the data are in demand in ever more domains of life. Demand for and usage of data have become ubiquitous, in ways that are normal to college students but still bewildering to many older people.

In this data episteme, a new type of power is exercised beyond the enduringly present sovereign power and biopower. That new type is *infopower*, determined by *infopolitics*. Infopower is exercised not only through increasing demands for data, but also through decisions about what Koopman calls their *formatting*. Data formatting concerns what type of data to collect, refine, process, or store; what use to make of them; how to share them; and whom to share them with. Infopolitics determines how infopower is deployed.

Infopolitics first concerns state surveillance in its ever more sophisticated approaches. The best-known surveillance system today is the Chinese Social Credit System, a large-scale effort advanced by the Chinese Communist Party over the last fifteen years to track reputations of individuals and businesses. (Standing at a traffic light, a driver's photograph might be captured by a camera and linked to a database with any amount of information about her life up to this point.) But while those efforts are extreme, it is common for cyberspace to become a battleground between excessively profit-seeking or outright criminal activities on the one hand and state reactions to them on the other. Such reactions might generate momentum, giving rise to tools that authoritarian governments can deploy to quench opposition. A typical example is software that prohibits users from accessing content deemed illicit, such as terrorist propaganda or child pornography, exercising the state's infopower to fight crime. But such software also can block access to any number of other websites the government wishes to keep beyond reach of its citizenry.[15] Moreover, years ago Edward Snowden revealed the extent to which governments, with the aid of corporations like Google and Verizon, collect and store records of digital activity of millions of people.[16]

---

[14] Koopman, *How We Became Our Data*. See also Cheney-Lippold, *We Are Data*. For a more optimistic take on Big Data, see Gilbert, *Good Data*. For Gilbert's take on Foucault, see his chapter 6.

[15] Deibert, *Reset*; Deibert, *Black Code*. Also see Angwin, *Dragnet Nation*; Schneier, *Click Here to Kill Everybody*; Ferguson, *The Rise of Big Data Policing*.

[16] Gellman, *Dark Mirror*; Greenwald, *No Place to Hide*. For the argument that changing capacities of government have depended on the implementation of new technologies, and

Infopolitics also determines what happens in the private sector, with the regulatory apparatus either shaping or distinctly omitting to shape the private sector. Therefore, infopolitics also concerns what is done about data-mining techniques used by private companies. These techniques have become so central to our economic system that Shoshana Zuboff coined the term "surveillance capitalism" for our current stage of capitalism.[17] Infopower is also exercised through design of social media. Facebook, Twitter, and others have created new possibilities for people to stay in touch, share views without depending on traditional media, form professional alliances, engage in campaigning, and so on. At the same time, social media can sow ignorance, prejudice, and chaos, through the use of excessively attention-grabbing algorithms or in other ways.

Moreover, infopolitics concerns online cryptocurrencies (like Bitcoin) and algorithmic finance, as well as the high level of data collection and unprecedented levels of data sharing via social media, the deluge of online file sharing, personalized genetic reporting, and the ever-quantifying wristwatches that capture the whole range of things people do. The humungous amount of data in digital lifeworlds makes possible (and often effectively requires) carefully managed online profiles, for purposes ranging from staying in touch with friends and finding mates to building professional networks. But infopolitics also includes resistance movements like digital rights advocacy groups, promoted by organizations like the Electronic Frontier Foundation.[18]

One characteristic of every episteme is that its participants tend to think that how they see the world is the only way possible or anyway acceptable. They are unaware of the extent to which the episteme makes them who they are. What this means in the data episteme, for instance, is that – the ubiquity of data notwithstanding – we naturally see ourselves as separate from data, taking them to be *about* us. We see ourselves as persons separately from our numbers, cards, certificates, accounts, and dossiers. Similarly, many people think that digital devices are tools they can opt to use or not. But for many people, it would be hard to even describe themselves in separation from all the data that characterize them or the tools that accompany them.[19] Data and devices help constitute our personality. We have become "digital persons,"[20] subject to what Donna Haraway calls the "informatics of domination."[21] Or to cast the point in the words of a technician in Don DeLillo's novel *White Noise*

---

that adoption of new technologies has depended on a certain vision of government, see Agar, *The Government Machine*.

[17] Zuboff, *The Age of Surveillance Capitalism*.

[18] See www.eff.org/; last accessed in December 2021.

[19] For the importance of computational devises for personality development and human interaction, see Turkle, *Alone Together*; Turkle, *Reclaiming Conversation*. For the argument that the Internet may cause defects in cognition that diminish capacities for concentration and contemplation, see Carr, *The Shallows*.

[20] Solove, *The Digital Person*.

[21] Haraway, *Manifestly Haraway*, 28.

(which appeared in 1985, one year after Foucault's death), "You are the sum total of your data. No man escapes that."[22]

As has been the case for biopower all along, in the age of infopower, participants make themselves compliant with power structures. As Koopman says,

> information's formatting is a work that prepares us to be the kinds of persons who not only can suffer these inequalities and unfreedoms, but can also eagerly inflict them, often unwittingly, on others who have also been so formatted. Information thus became political precisely when we became our information.[23]

Knowledge acquisition and production have changed profoundly through the Internet. People learn by using search engines. In the Western world, Google has become so central that questions about how to find out about something routinely deliver the answer "You should just google it."[24] For more sophisticated tasks, tools like Wolfram Alpha are widely used. Knowledge acquisition and production have changed profoundly through the Internet. People are *knowers* in this space, learning by using search engines. People are also *known* in new ways on the Internet. They leave electronic records of themselves (including what they search for). And whatever has been said about them and makes it to the Internet remains a few clicks away from anybody who cares to know.

The *World Wide Web* was conceived by Tim Berners-Lee to meet the demand for automated information sharing across academic institutions.[25] It has opened new possibilities for scientific collaboration, which has been able to flourish partly through availability of enormous amounts of data and tools to mine them.[26] "The web" has since become central to global communications. The *Internet* is the network of connected computers in which the web operates. In 2016, a panel of eminent scientists, academics, writers, and world leaders deliberating on behalf of the British Council ranked the invention of the Internet *first* in a list of eighty cultural moments that shaped today's world: "The fastest growing communications medium of all time, the Internet has changed the shape of modern life forever. We can connect with each other instantly, all over the world."[27]

---

[22] DeLillo, *White Noise*, 141. This is the quote I use as epigraph for this chapter.

[23] Koopman, *How We Became Our Data*, 155. For the view that the ubiquity of global communication flows in the present age has collapsed the separate spaces needed for critical reflection (and thus, in particular, undermined anything that might credibly be called critical theory), see Lash, *Critique of Information*.

[24] On Google, see Redding, *Google It*; Galloway, *The Four*; Vaidhyanathan, *The Googlization of Everything*. See also Peters, *The Marvelous Clouds*, chapter 7. On search engines generally, see Halavais, *Search Engine Society*. Google also comes in for heavy criticism in Zuboff, *The Age of Surveillance Capitalism*. Zuboff argues that Google originated the business model behind surveillance capitalism.

[25] Berners-Lee, *Weaving the Web*; Abbate, *Inventing the Internet*.

[26] For the social sciences, see Jemielniak, *Thick Big Data*. For the humanities, see Balkun and Deyrup, *Transformative Digital Humanities*; Schwandt, *Digital Methods in the Humanities*.

[27] "Eighty Moments That Shaped the World."

Search engines and other algorithms do not represent mere tools, creating access to knowledge, but reflect values and power. Much as in other contexts, design impacts social relations at economic and political levels.[28] Safiya Noble has argued that the power of algorithms in digital lifeworlds is especially pernicious because ours is also the *neoliberal* age.[29] Neoliberalism has delegated much social choice to markets. It has become profitable for private actors to develop information technologies that echo and reinforce oppressive social structures. As we noted in Chapter 2, Noble diagnoses a "technological redlining." For instance, online financial tools corral people of color into paying higher interest rates and premiums, especially in low-income neighborhoods.[30] And particularly for these and other marginalized communities, what one learns if one "just googles" something about them reflects the priority that Google, the company, assigns to particular bits of information. It is often pornographic themes that one encounters, for instance, if one googles what Black teenage girls are interested in. "Search results," Noble sums up,

> reflect the values and norms of the search company's commercial partners and advertisers and often reflect our lowest and most demeaning beliefs, because these ideas circulate so freely and so often they are normalized and extremely profitable.[31]

5.4 EPISTEMIC ACTORHOOD

Foucault's ideas about the episteme help us formulate a model of epistemic actorhood consisting of four roles. Capturing how individuals are involved in inquiry, these roles have each been affected by or become pronounced in digital lifeworlds in ways they were not before. With this framework we also open avenues for normative investigations. Individuals always acquire knowledge in particular contexts, within epistemes that are collectively maintained. However, as we reflect on inquiry, we must recognize humans not merely as individual knowers and as those who collectively maintain epistemes, but also as those who (wittingly or unwittingly) reveal information (individually or collectively). Much information that people seek is about other humans. Individuals – things about them, personal data – are *known to* others. We are *knowers* and also *knowns*.

We are more familiar with the role of knower or inquirer. But as revealers or bearers of information, we are also subject to rules that define success in terms of known-ness, one's own and that of others. These rules are a subset of those that apply

---

[28] On this theme, see again Chapter 2.

[29] Noble, *Algorithms of Oppression*.

[30] Also recall from Chapter 2 that Ruha Benjamin talks about "the new Jim Code," see Benjamin, *Race After Technology*.

[31] Noble, *Algorithms of Oppression*, 35f. For surveillance of Blackness in historical perspective, see Browne, *Dark Matters*. For use of digital technologies for purposes that create suspicion on more general social grounds rather than specifically racial grounds, see Eubanks, *Automating Inequality*; Zuboff, *The Age of Surveillance Capitalism*; O'Neil, *Weapons of Math Destruction*.

to successful inquiry generally (the subject of inquiry where the target is humans). What is distinctive about this subset is not the rationality that applies to seeking information, but the moral, social, or political standards expressing what information should or should not be available about people, and to whom. Moreover, as members of collectives, people maintain rules of revealing, and they collectively preserve the content of what is known about us (all of which, again, is part of the episteme, since knowers are also knowns).

Let us say an "epistemic actor" is a person or entity integrated into some communication network (system of information exchange) as seeker or revealer of information. In philosophical discourse, "actors" often are people who have agency ("agents"), common connotations being with choice or rationality. But the term also denotes performers who follow scripts provided by producers. This is the sense I enlist. Talking about epistemic actors rather than agents deliberately and appropriately de-emphasizes that they do things in ways reflecting both genuine choice and a background rationality these individuals themselves could expound. After all, epistemic actors, with their thoughts, feelings, and beliefs, play certain roles within communication networks. As seekers, they obtain, and as revealers, they generate information. In both cases, these processes occur according to prevalent standards, which vary in nature from rational to moral or sociological. These standards can be critically assessed or transgressed. However, individuals (the actors) do not normally noticeably contribute to these standards. Nor are they typically capable of reflecting on the standards systematically by taking a big step back from them. Foucault's episteme is an "unconscious" structure, one of which individuals are normally unaware. In terms of being knowers and knowns, actors fill roles by meeting expectations not of their making that reflect what is required by the episteme.[32]

To elaborate, and to embed my usage of this framework into a social-scientific context different from Foucault's, I use the term "actorhood" as sociologist John W. Meyer and his collaborators do in the "Stanford School's" world-society approach.[33] A *society* here is a system where values and norms are defined and implemented through collective mechanisms that confer authority. The system determines who gets to confer what kind of authority and how that occurs. The defining feature of a society is that it provides a set of norms and roles that the various actors, in the sense just explained, adopt. Through the implementation and spread

---

[32] For individual *knowns*, there is a difference between what people reveal about themselves and what is otherwise known about them, say, through observation or inference. These phenomena come together in the role of a known because they have much in common: It is about them being known. One could draw a parallel distinction in the domain of knowing. Some things we know because we actively investigate them. Others we merely pick up and repeat.

[33] See Krücken and Drori, *World Society*. See also Lechner and Boli, *World Culture*; Albert, *A Theory of World Politics*. For brief versions, see Boli, "World Polity Theory"; Boli, Gallo-Cruz, and Matt, "World Society, World-Polity Theory, and International Relations." For connections between world society theory and various questions of philosophy, see Meyer and Risse, "Thinking About the World: Philosophy and Sociology."

of various "scripts," society becomes an "imagined community," in Benedict Anderson's well-known sense.[34] A *world society* (which is what the Stanford School primarily explores), accordingly, is such a system with global dimensions. By recognizing such processes at the global level – processes that together constitute world culture – world-society analysis offers a unifying approach to global affairs.

With these clarifications, we can distinguish four roles that constitute epistemic actorhood: individual epistemic subjects, collective epistemic subjects, individual epistemic objects, and collective epistemic objects. Since I am interested in digital lifeworlds, I introduce these roles with an eye on such contexts. To begin with, people operate as *individual epistemic subjects*. They are learners, inquirers, or knowers whose endeavors are expected to abide by certain standards, ranging from standards of rationality (how best to obtain information) to moral standards or plain societal divisions of labor (who gets to have what kind of knowledge). To gather and process information, people must grasp established norms within the episteme. This includes finding appropriate uses for media, from books or newspapers to photos or videos. In digital lifeworlds, much has changed in terms of what this role amounts to. Information is stored and processed at astronomical scales. The Internet approximates H. G. Wells's *World Brain* that we encountered in Chapter 1.[35]

Secondly, people are part of a *collective epistemic subject*. In that capacity they help establish or (more commonly) maintain standards of inquiry, the various types of rules constitutive of the current episteme. Whereas in the first role we figure things out ourselves, in this second role we hold others to standards and help create standards. This role is about maintaining the episteme. How people fill the role of contributor to, or sustainer of, the information environment is rather passive for many individuals, largely consisting in compliance. Nonetheless, the role as such has been transformed in the digital age because the way we gather information has been affected considerably through availability of digital media: We may google things, or have information sent our way from platforms.

Thirdly, persons are *individual epistemic objects*. They get to be known by others as delineated by rules concerning what information about oneself may be shared. This role is that of an information holder (bearer) or provider (revealer) – the role of a *known*. It is about managing privacy, with its many complications. Expectations around the role of individual epistemic objects apply to both oneself and others: There are limits to what we are supposed to reveal about ourselves (depending on whom we interact with), and there are expectations around both *what* kind of information we are supposed to reveal about others and *how* we make it possible that they get to be known in certain ways. What we feel or believe increasingly constitutes data to be gathered or inferred from things we do (e.g., clicks). We can be traced in multifarious ways. We are subject to much surveillance. Accordingly, this

---

[34] Anderson, *Imagined Communities.*
[35] Wells, *World Brain.*

role has been much boosted in digital lifeworlds. Some people ("influencers") even become famous through the way they share things about themselves.[36]

Finally, individuals are part of a *collective epistemic object*. They maintain and contribute to the pool of what is known about us collectively and help ascertain what to do with that knowledge. This role is that of a contributor to data patterns, parallel to that of maintainer of the epistemic environment where information is gathered. Digital lifeworlds have brought lasting changes to data gathering. We can now be known collectively in ways that draw on an immense pool of indirectly inferred information about our inner lives and private acts. This kind of understanding of human patterns would have been unthinkable before.

With this vocabulary in place, we can distinguish among not only epistemic *successes*, *failures*, and *experiments*, but then also epistemic *entitlements*. Epistemic successes (or epistemic goods) are achievements in the acquisition of pertinent information. Depending on context, terms for such successes are knowledge and truth, but also justification, warrant, coherence, or interpretive fineness. Epistemic failures are breakdowns in the acquisition of information. Depending on context, such failures could be ignorance, falseness, delusion, misinformation, or disinformation. Such successes or failures could be obtained in the various roles we distinguished. Epistemic experimentation occurs if information-gathering tools are used for purposes other than inquiry or investigation, and thus in ways other than what can be evaluated in terms of epistemic success or failure. This would typically be art or entertainment, such as fiction or visual arts. This matters in Chapter 6 when we talk about deepfakes. Finally, we can also talk about epistemic entitlements, and among them primarily about epistemic rights and epistemic justice. We turn next to those topics.

5.5 EPISTEMIC RIGHTS

With this framework in place, we introduce some normative notions in terms of which epistemic actors can articulate entitlements and also concerns about being wronged in their roles. Some of the entitlements and wrongs engage actors as *individual* epistemic subjects or objects. Those we can assess in terms of epistemic rights. By contrast, entitlements and wrongs that occur as part of *collective* subjects or objects are structural issues, and thus are often plausibly captured in terms of epistemic justice. Epistemic rights can be formulated *within* the respective episteme, whereas epistemic justice concerns the shape of the episteme as such. Using this vocabulary allows us to formulate certain moral demands as they apply in the domain of inquiry. Linking epistemic rights to the individual roles and epistemic justice to the collective roles is an imperfect division of labor. But it captures the

---

[36] For advice on how to become an influencer, see Hennessy, *Influencer*.

basic sense that rights are articulated by individuals and directed at others, whereas the perspective of justice is that of the individual embedded into larger contexts.

Let us begin with epistemic rights and how they bear on the two individual roles. Rights are entitlements that justify performance or prohibition of actions, by the right-holder or other parties. Recall (from Chapter 4, Section 4.2) that in terms of the Hohfeldian scheme, rights can be privileges, claims, powers, or immunities.[37] For there to be something sensibly called *epistemic* rights that is not readily reduced to some other kind of right, there would plausibly be a range of objects (broadly understood) to the *awareness of* which individuals may have differential entitlements and that are of sufficient collective interest to merit efforts of limiting access to them (and of ensuring access, in other cases). Most straightforwardly, this kind of object would be *information*. Epistemic rights are rights that address who is entitled to what kind of information (with a sense of entitlement to be spelled out as a privilege, claim, power, or immunity). Such rights concern individual epistemic subjects and objects.[38]

Suppose I am tested for a disease. First consider the individual epistemic subject, the person understood as a knower. Normally I should be allowed to inquire about my result. I have a *privilege-right* to know the result (no duty not to). I also have a *claim-right* against the provider to learn my result: They have a duty to inform me (and thus ought not to refrain from informing me or misinform me). And I have a *power-right* to waive my claim-right and so not to know. Finally, an *immunity-right* protects me from the provider altering my entitlements regarding this information. There might be reasons to regulate entitlements some other way, but the point is to illustrate how the notion of an epistemic right operates for individual epistemic subjects.

Next consider the individual epistemic object, the person understood as a known. Normally nobody else will have a privilege-right to know my result. Others have a duty to refrain from investigating the matter. It is my privilege-right not to be known to others in such ways. Accordingly, nobody else normally has a claim-right against the provider to learn my result. I have a power-right to entitle others to know my result. Finally, an immunity-right protects me from other parties altering entitlements regarding this information.

But while epistemic rights (concerning knowers and knowns) are most readily understood in terms of information, we may evoke the distinction among various epistemic successes (or goods) to substantiate talk of rights *to know*, to *true and justified beliefs*, to *understand*, or to *truth*, and of rights to *privacy*, to *be forgotten*, or rights *against slander* or *theft of information*. One would need to spell out what type of right is meant (privilege, claim, etc.), and in what domain of data these rights

---

[37] Hohfeld, *Fundamental Legal Conceptions*. See also Wenar, "Rights."

[38] In this account of epistemic rights grounded in the notion of information, I follow Watson, "Systematic Epistemic Rights Violations in the Media."

operate. These more extended understandings of epistemic rights are thereby then reducible to the more basic one in terms of information. To the extent that I have a right to know my result, I have a right to understand my health situation and to the truth in that regard. But I might have no right to the truth about other things, such as other people's results. Similarly, I might have a right to privacy regarding my data, or the right that some of my data be deleted. But I might have no such rights regarding other matters. The sales price of my home is public for good reason.

For another illustration, consider the right to education. Again, first consider the perspective of the person as a knower. Unlike the earlier case, here we are not just concerned with one bit of information, but with a broad right *to know*, which covers an extensive range of information and the methods to acquire and evaluate them. Also, unlike the earlier case, the informational and methodological content of education is not normally a private matter. But here, too, we have a privilege-right to learn things, and a claim-right against one's community to make that happen (with specifics depending on how the community is organized). There normally is a legal requirement to attend school up to a certain age. Since that is so for good reason, there is no power-right to waive that right. An immunity-right protects me from the provider altering my entitlements regarding education. But this is so only within certain limits since the community needs to provide the schools (which makes my right subject to certain constraints under which the community operates). In addition, denial of education is an epistemic injustice. There are normally structural reasons at work that deny education to people with certain characteristics (often women or minorities) and make it appropriate to capture entitlements not in terms of one person's rights at a time but in terms of the episteme as a whole.

Let us next consider the perspective of the individual epistemic object regarding the right to education. Here we are not generally asking about the rights of others to the same informational content that I get to acquire. Obviously, many others will have the same privilege-right to enjoy such an education, and what is said about the claim-, power-, and immunity-rights applies to them as well. The perspective of the person as a known here is about how I am supposed to be known to others in the curriculum we go through. If this curriculum includes information specifically about me (a rare case) or information that influences how others relate to me and people relevantly like me (more common), I have a claim-right against curriculum designers that people like me not be represented in ways that initiate or perpetuate an oppressive status. I have a right *not to be thought of* in certain ways by others involved with the curriculum.

Pondering a right not to be thought of by others in certain ways generates complicated questions. It is more straightforward to see fair-minded treatment in curricula as a matter of epistemic justice. To see this, consider *testimonial injustice*. In a narrow sense, this occurs if a court disregards my testimony because I am a member of a certain group or otherwise for reasons that have nothing to do with epistemic competence. In the broader sense, this occurs if perspectives of people like me on history and culture are distorted, belittled, or ignored. Testimonial injustice of both sorts often results (at least in part) from inappropriate representation of certain people in curricula. These issues are better treated in terms of the overall design of the episteme. But we should acknowledge that they have counterparts in the violation of individual rights.

Epistemic rights are confined to the domain of inquiry: Beyond *learning of* X, I might not be entitled to anything regarding X. I might not even be allowed to share X myself, let alone market it, and so forth. Similarly, beyond being entitled to have my information protected in certain ways, I might have no claims against people I interact with. My entitlements *might* reach further, but the point is that epistemic rights are sui generis and not naturally reducible to other types of rights. In particular, epistemic rights are not the same as property rights in information (that is, intellectual property rights). Epistemic rights are about what I know and how I am known; intellectual property rights concern what economic use I can put ideas to.

My account uses the notion of information as foundational. This seems natural enough a starting point for a discussion of epistemic entitlements. However, another philosophical discussion about epistemic rights explores the nature of epistemic *justification*. The point is to assess what statements somebody is entitled to making even if they cannot do the work to justify them (which is the typical case in making assertions given how much, one way or another, we borrow from others in our quotidian beliefs).[39] According to my view, somebody has an epistemic right of sorts to a bit of information if they are entitled to being aware of it. According to this alternative view, for somebody to have an epistemic entitlement they must be able to do some work to establish its accuracy.

This is a different understanding of what epistemic entitlements are about. But the kind of question asked within the confines of that alternative view can also be articulated in the view I propose. To stay with the earlier example, we could ask whether I *ought to* have any right to medical information at all, as well as whether there are *limitations* to the use I may put it to. To answer these questions, it would arguably matter whether I actually can do the work to substantiate the information (the justificatory work). Today, what strikes most people as a conclusive consideration in favor of an affirmative answer to both questions is that I am the one whose medical information this is: my body, my concern. However, one can imagine someone arguing that, as the etymology of "patient" – which comes from the Latin for "suffering" – suggests, I should have no such right because I cannot provide and justify a diagnosis, and the ramifications of a diagnosis are beyond my ken. It should be at the discretion of medical professionals what to share with patients.

Apparently, something like this was long the standard view in medicine. To rebut such a view, one must argue that the right to be aware of information (and in this

---

[39] See, for example, Dretske, "Entitlement: Epistemic Rights Without Epistemic Duties?" See also Wenar, "Epistemic Rights and Legal Rights."

case also to do something with it) is not a matter of who can do justificatory work, but of whose life is affected. For other scenarios, these debates play out differently. The point is only that an account that grounds epistemic rights in information rather than in the nature of epistemic justification can still make room for matters of justification and so connect to this other usage.

Epistemic rights justify performance or prohibition of certain actions in the domain of epistemic goods. We can apply them to individual epistemic subjects and objects. But, as we keep noticing, people can be wronged in ways that involve *structural* features of communications networks. They would then be wronged as members of collective epistemic subjects or objects, rather than (exclusively) as individuals whose entitlements are thwarted. The language of justice would then be appropriate.

5.6 EPISTEMIC JUSTICE

Let me explain how epistemic justice relates to a general understanding of justice and to other kinds of justice. The perennial quest for justice is about making sure that each individual has an appropriate place in the environment our uniquely human capacities permit us to build, produce, and maintain, and that each individual is respected appropriately for their capacities to hold such a place to begin with. Under this umbrella, the distinction between *commutative* justice and *distributive* justice is familiar. The former maintains or restores an earlier status quo that set the stage for a given interaction or otherwise responds to violations. (If we trade things, then commutative justice demands that I reciprocate appropriately once you provide me with your goods, and that adequate measures are taken if I fail to do so – where the meanings of "appropriate" and "adequate" would need to be spelled out.) The latter is concerned with sharing out whatever communities hold in common. Major themes in the history of reflection on distributive justice have been to assess what communities hold in common, and what the relevant community is to begin with. For Rawls, the state is that community. What that community holds in common are social primary goods: rights and liberties, opportunities and powers, income and wealth, and the social bases of self-respect.[40]

Commutative and distributive justice are mutually exclusive – but not necessarily jointly exhaustive in light of my broad view of justice. And this observation creates space for a notion of *epistemic* justice separate from commutative and distributive justice. As we talk about what our uniquely human capacities permit us to build, produce, and maintain, we could (and plausibly should) also talk about methods and results of inquiry, about ways information is acquired and disseminated. Epistemic justice is justice to the extent that it is concerned with inquiry: It is about

---

[40] For distributive justice, see Risse, *On Justice*.

giving each person an appropriate place in how we conduct inquiry, and an appropriate place with regard to what inquiry makes possible.

Like commutative and distributive justice, epistemic justice can be and has been theorized in different ways. One way of making this point is to distinguish *concepts* from *conceptions* of commutative, distributive, or epistemic justice. To talk about *concepts* of these different kinds of justice is to assess the general human interest that is in the background of each. Inevitably any statement of what these kinds of justice mean generates a host of questions about the nature of the terms used, what principles would connect the concept to human practice, and how such principles would be justified. Responding to such questions is the task of *conceptions*.

As far as epistemic justice is concerned, the concept of epistemic justice, as we just stated, is about giving each person an appropriate place in how we conduct inquiry, and an appropriate place with regard to what inquiry makes possible. For any given time, one could identify the episteme(s) that is (are) in place. The relevant conception of epistemic justice would operate from within those epistemes to respond to questions about what each person's appropriate place in inquiry (its methods and results) is given how that episteme understands inquiry.[41] That kind of investigation, in turn, would be sorted into inquiry about a person's appropriate place in terms of the collective epistemic subject and object, respectively. That is, this investigation would, first, be about what possibilities for inquiry each person should have as part of that episteme, and second, about how people should be known. Since now we are not asking about rights but about justice, the standpoint is that of a critical investigation about the design or functioning of the episteme rather than directed demands of individuals.[42]

Let me present some examples of epistemic injustices, focused on digital lifeworlds. These include denial of education, testimonial injustice, silencing, and race-/nation-/gender-driven ignorance. Each time I spell out what the case amounts to for both the collective subject and the collective object. Let us begin with *denial of education*. This injustice occurs when people – typically women, minorities, and people at the lower end of the economic ladder – lack adequate access to education. One can see such exclusion as numerous violations of epistemic rights (as discussed before).

[41] For this overall methodological approach, spelled out in detail for distributive justice, see Risse, chapter 7.

[42] The term "epistemic *injustice*" was introduced by Fricker, *Epistemic Injustice*. Her concern was to identify *wrongs* to people in their capacity as knowers, rather than any embedding into a larger understanding of *justice*. (It should be clear, of course, that many people have articulated concerns sensibly understood as matters of epistemic justice prior to Fricker's work, especially from within communities primarily affected by epistemic injustice.) But to be clear about the distinction between epistemic rights and justice, we need to know how epistemic justice relates to the broader context of justice-related discourse. This view of how epistemic justice relates to other types of justice supersedes that in Kerner and Risse, "Beyond Porn and Discreditation." On epistemic justice in relation to distributive justice, see also Coady, "Epistemic Injustice as Distributive Injustice." For the role of epistemic justice in resistance movements, see Medina, *The Epistemology of Resistance*.

But that move misses a structural concern: As collective epistemic subject, we are systematically limiting access to information for certain groups, typically for the sake maintaining power relations. Members of excluded groups are prevented from acquiring skills to participate politically or economically. For digital lifeworlds, lack of education normally entails a highly diminished capacity to participate in anything other than mostly passive roles. The more our lifeworlds turn digital, the graver an injustice the denial of education is. From the standpoint of the collective object, these people and their standpoints will be neglected in what others learn. The other side of the coin of a denial of education often is a denial of presence in curricula that others go through.

Let us turn to testimonial injustice as another example of epistemic injustice.[43] Certain speakers have diminished credibility because recipients are prejudiced about their background. A narrow understanding, recall, is disregard of testimony in court. But since we acquire much orientation in the world through testimony (broadly conceived), testimonial injustice also occurs if perspectives are dismissed in ordinary exchanges, absent in textbooks, or sidelined in collective memory and its accompanying practices. In digital lifeworlds, occasions for inflicting such injustices directly are increasingly avoided through online echo chambers. But then, one common digital testimonial injustice is that such choices themselves reflect and reinforce prejudices even while permitting relatively few situations where injustices are committed to people's faces.[44] There is also little opportunity to examine underlying prejudices in the presence of all concerned. The collective epistemic subject of digital lifeworlds is increasingly fragmented. The collective epistemic object allows for people to be known only through lenses of fragmented processing. Recall also the infopower exercised through social media.

Let us discuss *silencing* next. Silencing – which often creates the conditions that bring about testimonial injustice – is the removal of one's ability to communicate through the creation of conditions under which one's utterances are disregarded. The term came into circulation through discussions about how pornography objectifies women in ways that imply that they are "not heard" when refusing sex.[45] Silencing also extends to politics when outlandish claims are made about public figures to such an extent that we would have no reason to believe anything they say (mutatis mutandis for other domains). Digital media provide new outlets to this form of epistemic injustice, for instance through competition for the wittiest short statement on an issue

---

[43] This is the main topic of Fricker, *Epistemic Injustice*. See also Lackey, *Learning from Words*; Coady, *Testimony*; Goldberg, *Relying on Others*.

[44] Recall our discussion of repetition in Section 4.6.

[45] MacKinnon, *Feminism Unmodified*; Langton, "Speech Acts and Unspeakable Acts"; Langton and Hornsby, "Free Speech and Illocution."

on Twitter. Often no amount of reasoned speech can offset a cleverly worded two-liner, no matter how devoid of substance this two-liner is. Again, this is a problem both for how we acquire knowledge and for how we are known in the world.

Or consider *race-/nation-/gender-driven ignorance*. This kind of epistemic injustice concerns the impact of collective identities on belief acquisition – that is, the formation of mistaken beliefs owing to suppression of pertinent knowledge within certain populations. This phenomenon might arise even without prejudicial attitudes. For instance, *White Ignorance* occurs if the absence of pertinent knowledge among white people about the historical trajectory of people of color (especially in countries with a fairly recent history of enslavement, like the United States) prevents white people from comprehending the extent to which many people of color are saddled with disadvantaged starting points.[46]

In the domain of Big Data, there has been much discussion of this type of epistemic injustice. To begin with, those who work in IT disproportionately come from certain segments of society and ask questions about data that reflect their experiences. Secondly, data collection might occur through devices that certain segments of the population own more commonly than the population as a whole does. Thirdly, the data themselves reflect what are often racist trajectories. In such ways, the prejudicial structures of the past might shape the future. And discrimination is harder to recognize if it is driven by factors *correlated* with odious phenomena, rather than by those phenomena directly. (Certain ethnic groups might display certain unique patterns of purchasing behavior that by themselves are unremarkable.)[47]

Let me conclude this discussion with two comments related to the topic of surveillance. To begin with, recall that we defined commutative and distributive justice so that a matter is either one of commutative or of distributive justice, not both. But, indeed, matters of epistemic justice can *also* be matters of commutative justice, for instance, if inappropriate treatment of people as knowers has created disadvantages for them that need correcting. And they can *also* be matters of distributive justice, for instance, if certain ways in which we are collectively known, like Big Data, bear on primary goods. This latter topic on distributive justice concerns us in Chapter 9. Large-scale collection of data is a matter of epistemic justice in the sense that it concerns the collective epistemic object. Data collection has made it possible for people to be known in ways they never have before. Earlier we talked about the Chinese Social Scoring System, which collects multifarious kinds of data and thus creates a pool of knowledge about the population that is deployed for governmental purposes. Knowledge and control are tightly connected.

---

[46] Mills, *Black Rights/White Wrongs*; Mills, "White Ignorance."

[47] Barocas and Selbst, "Big Data's Disparate Impact." See also Benjamin, *Race After Technology*; Noble, *Algorithms of Oppression*.

In capitalist systems, company-driven surveillance gathers myriads upon myriads of data, with the goal of predicting behavior for commercial purposes. So large-scale data collection sits at the intersection of distributive justice with epistemic justice. It concerns people's relative standing in society, and *also* how they fare as collective epistemic objects.

The second comment related to surveillance revisits the point that an episteme also covers possibilities for self-knowledge. A sense of self is constituted in part by what social relations make possible. What is striking in the data episteme is that any person's self-understanding develops in the constant presence of efforts to make people collectively known, with the goal of facilitating commercial exploitation. Since developing a sense of self increasingly involves digital devices, that sense evolves in the midst of countless efforts to throw light on the collective self, the intermediate results of which are constantly reflected back at people (e.g., through the answers they find on Google). Recall now that we have talked about three types of power: sovereign power, biopower, and infopower. Each type of power operates differently in the data episteme. For many people, the state's sovereign power – which involves actual exercises of violence – would materialize only occasionally. Biopower shapes the background conditions under which human life in a given society develops. But *infopower* is literally in people's faces or within earshot much of the time. It plays an all-encompassing role, leading Zuboff to talk about the commodification of all of our reality.[48]

5.7 CONCLUDING PERSPECTIVES

The vocabulary around epistemic actorhood in this chapter has focused on Life 2.0, and in a way still stands in the Baconian tradition. After all, Bacon championed a methodology that helped elevate humans above the rest of nature, enabling them to acquire knowledge and bring it to bear on their affairs. What Foucault shares with Bacon is a focus on humans who alone are theorized as knowers as part of an ontology that, for this reason, sets them apart from all other entities. The disagreement between Foucault and Bacon is about the status of knowledge as separate from power, not about the status of humans as knowers as separate from all other entities. This is a disagreement distinctly within Life 2.0. The roles of epistemic actorhood, as well as the notions of epistemic rights and justice, are formulated for Life 2.0, as part of a discourse *among* humans (who stand out in Life 2.0 in ways in which they no longer would in Life 3.0).

Humans make demands on each other that are articulated as part of a broadly shared understanding of, and a substantial amount of critical reflection on, the relative importance of goods. And they make their demands in the context of a

---

[48] Zuboff, *The Age of Surveillance Capitalism.*

background understanding of human capacities for action and thought. A person's right to life, for instance, is a right not to be treated in certain ways by other humans (and accordingly makes demands on all other humans). Mosquitos spreading malaria do not violate rights, nor do snakes inflicting bites. They do not make demands on humans, nor do humans make demands on them. They are not part of the discourse in which something like this would make sense. Or consider that there are good reasons to treat ecosystems certain ways. That is not because ecosystems and humans see themselves as part of a shared productive system, or any other system within which participants could make demands upon each other. Instead, it is because humans can recognize the value of ecosystems. Humans recognize its value but do not (for good reason) consider the ecosystem itself or other forms of life therein to be part of an interactive context in which participants make demands on each other. Therefore humans do not normally consider these other entities to have rights or to be able to violate the rights of humans.

To be sure, even from within Life 2.0, this focus on human affairs has been questioned. In the spirit of such questioning of the mainstream, the Whanganui River in New Zealand and other natural entities have obtained legal personhood.[49] Sue Donaldson and Will Kymlicka have encouraged us to see human life as unfolding in close collaboration with animals in a *zoopolis*.[50] Donna Haraway's "Cyborg Manifesto" is an appeal to break down binaries and contrasts and to live with nature in new ways. Bruno Latour has advocated for a "Parliament of Things," to make sure that perspectives of nature factor into decision-making.[51] So obviously, Life 2.0 has generated posthumanist tendencies, tendencies to reconsider the arrangements our species has made with other species and the way it has embedded itself into the material world.

To the extent that we have those posthumanist tendencies, these (possibly late) stages of Life 2.0 prepare us for how dramatically everything could change in Life 3.0. In addition, in Chapter 1 we encountered Dretske's approach to knowledge that does not limit such knowledge to humans. We also encountered Floridi's philosophy of information that sees Turing in line with Copernicus, Darwin, and Freud by way of relativizing human status in the world, this time vis-à-vis other interconnected informational organisms. In Life 3.0 itself, if it comes to that, rights will not only be rights vis-à-vis other humans; they will also have to be articulated in ways that defend the virtues of the distinctively human life against other kinds of intelligence. Distributive justice will not be exhausted by making sure that the accomplishments of humanity are shared out in ways that can be justified to all humans involved. Instead, what humans have jointly achieved will need to be shared out in the

[49] Kramm, "When a River Becomes a Person."
[50] Donaldson and Kymlicka, *Zoopolis*.
[51] Latour, *We Have Never Been Modern*; Latour, *Reassembling the Social*.

presence of other types of entities that might have claims of their own, or vis-à-vis whom human arrangements will have to be justified in any event. In Life 3.0, infopolitics would involve new kinds of entities that populate digital lifeworlds. These are questions similar to those with which we completed Chapter 3, and once again it will have to suffice for the time being to point out that we turn to these topics in Chapter 11. For now, we are going to do more work with epistemic rights.

6

Beyond Porn and Discreditation

Epistemic Promises and Perils of Deepfake Technology

AI-Assisted Fake Porn is Here and We're All Fucked.

—Samantha Cole[1]

6.1 THE BRAVE NEW WORLD OF SYNTHETIC VIDEO

Suppose you hear Barack Obama call Donald Trump a "complete dipshit" or Mark Zuckerberg boast about "control of billions of people's stolen data."[2] Chances are your source is a *deepfake*. Bringing photoshopping to video, deepfakes replace people in existing videos with someone else's likeness. They are named after their usage of deep-learning technology, a branch of machine learning that applies neural net-simulation to massive data sets. Artificial intelligence learns what a source face looks like at different angles to transpose it onto a target, as if that target wore a mask. The framework of epistemic actorhood from Chapter 5 lends itself to thinking about some central epistemological and ethical issues that we ought to keep in mind so that humanity can enjoy the promises of deepfake technology rather than suffer its perils.

While only time will reveal this technology's trajectory, we can identify some promises and perils to watch. They concern the way we acquire knowledge, and come to be known by others, in digital lifeworlds. Digital lifeworlds offer artistic possibilities unknown to the analog world. Synthetic media – media produced or modified through digital technology, especially AI – will contribute enormously to this change in what is possible. Such media might personalize, and revolutionize,

---

[1] This is the title of a 2017 article in *Motherboard*; see Cole, "AI-Assisted Fake Porn Is Here and We're All Fucked."

[2] See, respectively, www.youtube.com/watch?v=cQ54GDm1eLo&feature=emb_logo; www.youtube .com/watch?v=Ox6L47DaoRY; last accessed February 2022. This chapter draws on Kerner and Risse, "Beyond Porn and Discreditation."

education and personal development. For each learner, amazing opportunities could arise through technologies that capture people, including the learners themselves, in situations they have never inhabited. We might eventually conclude that – notwithstanding the downsides, which need appropriate regulation – "deepfakes" was an unfortunate choice of name. Possibly that choice resonated primarily for its association with "fake news," which began to play its infamous role in US (and global) culture in earnest only with the 2016 US presidential campaign. Talking about "synthetic media" might be more conducive to getting the whole range of relevant issues in sight. For the time being, however, deepfakes are mostly associated with pornography and with efforts to discredit people, most commonly and most egregiously women whose faces are projected onto the faces of porn actresses. So, we need closer scrutiny of the epistemic promises and perils of deepfake technology in the context of possibilities generated by digital lifeworlds.

To set the stage, Section 6.2 talks more about deepfakes, and Section 6.3 discusses some general epistemological issues around film. Sections 6.4 and 6.5 explore ways for epistemic actors to be wronged in their various roles, using the framework from Chapter 5. But while there decidedly are such perils, the underlying technology also offers some promises for each role. The range of both promise and peril is substantial, though a lingering concern will be that there is not enough of an upside to balance the downsides. At least it will take much thought and careful regulation to make sure that we can enjoy the promises without suffering too much damage, and that especially society's most vulnerable are protected from the perils. Also, media used to maintain epistemic actorhood (to bring about some kind of epistemic success) can be used for other purposes: to distort such actorhood (to bring about epistemic failure rather than success) and for non-epistemic, experimental purposes, like self-expression or self-discovery. Accordingly, Section 6.6 explores creative uses of deepfake technology. Section 6.7 concludes.

The goal here is not to come to bottom-line conclusions but to help set an agenda around some epistemological and ethical issues that we ought to keep in mind so humanity can enjoy the promises of an emerging technology. That agenda can only be further executed as the technology develops. On the technology side, this chapter reflects where things stand in mid-2020. But the philosophical framework in this book should provide guidance for the debate as the debate unfolds. Also note that – connecting back to Chapter 4 – we can readily say that deepfakes contribute to an erosion of truthfulness in the public domain (in any event, deepfakes whose content touches on matters that are of interest to citizens as such). But the angle we take in this chapter is not that of *truth*, but that of *knowledge*. That is, we investigate in what ways deepfake technology can either further or hamper individuals in their four roles of epistemic actorhood.[3]

---

[3] For a discussion of deepfakes in the context of virtual and augmented reality, see Chalmers, *Reality+*, chapter 13.

As a reminder, here is a summary of the approach to epistemic actorhood from Chapter 5. To begin with, people operate as *individual epistemic subjects*. They are learners, inquirers, or knowers whose endeavors are expected to abide by certain standards. Secondly, people are part of a *collective epistemic subject*. In that capacity they help establish or (more commonly) maintain standards of inquiry, the various types of rules constitutive of the current episteme. Thirdly, persons are *individual epistemic objects*. They get to be known by others as delineated by rules concerning what information about oneself may be shared. Finally, individuals are part of a *collective epistemic object*. They maintain and contribute to the pool of what is known about us collectively and help ascertain what to do with this knowledge. With these four roles in place, we can distinguish among epistemic successes, failures, experiments, and entitlements. Epistemic successes are achievements in the acquisition of pertinent information. Epistemic failures are breakdowns in the acquisition of information. Epistemic experimentation occurs if information-gathering tools are used for purposes other than inquiry or investigation, and thus in ways other than what can be evaluated in terms of epistemic success or failure. This would typically be art or entertainment, such as fiction or visual arts. Finally, epistemic entitlements, come in the form of epistemic rights and epistemic justice.

6.2 DEEPFAKES, CHEAPFAKES, AND WHAT ALL THIS HAS TO DO WITH PAMELA ANDERSON

Deepfakes got started in 2017 – in 2020 the term was recent enough for Word to underline it, though in 2021 that was no longer true – when an eponymous user of the online platform Reddit enlisted open-source software from Google and else-where to apply scattered academic research to face swapping. The user uploaded doctored clips mapping faces of celebrities such as Scarlett Johansson, Gal Gadot, and Taylor Swift onto bodies of porn actresses. Soon, others in the Reddit community r/deepfakes shared their creations, with nonpornographic videos often having actor Nicolas Cage's face swapped in.[4] Deepfakes came to public attention in December 2017, following a provocatively titled article in the online technology magazine *Motherboard* by tech writer Samantha Cole.[5]

Discreditation is another area where deepfakes have had an impact, as did the less sophisticated "cheapfakes," a coinage owed to Britt Paris and Joan Donovan.[6] Cheapfakes are media that have been edited without machine learning; they can involve audio-visual manipulations created via Photoshop, use of lookalikes, re-contextualization of footage, and the speeding up or slowing down of footage.

---

[4] For the technology and its emergence, see Westerlund, "The Emergence of Deepfake Technology: A Review."
[5] Cole, "AI-Assisted Fake Porn Is Here and We're All Fucked."
[6] Paris and Donovan, "Deepfakes and Cheap Fakes."

Such efforts can make people appear incapacitated, or as moving faster or slower than they did, to alter the nature of what occurred. In November 2018, CNN reporter Jim Acosta saw his credentials suspended after a cheapfake seemed to show him strike a White House intern when in fact he was staying her arm to hold on to a microphone to continue a tense exchange with Donald Trump.[7] But while that video distorted a real event, Indian investigative journalist Rana Ayyub found herself featured in a deepfake porn video in April 2018. While Ayyub's face was swapped in, the actress in the video was younger and had different hair. It would have been obvious to just about anyone familiar with Ayyub's appearance that she was not the person in the video. Still, going viral across India, the video created broadly shared knowledge of "witnessing" Ayyub in an intimate setting or of "finding out" about her side job in porn, damaging her standing as a journalist.[8]

Researchers and special-effects studios have long pushed the boundaries of video manipulation. For instance, the iconic 1994 film *Forrest Gump* (directed by Robert Zemeckis and starring Tom Hanks) uses footage of John F. Kennedy with altered mouth movements. The story of video manipulability resembles that of photography: Photos could be manipulated decades before digitalization, and increasingly powerful software enabled any competent user to do as good a job as Stalin's specialists did editing out erstwhile allies after their falls from grace.[9] What Zemeckis and others did to video was expensive and time-consuming and required artistic skill. Soon, deepfake technology could enable anybody to make convincing videos featuring themselves or just about anyone or to pay companies that do their processing in the clouds rather than in high-tech studios to make such videos. Deepfake technology can also create photos from scratch to help create fictional online personas.[10] Audio, too, can be deepfaked, to create voice "skins" or "clones" (digital assets that transform voices in real time, allowing anyone to speak as their chosen online persona).

For now, nonconsensual celebrity porn accounts for the lion's share of deepfakes, most others being jokes of the Nicolas Cage variety. But to gain some historical perspective on the current use of deepfake technology, recall the extraordinary role

---

[7]   Rothman, "The White House's Video of Jim Acosta Shows How Crude Political Manipulation Can Be."

[8]   Ayyub, "I Was the Victim of a Deepfake Porn Plot Intended to Silence Me."

[9]   See King, *The Commissar Vanishes.* One case (which after multiple revisions only leaves Stalin) is in the public domain: https://commons.wikimedia.org/wiki/File:Soviet_censorship_with_Stalin2.jpg; last accessed December 2021. It is worth noting that Winston Smith, the protagonist of George Orwell's dystopian novel *Nineteen-Eighty-Four*, is a clerk in the Records Department of the Ministry of Truth, rewriting documents to match the constantly changing party line. This involves revising articles and doctoring photographs to remove "unpersons," people who have fallen afoul of the party. See Orwell, 1984.

[10] A nonexistent Bloomberg journalist, "Maisy Kinsley," with profiles on LinkedIn and Twitter, was probably a deepfake. Another LinkedIn fake, "Katie Jones," claimed to work at the Center for Strategic and International Studies but is thought to be a deepfake created for a foreign spy operation; see Satter, "Experts: Spy Used AI-Generated Face to Connect with Targets."

that TV personality Pamela Anderson played in the spread of the Internet. Known through the widely watched 1990s series *Home Improvement* and *Baywatch*, Anderson has been featured on more *Playboy* covers than anyone else. She was the most searched-for person on the Internet between 1995 and 2005 – and thus she has evidently contributed enormously to its spread. But her shows eventually became television history. And even though as of 2017 porn sites still got more visitors each month than Netflix, Amazon, and Twitter combined,[11] and as of November 2021, the three most common pornography websites combined (Pornhub.com, Xvideos.com, Xnxx.com) were visited more often than Wikipedia, and around half as much as either Facebook or YouTube,[12] the Internet has outgrown its "original influencer." It has enabled new forms of activities and associations, ranging from networking and entertainment, electronic business, peer-to-peer philanthropy, telecommuting, and collaborative publishing to politics and even revolutions. So, while the Internet initially grew in no small part due to interests that relate to voyeurism and porn, it has expanded far beyond that in use and implications. Similarly, deepfake technology in time is likely to have implications for our increasingly digital lifeworlds far beyond porn and discreditation (a condition that should not belittle harms done in the meantime).

Deepfake detection in its current state is often referred to as a "cat-and-mouse" game, a term originally used to describe the competition between quickly evolving cybersecurity attacks and defenses.[13] Here, the adversarial game is between deepfake generators and the detectors designed to identify them. For example, one solution detects deepfakes based on the observation that deepfake generators rarely receive input frames with closed eyes. Accordingly, subjects in deepfakes do not follow natural blinking patterns. But the researchers acknowledged that *the very publication* of their paper would likely ensure that serious forgers consider blinking from now on. Comments by the researchers who developed the eye-blinking detector make this adversarial mindset clear:

> Lyu says a skilled forger could get around his eye-blinking tool simply by collecting images that show a person blinking. But he adds that his team has developed an even more effective technique, but says he's keeping it secret for the moment. "I'd rather hold off at least for a little bit," Lyu says. "We have a little advantage over the forgers right now, and we want to keep that advantage."[14]

[11] Kleinman, "Porn Sites Get More Visitors Each Month Than Netflix, Amazon and Twitter Combined."

[12] *Statista*, www.statista.com/statistics/1201880/most-visited-websites-worldwide/; last accessed July 4, 2022.

[13] Engler, "Fighting Deepfakes When Detection Fails."

[14] Quoted from Knight, "The Defense Department Has Produced the First Tools for Catching Deepfakes."

Much of the forward-looking literature on deepfakes (as of 2020) predicts the imminent arrival of the point when deepfakes obtain perfect photorealistic quality. At that point, detectors – however perfect themselves – will no longer be an effective solution.

6.3 CAPTURING REALITY: THE EPISTEMOLOGY OF FILM

In 1896, French engineer Louis Lumière released one of the first motion pictures ever, *L'Arrivée d'un train en gare de la Ciotat*. Only fifty seconds long, the film captures an unremarkable scene: a steam engine arrives at a station, passengers disembark, others board. With the camera set at an angle to the tracks, the locomotive grows ever larger in the frame until it appears to barrel into the theatre. The movie entered the annals of film owing to accounts that people screamed or fainted in the face of the onrushing train. Much about these accounts has been exposed as the "founding myth of film."[15] But like photography, film – originally a rapid sequence of photographs – has had an impact because "it is so real."

The epistemic value of photographs stems from their being true accounts of how things are. Kendall Walton has explained the epistemic value of traditional film by likening cameras to mirrors. By reflecting light, mirrors enable us to see objects outside of our line of sight, for example around a corner. Similarly, cameras capture light and enable viewers to see through time and across distances. Viewers can "see" objects through photographs, if only indirectly.[16] Walton's "transparency thesis" – that photographs enable literal perception – grounds much philosophical work on film in the analytical tradition.

To be sure, there has been much skepticism about how much encountering three-dimensional objects at time t_1 can be like encountering two-dimensional images of these objects at t_2. This has led to improved attempts at capturing the "realism" associated with photography. Dan Cavedon-Taylor, for one, has plausibly argued that the advantage of photography over painting is that the former generates *perceptual* knowledge but the latter only *testimonial* knowledge. ("I saw this," Francisco Goya wrote under one of the etchings in his harrowing series *The Disasters of War*, insisting on the value of his pictorial testimony.) Testimony leaves more space for doubt than perception does. As Cavedon-Taylor puts it,

---

[15] Loiperdinger and Elzer, "Lumiere's Arrival of the Train: Cinema's Founding Myth." The "Roundhay Garden Scene," recorded in 1888, seems to be the oldest surviving film; see Smith, "'Roundhay Garden Scene.'"

[16] Walton, "Transparent Pictures." Analytical philosophy came late to film. In continental thought, more work has been done (starting in the 1930s), drawing especially on Benjamin, *The Work of Art in the Age of Its Technological Reproducibility*.

"the conditions under which it is rational to believe the content of another's testimony are stricter than those under which it is rational to believe the content of another's photograph."[17]

What is most interesting for our purposes is Walton's reasoning for his transparency thesis, which is a view about the technology behind film. The process of capturing and developing a traditional photograph (and films, drawing on that process) is mechanical. So the experience of viewing it is connected causally to subjects in the real world: The fact that certain objects are the way they are out in the world is the direct *cause* for their representation on photographs or in films. This causality puts viewers "in contact" with objects in photographs the same way they would be if they were viewing those objects in real life. Knowledge can be as reliably acquired through seeing something in photographs as it can by visual perception. According to Robert Hopkins's development of this view, photographs are epistemically valuable because they present us with putative facts, generating what he calls a "factive pictorial experience."[18] That experience draws on causal processes of light capture and development used to produce film photographs, which, accordingly, *represent* objects in the real world. The facts they offer us cannot represent the world in ways other than it has been. It is for this reason that photography is a reliable source of knowledge, of not only true but also *justified* belief.[19]

By contrast, digital photography, which accounts for almost all image-based media consumed today, is *capable* of being fact-preserving, but does not *guarantee* the factivity of traditional photography. Digital images are captured by an entirely different process, one that Hopkins does not deem appropriately causal. To him, a subprocess called "interpolation," an engineering shortcut behind digital image capture, makes synthetic media incapable of factive guarantees. Also, owing to how they are stored, digital photographs are more easily manipulated than film photographs, rendering manipulated specimens indistinguishable from unmanipulated ones. Hopkins worries that it is possible to create a digital image out of a set of pixels such that they match exactly what cameras would capture if the scene *were* real. That is what deepfakes do now. As Barbara Savedoff warned not long after consumer digital photography first appeared,

> If we reach the point where photographs are as commonly digitized and altered as not, our faith in the credibility of photography will inevitably, if slowly and painfully weaken, and one of the major differences in our conceptions of paintings and photographs could all but disappear.[20]

---

[17] Cavedon-Taylor, "Photographically Based Knowledge," 288f.
[18] Hopkins, "Factive Pictorial Experience."
[19] Recall our discussion of knowledge in Chapter 1. The complications recorded there do not matter here.
[20] Savedoff, *Transforming Images*, 202.

To be sure, certain epistemological limitations of film – in addition to the fact that, with much effort, films could also be forged – have long been known but have not broadly undermined its authority. To begin with, anthropologists at the turn of the twentieth century enthusiastically deployed film to study non-Western cultures. They realized quickly, though, that film could not create deep enough an appreciation of how people interact in contexts utterly discontinuous with the viewers' own. Whatever impact Lumière's *L'Arrivée* had, for instance, it could have only because viewers knew trains and stations. Film can connect audiences with "what really happens" only if these audiences have a suitable frame of reference. Anthropologists soon switched to immersive fieldwork, producing monographs rather than films and addressing readers rather than viewers.[21]

Consider another epistemological limitation of film. To set the stage, note that Ukrainian-born clothing manufacturer Abraham Zapruder happened to capture on film the assassination of John F. Kennedy in Dallas on November 22, 1963.[22] The most complete footage of the events, Zapruder's film was used to corroborate (or debunk) accounts of thousands of eyewitnesses who were certain of dramatically different things. Complexities of speed, emotion, distance, and memory made it hard to judge whose testimony to trust. While Zapruder's film let investigators build a single narrative, however, they mistakenly assumed that the film captured the *entire* assassination. As it turned out, the first shot was fired before the camera was on. Trying to interpret all three shots within the film's timeframe generated inconsistencies that conspiracy theorists subsequently seized upon. The underlying problem is overreliance on the epistemological virtues of film.[23]

6.4 DEEPFAKES AND EPISTEMIC WRONGS: INDIVIDUAL AND COLLECTIVE EPISTEMIC SUBJECTS

Let us see how deepfakes might inflict wrongs in terms of the four roles of epistemic actorhood from Chapter 5. For each role, distinctive wrongs are created that we can capture in terms of either epistemic injustices or violations of epistemic rights. But each time, there are distinctive gains we can also capture in terms of the realization of either justice or rights. The challenge is to minimize the harms while cultivating the benefits. To be sure, there will be a lingering doubt that this can be done.

Let us begin with individual epistemic subjects. Inquirers are wronged if they have epistemic rights to specific information but receive deepfakes that provide false or misleading information. Straightforward examples are videos that misrepresent

---

[21] Griffiths, *Wondrous Difference*, chapter 4.
[22] Wrone, *The Zapruder Film*.
[23] See Holland, "The Truth Behind JFK's Assassination." This topic is helpfully discussed by Rini, "Deepfakes and the Epistemic Backstop." Also recall our discussion of conspiracy theories in Chapter 4, Section 6.

how events unfolded, for instance the Russian attacks on Syria in 2018.[24] In addition, to the extent that deepfakes become widespread, individual epistemic subjects are not merely wronged in *particular* instances when they fail to receive information to which they have a right. They are also wronged in their broader *role* as knowers to the extent that their ability, specifically the ability to perform any task for which they must be knowledgeable, declines. Inquiry becomes harder to complete with more parties aiming to undermine it.

But deepfakes can also empower people as knowers and make it easier for them to realize epistemic rights. Consider three kinds of examples. To begin with, deepfakes can stimulate interest in fields like art and history by making them come alive. For instance, the Dalí Museum in St. Petersburg, Florida, has used deepfake technology as part of an exhibition called Dalí Lives. To make good on that title, the museum created a life-size deepfake of the artist by having machine learning work with a thousand hours of his interviews.[25] This recreation could deliver a variety of statements that Dalí had spoken or written. To mention another example of this type, the Scottish company CereProc has trained a deepfake algorithm on recordings of John F. Kennedy. The company could thereby produce a delivery of the speech he was scheduled to give the day he was assassinated.[26]

Secondly, deepfakes might make it easier to convey certain messages effectively. In 2019, a British health charity used deepfake technology to have soccer champion David Beckham deliver an anti-malaria message in nine languages, many more than he was capable of even pronouncing. Celebrity might be dispatched effectively to convey information.[27] Thirdly, voice-cloning deepfakes can restore voices when people lose them to disease.[28] In such ways, inquiry, and thus exercise of epistemic rights, becomes easier through deepfakes. But to be sure, a sensible reaction to such examples would be that they fall short of making good on the harms done.

As far as the collective epistemic subject is concerned – the role in which individuals are maintainers of the episteme – the main impact is the changing role of video in providing testimony (and accordingly the changing role of video for inquiry). To begin with, deepfakes can allow people to produce recordings of events that never occurred, putting the burden on courts or competing parties to disprove that evidence. Fake videos can provide alibis, which can affect everything from custody battles or employment tribunals to criminal cases. In addition, deepfakes can mimic biometric data, tricking systems that rely on face, voice, or gait recognition. Similarly, deepfakes can be presented as long-lost evidence for untenable

---

[24] See Friedman, "Defending Assad, Russia Cries 'Fake News.'" For Russian information politics, see also Snyder, *The Road to Unfreedom*, chapter 5.
[25] Lee, "Deepfake Salvador Dalí Takes Selfies with Museum Visitors"; Chandler, "Why Deepfakes Are a Net Positive for Humanity."
[26] BBC News, "John F Kennedy's Lost Speech Brought to Life."
[27] Davies, "David Beckham 'Speaks' Nine Languages for New Campaign to End Malaria."
[28] www.projectrevoice.org/; last accessed December 2021.

viewpoints that some people nonetheless are eager to reactivate. Some people question the Holocaust, the moon landing, or 9/11, despite available video proof and numerous bits of corroborating evidence. Deepfakes can spread "alternative" versions, masquerading as long-oppressed evidence.

Moreover, to continue with the changing role of video for inquiry, the sheer possibility of deepfakes would create plausible deniability of anything reported or recorded. Doubts sown by deepfakes could permanently alter our trust in audio and video. For instance, in 2018, Cameroon's minister of communication dismissed as fake a video that Amnesty International believes to show Cameroonian soldiers executing civilians.[29] Similarly, Donald Trump, who boasted about grabbing women's genitals in a recorded conversation, later claimed that the tape was fake. He thereby enabled his followers to take this stance.[30] Such denials are then among the multifarious voices on an issue, making it ever harder to motivate people to scrutinize their own beliefs. We already discussed in Chapter 4 Nietzsche's rather plausible view that the truth has only limited value for many people.

For decades, video has played a distinguished role in human inquiry, both broadly (as discussed in Chapter 5, Sections 5.5 and 5.6) and specifically in the context of testimony. What was captured on film served as indisputable (or anyway least-disputable) evidence of something in ways that photography no longer could after manipulation techniques became widely available. Until the arrival of deepfakes, videos were trusted media: They offered an "epistemic backstop" in conversations around otherwise contested testimony, as Regina Rini puts it.[31] Without such a backstop, it is hard to maintain the trust that comes from reliance on established facts. Alongside other synthetic media and fake news, deepfakes might help create a no-trust society in which people cannot or no longer bother to separate truth from falsehood, and no reliable media can help them do so. Within generations, people might no longer even approach disagreements with a possibility of truth-finding in mind. This would also be a society where the varieties of epistemic injustice – especially testimonial injustice – would be pronounced in their application to digital lifeworlds.[32]

To assess in greater detail how problematic the loss of video as an epistemic backstop is for the collective epistemic subject, consider a related scenario. Ivan Illich and Barry Sanders (whom we encounter again in Chapter 10) offer an intricate discussion of "alphabetization," the penetration of human culture by the written word. As part of this exploration of the advent of literacy, Illich and Sanders investigate the changing role of the oath:

---

[29] Amnesty International, "Cameroon: Credible Evidence That Army Personnel Responsible for Shocking Extrajudicial Executions Caught on Video."
[30] Gambino, "Denying Accuracy of Access Hollywood Tape Would Be Trump's Biggest Lie."
[31] Rini, "Deepfakes and the Epistemic Backstop."
[32] Testimonial injustice is the main type of epistemic injustice discussed in Fricker, *Epistemic Injustice*.

My word always travels alongside yours [in the world of orality]; I stand for my word, and I swear by it. My oath is my truth until way into the 12th century: The oath puts an end to any case against a freeman. Only in the 13th century does Continental canon law make the judge into a reader of the accused man's conscience, an inquisitor into truth, and torture the means by which the confession of truth is extracted from the accused. Truth ceases to be displayed in surface action and is now perceived as the outward expression of inner meaning accessible only to the self.[33]

What they expound is how the oath ceased to be the epistemic backstop it could effectively be in a world of orality. To be sure, the oath – and the signed statement – still has special legal importance. However, today that importance does not lie in its being an epistemic backstop but in creating the possibility for people to incur special legal responsibilities. If Illich and Sanders are correct, there might not have been any such (broadly accepted) backstop between the demise of the oath in that function in the twelfth century and the advent of photography in the nineteenth.

In historical perspective, there normally simply is no epistemic backstop. In times when there is not, judgments must be made relying on the track record of, and one's willingness to trust, the source of the testimony. Otherwise, one would have to thoroughly investigate many background factors (witnesses, corroborating evidence, consistency with things known, etc.). In some ways, our testimonial practices might revert to such a world as synthetic video is perfected and as a result, we enter a world without any epistemic backstop. The difference is that, when we last inhabited such a world, we had no indisputable media to connect us to reality. In the future, when will reenter a world without any epistemic backstop, we do have such media, but their results can also be fabricated synthetically.

One way of seeing how much of a loss entering such a world would be is that during the period of history when democracies in territorial states became widespread, there actually *was* an epistemic backstop. Presumably having such a backstop has helped with the distant-state and overbearing-executive problems that beset modern democracies, as we saw in Chapter 3, drawing on David Stasavage.[34] In a way it is reassuring that by historical standards such a backstop was not normally part of the episteme: Our ancestors had to and somehow *could* manage without it. But they did not have to navigate the intricacies of large territorial democracies and the technological age.

In Chapter 4, Section 4.4, we encountered Origgi's work on reputation and focused on the reputation of individuals.[35] "Without consciousness of the interdependence between me and my image in the eyes of others, between my actions and my reputation," she writes, "I cannot understand either who I am or why I act."[36]

---

[33] Sanders and Illich, *ABC*, 85.
[34] Stasavage, *The Decline and Rise of Democracy*.
[35] Origgi, *Reputation*.
[36] Origgi, 254.

And without an epistemic backstop, managing this interdependence for each person involves judgments of trustworthiness of informational sources. In the future, that is, people must learn how to judge *for themselves* the *reputation* of information sources. If all goes well, the web might generate a form of collective wisdom. But even then, individuals must determine whom to trust. That in turn will have much to do with whom *others* trust. Origgi argues that we must orient ourselves by evaluating who is a trustworthy source and by then deferring to their expertise.[37] Regarding the individual epistemic subject, this means each person is much more on their own as far as both getting an orientation in the world and attaining a self-understanding are concerned – much more, that is, than in a world with an epistemic backstop. And regarding the collective epistemic subject, such a world is one in which no standards of epistemic success are available that depend on the existence of an epistemic backstop – and thus one that is populated by individual inquirers that must get on without that kind of objectivity.

With all that said, deepfake technology also has *upsides* for the collective epistemic subject, the ways we collectively acquire knowledge. Deep generative models – a type of machine learning – raise new possibilities in medicine and healthcare. For instance, use of deep learning to synthesize data might help researchers develop new ways of treating diseases without using patient data. "Fake" Magnetic Resonance Imaging (MRI) scans have already been created. Algorithms training primarily on these images, with real images representing only 10 percent of media used, became as good at spotting brain tumors as algorithms trained only on real images.[38]

In the medical world, synthetic data could also help with anonymization. It is often possible to identify individuals in anonymized data sets if ancillary sets can be cross-referenced. Synthetic data block such possibilities by "creating" new people.[39] New ways of generating knowledge that enrich our episteme thereby become available. "Deepfakes" as we know them would facilitate ongoing technological innovation, much as photos of Pamela Anderson have facilitated the spread of the Internet. At the same time, these benefits seem to come with much uncertainty and as of now feel remote.

6.5 DEEPFAKES AND EPISTEMIC WRONGS: INDIVIDUAL AND COLLECTIVE EPISTEMIC OBJECTS

Recall that as *individual epistemic objects*, persons get to be known by others as delineated by rules concerning what information about oneself may be shared. As parts of a *collective epistemic object* persons maintain and contribute to the pool of

---

[37] Origgi, chapter 7.
[38] Snow, "Deepfakes for Good: Why Researchers Are Using AI to Fake Health Data."
[39] Macaulay, "What Is Synthetic Data and How Can It Help Protect Privacy?"

what is known about us collectively and help ascertain what to do with that knowledge. So, the two roles under the heading of "epistemic object" capture persons *as knowns* rather than *as knowers*.

As far as the role of individual epistemic objects is concerned, people are wronged in their capacity as knowns primarily through efforts to spread falsities about them. Their epistemic rights are violated: What spreads about them is not how they should be known. But parallel to the individual-epistemic-subject scenario, there is more to this violation. In the case of the individual epistemic subject, the wronging occurs in particular instances and also through the creation of an environment where people can no longer operate as knowers. Similarly, in the case of individual epistemic objects, there is a rights violation not only if actual falsehoods about that person (the object) are conveyed, but also if the way that anything pertaining to that person is conveyed undermines her ability to come to be known in appropriate ways.

Recall journalist Rana Ayyub. Most people familiar with her appearance could detect that the woman in the video was not she. What was happening cannot be described as lots of men interested in Ayyub's body obtaining the opportunity to become privy to *her* sexual life (as it could be if a video of real events had been leaked). Instead, what the viral spread of the deepfake created was a kind of common knowledge – I know it, you know it, I know you know it, you know I know it, we know lots of others are "in" on it, and so on – that her intimate moments are fair game beyond individual fantasies about her and that these intimate moments could be alluded to as what people should *primarily think about* as far as she was concerned. That then lots of people were "in" on it damaged her ability to come to be known the right way. As a person Ayyub's dignity was violated, and as a journalist she was silenced.

This is the threat of deepfake porn: That women's fragile emancipation from being seen as sex objects more than as occupants of roles of professionals, citizens, or as human beings worthy of respect is damaged through depictions associated with objectification. Revenge porn has this effect, and on women more than normally on men, because men are not emerging from this kind of role. Such a fate could await many women since now unsophisticated perpetrators would no longer need to obtain nude photos or sex tapes to threaten women from elsewhere. They can manufacture such materials themselves and deploy them as they see fit. Similarly, deepfakes could do damage to how people from groups that are still overcoming prejudicial history get to be known.

Legally, all this is hard to address. As *Wired* noted, "You can't sue someone for exposing the intimate details of your life when it's not your life they're exposing."[40] In deepfake porn, it would not be *this* person's body, and the face could be ever so slightly altered: Everybody still realizes who it is, but there is plausible deniability, much as people look naturally similar. However, all this might change as the

---

[40] Ellis, "People Can Put Your Face on Porn – and the Law Can't Help You."

possibility of attacks like the one on Ayyub becomes commonplace. Perhaps to some extent what happened to her was so effective precisely because it was new. If something in principle could be done to everybody, seeing it done *to someone* might lose its thrill, and perhaps it would then be done less often.

To proceed to collective epistemic objects, deepfakes have the potential of changing the way people generally get to be known. We enter people's imaginations any number of ways. We come to be known to others in light of their prejudices, but also in ways that connect to their fantasies, traumas, or dreams. But all along these have been mental activities trapped in people's minds unless they captured their mental activities in words, drawings, or paintings. Now we all get to be known to others conscious of the fact that we could enter their artistic, possibly erotic, fabrications. ("We're all fucked," in terms of Samantha Cole's pathbreaking article on deepfakes.[41]) We are all potential actors in someone else's productions. But to be sure, this affects some persons more than others – those who have ways of catching people's imagination, which is sometimes consciously chosen and independently pursued, but often utterly unwilling and even forced upon people (which is important to emphasize as we are to some extent concerned here with the objectification of women).

Manipulated videos also do damage to democracy: People are harmed not only as knowers, but also as knowns. (To make collective decisions citizens need a decent level of knowledge about the people with whom they share a polity, lest these citizens be deceived, e.g., about how certain measures affect others or what such people's worries are – and if such deceptions occur those people would be harmed as knowns.) Our general infrastructure of how we get to know people will change for the worse in fast-moving political processes where fake news takes time to be rebutted (obviously especially if there is much fake news to be addressed). As these developments unfold, the various types of epistemic injustice discussed in Chapter 5 can be readily inflicted.

But as far as the role of the collective epistemic object is concerned, there is also empowerment, much as there was in the case of the subject. Deepfake technologies can amplify things for which people should be known. For instance, during the 2020 Delhi Legislative Assembly election, the Delhi Bharatiya Janata Party used deepfake technology to distribute a version of an English-language advertisement by its leader, Manoj Tiwari, translated into Haryanvi (a Western Hindi dialect) to target voters from the state of Haryana, where that dialect is spoken. An actor provided the voiceover, and video footage of Tiwari's speeches was used to lip-sync the video to the voiceover.[42]

Similarly, deepfake technology enables people to wear virtual masks on outlets like Snapchat to share experiences of abuse without revealing their identities. They

---

[41] Cole, "AI-Assisted Fake Porn Is Here and We're All Fucked."
[42] Dasgupta, "BJP's Deepfake Videos Trigger New Worry Over AI Use in Political Campaigns."

can remain anonymous while retaining human features and thereby the ability to convey emotion – which preserves the essential humanity of survivors of abuse.[43] But once again, readers might well leave this discussion with a lingering sense that the potential for more damage is enormous and already rather concrete, whereas the benefits are much more uncertain.

6.6 THE CREATIVE POTENTIAL OF DEEPFAKE TECHNOLOGY

Epistemic actorhood is concerned with both acquisition of knowledge and ways of being an object of knowledge. In these roles, there can be success or failure as far as inquiry is concerned. Inquiry occurs by means of certain tools, such as oral or written communication, imagery, or video. Such tools can also be used for purposes that are not knowledge-related but exploratory or artistic, concerned with self-expression or experimentation. Language can capture accurate information (success of inquiry) but also, as a flipside, convey inaccurate or misleading information (failure of inquiry). In addition, we use language to tell stories, entertain, and convey lessons about life, or in pursuit of a narrator's love for developing certain themes or for linguistic playfulness. Similarly, images can capture or falsify reality, but also play with reality or capture an author's imagination or sentiments about being in the world without any intention to misrepresent anything and without anybody engaging with the image as a successful or failed attempt to capture reality.

Creative use of language and imagery not only allows people to escape into fictional worlds. It also helps constrain power in ways that even the most relentless pursuit of truth never could, without falsifying anything. There is parody, satire, and caricature, which have ways of advancing political equality by taking a humorous look at the powerful, perhaps ridiculing them to overcome the seriousness that shapes power relations. Or think of a deepfake version of something like Montesquieu's *Persian Letters*, which cast his forbidden critique of the Ancien Régime as an extended commentary on the imagined court of Ancient Persia. Techniques that would be cruel when applied to the vulnerable or even to peers are liberating when applied to the powerful. As far as the word "parody" is concerned, its Greek origins are *para*, "beside, against," and *oide*, "song." Thus etymologically, a *parodia* is a "counter-song," an imitation set against some original, presumably a song of praise of those already well known.

Creative people have already discovered the potential of deepfake technology for artistic purposes. One example is German artist Mario Klingemann, a pioneer in the use of computer learning in art known for work involving neural networks, code, and algorithms.[44] Soon anyone could have their likeness inserted into most any scenario available on the Internet or have somebody else's inserted. This could

---

[43] Heilweil, "How Deepfakes Could Actually Do Some Good."
[44] For Klingemann's website, see http://quasimondo.com/; last accessed December 2021.

involve sexual fantasies. But as the technology develops, much as these things unfolded in the development of the Internet (recall Pamela Anderson), sexual visualization could be one among multifarious uses. Synthetic-video applications would enable users to produce porn clips, and it might be hard to set them up in such a way that this is one function they cannot fulfil. But they could also do numerous other things.

People fantasize about many things outside of sex. They can capture their fantasies using deepfake technology or develop fantasies in videos from scratch. Many of the mind's wanderings could find new outlets. So far, visual storytelling is expensive. Hollywood studios spend billions to create spectacles that transport audiences to other worlds.[45] Deepfake technology incorporates the ability to synthesize imagery, giving smaller-scale creators similar capacities for bringing imaginative creativity to life.[46] The common person's dream of a creative empire might materialize.

There is a thin boundary between inflicting an epistemic wrong by casting somebody in, say, a pornographic video produced with the intention or net effect of undermining how somebody else is perceived, and the living-out of fantasies that would be part and parcel of an expansion of creative possibilities from deepfake technology. Legal regulation must draw the line. Much will depend on whether one's creation is spread. In that regard, deepfakes are not very different from how we often think about fantasies in someone's mind and their execution, which is mediated through decisions. Fantasizing, one would think, should not be punishable and should arguably not be considered offensive even if dreamers avail themselves of deepfakes to capture their imagination (much as it should not be so considered if they captured their fantasies in private drawings that make only for themselves). However, what we presumably do *not* want is for such products to spread since such spreading would typically have pernicious effects on how somebody gets to be known.

In any event, virtual worlds have been around for a long time. Deepfake technology, to be sure, is likely to give a big push to them and create new possibilities of connecting to people in distant places. The great advantage of the Internet all along has been that it allows people in far-flung locations to do things together. Deepfake technology will enhance that possibility. More generally, this technology might make it possible for us to inhabit a world where what people dream about exists not merely in their minds but also in the clouds (and without thereby automatically becoming accessible to others). This would be an enormous change in how people's inner lives relate to the outer world, in the sense that there is the option of extending one's mind in such ways – ideally perhaps without otherwise acting back on the environment in any way, so that the virtual experience of one's fantasies can serve as

[45] Globe Newswire, "Global VFX Market Will Reach USD 19,985.64 Million By 2024."
[46] Sunny, "An Optimistic View of Deepfakes."

an outlet of sort, but how all this would play out is a difficult empirical question that would have to be assessed separately when the time comes. But ideally, indeed, we could then do things via cloud computing that so far we could only do in our minds or through paintings or other forms of art. The creative process as such thereby grows substantially.

The creative possibilities are immense, and worth exploring. Think about the television series *The Crown* (about Elizabeth II) with faces of actual royals mapped onto faces of actresses and actors, or *Thirteen Days* with the real faces of the protagonists of the Cuban Missile Crisis. Actors would still be important, but not for playing historical figures of whom we have enough images to let them literally speak for themselves. (The arguably odd connection between well-known actors and historically influential figures – as if it takes a Hollywood star to bring alive a famous leader – might then end, though it might also turn out that people are interested in that famous leader at least to a large extent *because* that person is played by a beloved actor.) The movie industry could not only improve dubbing on foreign-language films, but also, more controversially, resurrect dead actors. At the time of writing, James Dean is due to star in *Finding Jack*, a Vietnam War movie.[47]

Some may wish for Clint Eastwood or Meryl Streep to keep acting forever, and the two of them might wish for the same. Some actors and actresses have become timeless, and with deepfake technology, it might be appealing for many people to continue to see them featured in movies these actors might well have wanted to be in. And if you wanted your own movie to be narrated by Ronald Reagan, Morgan Freeman, or Michelle Obama, you might just make that happen. Also, finally, the ability to mimic faces, voices, and emotional expressions is one of the most important steps toward building a believable virtual human with whom we can genuinely interact. Such a process of creating virtual humans would come with an entirely new set of possibilities.

6.7 CONCLUSION: WHERE DO WE STAND?

Recognized as dangerous even by those who build them, deepfakes are mixed news, with the negative aspects of the technology more clearly in sight than any possible benefits. They bring change that will have positive and negative consequences as far as the various epistemic roles are concerned. Much thought and regulation are required to make sure that epistemic roles are strengthened rather than weakened, that epistemic rights and justice are respected rather than violated, and that human creativity is enhanced rather than hampered. Such regulation would especially have to make sure that society's most vulnerable receive protection. At the macrolevel, there is a risk of enormous danger to democracy. At the microlevel, there is a high

---

[47] Ritman, "James Dean Reborn in CGI for Vietnam War Action-Drama."

risk of damage to specific individuals whose dignity and standing could be undermined through deepfakes. The technology has come to stay and raises a host of questions, some of them philosophical. The goal here has been exploratory, to help set an agenda around such questions. We must remain vigilant to make sure the downsides do not outweigh the upsides. That will be a tall order.

7

The Fourth Generation of Human Rights: Epistemic Rights in Life 2.0 and Life 3.0

I told you so. You *damned* fools.

—H. G. Wells (a line he chose for his grave)[1]

7.1 INTRODUCTION

Providing myriads upon myriads of data, digital lifeworlds engage us much more as knowers and knowns than was ever possible in the analog world, with its limited capacities for storing, sorting, and processing information.[2] The digital age offers not only enormous opportunities but also colossal potential for epistemic intrusiveness much beyond the totalitarian surveillance of analog times. Chapter 5 provides a framework of epistemic actorhood and delineates notions of epistemic rights and justice. Chapter 6 deploys this framework to assess deepfake technology. Regarding our epistemic rights, humans need especially high levels of protection at this stage of Life 2.0. If we get to Life 3.0, these rights must include one to the exercise of the distinctively human intelligence in lifeworlds shared with entities that might surpass us enormously in certain ways. It is partly because of the relevance that epistemic rights have already and partly because of their relevance in a possible Life 3.0 that we should acknowledge them as *human rights*. Making that case is the main goal of this chapter.

The human rights movement is grounded in the 1948 Universal Declaration of Human Rights (UDHR) and has since given rise to a broad range of domestic and international laws, new institutions such as regional human rights courts and the International Criminal Court, and a globally disseminated network of grassroots movements and nongovernmental organizations. The human rights movement is dynamic in that it allows for an expansion of the scope of topics covered by

---

[1] Wells, *The War in the Air*, 277–80.
[2] This chapter is a descendant of Risse, "The Fourth Generation of Human Rights."

human rights.[3] Human rights are often classified in terms of three generations, partly to reflect the historical trajectory through which certain rights have become politically efficacious and partly to delineate subject areas. In the spirit of the dynamism of the human rights movement, there has long been talk of a *fourth generation*. I submit that epistemic rights should be components of that generation.

Among other things, human rights operate as standards of achievements that allow us to assess the performance of governments. Adding such a fourth generation means to develop and adjust these standards to the demands of the digital century. In this context, a comparison to China is instructive. The Chinese Communist Party – which rules autocratically and does not subject itself to democratic and human rights norms – has upgraded its governance system to a new technological level, drawing on stupefying amounts of data and electronic scoring in ways that reflect and respond to the possibilities of the digital century. By contrast, countries committed to democracy and human rights have not upgraded *their* governance systems. Instead they have either left the technological possibilities of the digital century largely to the private sector, creating a situation where companies take advantage of citizens by commodifying all of their lived reality without doing enough to use technology to bring the public sphere into the twenty-first century (and here the keyword is "surveillance capitalism" and the United States is the obvious example); or else they have so far only rather timidly embraced the current digital possibilities to begin with, especially the possibilities for improved governance (and here Germany is the obvious example).[4] But it is arguably vital for the flourishing and plain viability of democracy and human rights to undergo an upgrade to adjust to the digital century. Chapter 3 discusses democracy. Now we turn to human rights, drawing on the stage-setting in Chapter 5.

Sections 7.2–7.4 approach the subject of epistemic rights as human rights in three ways. Section 7.2 talks about the centrality that H. G. Wells gave to knowledge in his efforts at supporting a universal declaration of human rights. A celebrated science fiction writer and social commentator, Wells was a major advocate for such a declaration in the years before the passing of the UDHR. Wells grasped and articulated the central role that knowledge and its dissemination would (and already did) play in human affairs. His seminal ideas in that regard are still useful to bear in mind. From a philosophical standpoint, we must ask why epistemic rights, once recognized as such, would also be *human* rights. Section 7.3 addresses that question in terms of my own account of human rights, which regards them as membership rights in the world society. Section 7.4 explores the (substantial)

---

[3] For the human rights movement, see Lauren, *The Evolution of International Human Rights*; Forsythe, *Human Rights in International Relations*. For an assessment of its success, see Sikkink, *Evidence for Hope*. On the dynamic nature of the human rights movement, see Schulz and Raman, *The Coming Good Society*.

[4] The United States is the most prominent reference point throughout this book; for Germany, see, for example, Jacobi, *Reboot*.

presence of epistemic rights in the UDHR and beyond, and thus notes the recognition these rights have already received in the analog world for the protection of the distinctively human life. Section 7.4 also introduces the background to the discussion about a fourth generation of human rights.

Section 7.5 turns to epistemic rights in Life 2.0. Such rights are already exceedingly important because of the epistemic intrusiveness of digital lifeworlds in Life 2.0. They should be stronger and more extensive than what the UDHR provides. Section 7.6 is about the right to be forgotten, one of the epistemic human rights we should acknowledge. If Life 3.0 does emerge, we also need an entirely novel human right, one to exercise human intelligence to begin with. Section 7.7 discusses this matter. Human rights must expand beyond protecting "each of us from the rest of us" to protecting "us from them," much as such protection would have to prevail conversely. The point of a fourth generation of human rights is to protect human life in light of ongoing technological innovation and *also* in the presence of new kinds of intelligence that themselves eventually might need to be regarded as members of the same moral community, under an extended understanding of membership. The required argument for the validity of the right to the exercise of human intelligence draws on the secular meaning-of-life literature. Since my main purpose is to establish epistemic rights *as* human rights, I paint with a broad brush regarding the content of proposed rights. I offer them manifesto-style, much as the UDHR does.

7.2 EPISTEMIC RIGHTS AS HUMAN RIGHTS: WELLS ON THE CENTRALITY OF KNOWLEDGE

A prolific writer, Herbert George ("H. G.") Wells is best known for science fiction novels of enduring appeal such as *The Time Machine* or *The War of the Worlds*. He was also a clairvoyant social critic with global aspirations and socialist inclinations. Wells is of interest here not only because he so clearly saw the relevance of knowledge for human affairs in an era of technological innovation, but also because his views contrast both with strong techno-optimism and with the kind of "realist" approach to international affairs that dismisses his ideas as fantasies.

Wells began his public advocacy for the "Rights of Man" in a letter in the London *Times* on October 25, 1939, when World War II was erupting in Europe. Approaching the end of his long career, Wells hoped to articulate a view on what the fighting was about, a view broad enough for some enemies to be open to it too. Germans opposed to Hitler should also be able to look forward to a new world order rather than feel that they must prolong hostilities for fear of draconian punishment.[5] The letter triggered a

---

[5]   For Wells's political thought, see Wagar, *H. G. Wells and the World State*; Partington, *Building Cosmopolis*. For his work on human rights, see Partington, "Human Rights and Public Accountability in H. G. Wells' Functional World State." See also Dilloway, *Human Rights*

debate about a declaration of rights applicable at the global level. The debate itself was largely limited to British intellectual circles, but at that time the UK still ruled large parts of the world. So, a vision for a postwar world articulated in this manner was bound to be consequential.

The *Daily Herald*, a paper sympathetic to labor that would perish in the '60s, adopted the cause. Eventually a committee was established under chairmanship of John Sankey, 1st Viscount Sankey, a jurist and politician esteemed for his judgments in the House of Lords. With Wells as its dominant member, the Sankey Committee further developed his proposals. The Sankey Declaration of the Rights of Man appeared in 1940. Afterwards, Wells by himself published versions of this declaration between 1940 and 1944, making slight modifications each time. A public intellectual, he went to great lengths publicizing his work.[6]

As Wells saw it, his declaration offered a vision of a world that reasonable people would want now rather than a remote utopia.[7] The preamble notes that there has been a revolution in material conditions within the last century. Global communications have changed so dramatically that the importance of physical distance for international affairs has been largely erased. One concern is that "free play of the individual mind, which is the preservative of human efficiency and happiness" is increasingly constrained: Our minds can hardly roam freely without being burdened or troubled in times of uncertainty that results from such rapid change. Instead of us experiencing an "age of limitless plenty," which current potential makes possible, "war and monstrous exploitation are intensified," with a possibility that all progress perishes "in a chaotic and irremediable social collapse." Averting such a breakdown requires "a unified political, economic and social order" guided by a global assertion of rights.

The first right is the "right to live" (to *live*, rather than to *life*), which Wells formulates in the first of eleven articles as follows (explaining that by "man" he means every human):

Every man is a joint inheritor of all the natural resources and of the powers, inventions and possibilities accumulated by our forerunners. He is entitled, within the measure of these resources and without distinction of race, color or professed beliefs or opinions, to the nourishment, covering and medical care needed to realize his full possibilities of physical and mental development from birth to death.

---

and World Order; Ritchie-Calder, *On Human Rights*. For his influence on the UDHR, see Hamano, "H. G. Wells, President Roosevelt, and the Universal Declaration of Human Rights"; Smith and Stone, "Peace and Human Rights: H. G. Wells and the Universal Declaration."

[6] The final version appeared in Wells, *'42 to'44*. For publications during this period with the wording "rights of man" in the title, see Wells, *The Rights of Man, or What Are We Fighting For?*; Wells, *The Rights of Man: An Essay in Collective Definition*. For a contemporary edition, see Wells, *The Rights of Man*.

[7] I work here with Wells, *The Common Sense of War and Peace*, chapter 10. That version contains a wide-ranging preamble and formulates the right to knowledge in extensive ways.

Notwithstanding the various and unequal qualities of individuals, all men shall be deemed absolutely equal in the eyes of the law, equally important in social life and equally entitled to the respect of their fellowmen.

So, this right appeals to the importance of knowledge by insisting that each person be entitled to partake of the legacy of humanity (i.e., all the wonderful accomplishments accumulated "by our forerunners"). A "right to knowledge" then appears in Article 4:

It is the duty of the community to equip every man with sufficient education to enable him to be as useful and interested a citizen as his capacity allows. Furthermore, it is the duty of the community to render all knowledge available to him and such special education as will give him equality of opportunity for the development of his distinctive gifts in the service of mankind. He shall have easy and prompt access to all information necessary for him to form a judgment upon current events and issues.

Wells covers the right to freedom of thought and worship separately, in the next article. The remaining articles cover the right to work, the right to personal property, freedom of movement, personal liberty, freedom from violence, and the right of lawmaking.[8]

Even before formulating these rights, Wells stressed the importance of knowledge in his 1937 article on the *World Brain*, calling for universal organization and clarification of knowledge – that is, for a synthesis of widely scattered educational activities around the world. Such a synthesis would give us this World Brain, "operating by an enhanced educational system through the whole body of humanity."[9] Experts look at matters from their standpoints, which distorts decision-making on policy that requires bottom-line judgments that integrate disciplinary perspectives appropriately. To facilitate such integrative work, a *World Encyclopedia* would be invaluable, "an undogmatic guide to a world culture" to "hold the world together mentally."[10] Unless humankind pools its intellectual resources, Wells believes, we cannot solve the problems outlined in the preamble to his declaration.

His own denial notwithstanding, Wells's ambitions were utopian, certainly by the standards of his time. (Orwell, some decades his junior, thought him to be "too sane to understand the modern world."[11]) Let us acknowledge other pertinent voices from that time to put Wells's ideas in perspective. To begin with, consider US theologian Reinhold Niebuhr, a founder of modern international-relations realism. Niebuhr saw challenges similar to what Wells recorded but firmly believed that humankind

---

[8] Similar ground is covered in Wells, *The Rights of Man*, chapter 9; Wells, *The New World Order*, chapter 10.

[9] Wells, *World Brain*, 16.

[10] Wells, 30.

[11] This is from his 1941 essay "Wells, Hitler and the World State"; see Orwell, *The Collected Essays, Journalism and Letters of George Orwell*, 144.

was incapable of meeting them if doing so required the creation of international political or economic structures. Realists are wary of international structures, let alone global ones.[12] Niebuhr's influential 1932 book *Moral Man and Immoral Society* insisted that

> international commerce, the increased economic interdependence among the nations, and the whole apparatus of a technological civilization, increase the problems and issues between nations much more rapidly than the intelligence to solve them can be created.[13]

For realists, ever-tighter connections among states create more problems than they solve, preemptively encouraging states to block increased interconnectedness in the first place.

Wells believed that humanity's problems could *in principle* be solved, but indeed only within a global system that must be safeguarded for this purpose and to make sure that the World Brain can do its job. At the same time, he was not naively confident in humanity's technological future. His sober-mindedness also contrasts with an optimism common among technological innovators. For instance, Charles Steinmetz, a major figure in the early stages of the US electric-power industry and a leading scientist at General Electric, was interested in electricity partly for its promise to help realize socialism. While steam engines can do things by themselves, an electric grid requires coordination. Steinmetz believed that for this reason, electric power would push societies toward socialism.[14] Similarly, an AT&T chief engineer thought in the early days of the telephone that AT&T would eventually build a network to "join all the people of the Earth into one brotherhood." The innovators of modern weaponry (dynamite, machine guns, airplanes, etc.) typically thought – or persuaded themselves – that their inventions would annihilate war.[15]

Wells's view contrasts with such techno-optimism. In one of his last books, *Mind at the End of Its Tether*, Wells articulates the ominous possibility that the human mind would not meet the challenges. Instead, humankind would reach the (eponymous) "end of its tether." A different type of being – and such beings were much on the mind of Wells the fiction writer – might replace us, much as humanity once replaced other species in evolutionary competition. The species *Homo sapiens*, Wells knows, is "curious, teachable and experimental from the cradle to the grave." But we might not keep up with the "expansion and complication of human societies

---

[12] In fact, as an academic niche, international-relations realism came into its own by articulating critical perspectives on the potential of such structures. Mazower, *Governing the World*, 238–40.

[13] Niebuhr, *Moral Man and Immoral Society*, 85.

[14] Bly, *Charles Proteus Steinmetz*; Hammond, *Charles Proteus Steinmetz*. A genius in mathematics and engineering, Steinmetz was forced to leave his native Germany due to his socialist commitments.

[15] Recorded in Kelly, *What Technology Wants*, 191–92.

and organizations." Our ability to run our social and natural worlds might be inadequate; this possibility is "the darkest shadow upon the hopes of mankind."[16]

Another realist, Kenneth Waltz, wrote in his landmark 1979 study *Theory of International Politics* that "the domestic imperative is 'specialize,'" and "the international imperative is 'take care of yourself!'"[17] But opponents of realism who are of the Wellsian mindset do not overlook how international politics operates. They insist that, in light of what technology enables us to do, the world will founder if we fail to overcome our collective-action problems at the global level (and in that sense, one might say, they consider themselves the *real* realists). Already, Wells's 1907 *War in the Air* predicted the surge in aerial warfare that only fully materialized in World War II. In the preface to the book's 1941 reprint, Wells stated that "I told you so. You *damned* fools." We should do our best to make sure that this statement – which he wanted on his grave, and which I use as the epigraph to this chapter – will not come into play with regard to the mind reaching the end of its tether.[18]

7.3 EPISTEMIC RIGHTS AS HUMAN RIGHTS

For Wells, there would be no point in passing a declaration of rights without making access to and dissemination of knowledge central. To him, the right use of knowledge makes all the difference between humanity's flourishing and demise. Recall from Chapter 1 that Wells was writing only a decade shy of von Neumann's "Can We Survive Technology?", an article reflecting on the world that technology was creating (to whose relentless advance the mathematician added so much).[19] Von Neumann concluded that all we know for sure is that we need "patience, flexibility, intelligence" to get through. At that time, Wells had already suggested a way for the intelligence-part of von Neumann's outlook to materialize.

A universal declaration of rights should be in place to tackle problems that humanity faces as a whole. Let me now argue for the claim that epistemic rights are *human rights* from the perspective of my own account of human rights, which understands them as *membership rights in the world society*.[20] I first introduce my account, in three steps, and then explain how epistemic rights can be integrated in it (and thus register as human rights according to my account). In a first step note that conceptually speaking, I take human rights to be rights with regard to the organization of society that are invariant with respect to local conventions, institutions,

---

[16] Wells, *Mind at the End of Its Tether*, 34.
[17] Waltz, *Theory of International Politics*, 107.
[18] Wells, *The War in the Air*, 277–80. Emphasis in original.
[19] von Neumann, "Can We Survive Technology?"
[20] See Risse, *On Global Justice*, chapters 4 and 11; Risse, "Human Rights as Membership Rights in World Society." Those earlier pieces discuss many philosophical questions about human rights – in particular, just what makes them *rights* and what generates *duties* on the side of other actors. Here I treat these matters only superficially. For world-society analysis, see again Section 5.4.

culture, or religion. These are rights whose realization is a genuinely global responsibility, which involves corresponding obligations appropriately disseminated across the world society. There is a difference between rights that should hold everywhere, but that do so respectively vis-à-vis the local political community, and rights that entail genuinely *global responsibilities*. And only the latter, I submit, should be considered human rights. There are different reasons that some rights would entail such responsibilities.

In a second step, let us note that one reason for rights to entail global responsibilities is that they are "natural" rights, by virtue of their contrast with "associative" and "transactional" rights. What makes rights natural is that they are derived in ways that do not dwell on affiliation (e.g., membership in political communities in which, say, fair-play obligations arise because membership generates certain benefits that it takes efforts to maintain), or on transactions like promises or contracts (which explicitly articulate commitments among the transacting parties). Instead, natural rights have justifications that depend on attributes of persons and facts about the nonhuman world *rather than* affiliations or transactions. Justifications of natural rights accordingly do not appeal to contingencies – matters that are empirically true, rather than as a matter of logical necessity – other than laws of nature, general facts about human nature, or the fact that certain beings are human. For instance, we can argue for a right to life by talking about features of the human body, most importantly the brain, and about human capacities, say, for cooperative behavior – and thereby argue for a natural right because all this can be done without mentioning specific affiliations or transactions. Accordingly, natural rights formulate entitlements that draw on our common humanity (our common human nature), or, as one may say alternatively, on the distinctively human life.

If human rights were understood *entirely* in terms of common humanity, or of a distinctively human life, they would all be natural rights as explained. There would then be no human rights that are not natural rights. One hallmark of natural rights (given how they are derived) is that their force should be recognizable by all reasonable people, independently of any provisions of positive (domestic or international) law. Since affiliations or transactions play no role in the derivation of natural rights, corresponding obligations to realize such rights for certain people are not limited to parties with whom these people share an affiliation (e.g., a political community), or to whom they are linked through certain transactions. Rather than being limited to certain groups in such ways, any such responsibilities apply to all human beings and are thus in principle global in reach (which means that in a separate investigation one would need to assess just how such responsibilities are to be shared out among actors in the world society).[21]

---

[21] For a discussion of this understanding of natural rights in contrast to a different understanding of natural rights (whose essence is that these rights are grounded in a realty outside of humanity), see Risse, "On American Values, Unalienable Rights, and Human Rights."

So natural rights are one kind of right that comes with global responsibilities. Since I understand human rights as specifically those rights that come with global responsibilities, we can now – and this is the third step in the presentation of my account of human rights – turn around the direction of inquiry and ask *how else* (i.e., other than by being natural) there could be rights with global responsibilities. That is, we can state that the distinctively human life that leads to natural rights is one *source* of human rights (or one source of global responsibilities) – and inquire about what other sources of human rights (i.e., rights with global responsibilities) there could be.

Such additional sources include *enlightened self-interest* and *interconnectedness*. For enlightened self-interest, one must show that certain matters give rise to rights domestically, and a self-interest argument would then show why such matters are globally urgent. As an example, one might think of a right not to be enslaved, even under relatively benign conditions. A pure natural-rights derivation of such a right might be difficult because the distinctively human life might not be destroyed through bondage if the conditions indeed are relatively benign. However, one could argue instead that *any* kind of enslavement violates one's status as a citizen (and therefore that even benign enslavement is precluded domestically); and in a next step one could argue that there needs to be a global responsibility to prevent any kind of enslavement since otherwise human trafficking will bring enslaved people into a domestic context where there is a right even against benign enslavement.

As far as interconnectedness is concerned, one could argue that certain labor rights are human rights because global economic structures create incentives for exploitation of workers in poor countries. Various sources of human rights can readily operate together, especially enlightened self-interest and interconnectedness. For instance, interconnectedness supports my discussion above about why there is a human right not to be enslaved even under benign circumstances (since the global transportation infrastructure creates incentives for human trafficking). One other source of global responsibilities (and thus of human rights) is very different in nature. That is, one way in which concerns can become shared at the global level is for them to be regarded as such global concerns by an authoritative process both across and then also among countries. In this case we could talk about a *procedural* source of global responsibilities: Something is a global responsibility if in an authoritative sense the world society as such sees it that way.

The point of this conception of human rights as membership rights in the world society is to articulate entitlements and corresponding responsibilities that arise, one way or another, from all of humanity *living together in this world*, as one intercon-nected world society.[22] By recognizing sources other than the distinctively human

---

[22] One other source I have done much work with is humanity's collective ownership of the earth – which develops the theme of us living together in this world by making our planet central as humanity's habitat – but that topic is harder to integrate into our current discussion;

life, this conception uses contingent facts more freely than derivations of natural rights do, enlisting features of an empirically contingent but relatively abiding world order. And instead of thinking of human rights exclusively as rights individuals hold *in virtue of being human* (as is very common), my own view understands human rights more broadly as rights that involve global responsibilities and, in that sense, as membership rights in the world society.

Wells's insistence on the centrality of knowledge can easily be integrated into this understanding of human rights. This is most straightforward for the distinctively human life as a source. The human brain has evolved in ways that make it suitable for – and good at – cooperating, including in amassing and sharing both information itself and ways of structuring information. Accordingly, the distinctively human life is one of producing and sharing knowledge. Historian David Christian calls us "networking creatures," emphasizing that collective learning characterizes our species.[23] Friedrich August von Hayek once stated the related thought that "civilization rests on the fact that we all benefit from knowledge which we do *not* possess."[24] Once we see the centrality of knowledge to the distinctively human life, it also becomes plausible to say that certain entitlements and protections around knowledge and its acquisition and dissemination register as human rights with accompanying global responsibilities. Thus, it becomes plausible that some epistemic rights are among the human rights.

In a globally integrated economy driven by knowledge-based innovation, enlightened self-interest and interconnectedness also support the case for some epistemic rights being human rights. Parallel to what I said above about the case of benign enslavement one can make a case that, domestically, certain ways of partaking of the economy are any citizen's right. The more economies are knowledge-driven, the more this case includes epistemic entitlements. But then, to the extent that refugee crises and other international spillovers of domestic challenges are driven by economic calamity, we can make an enlightened-self-interest argument for a broadly (globally) shared responsibility also as far as epistemic rights are concerned. Interconnectedness supports this line of reasoning. Interconnectedness also supports an argument for the broad availability of knowledge to fight global challenges like pandemics through the development and dissemination of medications and vaccinations.[25] Such considerations support the case for some epistemic rights being human rights according to my understanding of human rights.

---

see Risse, *On Global Justice*, part II. Chapter 9 also touches on the subject of collective ownership.

[23] Christian, *Maps of Time*, part III.

[24] Hayek, *Law, Legislation, and Liberty*, 32. Emphasis is in the original.

[25] For discussion of these matters in the pharmaceutical domain, see Risse, *On Global Justice*, chapter 12; Risse, "Is There a Human Right to Essential Pharmaceuticals?"

7.4 EPISTEMIC RIGHTS AS HUMAN RIGHTS: THE UDHR AND THE GENERATIONS OF HUMAN RIGHTS

As our discussion of Wells has shown, epistemic rights were on the radar of advocates for a universal declaration. As my philosophical account of human rights reveals, it is plausible to regard certain epistemic rights as human rights. As far as the history of actual human rights documents is concerned, the term "knowledge" did not make it into the UDHR. Still, the declaration does bring epistemic rights into view, rights we can understand as protecting both individual and collective knowers as well as individual knowns. What is missing is rights protecting collective knowns.

The individual epistemic object is safeguarded in Article 12 through protection from arbitrary interference with privacy, family, home, or correspondence and from attacks upon honor and reputation. But the bulk of epistemic rights in the UDHR are about protecting the knower. We find freedom of thought and conscience in Article 18. Freedom of opinion and expression, including freedom to hold opinions without interference and to seek, receive, and impart information and ideas through any media regardless of frontiers, appear in Article19. Cultural rights – indispensable for dignity and free development of personality – appear in Article 22. We can read cultural rights as rights protecting the collective knower, the ways in which the overall episteme is maintained. Article 26 formulates a right to education, crucial for protecting individual knowers. Finally, Article 27 articulates the right freely to participate in cultural life, to enjoy the arts and to share in scientific advancement, which again register as epistemic rights protecting the collective knower. From here epistemic rights have found their way into legally binding conventions and other fundamental legal documents, domestic and international.

These and other efforts have unfolded in the context of discernible types (and phases) of human rights. Since the late 1970s, scholars and activists have distinguished among three generations of human rights, the first comprising civil and political rights; the second involving economic, social, and cultural ones; and the third ushering in collective or solidarity rights.[26] The distinction was inspired by the themes of the French Revolution: liberty (*liberté*), equality (*égalité*), and fraternity (*fraternité*). First-generation rights deal with liberty and participation in political life, protecting individuals from excessive state power. They trace their origins as far back as the Magna Carta of 1215, the English Bill of Rights of 1689, the US Declaration of Independence of 1776 and the US Bill of Rights of 1791, and the French Declaration of the Rights of Man and of the Citizen of 1789. Second-generation rights became prominent after World War II. Economic, social, and cultural rights guarantee an equal status to people as citizens that is beyond civil and political rights. Third-generation rights cannot be exerted by individuals in isolation: They necessarily

---

[26] This distinction seems to go back to Czech jurist Karel Vasak; see, for example, Vasak, "Human Rights: A Thirty-Year Struggle."

involve a group context. They include not only rights to self-determination, economic development, humanitarian assistance, and a clean environment, but also the respective rights of ethnic, religious, linguistic, and sexual and gender minorities.

Epistemic rights to the extent that they have been recognized so far would be subsumed under these generational categories, the word "knowledge" making no explicit appearance. To be sure, the generational analogy hardly intends to capture linear progression with one generation giving rise to the next, only to then disappear. The "generations" are interdependent and interpenetrating, much as needs once recognized continue to be needs even after more needs are acknowledged. However, once such a generational model is available, one is naturally inclined to ask what the next generation would be. And indeed, for almost as long as there has been talk about generations, there has been sporadic talk about a *fourth*, which captures the dynamism of the human rights movement. The topics that fourth-generation rights are supposed to cover have varied, ranging from future generations or genetic lineage to women, indigenous people, or technological change.[27]

For two reasons, human rights as they apply *in digital lifeworlds* should count as that next generation, and then prominently include epistemic rights. To begin with, digital lifeworlds only emerged after the first three generations had been formulated in analog lifeworlds. Given the overwhelming importance of digital lifeworlds for human life and their role in the trajectory of human history (as discussed in Chapter 1), it is fitting to see this fourth generation as connected to them. Again, China has updated its governance system in the last decade, reasserting its operations for digital lifeworlds. In the part of the world shaped by liberalism, democracy, and capitalism, the tendency has been to strengthen capitalism *rather than* liberalism or democracy. Accordingly, we now find ourselves in surveillance capitalism rather than in democratized digital lifeworlds with strong rights protection. A fourth generation that emphasizes epistemic rights would help parts of the world that have embraced previous generations of human rights to understand the need to upgrade their systems for digital lifeworlds.

Secondly, while it remains to be seen to what extent digital lifeworlds take us beyond Life 2.0, it is plausible that Life 3.0 could emerge *only* from these lifeworlds. Therefore, reflection on digital lifeworlds is a suitable starting point for the rights needed in any possible Life 3.0, a life that would put into a new place a species that has become so dominant that it could name the present geological era

[27] For an overview, see Thorp, *Climate Justice*, chapter 1. (Footnotes toward the end contain references to various articulations of fourth-generation rights.) For an influential effort to declare a fourth generation to be about women's rights, see Coomaraswamy, "Reinventing International Law." For the effort to connect fourth-generation rights to integrity of genetic lineage, see Bobbio, *The Age of Rights*. For discussion, also see Falcón y Tella, *Challenges for Human Rights*, 66.

after itself ("Anthropocene"). Accordingly, a fourth theme might be inclusiveness (*inclusivité*, to stick with the French), the integration of humans into the rich possibilities of digital lifeworlds that include entities surpassing human intelligence. After the first generation was concerned with protecting personhood, the second with relative status, and the third with collective endeavors, the fourth concerns humanity's relationship with entities of similar or larger general intelligence that would share our lifeworlds.

If this much is plausible, epistemic rights – based on those that already exist, but considering current realities and future possibilities – should be core components of that fourth generation, next steps in the human rights project. We can now make this claim both as a proposal directly for the human rights movement and as something warranted by my philosophical account introduced above. Epistemic rights are already extraordinarily important because of the epistemic intrusiveness of Life 2.0 but must be stronger and more extensive than what the analog world has provided. In Life 3.0, these rights also need to secure the distinctiveness of human life in the presence of other intelligences (which would have a substantial moral status themselves). Epistemic rights in that scenario would include a right to exercise *human* intelligence.

7.5 EPISTEMIC RIGHTS IN THE DIGITAL LIFEWORLDS OF LIFE 2.0

What additional protection is needed for epistemic actorhood, first in the digital lifeworlds of Life 2.0 and then (possibly) in Life 3.0? In Life 3.0, human rights must be reconsidered. They were meant to protect against threats from other humans when the only other intelligent life around was other animals that had arisen alongside humans in the evolution of organic life. Amazing adaptation to their niches notwithstanding, other animals are inferior to humans in general intelligence. If Life 3.0 does arise, human rights would also need to secure a moral status potentially threatened by synthetic life of a possibly enormously larger intelligence. But before it comes to that, epistemic rights must be formulated and secured for the last stage of Life 2.0 – an endeavor immensely important for its own sake and one that, as it turns out, puts humans in a position to argue that human intelligence is *worth* protecting.

So let us deal with Life 2.0 first. What kind of protection is needed in the four roles of epistemic actorhood to rein in infopower in our data episteme (the power to control data and what is done with them), and, to the extent that biopower and sovereign power are also affected by data and information, also to rein in these other forms of power? To formulate a proposal, I work with four values that guide us toward protections and entitlements that epistemic actors need in their four roles in the data episteme of digital lifeworlds. These values are *welfare* (well-being and prosperity), *autonomy* (independent decision-making), *dignity* (respectful, non-infantilizing, and nonhumiliating treatment), and *self-government* (control over leadership). To be sure, these values have nowhere been explicitly endorsed as the key values of the human rights movement, but they arguably do capture what the human rights movement has been all about. They also reflect the human concerns toward whose protection or promotion knowledge should be deployed. They give cues as to how we should translate the centrality of knowledge to the distinctively human life into entitlements and protections. So, these values cohere with both the human rights movement and my philosophical account of human rights.[28]

The upcoming list should be understood cumulatively: Rights introduced to protect epistemic actors in one role also protect them in others, but I do not mention such rights again. The most important addition to the set of epistemic rights that the human rights framework already contains are rights to protect persons in their roles as parts of the collective epistemic object.

(1) Rights to protect individuals as individual epistemic subjects (individual knowers)

Welfare: What is primarily needed is a substantially boosted right to education, including basic literacy in digital lifeworlds. Future economic and political possibilities in the data episteme increasingly depend on such a capacity.

Autonomy: Freedom of thought, expression, and opinion, including the right to seek information, are already established as human rights. What is also needed is an explicit right to have governments and companies take measures to moderate content, preventing the use of the tools that digital lifeworlds provide for the systematic spread of falsehoods that would undermine people's ability in independent decision-making.

Dignity, Self-government: Nothing more to be added with the aforementioned rights in place.

---

[28] (1) I take the focus on these values from Sunstein, *The Ethics of Influence*. Sunstein explores the extent to which core values (those four) are affected by governmental use of behavioral economics (nudging). That is a nice parallel to what I do here: explore how core values are affected by the epistemic intrusiveness of digital lifeworlds. Inquiring about that matter sensibly involves the same values. While Sunstein was not concerned with human rights, the way he draws out the differences among autonomy, dignity, and self-government is useful for human rights purposes. (2) I have argued for the thesis that some epistemic rights are human rights in two ways: I have argued that this conviction has always been part of the human rights movement, and I have also argued that my own philosophical account of human rights delivers that conclusion. In this section I only work with the first strand of this earlier discussion. That is, I proceed by enlisting what I take to be four recognizable core values of the human rights movement to make a proposal, for which epistemic rights should count as human rights. I do not go through the exercise of showing that each of these proposed rights can also be backed up by resources that come from my philosophical account. But I think this work can be done.

(2) Rights to protect individuals in their roles as belonging to the collective epistemic subject (collective knowers)

Autonomy: There already are cultural rights indispensable for dignity and free development of personality and the right to freely to participate in cultural life, to enjoy the arts, and to share in scientific advancement and its benefits. These need to be adjusted to the data episteme (and actually taken seriously). The way infopower is exercised can be legitimate only if rights are in place that generate possibilities of participation in the design of the data episteme.

Welfare, Dignity, Self-Government: Nothing more to be added with the aforementioned rights in place.

(3) Rights to protect individuals as individual epistemic objects (individual knowns)

Autonomy: There need to be rights to protection of personal data, combined with much education about how important such protection is. There also needs to be a right to be forgotten (on which Section 7.6 elaborates).[29]

Dignity: There already are rights to be protected from arbitrary interference with privacy, family, home, or correspondence; and from attacks upon honor and reputation. These rights must be adjusted for digital lifeworlds with their new possibilities of synthetic media (e.g., deepfakes).

Welfare, Self-Government: Nothing more to be added with the aforementioned rights in place.

(4) Rights to protect individuals in their roles as belonging to the collective epistemic object (collective knowns)

Self-Government: There need to be rights to substantial control over collected data. One hallmark of the data episteme is a humungous amount of data collection. Control over them needs to be broadly shared. *This is the most important genuine addition to the body of existing human rights.* When the UDHR was passed in 1948, nothing like this data deluge and its possible uses by government and companies was on the radar.

Welfare, Autonomy, Dignity: Nothing more to be added with the aforementioned rights in place.

Since my main purpose is to establish epistemic rights as human rights and indicate only roughly what kind of rights that involves, I have proposed rights manifesto-style.

---

[29] The right to be forgotten does not appear on that list in Risse, "The Fourth Generation of Human Rights." That was a regrettable omission.

While I take it that these rights are intelligible as stated, they require refinement and specification. We must spell out not only how such more refined and more closely specified rights give moral guidance, but also how to conceptualize them legally. Doing so generates new agendas, as the above demand that "control over collected data must be broadly shared" illustrates. For this particular demand, Chapter 9 does that work.

7.6 THE RIGHT TO BE FORGOTTEN

The "right to be forgotten" sounds rather broad. But as commonly understood, it is a person's right to have information about themself removed from internet searches or other places that store information. This right has been discussed not only but especially intensely in the legal framework of the European Union, so much so that some have asked whether such a right constitutes a form of European data imperialism – the imposition of parochial preferences – rather than a human right.[30] It is challenging to spell out the details of either content or implementation for a right to be forgotten. Such a right must be related adequately to legal understandings of other rights, such as freedom of expression and privacy. And it must be balanced against a collective interest in accurate record keeping, as well as against interests of other parties in information. Here I merely present some considerations to the effect that a suitably narrow version of such a right indeed is a *human right*. I do so by making a moral case for such a right rather than a legal one (which would have to engage with competing considerations arising from existing law). To that end, I revisit our discussion of repetition in Chapter 4, especially some ideas from Kierkegaard.

The default for human memory is *to forget*, and most information that individuals encounter never becomes part of (personal or collective) long-term memory.[31] Still, we remember many things, and communication channels keep memories alive. Unsurprisingly, then, since the onset of communication people have had an interest

---

[30] Gstrein, "Right to Be Forgotten: European Data Imperialism, National Privilege, or Universal Human Right?" See also Rosen, "The Right to Be Forgotten." For philosophical aspects of memory, see Michaelian and Sutton, "Memory." For moral considerations around a right to be forgotten, see Ghezzi, Pereira, and Vesnic-Alujevic, *The Ethics of Memory in a Digital Age*. On a related duty to forget, see Matheson, "A Duty of Ignorance."

[31] That forgetting is good for individuals is an important theme for Nietzsche. See, for example, Nietzsche, *On the Genealogy of Morality*. Forgetting keeps people from letting harmful thoughts derail them. For discussion, see Risse, "Origins of Ressentiment and Sources of Normativity." By contrast, a key idea of Plato's epistemology, as expounded, for example, in his *Phaedo*, is that learning is the development of ideas buried in the soul, often under guidance of interrogators. Souls existed before birth, and at this early stage acquired knowledge of Platonic Forms. When such a Form is "learned," it is actually "recalled." See, for example, Shorey, *What Plato Said*.

in getting certain things about them removed from those channels. Reputation shapes what one can do in life. Individuals are therefore keen on having their reputation protected and thus on having offensive or embarrassing occurrences stripped from the complex entanglements that constitute their reputation. Such an interest has become ever stronger as not only improved ways of keeping records (especially through the invention of scripts) but also artistic techniques have made it easier to keep memories alive. Eventually there was the printing press, newspapers with ever larger circulations, mass media, and finally the digital age, with its novel forms of external memory that could be copied, stored, and accessed quickly and easily.

As we reconnect to Kierkegaard, it is worth mentioning that he was a serious critic of the newspaper business of his day.[32] He accused the press of an unhealthy influence on intellectual life through the power that comes from circulation and through the incentives the pursuit of a large circulation generates. Kierkegaard himself fell prey to that power when a frivolous review of one of his works appeared in the magazine *The Corsair*. "A newspaper's first concern has to be circulation," he writes.

> [F]rom then on, the rule for what it publishes can be: the wittiness and entertainment of printing something without any relation to communication through the press. How significant! How easy to be witty when misuse of the press has become the newly invented kind of witticism.[33]

It was the *repetition* associated with newspaper circulation that bothered Kierkegaard. Instead of that offensive review being articulated orally and falling into oblivion quickly, the written version that fixed it on paper and the newspaper that brought it into circulation prevented him from having even a chance at having this occurrence forgotten. In the digital age, the potential for damage through the wrong kind of repetition has become much larger. For human memory, the default indeed is to forget, which undermines possibilities for repetitions. Meanwhile for computer memory, the default is to remember, which enables repetition.[34]

In Chapter 4, we turned to Kierkegaard to appreciate the essential importance of repeating for the flow of one's life. How the repeating is done, along with what enables the repetitions, matters greatly, not only for that flow but also for the formation of remembering selves.[35] It does so especially in digital lifeworlds, with

---

[32] See especially "The Present Age," Kierkegaard, *Kierkegaard's Writings*, XIV, Volume 14, 68–112.

[33] Kierkegaard, *Kierkegaard's Writings*, XIII, Volume 13, 220. Or also: "Certain phrases and observations circulate among the people, partly true and sensible, but devoid of vitality, but there is no hero, no lover, no thinker, no knight of faith, no great humanitarian, no person in despair to vouch for their validity by having primitively experienced them;" Kierkegaard, *Kierkegaard's Writings*, XIV, Volume 14, 129.

[34] For the argument that the default should be shifted back from retaining information forever to deleting it after some time, Mayer-Schönberger, *Delete*.

[35] Kahneman, *Thinking, Fast and Slow*, Part 5.

their ubiquitous possibilities for copying data. The combined force of the import-ance of repetition in human life and the enormous potential for generating repeti-tions of the pernicious sort support a moral right to the truth. That argument had to be balanced against the need for narratives (which inevitably involve an abundance of half-truths) to provide an orientation for people in the world. In the end, I submitted that no broad right to truth was forthcoming, not even as a way of protecting the public sphere. While the value of truth must be upheld in the public domain, the issues at stake do not normally straightforwardly translate into demands particular individuals can make.

By contrast, the combined force of the importance of repetition in life and the potential for generating repetitions of the pernicious sort in digital lifeworlds does support a right to be forgotten. Repetition of actual truths (rather than untruths) might become pernicious, in ways about which *specific persons* have legitimate complaints. This would be so if offensive or embarrassing actions from the past no longer have any predictive value for the present (and thus reveal nothing others legitimately should know) but continue to be in or are returned to circulation. Under appropriate circumstances, as a matter of protection their autonomy (which is the value with which I associated a right to be forgotten in the previous section) people should have an opportunity for a new beginning after engaging in inappro-priate behaviors. They have a human right to that effect.

Let me elaborate on why the combined force of the importance of repetition in human life and the enormous potential for generating repetitions of the pernicious sort ultimately fails to support a broad right to truth but *does* support a right to be forgotten. Reflecting on the different roles of *half-truths* in relation to these rights helps with this matter. In the context of a broad right to truth, half-truths are needed for valuable human purposes (since they are inevitably part of the narratives people devise and deploy to orient themselves in the world) – which outweighs that combined force. By contrast, in the context of a right to be forgotten, and thus in the context of a person's reputation, half-truths are *not* needed for any valuable human purposes. So, in this case, the combined force of the significance of repeti-tion in human life and the enormous potential for generating repetitions of the pernicious sort prevails, and we can have a right to be forgotten.

Still, competing considerations must be taken into account. Making it easier for people to lead lives untarnished by a reputation that does not shake certain occur-rences from the past should not involve falsification or distortion of history. But information about individuals that does not provide useful information for present matters should be considerably harder to find than information about tomorrow's weather or yesterday's police reports. And as we noted, there are potentially conflict-ing *rights* to be considered. How to do so is a matter for context-specific legal interpretation that will often have to resolve reasonable disagreement. But we have now laid out a moral case for a person's human right to have information about themselves removed from internet searches and other places that store information.

7.7 EPISTEMIC RIGHTS IN THE DIGITAL LIFEWORLDS OF LIFE 3.0

If a full-fledged Life 3.0 emerges, it will likely come from within digital lifeworlds. This stage might be populated by genetically enhanced humans, cyborgs, uploaded brains, and advanced algorithms embedded into any kind of physical device. Technologically or genetically unenhanced humans would be intellectually inferior to other inhabitants. Creatures from Life 2.0 would be unable to design their shapes and thus would also be inferior in terms of longevity and abilities to entities that are able to do so. The likely response would be for humanity to enhance itself, in a transhumanist spirit. This might well happen regardless of whether Life 3.0 emerges, as a response to improved technological capacities that create comparative advantages vis-à-vis other humans.[36]

Normative practices would change in Life 3.0. The new entities that human ingenuity will have made possible must be accorded a moral status all their own. New moral and legal standards must delineate the complex relationships among such entities.[37] Human rights must expand beyond protecting "each of us from the rest of us" to protecting "us from them," much as such protection should prevail conversely. As far as epistemic rights are concerned, we need a *right to the exercise of genuinely human intelligence*, to use the human mind with its power and limitations that reflect millions of years of evolution of organic life. Such a right needs to hold even as we are surrounded by intelligences vastly larger than ours. Again, I propose this right manifesto-style, aiming to establish its basic plausibility by way of two arguments.

The first argument draws on how new intelligences might regard and relate to us. In the extreme, new intelligences might extinguish us, as Stephen Hawking feared.[38] They will study us and come to mixed results, drawing on humanity's historical record and insights from fields like evolutionary psychology and anthropology. It is a reasonable guess that what they will find is in line with what Fyodor Dostoevsky found when he became a student of human nature, during several insufferable years in a Siberian camp as a political prisoner. Dostoevsky is celebrated for his profound insights into human nature, and we will profit from letting a quick account of his findings guide our discussion. In Siberia, Dostoevsky encountered humble and considerate people who nonetheless had perpetrated awful crimes. Treated with fraternal kindness by men capable of immense cruelty, Dostoevsky acquired a profound appreciation of the complexities of personhood. He realized that good and evil inclinations could

---

[36] On transhumanism, see Livingstone, *Transhumanism*; More and Vita-More, *The Transhumanist Reader*.

[37] For an exploration of possible arrangements among humans and artificial intelligences in Life 3.0, see Tegmark, *Life* 3.0, chapter 5.

[38] Cellan-Jones, "Stephen Hawking Warns Artificial Intelligence Could End Mankind." Such concerns are shared by Elon Musk, Martin Rees, and Eliezer Yudkowsky, among others. For a rebuttal, see Pinker, "Tech Prophecy." See also Bostrom, *Superintelligence*.

coexist, conditioning and constraining each other in the same person. He would later write several masterpieces to investigate human nature. Nikolai Vsevolodovich Stavrogin – the main character of his novel *Demons* – is among Dostoevsky's most sophisticated characters.[39] It is also true that Stavrogin rapes an eleven-year-old and drives her to kill herself, listening to the girl as she hangs herself.

Superintelligences will similarly see the mixed qualities of human nature (backed up by scientific inquiry).[40] So how would such entities possibly respect a right to exercise human intelligence? To begin with, these new entities would be designed by us, or anyway spring from technologies that emerged from digital lifeworlds. Despite its profound shortcomings, human intelligence and the larger context of organic life make synthetic intelligence possible. This might well be the foundation of a decent respect for human intelligence. Such respect, in turn, might generate support for certain protections and provisions for human beings, also as a way of keeping them from inflicting the kind of evil *on each other* that Stavrogin inflicted on that girl. At least, the fact that synthetic intelligence understands its derivation from intelligence that arose in an evolutionary process should trigger the observance of certain conduct with regard to this latter intelligence, one that would include acceptance of that aforementioned right. What is less clear is whether this line of reasoning could establish shared normative practices that would include an outright duty that such superintelligences would have directly *to* humans.[41]

Support for such an argument from respect comes from the recent secular meaning-of-life literature. The reasons philosophers have offered for why human life would not be pointless in a godless universe could also show that nonhuman life has reason to endorse a right to the exercise of a genuinely human intelligence. Let me make this second argument through some references to Bertrand Russell's celebrated 1903 article "A Free Man's Worship."[42]

Russell is a seminal figure in multiple areas of mathematics and philosophy. A classic contribution to the secular meaning-of-life literature, "A Free Man's Worship" is among his best-known pieces. It has done important work to establish the view that there is meaning to life – a justified sense of personal significance – even outside any kind of theistic framework. The purpose for which I deploy Russell's piece could be met in other ways. But there is a certain historical importance to this piece. And much as thinking about personal significance had to be

---

[39] Dostoevsky, *Demons*.

[40] A different way of making the same point is to say that the new intelligences would know the kind of thing about us that is recorded in Glover, *Humanity*.

[41] For some complexities in moral practices with regard to establishing claims between two actors, see Darwall, *The Second-Person Standpoint*. These complexities might take on new forms in the normative practices of Life 3.0.

[42] Russell, "A Free Man's Worship." The meaning of life concerns us again in Chapter 10.

unmoored from a theistic framework once, so discussions of moral entitlements might eventually have to be unmoored from the human contexts to which our normative practices have been largely confined so far. It is worth noticing that these two tasks can be met by the same set of ideas.

Russell takes account of the intrinsic meaninglessness of the physical universe to explore what this implies for comprehending the point of human existence. Advances in human understanding (especially progress in the natural sciences) undermined all thinking that sees us elevated in a metaphysical "great chain of being."[43] Nothing in or about the world can answer questions about point or purpose of life. We can provide these answers only from within ourselves, from an internal human standpoint. But we can indeed do this much because we have the kind of mind that allows us to do so. As Russell writes, in the heavy prose he used at the time:

> Man is yet free, during his brief years, to examine, to criticize, to know, and in imagination to create. To him alone, in the world with which he is acquainted, this freedom belongs; and in this lies his superiority to the resistless forces that control his outward life.

From a first-person standpoint, that is, we understand ourselves as having choices, and these choices involve the ability to assess the world critically. While this ability is itself a result of evolution (and of background physics), and the mind is reducible to the brain, there is a first-person perception of choice (i.e., the perception that we make decisions rather than do something that is predetermined through laws of nature). We can scientifically reduce that perception to brain operations, but we can opt to also take it at face value. A bit later we read the following, as an elaboration of what that first-person standpoint contains:

> In this lies Man's true freedom: in determination to worship only the God created by our own love of the good, to respect only the heaven which inspires the insight of our best moments. In action, in desire, we must submit perpetually to the tyranny of outside forces; but in thought, in aspiration, we are free, free from our fellow-men, free from the petty planet on which our bodies impotently crawl, free even, while we live, from the tyranny of death. Let us learn, then, that energy of faith which enables us to live constantly in the vision of the good; and let us descend, in action, into the world of fact, with that vision always before us.

And yet a bit later:

> The life of Man, viewed outwardly, is but a small thing in comparison with the forces of Nature. The slave is doomed to worship Time and Fate and Death, because they are greater than anything he finds in himself, and because all his

---

[43] On that theme, see Lovejoy, *The Great Chain of Being*.

thoughts are of things which they devour. But, great as they are, to think of them greatly, to feel their passionless splendor, is greater still. And such thought makes us free men ... To abandon the struggle for private happiness, to expel all eagerness of temporary desire, to burn with passion for eternal things – this is emancipation, and this is the free man's worship.[44]

Humans vis-à-vis each other, that is, can put their brains to work in ways that reflect that most things we care about (everything associated with human accomplishment) are grounded in *lifeworlds* of shared experience. We literally live the life of the mind: That the human brain enables that kind of life makes it an awesome thing worthy of respect, a respect due from *all* manner of intelligence.

Ronald Dworkin has echoed this thought, in a related context. His purpose is to articulate a secular understanding of sacredness, to show that the essential components of what religious people have aimed to express under the heading of sacredness can also be captured in secular ways.[45] Dworkin sees human life as the highest product of evolution, in the secular sense that it features enormous complexity, mental abilities, and self-awareness. In addition, each life reflects efforts of civilization, parental care, and so on. All of this should be enough to make human life valuable *intrinsically* (rather than merely instrumentally, for the sake of something else) and *objectively* (as opposed to merely subjectively, in a perspective-dependent manner). Human life *rightly* generates awe in us, both admiration and inspiration. This intrinsic and objective value of human life should suffice to generate a right to the exercise of genuinely human intelligence in the presence of more intelligent creatures. If we can successfully realize the epistemic rights that apply in the digital lifeworlds of Life 2.0 we will greatly support the flourishing of the life of the mind at this stage of life. We would thereby also demonstrate to maximal effect to other intelligent beings that might subsequently emerge how we are worthy of a right to the exercise of human intelligence in Life 3.0.

This section brought into view two arguments for why a right to the exercise of genuinely human intelligence is both appropriate and needed. The earlier argument draws on the fact that synthetic intelligence has been designed by human intelligence. That argument thus makes a claim explicitly based on a shared context in which one kind of intelligence *relates* to another in certain ways. By contrast, the second argument should appeal to any kind of intelligence, in principle also to an extraterrestrial intelligence not connected to us the way human-designed AI is. But here, too, the basic capacities of human beings should at least trigger the observance of certain conduct toward human intelligence (conduct that would include

[44] Russell, "A Free Man's Worship."
[45] Dworkin, *Life's Dominion*, chapter 3.

acceptance of a right to the exercise of genuinely human intelligence) if not an outright duty *to humans*.[46]

In contrast to China's efforts to upgrade its governance system to new technological heights, built around a stupefying amount of data collection and electronic scoring, countries committed to democracy and human rights have not upgraded their systems. It is vital for the ongoing relevance of those ideas about governance to perform such an upgrade. Protecting epistemic actorhood, in turn, is crucial to that project. The distinctively human life (which human rights protect) now increasingly unfolds in digital lifeworlds. Accordingly, interactions in the world society (in which global responsibilities arise to which human rights are one significant response) also increasingly involve or take place entirely in digital lifeworlds. A set of epistemic rights that strengthen existing human rights – as part of a fourth generation of human rights – is needed to protect epistemic actorhood in such lifeworlds. Democracy, too, occurs in digital lifeworlds and can flourish there only if citizens are protected as knowers and knowns, both individually and collectively (and here this chapter connects back to Chapter 3). Otherwise power, especially infopower, will be wielded by only a few.

If we do indeed progress into Life 3.0, we need a new kind of human right, one to the exercise of genuinely human intelligence. To the extent that we can substantiate the meaning of human life in the godless world science describes, we can also substantiate such a right vis-à-vis artificial intelligence. If it comes to that, we must hope that such arguments can persuade a superior intelligence, and thus that such an intelligence might even be willing to participate in shared normative practices with others (rather than just concede certain protections and provisions to us, *if that*). But such intelligence, by definition, would be beyond ours, and thus is hard for us to anticipate. We return to Life 3.0 in Chapter 11.

---

[46] The point is not to ascribe to humanity an absolute value, as often associated with the Kantian tradition with the centrality it gives to dignity. For Kantians humans have "dignity," in the sense that they are "ends in themselves," because they are capable of necessitation, and so of morality. ("Morality is the condition under which alone a rational being can be an end in itself," Kant says in the *Groundwork of the Metaphysics of Morals*, 4:435; also Kant, *Practical Philosophy*, 37–108.) We treat others as ends in themselves if we recognize this capacity in them and act accordingly. For a defense of such a view in the context of human rights, see Rosen, *Dignity*. On these topics, also see Theunissen, *The Value of Humanity*. Instead of an absolute view, Theunissen articulates a nuanced relational view of that value that avoids complications that support for its absolute value would face. "People are of value because we are constituted in such a way that we are able to be good for ourselves in the sense that we are able to lead flourishing lives;" Theunissen, 2. We are good for ourselves insofar as our capacity to value enables us to lead good lives. That is something other intelligences could also see (and we do not have to appeal to an absolute value of humanity to make this point).

8

On Surveillance Capitalism, Instrumentarian Power, and Social Physics

Securing the Enlightenment for Digital Lifeworlds

Private property has made us so stupid and narrow-minded that an object is only ours when we have it, when it exists as capital for us or when we directly possess, eat, drink, wear, inhabit it, etc.

— Karl Marx[1]

8.1 INTRODUCTION: KANT AND THE MACHINES

Immanuel Kant's 1784 essay "What is Enlightenment?" offers a famous answer to his title question: Enlightenment is emergence from a mindset in which one refuses to exercise one's capacities for thinking and takes guidance from others instead.[2] "If I have a book that understands for me," Kant explains, "a spiritual advisor who has a conscience for me, a doctor who decides upon a regimen for me, and so forth, I need not trouble myself at all." He continues, "I need not think, if only I can pay; others will readily undertake the irksome business for me."[3] Articulating the significance of and the strains in developing one's *individuality*, Kant offers an influential account of what enlightenment is (and so of what the eponymous era is about). "What is Enlightenment?" is a paradigmatic text of a period that is arguably still ongoing, in which free development of one's personality is a much-praised goal. That goal is also essential to the human rights movement. Safeguarding the goals of the Enlightenment is always challenging, especially so in digital lifeworlds.

[1] McLellan, *Karl Marx: Selected Writings*, 100.
[2] Kant, *Practical Philosophy*, 16–22. This would be quoted as "Kant, 8:33–42" according to volume and page numbers of the standard edition of Kant's works. I capitalize "Enlightenment" when talking about the period and not when talking about this process.
[3] Kant, 8:35. There are interesting parallels to Marx's discussion of money in his *Economic and Philosophical Manuscripts*; see McLellan, *Karl Marx: Selected Writings*, 118–21. Section 3 discusses that passage.

Independent thinking is easily thwarted by those who provide advice for a living, the professional class. Their standing depends on wielding influence that way. One way to show independence of mind is to stand up to this professional class: Kant praises thinkers who go against the grain. But even for Kant, the champion of this ideal, independent thinking is a difficult ideal. For the societies he is familiar with – the kind that is nowhere near the full realization of enlightenment ideals – Kant does not recommend independent thinking across the board, at least not the kind that translates into action. After all, the community is a "machine" that requires rule-following to remain functional.[4] The word "machine" reappears at the very end of the essay. Once society has not only broadly adopted the ideal of independence of mind but also reached a high level of maturity, this ideal is no longer overruled or even qualified by the societal need to remain functional. And then, but only then, Kant says, individuals will be *"more than a machine."* And at this later stage, it behooves the government to treat people in accordance with their dignity (whereas at earlier stages, the government would presumably need to consider that many citizens remain rather immature).[5]

So Kant deploys the term "machine" with two related meanings: one on the political and economic system in which people operate, and the other on the contrast between following along and thinking for oneself. The relationship between these uses – which draws our attention to the difficulties around the ideal of independence of mind – seems to be this: When individuals are mature enough to think for themselves, they also can exercise their judgment as to when they should or should not oppose prevailing norms. In this way, they become importantly different from machines. Once this happens, one does not need to worry about people exercising their intellectual independence in ways that undermine the smooth functioning of state or society. And because this is no longer a worry, one also does not need to actively curtail the exercise of people's judgment out of fear that public life would otherwise founder through the pigheadedness and recalcitrance of immature individuals. In other words, intellectual maturity means for people to be unlike machines in ways that, their independence of mind notwithstanding, do not undermine the functionality of state and society.

While our era continues to celebrate individuality, we live in digital lifeworlds structured around electronic devices and numerically coded information. Especially the advent of AI makes it simultaneously more real and more problematic than Kant presumably meant it when he said that we are small parts of a large machine, one that increasingly tries to do the thinking *for us* and to extract information *from us* in pursuit of commercial gains. After all, one thing this machine does now is to collect humungous amounts of data about us to influence decision-making. Such

---

[4] Kant, *Practical Philosophy*, 8:37.
[5] Kant, 8:42. Emphasis is in the original.

practices have assumed such importance that Shoshana Zuboff has coined the term "surveillance capitalism" for this stage of capitalism.[6]

Kant worried about threats to individuality – by which he typically meant a person's ability to develop their personality through learning and thinking – from books or professionals. Today we must worry about our independence especially vis-à-vis surveillance. Surveillance embodies a powerful social-scientific, philosophical, and engineering outlook that encourages dismissive and even hostile attitudes toward individuality. What characterizes that outlook (and thus shapes surveillance capitalism) is the desire to exercise what Zuboff calls "instrumentarian power": power that aims to predict, modify, and monetize behavior through multifarious data-collection devices and the creation of a mentality that unhesitatingly commodifies human experience. Instead of civic or emancipatory purposes, surveillance capitalism pursues commercial ones.

My first (and primary) goal here is to discuss how surveillance capitalism in digital lifeworlds threatens the ideal of individuality and what it takes to secure the Enlightenment for digital lifeworlds. Kant offers a celebrated discussion of individuality. To get individuality, its various meanings, and its relevance for our age into focus, Section 8.2 starts with a less well-known but even more illuminating essay on individuality by Émile Durkheim. Our encounter with Durkheim also allows me to introduce his famous notion of "social facts," of which I make ample use in Chapter 9.

Section 8.3 explores Zuboff's notions of surveillance capitalism and instrumentarian power to capture ways in which the individualism that Durkheim praises is under siege. Zuboff traces instrumentarian power to B. F. Skinner's radical behaviorism and identifies computer scientist Alex Pentland as a major contemporary representative. Section 8.4 introduces Skinner's radical behaviorism and what Pentland calls "social physics," the deployment of quantitative social science in our age of Big Data to shape society. Section 8.5 explores what can be done in response to these divergent assessments of the current trajectory of the digital age, and thus what it takes to secure the Enlightenment for digital lifeworlds. My answer draws on Chapter 3 (which discusses democracy) and Chapter 7 (epistemic rights/human rights).

With that account in place, this chapter turns to its second goal, to argue that an assignment of rights by itself cannot secure the Enlightenment for digital lifeworlds, but that solutions must give prominence to structural considerations that make democracy and justice central. We have already talked a lot about both democracy and justice, especially epistemic justice. Section 8.6 addresses readers who nonetheless entertain the idea that rights, especially human rights, offer a plausible normative vision *partly because* such rights render further-reaching discussions of democracy and justice superfluous or misguided. That is, according to such a view, a set of rights is all that a plausible ideal of a good society requires, and reflection on democracy and justice beyond a purely rights-based view would merely add

---

[6]   Zuboff, *The Age of Surveillance Capitalism.*

demands that then also go beyond what is warranted – a view that might be attractive to people who fear they have much to lose from such additional demands. We discuss this material here because it completes our discussion of epistemic rights while also setting the stage for a chapter on matters of justice.

Perhaps few readers hold the view I just mentioned (and if they do, it will presumably at least not *consciously* be because they have much to lose from such additional demands). Still, one factor that arguably explains the success of the human rights movement *in a neoliberal age* is that, in the eyes of many (especially those with much to lose through further-reaching changes), human rights offer *enough* of a normative vision for the world for which no further-reaching structural considerations around democracy or justice are needed.[7] So it is useful to have arguments as to why rights are *not enough*. To that end, I turn to some long-standing concerns about rights from the Marxist tradition, drawing on Max Horkheimer and Theodor W. Adorno's *Dialectic of Enlightenment*. Their criticism of the Enlightenment in terms of the instrumentalization of reason dovetails with Zuboff's account of instrumentarian power, a connection that by itself is worth acknowledging. The digital age, with its omnipresence of surveillance, makes it very difficult to live up to Kant's ideal of intellectual maturity, an ideal that envisages for people to possess genuine independence of mind while also remaining contributors to society. For that ideal to be realized at a broader scale, we need to have ideals of democracy and justice in place in addition to rights.

8.2 DURKHEIM'S PRAISE FOR INDIVIDUALISM

To get the Enlightenment ideal of individualism more into focus, let us discuss Émile Durkheim's 1898 essay "Individualism and the Intellectuals," which articulates the enduring importance of individualism for modern societies.[8] Setting the stage for sociology as a field, Durkheim's work revolves around the study of "social facts," a term he coined to describe phenomena that are not tied to actions of individuals but have a compelling influence on them. We need social facts to explain social phenomena. Durkheim talks about a collective consciousness – a mindset that members of a society share, at least in some rough way – that forms the moral basis of society and creates integration. While individuals produce collective consciousness through interaction, that consciousness produces society and holds it together.

Durkheim explores not only how religion sustains such consciousness, but also how societies can remain cohesive once traditional social and religious ties vanish. A main feature of modern societies is the significance ascribed to *the individual*. At the center of rituals that tie societies together, individuals are bearers of rights and

---

[7] As articulated by Moyn, *Not Enough*.
[8] Lukes, "Durkheim's 'Individualism and the Intellectuals.'" For Durkheim's work overall, see Lukes, *Emile Durkheim*; Alexander and Smith, *The Cambridge Companion to Durkheim*.

responsibilities. Individualism is a central social fact in modern societies. There is an outright cult of the individual. Instead of there being a fundamental antagonism between individuals and society, that cult is a product of society and the very glue that holds it together.

Durkheim wrote during the Dreyfus affair, a political scandal around the sentencing of a Jewish officer, Alfred Dreyfus, that divided France for years after 1894. Part of that conflict was a dispute between the French army and its champions, who saw themselves as stalwarts of stability and tradition (insisting that the word of high-ranking officers condemning Dreyfus remain unquestioned), and parts of the intellectual class, who defended standards of evidence and due process. Intellectuals were accused of being "individualistic," unwilling to play their proper social roles by resisting traditional sources of authority. It was in response to this charge that Durkheim wrote his essay, not only in defense of an appropriately understood individualism (reclaiming the term for a position with positive connotations) but also to insist on its foundational relevance for the modern age.[9]

Durkheim defends an individualism that he traces to Kant, but also to Jean-Jacques Rousseau (who wrote a bit earlier than Kant and had much influence on Kant's thinking), placing himself in the tradition of "What is Enlightenment?" Durkheim traces another version of individualism to utilitarianism but associates it with a deplorable egoism that is merely aggregated if collective decisions are made that way. The kind of individualism Durkheim considers himself to be defending – according to which each person should be in a position to develop their own personality with its capacities for reason while being protected not only in these efforts but also in their ability to make a living – is the kind that he thinks the 1789 French Declaration of the Rights of Man and of the Citizen translates "into formulae."[10] What Kant and Rousseau share and Durkheim endorses is the view that moral agency amounts to acting in ways "fitting for all men equally, that is to say, which are implied in the notion of man in general." Accordingly, "the human person . . . is considered sacred," capturing the kind of "transcendental majesty which the churches of all times have given to their Gods."[11] Humanity – as it exists in each person equally – is sacred and worthy of respect in light of the rational capacities inherent in everyone.

Such individualism amounts to a kind of religion "of which man is, at the same time, both believer and God," a "cult of which he is at once both object and follower, which does not address itself to the particular being that constitutes himself and carries his name, but to the human person, wherever he is to be found, and in whatever form it is incarnated."[12] More traditional views of religion or codes of ethics

[9]   For the history of the word "individualism" in English, see Claeys, "'Individualism,' 'Socialism,' and 'Social Science.'" For a comparative perspective across countries, see Lukes, *Individualism*, Part I. The political and moral connotations of this term have varied greatly.
[10]   Lukes, "Durkheim's 'Individualism and the Intellectuals,'" 21.
[11]   Lukes, 21.
[12]   Lukes, 22f.

increasingly fail to bind people, lacking resources to persuade sprawling populations in ever more different lines of work. "The communion of minds can no longer form around particular rites and prejudices," Durkheim explains, "since rites and prejudices have been swept away in the natural course of things. In consequence, there remains nothing that men may love and honor in common, apart from man himself."[13]

Accordingly, any individual who defends the rights of one person also defends the vital interests of society as such, "for he is preventing the criminal impoverishment of that final reserve of collective ideas and sentiments that constitute the very soul of the nation," much as Roman citizens safeguarded their rites against reckless innovators.[14] Individualism is a social product, much as those rites were. What Kant and Rousseau failed to grasp, however, is that "the individual receives from society even the moral beliefs which deify him." Instead, these earlier thinkers tried to deduce an individualist ethic from the notion of the isolated individual – the idea that the moral value assigned to individualism is so assigned by each person on their own – which Durkheim thought entailed logical difficulties. In other words, Kant and Rousseau failed to grasp the extent to which individualism was a *social fact*.[15]

Durkheim rebuts a response by conservative detractors that such individualism contradicts Christianity. On the contrary, he argues that Christianity was "the first to teach that the moral value of actions must be measured in accordance with intention, which is essentially private, escapes all external judgments and which only the agent can competently judge."[16] Individuals thereby became judges of their conduct, absent others who could perform that task. In addition, the separation of the transcendent world from the present world and the former's superiority opened the latter to scientific inquiry with accompanying standards of freedom of thought: After all, the transcendent world is the eternal world, but it is also a world we cannot readily observe but must inquire about in other ways – and once the pertinent kind of inquiry is encouraged, that same kind of inquiry or related forms also have much to teach us about the present world. Accordingly, individualistic morality is not antagonistic to Christian morality but rather its continuation in times when Christianity's ritualistic and metaphysical prescriptions have lost persuasive force. As far as Durkheim is concerned, the Enlightenment descends from Christianity.

Durkheim's discussion is many things: an assertion of the role of social facts for the foundations of moral practices versus philosophical argumentation; a deeply searching analysis of the foundations of at least European societies shaped by a Christian past in which seemingly divergent viewpoints ultimately still derive from the same mindset (which leads to questions about how broadly applicable that

---

[13] Lukes, 26.
[14] Lukes, 27f.
[15] Lukes, 28, footnote 1.
[16] Lukes, 27.

analysis is globally); and also a piece that reveals that "individualism" is hardly one concise position but a family of views. It is unsurprising that it would be Steven Lukes (who did much to bring Durkheim's work, including the essay we are discussing, to greater prominence in English-speaking countries) who also provided a classic study of individualism.[17]

Lukes has analyzed the breadth of what is covered under "individualism," organizing that domain around four "unit-ideas": respect for human dignity, autonomy, privacy, and self-development.[18] These ideas feature prominently in moral and political positions ranging from romanticism to existentialism, from Rousseau and Kant's ideas of a morality grounded in individual reason to radical ideas of personal freedom captured under "rugged individualism," from social-contract theories to social Darwinism, from various versions of liberalism and libertarianism to anarchism, and from humanism to ethical egoism. Many philosophical ideas meet in these four unit-ideas, which shows that the Enlightenment is a broad movement.

Still, this breadth does not render individualism so broad that just about everybody could subscribe to it, in any event not in any version that Durkheim too could endorse. In his book *Beyond Good and Evil* (which we encountered in Chapter 4) Nietzsche explores the role of religion in human life. There he says that "ordinary men" – "the majority of people" – merely "exist for service and general utility, and are only so far entitled to exist."[19] Such a view is compatible with an elitist version of individualism (one that limits praise of individual virtues to a select few); meanwhile, it stands opposed to any "cult" of the individual that could become a Durkheimian social fact.

Nietzsche's anti-Durkheimian view remains relevant today, as a reference point in our discussion. For, in fact, one way of thinking of Shoshana Zuboff's critical assessment of surveillance capitalism in digital lifeworlds is that it treats people as if they existed "for service and general utility." In the commercial context that she discusses, this means something more subtle and refined than the cruel scenario Nietzsche presumably envisaged. (After all, surveillance capitalism does not stand accused of implying that anyone's very "entitlement to exist" is limited to their having general utility.) But both commercialization of experience and efforts at directing people's thinking to facilitate further commercialization do treat humans as mere instruments for enrichment. Such a system would be in violation of any plausible articulation of what respect for human dignity, autonomy, privacy, and self-development involve.

Recall from Chapter 1 how we characterize digital lifeworlds:[20] They are *pervasive* in that ever more devices complete tasks while linked to the Internet; *connective* in

---

[17] Lukes, *Individualism*.
[18] Lukes, Part II.
[19] Nietzsche, *Beyond Good and Evil*, section 61.
[20] Drawing on Susskind, *Future Politics*, chapters 1–2.

letting people in far-flung locations interact more or less instantly; *sensitive* in that sensors trace ever more things and information; *constitutive* in that machines are essential to our reality, rather than representing cyber add-ons to a life otherwise focused; and *immersive* by offering more and more augmented or virtual reality to supplement and enrich the physical reality we inhabit with our bodies. Such an environment creates enormous possibilities for individuals, among other things by furthering individualism's four "unit-ideas." But such an environment also enables all the mechanisms that threaten the sheer possibility of implementing these ideas in people's lives. We must therefore ask how the Enlightenment itself can be secured for digital lifeworlds.

8.3 SURVEILLANCE CAPITALISM AND INSTRUMENTARIAN POWER

In the US legal tradition, a right to privacy was introduced in an 1890 article by attorneys Samuel Warren and Louis Brandeis.[21] Anxieties around intrusion into what people consider to be nobody else's business have presumably been around for as long as humans have. Over time, technology has massively increased possibilities for intrusion. Unsurprisingly, the two jurists investigated the "right to be let alone" in light of intrusions by "mechanical devices." One such device was the printing press, with the newspaper circulations and journalistic practices it had enabled over time. But there also were more recent inventions: cameras corresponding to the state of photography at the time, and the telephone.

So the articulation of privacy concerns as a legal matter was triggered by late nineteenth-century technological advances. Decades later, in 1928, Brandeis was serving as Associate Justice on the Supreme Court. In a dissenting opinion, he writes that "the progress of science in furnishing the Government with means of espionage is not likely to stop with wiretapping." In fact, he continues presciently, "ways may someday be developed by which the Government, without removing papers from secret drawers, can reproduce them in court, and by which it will be enabled to expose to a jury the most intimate occurrences of the home."[22] More generally, much of the history of the United States can be told as a story of anxieties about privacy.[23] Or to connect to the previous section, the history of a country much committed to individualism in numerous guises can also be told as a history of anxiety about the underlying unit-ideas of individualism. Eventually there were debates around privacy explicitly in terms of surveillance; for instance, there were already debates around "data surveillance" in the 1960s. These and other debates

---

[21] Warren and Brandeis, "The Right to Privacy."
[22] Brandeis wrote this as part of a dissenting opinion in *Olmstead v United States*, 277 U.S. 438 (1928), a case in which the government illegally wiretapped a suspected bootlegger.
[23] See Igo, *The Known Citizen*. Igo discusses the Warren/Brandeis article in chapter 1.

represented a reckoning with the place of records in American life.[24] And in a 2021 publication, legal scholar Neil Richards defines privacy right away in terms of the vocabulary that is foundational to the digital age: *"Privacy is the degree to which human information is neither known nor used,"* thereby declaring "information privacy" to be the central issue of our time to be covered under the heading of "privacy" (in contrast in particular to "spatial privacy").[25]

Zuboff's *Age of Surveillance Capitalism* investigates surveillance and its implications for the digital age. She explores a "rogue mutation of capitalism marked by concentrations of wealth, knowledge, and power unprecedented in human history."[26] Surveillance capitalism is "a new economic order that claims human experience as free raw material for hidden commercial practices of extraction, prediction, and sales."[27] Its mechanism is the digital capture of online (and increasingly offline) human experience for commercial exploitation and later both the modification and outright control of behavior.[28]

To grasp the problem's nature and magnitude, consider how Marx characterizes the kind of commodification he thinks is typical of capitalist societies generically. The following is from Marx's discussion "On Money" in his 1844 *Economic and Philosophical Manuscripts*:

> What I have thanks to money, what I pay for, i.e., what money can buy, that is what I, the possessor of the money, am myself. My power is as great as the power of money. The properties of money are my – (its owner's) properties and faculties. Thus what I am and what I am capable of is by no means determined by my individuality. I am ugly, but I can buy myself the most beautiful women. Consequently, I am not ugly, for the effect of ugliness, its power of repulsion, is annulled by money. As an individual I am lame, but money can create twenty-four feet for me; so I am not lame; I am a wicked, dishonest man without conscience or intellect, but money is honored and so also is its possessor. Money is the highest good, so its possessor is good. Money relieves me of the trouble of being dishonest; so I am presumed to be honest. I may have no intellect, but money is the true mind of all things and so how should its possessor have no intellect? Moreover, he can buy himself intellectuals and is not the man who has power over intellectuals not

---

[24] Igo, chapter 6. For philosophical issues around privacy, see DeCrew, "Privacy." For pioneering work on privacy in the digital age, see Nissenbaum, *Privacy in Context*. For the recent legal debate in the United States, see Richards, *Why Privacy Matters*. See also Hartzog, *Privacy's Blueprint*. For important discussions of privacy from before digital lifeworlds took over, see Thomson, "The Right to Privacy"; Rachels, "Why Privacy Is Important." For current challenges in the United States, see Shattuck, Raman, and Risse, *Holding Together*, chapter 15.

[25] Richards, *Why Privacy Matters*, 22. Emphasis is in the original.

[26] Zuboff, *The Age of Surveillance Capitalism*, vii.

[27] Zuboff, vii.

[28] On surveillance from a virtue-ethics standpoint, see Vallor, *Technology and the Virtues*, chapter 8.

more intellectual than they? I who can get with money everything that the human heart longs for, do I not possess all human capacities? Does not my money thus change all my incapacities into their opposite?[29]

So among the basic features and fundamental evils of capitalism is that money determines what people can *do* and *be* to begin with. Relationships among and the status of people in capitalism are bound up with money. Relationship and status might not be for sale the way supermarket items are. But what people do to maintain relationships and to respond to status directly or indirectly reflects how much money is associated with them. Relationships and status thereby do turn into commodities (something with a market value of sorts) and are commercialized (exchanged in ways that generate monetary value).

This much is long-standing leftist criticism of capitalism for the centrality it bestows upon ownership, especially ownership of means of production. What the critique of *surveillance* capitalism adds is that increasingly the *totality* of human experience is becoming commodified and commercialized, through surveillance by multifarious electronic devices or through inferences about behavior enabled by data-mining techniques. The harm caused thereby is both unique and irreducible to what is happening to specific individuals or groups. It implicates the very "stuff of human nature."[30]

Google is to surveillance capitalism what Ford and General Motors were to mass production. Facebook, Amazon, and others subsequently adopted Google's economic model. Increasing data collection and its commercial use "destroyed the reciprocities of its original social contract with users."[31] Users click on items or links on platforms, in a certain order and at a certain speed. Until roughly 2002, Google used data generated by such acts of use to improve speed, relevance, and accuracy or to launch ancillary services such as translation. Subsequently, surveillance capitalism involved first a more comprehensive appropriation of what is known as "behavioral surplus," then the creation of predictive products, and finally the implementation of behavioral modification for the sake of control and monetization.

Behavioral surplus is a byproduct of interactions with multifarious devices, from phones and self-tracking devices to social-media interfaces and smart-home tools (a new kind of social fact drawing on a different kind of interactions, as one might say). Usage records track communications but also movement, domestic habits, sleep patterns, and physical conditions. The more of this byproduct there is, the more such a surplus permits ever more detailed assessments of behavior. Over time, the number of devices that generate usage records has risen enormously. Machine learning takes this yield as input to generate products that forecast what people feel, think, or do.

[29] McLellan, *Karl Marx: Selected Writings*, 118.
[30] Zuboff, *The Age of Surveillance Capitalism*, 94.
[31] Zuboff, 88.

Surveillance capitalism involves a distinctive type of power, "instrumentarian" power. Zuboff defines it as "instrumentation and instrumentalization for the purposes of modification, prediction, monetization, and control."[32] "Instrumentation" characterizes an ensemble of instruments, such as musical instruments in an orchestra or measurement devices on a plane. For Zuboff, instrumentation is "the ubiquitous connected material architecture of sensate computation that renders, interprets, and actuates human experience."[33] It is the ensemble of devices used in surveillance. Expounding her definition, Zuboff talks about "puppets" and "puppet masters," where the puppets are the devices just mentioned, and the masters are those who deploy them. "Instrumentalization" normally denotes the process of using something as means to some end. For Zuboff, it denotes "the social relations that orient the puppet masters to human experience as surveillance capitalism wields the machines to transform us into means to others' market ends."[34] Instrumentalization captures the essence of the relationships that prevail in this mode of capitalism, which are so means-end oriented that the deployment of devices to monetize experience becomes acceptable.

Instrumentarian power, accordingly, is power exercised through use of such devices in an environment that renders the widespread deployment of these tools acceptable to harvest profits. Zuboff contrasts instrumentarian with totalitarian power as understood by Arendt through multiple lenses.[35] First, the *central metaphor* in totalitarian power is Big Brother, the all-encompassing power of the state. In instrumentarian power, it is Big Other, the digital apparatus (largely provided by relatively few companies) that accompanies us throughout the day, syphoning off data about everything we do. The *goal* of totalitarian power is full possession: It aims for a scenario where it faces no obstacles that it cannot circumvent. For instrumentarian power, it is complete certainty, the unfailing capacity to predict what people will do or think or say next.

To continue with the comparisons, the *locus* of totalitarian power is control of means of violence, thus preventing opposition from representing an obstacle; that of instrumentarian power is the division of learning in society, thus preventing citizens from obtaining enough knowledge and mental independence to escape from the prescriptions provided. Instrumentarian power obtains certainty by availing itself of the full range of learning in society. The *means* of totalitarianism lie in administrative capacities; those of instrumentarian power lie in ownership of means of behavioral modification ("instrumentation"). The *foundational mechanism* of the former is terror; of the latter, it is dispossession of behavioral surplus. The *ideological style* in the totalitarian case is a political religion since what matters is profound

---

[32] Zuboff, 352. Italics in the original.
[33] Zuboff, 252.
[34] Zuboff, 352.
[35] Arendt, *The Origins of Totalitarianism*.

allegiance. In the instrumentarian case, it is radical indifference since the aim is monetization. Finally, the *core social process* in totalitarianism is in-group/out-group differentiation to reinforce obedience. In the instrumentarian case, it is creation of a hive mind to generate predictability.[36]

As Marx wrote in his *Economic and Philosophical Manuscripts* (an excerpt I also use as epigraph to this chapter),

> Private property has made us so stupid and narrow-minded that an object is only ours when we have it, when it exists as capital for us or when we directly possess, eat, drink, wear, inhabit it, etc. In short, when we use it.[37]

The core of the alienation – the sense that one lives in a society whose workings one cannot comprehend and that do not even aim to meet one's needs or values – that capitalism generates lies in the centrality of private ownership. Where private ownership is central to the economic system (most importantly, of course, private ownership in the means of production) and to the political system (whose institutions are busy protecting people's private holdings) possibilities of human flourishing *other than* what can be monetized are neglected across the board. It is in this sense that private property makes us stupid. As discussed in Chapter 2, a century after Marx, Herbert Marcuse argued that capitalism, technology, and entertainment align to create forms of social control to make people complacent.[38] Zuboff's analysis of instrumentarian power develops these themes for surveillance capitalism.

The specific evil of *surveillance* capitalism is usurpation of control over data about people's lives. Zuboff talks about domination, dispossession, expropriation, and robbery.[39] Surveillance capitalism deprives us of "the life-sustaining inwardness, born in sanctuary, that finally distinguishes us from the machines."[40] The instrumentarian power that surveillance capitalism involves aims to predict and modify behavior. If the advertising we see reflects our (predicted) preferences, we can give up the irksome business of thinking for ourselves and instead follow along, taking guidance from others. If the media targeted at us entrench our attitudes, assuring us of what to believe, then we need not think. When we are small parts of a large machine that increasingly tries to do the thinking for us and to extract information from us in pursuit of commercial gains, our decision-making is influenced and independent thinking is thwarted.

Surveillance capitalism threatens each of Lukes's four unit-ideas of individualism. Commodifying the totality of human experience (as free raw material for hidden commercial practices of extraction, prediction, and sales) and treating humans as mere instruments for enrichment undermines *respect for human dignity* and the

---

[36] Zuboff, *The Age of Surveillance Capitalism*, chapter 13.
[37] McLellan, *Karl Marx: Selected Writings*, 100.
[38] Marcuse, *One-Dimensional Man*.
[39] Respectively, Zuboff, *The Age of Surveillance Capitalism*, 10, 100, 128, 158.
[40] Zuboff, 492.

sacredness of the person articulated by Durkheim. Efforts to direct people's thinking to facilitate further commercialization and the outright control of behavior violate *autonomy*. The capture of online (and increasingly offline) human experience and the dispossession of detailed assessments of behavior by individuals whose experiences have been captured erodes (if not eliminates) our *privacy*. (Recall Neil Richards's definition: *"Privacy is the degree to which human information is neither known nor used"*; under surveillance capitalism, this degree is rather low.) And the manipulation of the information we see and of our ways of engaging with that information warps the free development of one's personality: one's *self-development*. Surveillance capitalism, that is, is dramatically at odds with what the Enlightenment is all about. To the extent that digital lifeworlds nurture surveillance capitalism, the continuation of the Enlightenment in such lifeworlds becomes questionable.[41]

8.4 RADICAL BEHAVIORISM, SOCIAL PHYSICS, AND THE "DEATH OF INDIVIDUALITY"

Zuboff traces the intellectual roots of surveillance capitalism to B. F. Skinner's "radical behaviorism." For Skinner, humans are controlled by their environment and genes. Contrary to the views of Freud and many others, Skinner's perspective is that appeals to "inner" notions are unnecessary (and useless) to explain behavior. If society wishes to improve collective habits, it must change people's environment through social engineering. Skinner's 1971 *Beyond Freedom and Dignity* is a wide-ranging engagement with philosophical ideas about the kind of individualism Durkheim defends. Skinner argues for a more orderly structuring of society than what happens if people get to make their own choices – which not only often do not work out on people's own terms but also create undesirable outcomes at the social level. Such more orderly structuring requires a "technology of behavior."[42]

Moral vocabulary, such as "freedom," "autonomy," or "dignity," offers mere placeholders for actual explanations of behavior. We customarily explain, praise, or criticize action in such terms, but should cease to do so once better explanations reveal how environmental or genetic factors cause actions. For instance, we recognize someone's dignity or worth when praising them for something they do. The credit we give, Skinner submits, is inversely proportional to the *conspicuousness* of the causes of a person's behavior: The more it is obvious how someone was influenced to act in certain ways, the more we are inclined to explain their behavior in terms of that influence, and the less we are inclined to praise or blame them – and

---

[41] For intellectual resistance to the idea that "privacy is dead," see Richards, *Why Privacy Matters*, chapter 3. "Privacy isn't dying," he writes, "but claims of its decline mask the real issue, which is that the content of privacy rules—the rules that govern our human information—are very much up for grabs;" Richards, 108.

[42] Skinner, *Beyond Freedom and Dignity*, 10. What he has in mind is illustrated in Skinner, *Walden Two*.

vice versa. If we cannot otherwise explain a person's behavior, we attribute it *to them*, deluding ourselves into thinking that we have achieved some level of understanding.[43] As long as we find such attributions satisfactory, we will fail to investigate how modifications of the environment could improve behavior. But humans can reach full potential only with the assistance of a technology of behavior. The only alternative to embracing this technology is for our poor choices to destroy us and the environment.

A technology of behavior requires us to radically reassess our moral vocabulary.[44] In this process, Skinner explains,

> What is being abolished is autonomous man, the inner man, the homunculus, the possessing demon, the man defended by the literatures of freedom and dignity. His abolition has long been overdue. Autonomous man is a device used to explain what we cannot explain in any other way. He has been constructed from our ignorance, and as our understanding increases, the very stuff of which he is composed vanishes. Science does not dehumanize man, it de-homunculizes him, and it must do so if it is to prevent the abolition of the human species. . . . Only then can we turn from the inferred to the observed, from the miraculous to the natural, from the inaccessible to the manipulable.[45]

For instance, freedom according to radical behaviorism is not about a state of mind, as champions of "inner" notions claim. It is about inhabiting a well-structured environment. Contrary to Durkheim's view, we should abandon individuality as an ideal. But "is man then 'abolished'?" Skinner asks. Continuing the passage just quoted, he responds, "Certainly not as a species or as an individual achiever. It is the autonomous inner man who is abolished, and that is a step forward."[46] Based on his analysis, Skinner ends on a note of optimism: "A scientific view of man offers exciting possibilities. We have not yet seen what man can make of man."[47]

Skinner questions our quotidian ways of making sense of ourselves and each other, as well as established legal patterns based on these ways. Radical behaviorism rejects much established psychology and was not received favorably by many in the discipline.[48] Nonetheless, for Zuboff, Skinner's once-reviled views define the frontier of instrumentarian power.[49] Among the contemporary champions of (at least some key aspects of) Skinner's approach is computer scientist Alex Pentland, who became known for his pathbreaking work on wearable computing and subsequently focused on "social physics." As Zuboff argues, Pentland

---

[43] Skinner, *Beyond Freedom and Dignity*, 61.

[44] Skinner, *Walden Two*.

[45] Skinner, *Beyond Freedom and Dignity*, 196.

[46] Skinner, 210.

[47] Skinner, 210.

[48] One example is Noam Chomsky's negative assessment of Skinner's scientific outlook; see, for example, Chomsky, "A Review of B. F. Skinner's 'Verbal Behavior.'"

[49] Zuboff, *The Age of Surveillance Capitalism*, 431.

"completes" Skinner, fulfilling his social vision with big data, ubiquitous digital instrumentation, advanced mathematics, sweeping theory ... and corporate friends without having attracted the worldwide backlash, moral revulsion and naked vitriol once heaped on Harvard's outspoken behaviorist.[50]

Social physics traces mathematical connections between information and behavior. Quantitative social science illuminates how ideas are spread through mechanisms of social learning and how this flow shapes norms, productivity, and creative output of firms, cities, and whole societies. Subsequently, we can predict productivity and tune communication networks to improve decision-making.[51] Echoing Skinner (whom he does not mention), Pentland writes that we have come to realize "that human behavior is determined as much by social context as by rational thinking or individual desires ... Both people's desires and their decisions about how to act are often, and perhaps typically, dominated by social network effects."[52] Writing in 2015, Pentland is enthusiastic about possibilities generated by Big Data and the analytical tools constitutive of social physics:

> In just a few short years we are likely to have incredibly rich data available about the behavior of virtually all of humanity – on a continuous basis. The data mostly already exists in our networks, credit card databases, and elsewhere, but currently only technical gurus have access to it. As they become more widely available for scientific inquiry, however, the new science of social physics will gain further momentum. And once we develop a more precise visualization of human life, we can hope to understand and manage our modern society in ways better suited to our complex, interconnected network of humans and technology.[53]

Some years before the world got hit by COVID-19, one of Pentland's common examples is pandemics, which could become more manageable through social physics. We could also avoid financial clashes, use resources more wisely, and so on. In Skinnerian spirit, Pentland states that

> because modern culture puts so much emphasis on independence and personal choice, it is often difficult to realize that it is a *good* thing that most of our life is highly patterned, and that we are all quite similar rather than being completely different individuals with different patterns of behavior. The fact that most of our attitudes and thoughts are based on integrating the experiences of others is the very basis for both culture and society.[54]

---

[50] Zuboff, 418.
[51] Pentland, *Social Physics*, 4.
[52] Pentland, 59.
[53] Pentland, 12f.
[54] Pentland, 191.

An accompanying article even talks approvingly about the "death of individuality" – a death that would come with rewards, rewards from the good things that "we" would do.[55]

8.5 WHAT TO DO?

Zuboff and the (wittingly or unwittingly) Skinner-inspired Pentland respectively represent pessimistic and optimistic takes on social physics. Zuboff continues the Marxist tradition of criticizing capitalism for its negative effects on human life. But while Marx himself recognized technology as political in the foundational and interactive senses, it was later writers, especially Marcuse, who saw technology as political in the enframing (and dystopian) sense. For Marx, capitalism *rather than* technology was the problem. For Marcuse (as well as his teacher Heidegger), capitalism cannot be separated from technology that way. Zuboff's coinage "surveillance capitalism" indicates that, to her, the impossibility of performing such a separation has become entrenched in the digital age.

Zuboff worries that Pentland never defines the "we" that would do the good things he dangles before us as rewards from the "death of individuality."[56] She insists that what appears like a democratic "we" predictably would be Big Other's profit-seeking "we." For Zuboff, Pentland at best is naïve and at worst legitimizes harmful large-scale data collection. For us to avoid turning into a hive, she submits, everybody needs a domain of psychological privacy, a "backstage," to recuperate from the strains of the social world.[57] Our secluded selves can thereby also gather strength to fend off efforts to become data points – and instead engage with the Enlightenment project in their own ways.[58]

A society of such selves might forfeit considerable benefits. With these very lines written in times of COVID-19, we know that is no small matter. It is also worth noting that there is another side to Pentland's techno-optimism, which becomes visible in the connection to Skinner. Skinner was adamant that the only alternative to a technology of behavior – which would improve collective habits and create a more orderly structuring of society – is for our poor choices to destroy us (individually and collectively) and the environment. As it turns out, the Skinner-Pentland nexus also ushers in Henri Saint-Simon, who in the nineteenth century proposed that a small elite should control society through central planning. He introduced the term "industrialiste" for the elite of the diligent, such as entrepreneurs, artisans, artists, managers, bankers, and scientists. Being wealth creators, the industrialists

---

[55] Pentland, "The Death of Individuality." For another optimistic take on the possibilities of Big Data, see Gilbert, *Good Data*. That book was written in response to Zuboff.

[56] Zuboff, *The Age of Surveillance Capitalism*, 430.

[57] Zuboff, 470–72.

[58] For the advice that a good strategy not to become a data point is to obfuscate industry efforts to collect data from us, see Brunton and Nissenbaum, *Obfuscation*.

should rule in a government of elite chambers.[59] The Skinner-Pentland mindset could readily adopt something like this position, and argue that only a coalition of talent, enlisting available technologies (much beyond what Saint-Simon could have envisaged), can safeguard our future. Only such a coalition – or so Skinner, Pentland, Saint-Simon, and like-minded thinkers might well insist – can ensure that humanity has the "patience, flexibility, intelligence" that (recall from Chapter 2) John von Neumann argued we need to survive technology.[60]

That is, one could respond to Zuboff's view and object, in the first instance, that human personalities and potential to some extent change with available technologies and that we need to try harder to delineate appropriate legal and regulatory protections to make sure the gains outweigh the losses, and avoid certain losses altogether.[61] One can also object, more strongly, that it is not the alliance of capitalism and technology that might "cost us our humanity," as Zuboff fears.[62] Instead, so this objector would argue, Skinner was right that the threat comes from leaving decision-making to individuals instead of being governed by a capable elite with suitable technological tools. And this threat – which Skinner correctly identifies, according to this objector to Zuboff – emanates directly from the Enlightenment ideal of individuality as defended by Kant and Durkheim.

Now that we see the contours of Zuboff's position and what I take to be the major objections to it, where does all this leave us? The reply to this second objection is that, regardless of what is true of capitalism more generally, under surveillance capitalism specifically the dangers associated with Big Other being in charge are already too large to entrust power to any such elite (or even to leave the current elite empowered). What is also clear (and this speaks to *both* objections) is that, as Zuboff points out, frameworks like current privacy or antitrust laws cannot on their own protect us from the unprecedented surveillance of recent decades or secure the Enlightenment project for digital lifeworlds. What it takes instead is a broader vision for society that adopts considerations from democratic theory, theories of justice, and an account of rights. We have already discussed all these topics to some extent, and Chapter 9 has more to say about justice.

Chapter 3 explores how AI, in particular, can be designed to harness the public sphere, political power, and economic power for democratic purposes and thus make them akin to Winner's inclusive traffic infrastructure. In that chapter I have made several suggestions: that we need digital public infrastructure to engage in

---

[59] Ionescu, *The Political Thought of Saint Simon*; Manuel, *The New World of Henri Saint-Simon.* Marx emphasized conflicts within that group. Saint-Simon saw what productive people had in common (contrasting the working class thus broadly understood with the idling class, which society should abolish).

[60] von Neumann, "Can We Survive Technology?"

[61] For helpful reviews of Zuboff's book, see Cuélla and Huq, "Economies of Surveillance"; Morozov, "Capitalism's New Clothes."

[62] Zuboff, *The Age of Surveillance Capitalism,* 347.

public and civic life in digital spaces, with norms and affordances designed around civic values (which will strengthen the grassroots part of democratic engagement, cementing democracy as a way of life); that the same digital public infrastructure and other tools of the digital age should also be used to improve communication between politicians and electorate, as well as citizen services; that large technology companies should be broken up; that technology should be deployed to transform the domain of work to create much more leisure time for average people – partly to give them more meaningful lives, but also to allow them to assume more political responsibilities; and that government should ensure political oversight over such measures, rather than leaving them to the private sector. All this is a tall order because democracy and technology are not natural allies. But a strengthened form of democracy is essential for harvesting at least some of the advantages of social physics (those that survive democratic scrutiny) while supporting the "unit-ideas" behind individualism: respect for human dignity, autonomy, privacy, and self-development.

Epistemic rights – which appear in Chapter 3 and are developed at greater length in Chapter 7 – also have a role to play in strengthening democracy for the digital age. Mature democracies in the digital age require technological literacy, which is covered by the right to education. Governments should take measures to prevent use of the tools of digital lifeworlds for the systematic spread of falsehoods that undermines independent decision-making. The rights of individuals to participate in cultural life, enjoy the arts, and share in scientific advancement and its benefits must be adjusted to the data episteme. Individuals have rights to the protection of personal data, including a right to be forgotten. As far as the collective epistemic object is concerned, control over collected data should be broadly shared (as discussed in Chapter 9, in ways that draw on considerations of justice).

These considerations capture my own response to the dispute between Zuboff and the techno-optimistic outlook defended by Skinner and Pentland (which we also traced back, in certain ways, to Saint-Simon). They also capture my account of what it takes to secure the Enlightenment for digital lifeworlds. Much is at stake, as there is reason for us to continue the Enlightenment while also benefiting from a good deal of the technological potential of digital lifeworlds. A broad, demanding normative vision for society is the way to do so, a vision that strengthens democracy and pushes considerations around rights and justice and thereby makes sure that gains do not disproportionately accrue to the commercializing "we" of Big Other.

8.6 THE DIALECTIC OF RIGHTS

There is one more subject to cover in this chapter: that an assignment of rights *by itself* cannot secure the Enlightenment for digital lifeworlds. Solutions must give prominence to structural considerations around democracy and justice (as we did in Section 8.5). The upcoming discussion addresses readers who entertain the view that a set of rights is all that a plausible ideal of a good society requires, and that reflection on democracy and justice that go beyond rights would merely add demands that go beyond what is warranted.[63] This discussion completes our exploration of epistemic rights while also setting the stage for the next chapter, which deals with matters of justice.

There are some long-standing concerns about deploying rights to improve society that arise forcefully in digital lifeworlds. One is the *emancipatory concern*: Rather than advancing emancipation, rights stifle society. This is articulated classically in Marx's essay "On the Jewish Question."[64] For Marx, an assignment of rights strengthens the social isolation characteristic of capitalist societies instead of encouraging a flourishing human "species-being." Another concern, the *dialectic concern*, is that the very exercise of rights in due course undermines them. The problems that rights are meant to address eventually become exacerbated by their very realization

I call this the "dialectic" concern because we can develop it effectively by drawing on Horkheimer and Adorno's *Dialectic of Enlightenment*.[65] To be sure, their topic is reason generally rather than rights. But one aspect of the process they are interested in is arguably that *exercising rights* leads to the instrumentalization of persons, which eventually undermines the very possibility of that exercise. The fact that Zuboff worries about *instrumentarian* power makes a discussion of *instrumentalization* resulting from the exercise of rights illuminating as we assess how *more rights* can help in response to instrumentarian power. The dialectic concern articulated by the founders of the Frankfurt School encapsulates the emancipatory concern, but not vice versa. Therefore, I only develop and deal with the former.[66]

---

[63] Again, for the view that such an attitude has fueled much of the success or in any event political acceptance of human rights, see Moyn, *Not Enough*.

[64] McLellan, *Karl Marx: Selected Writings*, 46–70.

[65] Horkheimer and Adorno, *Dialectic of Enlightenment*. For background, see also Held, *Introduction to Critical Theory*; Jarvis, *Adorno*. For the Frankfurt School, see Wiggershaus, *The Frankfurt School*.

[66] But let me elaborate just a bit more on the *emancipatory concern*. Marx's "On the Jewish Question" ostensibly assesses his contemporary Bruno Bauer's reflections on Jewish efforts to achieve political emancipation in Prussia. For Bauer, true political emancipation requires abolition of religion rather than protection of religious affiliations. But for Marx, Jews could readily achieve emancipation in terms of rights without renouncing religion. By focusing on religion, Bauer misses the true obstacles to genuine emancipation. Marx questions the potential of rights to create genuinely human emancipation. The "so-called rights of man," Marx states, are "rights of the member of civil society, i.e., egoistic man, man separated from the other men and the community"; McLellan, *Karl Marx: Selected Writings*, 60. Rights keep people isolated, protecting them only in their pursuit of private interests (especially property). Emancipation is complete only when "as an individual, man in his empirical life, in his individual work and individual relationships becomes a species-being"; McLellan, 64. Species-being is about a communally richer experience than emancipation in terms of rights makes possible. It is notoriously difficult to assess how important Marx thought considerations of justice should be; see, for example, Lukes, *Marxism and Morality*; Geras, "The Controversy about Marx and Justice." Any kind of moral talk Marx normally relegates to society's ideology,

The gist of Kant's essay on enlightenment is that exercising reason helps overcome *domination*: Those who dare think are no longer dominated by intellectual forces. Domination occurs where others prescribe one's goals and the means of attaining them. Once domination by intellectual forces ceases, liberation from other forms of domination can follow. Power depends on compliance, and citizens who think for themselves are more likely to resist domination generally. By contrast, for Horkheimer and Adorno, such emancipation can be only temporary. Exercising reason gets entangled with domination; in fact, it becomes a *device* for domination. As the opening of the *Dialectic* states, "In the most general sense of progressive thought, the Enlightenment has always aimed at liberating men from fear and establishing their sovereignty. Yet the fully enlightened Earth radiates disaster triumphant."[67] These words were written in 1944, while Hitler ruled the authors' homeland. Their text engages totalitarian power. But it also does much more.

One way of thinking about enlightenment is that it seeks to supplant *mythology* of various sorts. Mythology tells stories that provide answers to people with questions about the world. But thereby it also deprives them of the need to investigate for themselves (which is the essence of Enlightenment). It therefore comes as a surprise that Horkheimer and Adorno's key thesis is that "myth is already enlightenment; and enlightenment reverts to mythology."[68] Let us investigate this claim.

Differences notwithstanding, mythology and independent thinking both seek to make sense of the world. Mythology did so long before the Enlightenment. Horkheimer and Adorno argue that enduring practices of enlightenment eventually re-instantiate social conditions over which individuals have, and realize they have, little control. The very practice of enlightenment reverts us to domination, to the heteronomous condition from which Kant's encouragement to think for oneself was supposed to be an escape. The reason for this is that the liberation that enlightenment entails *also* ushers in new possibilities for people to acquire knowledge. In Baconian fashion (see Chapter 5), this involves possibilities and encouragement to subject *nature* to one's own projects. The value of nature is then increasingly conceptualized instrumentally, rather than in ways that do not turn on human purposes. That is, the more people know and understand, and the more they take charge of their own lives, the more they are inclined to instrumentalize what is around them for their own purposes.

---

ideas that reflect class interests. Instead, he makes his point in terms of species-being. A century later Rawls echoes Marx's point but in terms of distributive justice. Rawls formulates two principles of justice. The first talks about civil and political rights, demanding each person have as broad a range of them as compatible with any other person having the same. The second supplements the first by demanding fair equality of opportunity as well as a distribution of wealth and income in society in a manner that pays special attention to the least advantaged. Like Marx, Rawls hopes for a richer communal life, *beyond* what rights can accomplish. Unlike Marx, he did so in terms of social justice. That is the right move, especially in a digital age.

[67] Horkheimer and Adorno, *Dialectic of Enlightenment*, 3.
[68] Horkheimer and Adorno, xvi.

But this instrumentalization of nature is only a first step. In societies that champion this kind of exercise of reason, ways for reason to be deployed other than for purposes of instrumentalization are increasingly marginalized. Eventually such marginalization includes reason's ability to negotiate reasonable agreements for all concerned rather than constellations of rational (instrumentalizing) pursuits. Instrumentalization even extends to other human beings. "What men want to learn from nature is how to use it in order wholly to dominate it and other men," Horkheimer and Adorno write. "Ruthlessly, in spite of itself," they continue, "the Enlightenment has extinguished any trace of its own self-consciousness. The only kind of thinking that is sufficiently hard to shatter myths is ultimately self-destructive."[69] Persons see their value reduced to a market (or some other instrumental) value. One stunning symptom is that enslavement continued throughout the Enlightenment, and in fact got exacerbated through the new manufacturing possibilities that the Industrial Revolution set in motion (think of cotton plantations in the American Deep South that became big business only once there was a textile industry that manufactured clothes from cotton). More generally, societies were not organized in ways that aimed for reasonableness. Instead, organization reflected successful implementation of some people's instrumental ambitions to the detriment of those of others.

Horkheimer and Adorno also touch on human rights. "For the Enlightenment, whatever does not conform to the rule of computation and utility is suspect," they explain. "So long as it can develop undisturbed by any outward repression, there is no holding it. In the process it treats its own human rights exactly as it does the older universals. . . . Enlightenment is totalitarian."[70] At some stage, the pursuit of enlightenment naturally involves a recognition of rights that all humans possess to safeguard their ability to exercise reason. To that end, individuals need some protections and provisions. But as people use these rights, their exercise by some undermines the rights of others. Rather than a society where autonomy is widespread, these developments lead to an increasingly heteronomous social order over which most people have little control. That order is systematically indifferent to persons and their sufferings.

To explain this last point a bit more, persons themselves ultimately become mere objects of the form of reason we have created through the exercise of reason generally and the exercise of rights specifically. Eventually the very idea that humans as such have rights will be treated within the Enlightenment like the guiding ideas of pre-Enlightenment mythologies. Enlightenment is totalitarian also in the sense that its machinations eventually turn against its own ideals: It provides answers of sorts but does not enable people to genuinely act on their own. As Horkheimer and Adorno state,

---

[69] Horkheimer and Adorno, 4.
[70] Horkheimer and Adorno, 6.

men pay for the increase of their power with alienation from that over which they exercise their power. Enlightenment behaves towards things as a dictator toward men. He knows them in so far as he can manipulate them. The man of science knows things in so far as he can make them. In this way, their potentiality is turned to his own ends.[71]

People succeed in such a world only by conforming to instrumental reason. Inquiry aids and abets this order, since intellectuals merely seek to mirror that reality without showing the way beyond it. We revert to mythology in that individuals receive explanations but are not endowed with a sense of agency. We reach this point partly because we built a society that recognizes rights for everyone, and this recognition sets dynamics in motion that eventually generates an order that is oppressive for most people. Typically, individuals will not even be aware of the oppression that shapes their life circumstances because they are not inclined to question the circumstances that shape their thoughts and activities. But they would become more aware of these matters if they tried to intellectually engage with these circumstances or decided to pursue courses of action that deviate from what is broadly accepted. Both mythology and enlightenment are ultimately about domination of nature and persons.

8.7 CONCLUSION

We should acknowledge that our neoliberal age vindicates a good deal of what Horkheimer and Adorno worried about. Rights matter, but if indeed they are implemented in a society without additional reflection on how to strengthen democracy or on what justice requires in a more structural way, they empower some people much more than others (about whom it will nonetheless be said that they too have "the same rights"). Eventually, rights talk is more so handed down like a mantra than it is treated as anything designed to empower people. So, as we think about how we want the digital age to turn out, adding epistemic rights to a fourth generation of human rights clearly is important – but that kind of addition must happen while we are *also* aiming to make democracies stronger and societies more just.

Zuboff's analysis of instrumentarian power reflects the understanding of the workings of reason that the founders of the Frankfurt School have offered. Tendencies toward instrumentalization are especially pronounced in a context shaped by instrumentation to the extent that digital lifeworlds are. But one must then wonder whether an assignment of rights could ever improve the situation. It is because Zuboff's account of instrumentarian power illuminates so much about the kind of capitalist society that has become the norm in the Enlightenment era that we can see why recognizing more rights *by itself* would not help. Adorno famously states

---

[71] Horkheimer and Adorno, 9.

that "Es gibt kein richtiges Leben im falschen" (There is no correct life amidst a wrong one).[72] For problems at the level of society as a whole, changes at a small scale will not make any difference. Recognizing more rights *and doing nothing further* would amount to such an effort.

What it takes instead to bring about change for society as a whole is larger-scale thinking at the level of democracy and justice. We must work on the background structures within which a firm rights protection, including that of epistemic rights, can flourish. Rights are not enough. The digital age, with its omnipresence of surveillance, makes it immensely difficult to meet Kant's ideal of intellectual maturity, an ideal that envisages for people to possess genuine independence of mind while also remaining contributors to society. For that ideal to be realized at a broader scale, we need to have ideals of democracy and justice in place *in addition* to rights. Active implementation of these ideals is needed to rein in the pernicious tendencies (as laid out by Horkheimer and Adorno) that might arise from the implementation of rights in isolation.

Readers familiar with the Marxist tradition will be wary of a reply to concerns *about rights* that appeals *to justice*. After all, at least for a certain kind of Marxist, any theorizing about justice would readily stand accused of being *ideological* – that is, of being explicable largely in terms of underlying class-interests and of being incapable of driving change on its own (which instead comes from changes in material circumstances, see again Chapter 2).[73] One way of expressing that wariness is that Horkheimer and Adorno make their points in terms of reason rather than rights. The sheer *breadth* of their formulation includes efforts at realizing justice and other values – or so one might insist, also by way of worrying that my narrowing of their concerns to matters of right distinctly understates what Horkheimer and Adorno were after.

And this worry is well taken, certainly in the sense that appeals to justice will not fully dissolve their concerns. Nonetheless, the broader realization of justice (and other values) is what in the first instance we need specifically in response to the dialectic concern about rights. That the same concern then also arises about justice is a point of which we must remain keenly aware in the political process.[74] We must deal with it as best we can, but it is also true that this challenge only arises once justice is taken *much more* seriously than it is now. So this is a bridge we will indeed have to cross once we get there – but not before. In fact, we would be fortunate if we ever got there.

[72] Adorno, *Minima Moralia*, 42.
[73] Again, for the role of justice in Marx's work, see, for example, Lukes, *Marxism and Morality*; Geras, "The Controversy about Marx and Justice."
[74] For one articulation of that point, see Derrida, "Force of Law." For discussion, see Risse, *On Justice*, chapter 1.

9

Data as Social Facts: Distributive Justice Meets Big Data

A social fact is any way of acting . . . which is general over the whole of a given society whilst having an existence of its own, independent of its individual manifestations.

—Émile Durkheim[1]

9.1 INTRODUCTION

The perennial quest for justice is about making sure that each person has an appropriate place in what our uniquely human capacities permit us to build, produce, and maintain, and that each person is respected appropriately for their capacities to hold such a place to begin with.[2] That is, justice is concerned with making sure that each person has their proper place in what human ingenuity has made possible over millennia.

Using a distinction we owe to Aristotle, we can distinguish *commutative* justice from *distributive* justice under this umbrella. The former either restores an earlier status quo that set the stage for a certain interaction (the one that triggers the need for commutative justice) or otherwise responds to violations. For concreteness, one may think here of tort law or criminal justice. The latter is concerned with sharing out whatever a community does or plausibly should hold in common. For concreteness, today one may think about property and tax law, but also much beyond that. After Aristotle, theories of distributive justice needed to explain how to think of the communities that are said to hold anything in common. That is, such theories needed to determine whether there was only one such type of community (e.g., people sharing citizenship, where then it might be in virtue of that shared citizenship that these people have claims to the proceeds of the economy to which they jointly contribute), or whether there might be different communities that

---

[1]   Durkheim, "What Is a Social Fact?," 59.
[2]   I develop this view of justice in detail in Risse, *On Justice.*

respectively hold different things in common (the citizens/inhabitants of one country, but perhaps also the global population or other groups, which would respectively have claims to different things).

Theories of distributive justice have also needed to explain *what* the respective community should hold in common, a thing whose availability or accessibility among the population therefore ought to be justifiable to each member. The technical term that philosophers use here is *distribuendum*, "the thing to be shared out." For Aristotle, that distribuendum is honors, wealth, and security. The population among which those are supposed to be shared out is the citizenry of the *polis*.

Millennia later, Rawls sought to describe a just arrangement of the major political and social institutions of a liberal society: political constitution, legal system, economy, family, and so on. Their arrangement is the *basic structure*. These institutions distribute among the citizens the main benefits of social life, the *social primary goods*, which include basic rights and liberties, freedom of movement and free choice among a wide range of occupations, the powers of offices and positions of responsibility, and income and wealth, as well as the social bases of self-respect (that is, recognition by social institutions that gives citizens a sense of self-worth and the confidence to implement plans).[3]

The use of social primary goods as distribuenda in a contemporary theory of distributive justice reflects the sheer range of things we provide to each other through joint activities. Recall from the Preface that Rawls proposes the following principles to regulate the distribution of the social primary goods. The first – which deals with political status – states that each person has the same indefeasible claim to a fully adequate scheme of equal basic liberties, a scheme that is compatible with the same scheme of liberties for all. The second principle – which deals with relative economic standing – falls into two parts. The first part states that social and economic inequalities are to be attached to offices and positions that are open to all under conditions of fair equality of opportunity. The second states that remaining social and economic inequalities should be to the greatest benefit of the least-advantaged members of society (Difference Principle).[4]

How do data fit in with these long-standing ways of thinking about distributive justice generally and the Rawlsian principles specifically? Access to data allows for detection of patterns that enable predictions for what individuals do, say, or think next or what happens to them. For instance, Amazon Web Services controls vast arrays of cyberspace, which enables data collection at a breathtaking scale. This data collection, at least in principle, could be used to guide customers on Amazon's website. The more data there are, the more accurate such efforts become, and the harder it is for competitors to enter markets. In the aggregate, such predictions

---

[3] See, for example, Rawls, *Restatement*, 58f.

[4] Rawls, 41–43. Fulfillment of the first principle, on political status, takes priority over the second. Within the second, fair equality of opportunity takes priority over the Difference Principle.

anticipate societal trends. Whoever can make such predictions can redirect behavior and to that extent also shape societies. Accordingly, *control over data*, which may or may not amount to data *ownership*, is genuine power. Who should hold that power? How should data be controlled?[5] And how do such questions connect to theorizing distributive justice?

Data understood as personal information, which reveals something essential about somebody that is subject to misuse in the wrong hands, have long concerned political thinkers. Data of that kind, after all, have a direct connection to personal liberties, and the need to protect such data is typically discussed under the heading of "privacy."[6] However, control over data that mostly matter *in the aggregate*, for the predictions they allow for what people of certain characteristics will do, has not been a traditional subject in theories of distributive justice. It has only been within economies that have emerged through digital lifeworlds that this subject has gained political relevance. But it now behooves us to think about control over data from the standpoint of distributive justice.

Data in the sense we worry about are not themselves primary goods. But in digital lifeworlds, data help shape the nature of all primary goods one way or another. Most obviously that is the case for income and wealth in an increasingly data-driven economy. Control over data, then, might not seem to require special attention from the standpoint of distributive justice: Bringing our understanding of social primary goods up to date would be all that is needed and appropriate to integrate control over data into a theory of distributive justice. But Big Data change our lives, and especially the way the economy works, so dramatically that it behooves us to see if – within the approach to distributive justice that Rawls offers – a specific principle or perhaps at least a general guideline can govern control of data. Such a principle would then be essential to how Big Data help define the nature of primary goods.

The importance of control over data for distributive justice explains why it has been analogized to other domains where legitimate control is better understood. Several *data-as* proposals are available: Data as Oil, as Intellectual Property, as Personhood, as Salvage, and as Labor.[7] Each time the point is that data *essentially is*, or *is relevantly like*, something else about which we have established views on how to control it legitimately. Data-as proposals do or contribute to three things. To begin with, each proposal makes a suggestion for what it is about data that makes them valuable; secondly, by identifying what makes data valuable, the proposal points to who should control them (typically, who should *own* them); and thirdly, ipso facto the proposal also points to how data should be controlled (owned), through the kind of rights involved.

---

[5] For conceptual discussion of "data," "information," and related notions, see again Chapter 1.
[6] For recent discussions of privacy specifically with an eye on digital lifeworlds, see Richards, *Why Privacy Matters*; Hartzog, *Privacy's Blueprint*.
[7] I switch to capital initials because these are names of specific positions.

To explain why I say "points to": What arguments are needed to make such proposals plausible depends on the details, especially on how much mileage can be gained from what is said about how data are valuable. To illustrate, according to Data as Labor, data are valuable because they amount to labor provided by specific people; therefore, the data provided should be owned by whoever does this labor; and the data should be owned the way that labor normally is controlled (owned) in that society. Reducing data to labor greatly helps with questions about the who and how of control over data.

Like the aforementioned data-as proposals, my view characterizes data in ways that illuminate how they can legitimately be controlled and can be expressed as a data-as view: *Data as Social Facts*. Unlike some alternatives, Data as Social Facts creates no equivalence with another domain where legitimate control is well understood. Questions around the who and how of control are not advanced in such a fashion. But what this proposal does – unlike its competitors – is identify just what it is about data that makes them economically relevant and so makes regulation of control over them politically important: to wit, that they capture regularities that allow for (probabilistic) predictions, and thereby are social facts in Durkheim's sense (as discussed in Chapter 8).[8] The bulk of this chapter develops an argument to the effect that such social facts should be privatized only within certain limits. This does not deliver complete answers regarding the who and how of control over data. But it does constrain plausible accounts of these matters substantially, and in that sense Data as Social Facts also delivers the principle – though not a crisp one, but instead something closer to a general guideline – that shows how Big Data help define the nature of primary goods.

I normally talk about (legitimate) *control* rather than *ownership* since I seek to avoid specific legal questions. Such questions typically go beyond my basic philo-sophical point, and the fact that I leave them open does not embarrass that point. But the more one thinks of ownership detached from legal specifics, the closer ownership and control become. Moreover, the competing data-as proposals are formulated to some extent in terms of ownership rather than control. So ownership language is already part of this discussion. I also think there are good reasons to integrate control over data into legal systems of ownership. Accordingly, Section 9.2 explores why ownership considerations matter here to begin with.

Section 9.3 introduces and rebuts various data-as proposals. Section 9.4 presents Data as Social Facts. Sections 9.5–9.7 show that social facts of this sort can be

---

[8] Durkheim, "What Is a Social Fact?" For a philosophical account that deploys a Durkheimian notion of social facts, see Gilbert, *On Social Facts*. Also see Gilbert, "Durkheim and Social Facts." I used to refer to "Data as Social Facts" as "Data as Collectively Generated Patterns"; see Risse, "Data as Collectively Generated Patterns." The latter term is more descriptive and sidesteps ontological debates that come with introducing Durkheimian terminology. But "Data as Social Facts" is a more elegant name, and the connections to Durkheim and Gilbert are welcome. I still talk about collectively generated patterns later.

privatized only within certain limits. I enlist an approach to ownership proposed by Hugo Grotius in his 1609 *Mare Liberum (Free Sea)*. I develop this approach gradually, beginning with the original context of the high seas. Next, I transfer this approach to intellectual property, and ultimately to social facts. That a seventeenth-century figure would appear as we try to throw light on a twenty-first-century problem might startle and even irritate. But Grotius's account of the ownership of the seas formulates basic – and plausible – ideas about what kind of thing should and should not be privatized. His account offers lessons that it behooves us to heed. Since control over data matters enormously but is poorly understood, we should treat questions about it as *genuinely open*. This is a good time to consider unorthodox thinking on the matter. Section 9.8 concludes by exploring some objections.

Let me create some more context for the discussion in this chapter. Chapter 5 introduces epistemic justice in addition to commutative and distributive justice. I understand commutative and distributive justice such that matters cannot come under the purview of both. But matters of commutative and those of distributive justice can both come under the purview of epistemic justice. Both epistemic and distributive justice enter once we investigate how ways in which we are collectively known (such as Big Data) bear on, say, primary goods. So, while this chapter deploys the language of distributive justice, we could conduct this investigation in terms of the collective epistemic object and thus under the heading of epistemic justice. Chapter 7 introduces new epistemic human rights. One of them, meant to protect individuals in their roles as belonging to the collective epistemic object, is a right to substantial control over collected data. This is a right to the collective epistemic object being a certain way. This right is the most important addition to the body of existing human rights that I propose in this book. The current chapter spells out what that right is an entitlement *to*.[9]

9.2 WHY OWNERSHIP?

One might think ownership is not the right way to address concerns about data use. So, to the extent that control over data matters, we should develop the concerns in other ways. This objection appears in two versions. The first is that concerns about data ownership often involve privacy and should be assessed directly in ways that neither enlist nor benefit from considerations of ownership. Ownership language is

---

[9]   (1) For the argument that AI should be integrated into the Rawlsian framework by way of seeing it as part of the basic structure, see Gabriel, "Towards a Theory of Justice for Artificial Intelligence." (2) For Rawls, property rights are (at least largely) conventional. So, the considerations in this chapter should be understood as informing a debate within a political community committed to the Rawlsian understanding of distributive justice that needs to assess how to integrate data ownership into its legal framework. Some considerations we encounter (especially those drawing on Grotius) originate in a natural-law context. But their origins notwithstanding, the content of these considerations can be rearticulated for discussions about the contours of conventional arrangements around control or ownership.

inappropriate. The second is that, while ownership considerations might matter, little hangs on how we determine the ownership status of data. Regardless of whether data can be privately or publicly owned, concerns expressed in terms of privacy would compete with them and entail the same conclusions. Ownership language is redundant. Taken together, these objections call into question whether ownership considerations have a role in addressing concerns about data use. Consider some cases to develop these matters:[10]

> **Case 1:** Data analysis reveals that a certain pattern of typing on keyboards indicates the onset of a debilitating muscle disease. Insurance companies pay for such information because it allows them to reject potential clients or adjust premiums.
>
> **Case 2:** Data analysis reveals that someone's reading tastes make it likely that she would be receptive to advertising for a new book on internet privacy. Internet sellers that carry this title pay for this information to improve their marketing.
>
> **Case 3:** Data analysis renders it likely that somebody is the kind of voter who could be persuaded to favor a particular candidate in response to suitable messages (whose truthfulness she would not be able to validate). Political campaigns pay for such information because it increases their chances at winning elections.

In such cases, so objectors insist, deliberation about the appropriateness of using data in such ways could proceed without consideration of ownership. In Case 1, that debate revolves around the kind of intrusion constituted by a transfer of information from one context (being active on a keyboard) to an entirely different one (medical assessments).[11] In Case 2, a commodification of day-to-day behavior occurs that requires justification. In Case 3, the discussion revolves around the permissibility of particular means in the process of opinion formation.

But upon reflection, ownership considerations do enter. In Case 1, one may be appalled at the intrusion, but such matters are not entirely simple. Any conclusion we may reach involves pondering multiple considerations, and ownership consider-ations would be among them. One concerns what obligations insurance companies have or how they should be regulated. Sharing insurance means sharing risk: Risk-sharing is the point of insurance. If an insurance company knows that somebody is at a higher risk but does not act on this information, it would thereby also impose higher average costs on others not connected to the fate of the high-risk client. These others may reasonably complain if information about risk profiles is available but not used to assess premiums. But if the case is controversial in such ways,

---

[10] Versions of these examples were brought up by Lawrence Lessig in seminar discussion in February 2019.

[11] On that point about the relevance of context, see Nissenbaum, *Privacy in Context*.

ownership considerations might enter by suggesting that decisions about data use should be made by the person who owns the data. This may or may not be conclusive, but in any event ownership considerations would enter by helping to fend off competing claims of other members of the insurance scheme.

In Case 2, the commodification involved is rather trivial. In such cases, commodification would likely be welcomed, or at least tolerated, by potential buyers. Targeted advertising is a way of protecting people from a flood of pointless marketing. So a judgment must be made about whether (and what) data can be used for such advertising – and arguably it should be made by the person who has ownership claims to the data, which would again reveal ways for ownership considerations to matter after all. Finally, in Case 3, there will be reasonable disagreement about the scope and limits of legitimate means of persuasion, which again would point to a role for ownership considerations. So the response to all cases – and thus to the objections that call into question whether ownership considerations have a role in addressing concerns about data use – is that ownership may not be the whole story: Even within the domain of rights, other types of right may enter, such as some type of liberty- or personality-related rights. But this response is consistent with ownership being among the relevant considerations. And in each case, there is reason to say that it is indeed so.

Another way of highlighting the relevance of ownership is to resist the importance of privacy considerations.[12] The term "privacy" merely points to a relevant distinction between something that should be left to individual decision-making, be hidden from eyes and ears of others, or not be subject to scrutiny or assessments, on the one hand, and other matters that should not be set aside in such ways, on the other. "Privacy" or "the private sphere" is not *independently* understood. Therefore, considerations of privacy do not limit the relevance of ownership in plainly obvious ways. We need arguments to establish a particular way of drawing such distinctions. Clarifying the work that ownership considerations do could help with that.

The point of ownership is to generate a set of claims, liberties, and powers to do with certain things as one pleases within certain legal and arguably also moral constraints.[13] In none of these cases do ownership considerations by themselves settle the matter conclusively. But nor do such considerations just not matter at all. And as the old adage has it, possession is nine-tenths of the law. The bundle of claims, liberties, and powers that constitute ownership are, for better or worse, key components of our social lives because they help with assignments of responsibilities and shape expectations. Reflection on data ownership is reflection on how to make room for data in a world that works this way. That is the general point of bringing up ownership considerations here.

---

[12] For philosophical issues around privacy, see DeCrew, "Privacy."
[13] See the classic discussion in Honore, "Ownership."

But now that we see that ownership considerations are not inappropriate (which is a response to the first objection previously), what about the second objection, that it would not matter how the ownership status was resolved and thus that ownership language is redundant? This would be so if considerations of private ownership in combination with moral constraints on such ownership would always deliver the same conclusions as considerations of public ownership of sorts. If such an equivalence could be shown (for suitable understandings of private and public ownership), that would be remarkable. But in any event, the task at hand is to clarify the nature of ownership in context of data patterns to begin with, and only then to wonder how this might be different from or equivalent to other ways that ownership questions can be resolved.

9.3 DATA-AS PROPOSALS

Absent legislation that makes different provisions, data once collected are under control of whoever gathers them – normally companies that provide smart phones, tablets, personal computers, digital assistants, electronically linked household appliances, positioning systems, or search engines. The argument for "finders, keepers" is that it is only in virtue of the platform-mediated character of interactions that we detect previously unobservable behavior, which enables transactions that were unfeasible before. Regulation that contradicts such an approach would either constrain ways in which data can be obtained or aggregated to begin with or constrain the use to which data could be put once collected. Either way, it is at this stage that the question of data control becomes significant.

Humanity has never had much difficulty increasing the range of things that can be privately controlled (and then normally *owned*), first and foremost things essential to creating wealth and status. Land, hardware, labor, ideas: All these have met that description over the centuries. Each of them is regulated by a comprehensive set of laws accompanied by much reflection on, and mobilization around, the adequacy of any given set of such laws compared to alternatives. Data as understood in the digital world are newcomers in the domain of things that can be privately controlled. Given the novelty and elusiveness of the topic, it is unsurprising that several answers have been formulated in ways that analogize data to things in whose regulation ownership considerations have long been prominent.

The more prominent among these proposals are *Data as Oil, Data as Labor, Data as Personhood, Data as Salvage,* and *Data as Intellectual Property*. My main point about them is that they all run afoul of a basic insight about what makes data valuable to begin with. To wit, among the myriad of data that are collected, those data are valuable that form overall patterns generated from the activities of multiple, often very many people that allow for predictions of other actions or events, which in turn can be monetized or otherwise exploited by whoever has the mathematical tools to draw such inferences.

One attempt to bring data specifically under the purview of ownership is to analogize them to natural resources. Obviously, data are not themselves such resources since they are generated through human activities. But data might still be relevantly like natural resources. This argument says that much like oil, for example, data are *just there*. If we ask who should get to use them, the answer evokes methods of extraction. It is those who do the work of collecting data who get to exploit them, much as it is those who extract oil who get to put it to commercial use. Since oil is the most referenced resource in this context, I call this proposal *Data as Oil*.[14]

For the last 150 years or so, oil has been crucial to enabling global transportation systems, in the form of gasoline, diesel, jet fuel, home-heating fuel, lubrication oil, or asphalt. Petrochemicals based on crude oil enter production of plastic, synthetic fiber, drugs, soap, and paint. To the extent that oil generated profits as an original ingredient of all these products, these profits accrued to a large extent to those who *extracted* the oil. Unsurprisingly, Data as Oil has appealed especially to representatives from certain business sectors. After all, the analogy highlights the fact that much as oil requires extraction and distillation to be useful (and thus work done by commercial enterprises), so data require collecting devices and mechanisms as well as mathematical analysis to be useful (and thus again work done by commercial enterprises). The term "data mining" echoes this analogy.

However, the disanalogies between oil and data are glaring. Oil is relatively scarce, fungible (in that oil from different regions is largely interchangeable, controlling for grade), and rivalrous (it can only be used by one party). Data are neither scarce nor fungible nor rivalrous. Most importantly, Data as Oil ignores that data are generated by human activities and are valuable precisely because they are generated by the kind of activities that allow for predictions of additional activities. By sidestepping the ways in which data are produced, Data as Oil forecloses the sheer possibility of diagnosing any type of *mis*appropriation. Lauren Scholz is right that the *only* meaningful similarity between data and oil is that both are valuable for commerce.

Another attempt to bring data under the purview of ownership is *Data as Labor*. Data should be owned by those who provide them: Acts of generating data are labor. If so, such labor should be compensated in the variety of ways that labor is commonly compensated. In the first instance, this would mean companies that collect data must find ways to compensate people for the time needed to generate data. Actual wages may be impractical, but one could imagine other forms of compensation, such as privileges of sorts on the platforms through which data are collected that would be equivalent to wages. Moreover, if data is labor, laborers

---

[14] My discussion follows Scholz, "Big Data Is Not Big Oil." According to Scholz, data scientist Clive Humby coined the phrase "Big Data Is the New Oil" in 2006.

should have control over whom to sell that labor to and in what manner. They might even have claims to a share in profits based on their contributions.[15]

One thing to note is that this proposal involves a broad notion of labor. Based on the rather attractive Marxist understanding, labor allows workers to leave their mark on the world. This would involve an actual shaping with hands and minds, rather than something that arises as a byproduct. But let us set this aside.[16] One objection to Data as Labor is that any payment would be minuscule if it is based on time expended or skills needed to this effect. Such payments would not stand in much of a relation to what platforms do with the data and thus to the value of the product of the labor. On the other hand, if payments are based on the profits obtained based on the data collected, then Data as Labor moves closer to my own proposal, Data as Social Facts. A second objection is that Data as Labor treats the data collected on platforms as if they were any one person's data. However, data that one provides as a user reveal much about others with whom one is connected in multifarious ways, much as genetic information does. For the *labor* any one person invests in providing data to be considered an adequate way of capturing the value *of data* would miss out on the fact that thinking of data in person-by-person ways is incoherent.

A third approach, Data as Personhood, insists that – in virtue of having been produced by humans – data express aspects of personhood, one way or another.[17] Any applicable regulation should be concerned with protection of personhood. Whereas Data as Oil and Data as Labor draw attention to ways data could in fact be owned (parallel to how natural resources could, or to how workers would be remunerated), the most straightforward understanding of this proposal encourages us not to think of data as owned at all. Data generated by human activity extend personhood and ought to receive protection accordingly. Use should be guided by rights protecting personal integrity. But there is also a different understanding of this argument, in terms of self-ownership, that would allow us to see Data as Personhood as a proposal about ownership after all.[18]

To be sure, property and personality are connected.[19] But this approach should be considered as *complementing* considerations pertaining to control over or ownership of data, rather than as *informing* those very considerations. What renders questions about control or ownership significant is that data have market value, which comes from *collective* activity. But there is then also another (complementary) way of thinking about data: *Individually*, data are expressions of personality,

---

[15] For Data as Labor, see Posner and Weyl, *Radical Markets*, chapter 5; Arrieta-Ibarra et al., "Should We Treat Data as Labor? Moving beyond 'Free.'"

[16] This Marxist understanding of work makes another brief appearance in Chapter 10, when we note how Hannah Arendt deploys the notion of action to put the significance of Marxist labor in perspective.

[17] See, for example, Balkin, "Free Speech in the Algorithmic Society."

[18] Such an argument could draw on Nozick, *Anarchy, State, and Utopia*.

[19] Hegel was basically right here; see Hegel, *Philosophy of Right*. For discussion, see Waldron, *The Right to Private Property*, chapter 10.

though the extent to which they are varies across contexts. Often data generated as byproducts of activities by themselves say little about persons and only amount to anything substantive once combined with a myriad of other activities that again in each case are trivial on their own. These are potentially competing but also supplementary perspectives. So while considerations of control and ownership do have a role in this version, Data as Personhood as such does not sort out those considerations.[20]

Next let us discuss Data as Salvage.[21] *Black's Law Dictionary* defines "salvage" as "rescue of imperiled property." A salvage award is compensation for people who helped to rescue property, especially property lost at sea. Those who salvage objects that would otherwise perish have some claim to the value of these objects in virtue of the work they invested. Nonetheless, they are not the owners of such objects. As Scholz notes, in the context of data collection, this approach captures the intuition that "data miners" should be compensated for work done to generate marketable outputs while acknowledging that the data are traceable to someone else. Without "data miners," these data likely would not survive *as* data. Even if they did, they would be of no value, and so be lost to commerce. But prior to such work being done on them, they were recognizably somebody else's. Most importantly, however, this approach likewise runs afoul of the basic insight that what makes data valuable is that they are collectively generated. This approach focuses on how somebody *other than* producers or original owners can have an ownership claim to something. But it does not articulate the nature of the original thing and illuminate how it becomes valuable.

Finally, consider Data as Intellectual Property. Intellectual property typically includes scientific, musical, literary, and other artistic works and inventions, but also images, names, symbols, and design patterns – so ideas, broadly conceived. Again, unlike oil, data are non-scarce, non-fungible, and non-rivalrous. These are features that data share with intellectual property. Also, both data and intellectual property are key assets in the knowledge economy. To that extent, it is plausible to treat data in similar ways, a thought taken up in European law.[22] But there are important differences. To begin with, ideas are valuable individually and separately for the patterns they generate, but data (of the sort we are interested in here) are valuable in this way only in large quantities. Moreover, legal protection of ideas is normally grounded in acts of creativity, beyond how algorithmic collection of data would be creative. But anyway, the approach I am about to suggest also has much to say about intellectual property. So as far as Data as Intellectual Property is concerned, I work with the similarities more than with the differences.

---

[20] For a critical take on Data as Personhood, see also Cohen, "Examined Lives."
[21] The discussion of Data as Salvage again draws on Scholz, "Big Data Is Not Big Oil."
[22] Grosheide, "Database Protection—The European Way."

9.4 DATA AS SOCIAL FACTS

These data-as proposals neither explain nor even highlight what is valuable about data. This insight ushers in my own proposal: *Data as Social Facts*. The basic idea is that the value of data does not reside in individual items but in collectively generated patterns that allow for predictions regardless of whether people's actions have aided the identification of the pattern, as long as those people who have not are relevantly like the ones who have. Unlike personal data that reveal something important about someone, the data that drive surveillance capitalism do not matter piece by piece but rather for the patterns they reveal.

By a collectively generated pattern, I mean something like this:

> Under social parameters $P_1, \ldots, P_n$ as they prevail in country C (or perhaps in countries $C_1, \ldots, C_n$), individuals with features $F_1, \ldots, F_n$ will with probability p do action A under circumstances $CI_1, \ldots, CI_n$.

This could be anything from people with certain features hailing a cab or ordering pizza to them participating in marriage, home-buying, or loan-taking behavior or political actions. Past behavior predicts what happens next, at least probabilistically. Data generated from the behavior of many people are valuable to the extent that they permit such inferences. In increasingly sophisticated ways, data-mining techniques use large quantities of data to identify such patterns. Unlike its competitors, Data as Social Facts does not create any equivalence with another domain where control or ownership is already well understood. We must explore separately how ownership considerations enter, which we do in Sections 9.5–9.7.

Collectively generated patterns are "social facts" in virtue of being facts about group behavior that is systematic enough to generate predictions about the future. For Durkheim, a social fact is "any way of acting, whether fixed or not, capable of exerting over the individual an external constraint; or: which is general over the whole of a given society whilst having an existence of its own, independent of its individual manifestations."[23] This definition makes it possible to study behavior of societies per se, parallel to and unreducible to behavior of individuals. Behavior of societies as such is captured by institutions like marriage, kinship, and political organization, but also language and religion. Individual actions register as instances or representations of different types of actions. Durkheim's best-known illustration for how social facts operate is his pathbreaking study of suicide, which revealed that suicide rates (when he conducted his study) varied across religious communities – and thus at that time were collectively generated patterns relative to such groups.[24]

The nature and plausibility of stipulating social facts has generated much foundational debate in sociology and beyond. A broadly discussed contrast is between

---

[23] Durkheim, "What Is a Social Fact?," 59.
[24] Durkheim, *Suicide*.

Durkheimian "holism" (which foregrounds such social facts that concern societies as a whole) and a "methodological individualism" associated with Max Weber.[25] Weber aims to explain social phenomena by showing how they result from individual actions, which reflect intentional states of those actors. Social facts accordingly play no role in Weber's outlook. In a book suggestively called *On Social Facts*, Margaret Gilbert sympathetically reassesses some of Durkheim's ideas. For Gilbert, the essence of a social group or collectivity consists in a certain mental state. Individuals in this state form a locus of agency, a "plural subject" (a term Gilbert uses to sidestep the baggage that debating the term "social" has amassed over decades of foundational debates in the social sciences, also in an attempt to make overtures to the Weberian standpoint). Actions and intentions of a social group do not distribute and thus are irreducible to those of individuals.[26]

To be sure, my definition of collectively generated patterns is noncommittal as far as the Durkheim – Weber dispute is concerned. It makes sense to refer to collectively generated patterns as "social facts" in the intuitive sense that statistical techniques reveal a certain underlying social cohesiveness. They reveal certain aspects of the *group's* behavior, the kind of phenomenon Durkheim seeks to capture with this notion. To this extent, there is an important overlap with Durkheim. Whether in the end his holism proves misguided or unnecessary is not a matter on which we must take a stance.

For those who collect or mine data, it might be perplexing that what they deal with is anything other than vectors in multidimensional spaces that would not exist (in any interesting sense) were it not for certain platforms and hardware to connect them, and that would yield no insight were it not for analytical techniques. But the reason such work actually yields results is because those vectors reflect an underlying social reality. So, there is more to them than their mathematical existence *as* such vectors and the work that leads to their presence in the data miner's storage.

9.5 THE LIMITS OF PRIVATIZATION: WATER AND IDEAS

First published in 1609, Hugo Grotius's *Mare Liberum* (*Free Sea*) is a classic work in property theory. Its systematic import has been neglected in important ways, but it is of surprising value also when it comes to control over data.[27] Grotius's topic is ownership of the seas in the context of seventeenth-century European expansionism. He held that the high seas should remain non-privatized. That view was controversial in Grotius's time – after all, if far-flung lands could be claimed, why not the

---

[25] Weber, *Economy and Society*, chapter 1. See also Lukes, *Individualism*, chapter 17.
[26] Gilbert, *On Social Facts*; Gilbert, "Durkheim and Social Facts." See also List and Pettit, *Group Agency*.
[27] Grotius, *The Free Sea*.

waterways one must traverse to reach them – but this particular view of his has, by and large, prevailed in international law.

Mare Liberum is of interest here because it offers pro-tanto considerations against appropriation *in any domain*. It is doubtful that today these considerations succeed for the seas, but they readily apply to intellectual property. In this way, much less extensive ownership rights to ideas are justifiable than in the dominant approach that goes back to John Locke (which we discuss later). These Grotian considerations then also apply to social facts like collectively generated patterns. As a result, ownership rights to data, much as ownership rights to the seas and to ideas, can be justified only to a limited extent, considerably less than is reflected in current practice. It would be immensely desirable, in particular, for a new kind of Internet to be designed that reflects a revised ownership structure.

The idea that humanity *collectively owns the earth*, and thus that the earth is a Global Commons, mattered greatly to seventeenth-century political philosophy. That idea draws on the Old Testament, which records God's gift of the earth to humanity in the First Book of Genesis. Grotius, Samuel Pufendorf, Locke, and others debated how to capture this status and the conditions under which parts of this Global Commons could be privatized.[28] These ideas were prominent at the time, since the object whose appropriation mattered most was land; a crucial question was how European powers could rightly claim land far from home and make such claims stick vis-à-vis competing European powers (rather than indigenous populations, whose interests were disregarded).

We can no longer deploy revelation to make substantial arguments about the politics of pluralist societies. Moreover, we must acknowledge the tarnished history of the interpretation of this bit of scripture in the context of colonialism. For a suitably limited understanding of collective ownership, however, the idea that humanity collectively owns the earth – as in, whatever claims to its resources and spaces that humans have, any two of them have such claims in the same way, no matter where they live and when they are born – remains intellectually viable. This is so especially in the twenty-first century, with its list of problems that concern the maintenance of our planet as humanity's living space. The basic idea behind this approach is that the original resources and spaces of the earth have come about without human agency but are needed for all human activities to unfold.[29]

Grotius reflects not only on how what is originally collectively owned can be privatized, but also on how parts of the earth should *not* be. It is for his work on the morality of appropriating the sea, specifically his arguments against such a possibility, that Grotius is best known. Throughout his writings, he argues in different ways that the seas cannot be owned. The seas are free in the sense that all human uses of them, from fishery to mere passage, are permissible for everybody who can get there.

---

[28] See Buckle, *Natural Law and the Theory of Property*; Tuck, *The Rights of War and Peace*.
[29] I develop this at length in Risse, *On Global Justice*, part II.

Grotius's reasoning also bears on a very different domain, the *products of the mind* – those aforementioned ideas such as scientific, musical, literary, and other artistic works and inventions, but also images, names, symbols, and design patterns – and subsequently also on social facts. Those products are subject to intellectual property law, which, among other things, includes patents, copyrights, and trademarks. To be sure, a Grotian approach to intellectual property law would be consistent both with *compensation* for those who transform ideas into marketable products and with *setting incentives* for such work (and the same points will apply to the exploitation of social facts). But once we think of ideas (and social facts) as parallel to water and of water as not amenable to privatization, the same would be true of ideas (and social facts) as well. Ex ante, they belong to everybody, and it is hard to see how there could be legitimate benefits to developers of ideas (or of social facts) *beyond* what I am in the process of sketching here.

Since I do not think Grotius's ideas ultimately succeed for the seas (certainly not given current maritime realities), let me introduce his arguments with an eye on how they transfer to intellectual property. First, Grotius points out that any one person's use of the seas is consistent with everybody else's use of it. For water, this was arguably true in the seventeenth century, when, for instance, fishing would have involved sufficiently few fishermen with sufficiently limited carrying capacity that overfishing typically was a highly unlikely outcome. But things are very different today, and so it is no longer the case that one person's use is consistent with everybody else's. However, this claim *is* plausible for the realm of ideas, as much in the seventeenth century as today. Two centuries after Grotius, in a letter from 1813, Thomas Jefferson makes this very point about intellectual property in timeless fashion:

> If nature has made any one thing less susceptible than others of exclusive property, it is the action of the thinking power called an idea.... Its peculiar character ... is that no one possesses it the less, because every other possesses the whole of it. That ideas should be freely spread from one to another over the globe, for the moral and mutual instruction of man, and improvement of his condition, seems to have been ... designed by nature ... Society may give an exclusive right to the profits arising from them, as an encouragement ... to pursue ideas which may produce utility, but this may or may not be done, according to the will and convenience of the society, without claim or complaints by anybody.[30]

There is a point to having private property in things like apples, since only one person can make certain uses of them. But as Grotius insists regarding the seas and Jefferson does regarding ideas, there is no such point in having private property in either of these spheres. Crucially, gains for occupiers, certainly in the case of ideas,

[30] Jefferson, "The Invention of Elevators," quoted in Shiffrin, "Lockean Arguments for Private Intellectual Property," 138.

do not depend on excluding others (if we talk about actual use of ideas rather than profits *from excluding* people).

In addition to arguing for freedom of the seas by pointing out that nobody's use of the seas interferes with anyone else's (which, again, is much more plausible for the realm of ideas), *Mare Liberum* also appeals to the relevance of sea travel for trade to establish that *everybody benefits* from leaving the seas free (and this point most readily speaks to our current reality):

> For even that ocean wherewith God hath compassed the earth is navigable on every
> side round about, and the settled or extraordinary blasts of wind, not always blowing
> from the same quarter, and sometimes from every quarter, do they not sufficiently
> signify that nature hath granted a passage from all nations unto all?[31]

Similarly, use of ideas by some people subtracts nothing from their usefulness for others. Rather, it *adds* to it by increasing the overall amount of intellectual activities that inspire yet more such activities and thereby also increase the availability of whatever benefits such activities may have. *Everybody* benefits – at least with appropriate regulation put into place – if ideas are left unappropriated (and also given that anybody's use of them does not interfere with everybody else's), whereas only a few do if social and legal norms protect appropriation of ideas.[32]

Let us proceed to Grotius's third point about the seas: They cannot be *meaningfully occupied*. One cannot do anything to water parallel to how for land "the beginning of Possession is joining Body to Body."[33] Body A's being joined to B (A's getting physically connected to B) literally decreases the space for C to be joined to B. Such joining might either affect the object itself in ways that make it impossible for other people to be connected to the object the same way, or else create a situation where others could do so only by violating more basic moral rights of the person who did the original joining (say, because she needs to be pushed away, as a person might have to be pushed away from a certain bit of land if others insist on being there). These considerations fail to apply to water: One simply could not physically connect anything to water in such ways. Therefore water cannot be meaningfully occupied.

In straightforward ways of understanding what it is to occupy something, it is in a parallel manner true of ideas that they cannot be occupied. One can keep ideas secret or distract people from them. But one's own mind's grasping an idea decreases no other mind's capacity to do so. Such grasping does not affect the idea itself in

---

[31] Grotius, *The Free Sea*, 10. See also pp. 49 and 51.

[32] Were we to change intellectual property arrangement *now*, some would be made worse off (so not everybody would benefit *from these changes*) – namely, those who so far have been allowed to appropriate ideas. What I argue holds from an *ex-ante* standpoint where no property arrangements have been made yet and from where we must assess what private rights to intellectual property (if any) there should be.

[33] Grotius, *The Rights of War and Peace*, book II, chapter 8, section VI.

ways that make it impossible for others to grasp the idea, nor does it create a situation where others could do the same only if they violated more basic moral rights of the original grasper. Like water, ideas cannot be meaningfully occupied. In the case of water understood as physical spaces ("the seas"), contemporary technology might even allow for new ways of conceptualizing occupancy (contrary to what I just stated in the previous paragraph). But in the case of ideas, such innovation seems to make no difference.[34]

A Grotian approach delivers much more restrictive private intellectual property rights than Locke's enormously more influential approach.[35] But while Grotius indeed is famous for his work on ownership of the sea, there is basically no tradition of applying his thoughts in the domain of intellectual property. By contrast, there is such a tradition – and a rather influential one – that follows Locke.

In chapter V of his 1689 *Second Treatise of Government*, Locke merges his own account of humanity's collective ownership of the earth with a labor-based ("mixing") approach to privatization.[36] Individuals could privatize parts of the divine gift of the earth by working on the land. They would mix their labor with the land to stake out a better claim to it than others could muster. To be sure, there were constraints to how much of such appropriation there could be. "Enough and as good" land had to remain in common possession for later arrivals to privatize it the same way, and people could claim only an amount of land such that no spoilage would occur.[37] Subsequently, many commentators thought these ideas transferred readily to intellectual property. That is, parallel to how there is a Global Commons (the earth), so the totality of ideas forms an Intellectual Commons. Those who "have" ideas are then not inventors or creators, but explorers or discoverers. The scope of permissible claims to controlling the use of ideas must be evaluated in light of the fact that such ideas originally belong to a Commons. But then, ideas about "mixing labor" stemming from the debate about land ownership can be re-articulated to allow for far-reaching rights to privatization in the domain of ideas.

The "mixing" would consist in whatever labor is necessary to develop an idea into a marketable product. The constraints – leave "enough and as good," do not

---

[34] One might object that one can "occupy" ideas in the sense that there could be (and, in fact, are) norms of intellectual ownership, such as patent and copyright law. However, "occupation" (of sorts) of ideas is possible *only* through acceptance of such norms, which require of people other than the rights holder to renounce the option of making use of ideas although their making such use could occur consistently and simultaneously with everybody else's doing the same. This raises the question of why anybody ought to accept such norms, a question that returns us to the other two considerations against privatization.

[35] For the philosophical concerns behind intellectual property law, see Shiffrin, "Intellectual Property." See also Kuflik, "Moral Foundations of Intellectual Property Rights"; Fisher, "Theories of Intellectual Property." For the more recent development of the law of the seas, see Malanczuk, *Akehurst's Modern Introduction to International Law*, chapter 12.

[36] Locke, *Second Treatise of Government*, chapter V.

[37] For discussion of Locke's theory, see Waldron, *The Right to Private Property*, chapter 6; Sreenivasan, *The Limits of Lockean Rights in Property*.

generate spoilage – are readily satisfied for the Intellectual Commons. Since there plausibly would be infinitely many ideas, there will always be "enough and as good left" for people to exploit the Intellectual Common. And intellectual products cannot "spoil." In the Grotian approach, recall, it is fair for people to be compensated for developing certain ideas and permissible to set incentives for people to discover and develop ideas. But the extent to which they can profit should be limited to these considerations. The Lockean approach can justify much more generous entitlements to proceeds from intellectual property.

Again, Grotius's ideas on water were never transferred to intellectual property. By contrast, chapter V of Locke's *Second Treatise of Government* has obtained "totemic status" in theorizing intellectual property.[38] This transfer of Lockean ideas from land acquisition to intellectual property is regrettable. Locke took little interest in the possibility of not accepting privatization *of certain parts* of the collectively owned earth, especially the seas. But the considerations that Grotius deploys to show that the seas should be left non-privatized apply to ideas (indeed more so than to the seas). Constraints on privatization for domains where privatization does make sense (as Locke formulates them *for land*) therefore apply neither *to the sea* nor *to ideas*. That Locke's discussion has obtained "totemic status" in theorizing intellectual property rests on an intellectual error.

9.6 MORE ON THE PRIVATIZATION OF IDEAS

We are not yet ready to transfer these results to the case of social facts but must attend to some more complexity in the domain of intellectual property that also matters for social facts. We have seen that, for intellectual property, certain considerations *would* support limitations on privatization were there a presumption against privatization, parallel to how there was one in the domain of land and water. After all, the earth was considered humanity's collective property. A ready way of arguing for such a presumption in the intellectual domain and thus of making the transfer of these considerations to that domain uncontestable is to show that there actually is an Intellectual Common in relevantly similar ways to how there is a Global Common. A straightforward way of doing so is to defend a kind of *realism* about intellectual products.

Such realism denies that scientific, musical, literary, and other artistic works are literally "products" of the mind. Instead, they exist outside the realm of either material or mental objects. They belong to a "third realm" of nonmental supersensible entities, as articulated prominently by Gottlob Frege and Karl Popper, distinct from both the sensible external world and the internal world of consciousness.[39] Alleged "products" of the mind would be such products only in the sense that conscious minds can

---

[38] Drahos, *A Philosophy of Intellectual Property*, 41.

[39] (1) Gottlob Frege's 1918 essay "The Thought" is a *locus classicus* for this view; see Frege, "Der Gedanke. Eine Logische Untersuchung." For the sake of the argument, I offer an extreme

discover them. There is no invention, no refinement, nor even any *contribution* to these entities. This view delivers a presumption against privatizing elements of this third realm (which exists prior to any human activities). In a second step we could add the considerations against privatization from Grotius's discussion of the seas: They show that this presumption is hard to overcome.

To be sure, this presumption *can* be overcome. First, individuals may fairly claim *compensation* for investments in making ideas accessible, compensation that might consider opportunity costs of relevant individuals. Second, it is consistent with the argument for limited private intellectual property rights that emerges if there is such a "third realm" for societies to *set incentives* to stimulate creativity. To be sure, acknowledging compensation and incentive-setting as reasons for creating private intellectual property rights, we still leave open much potential for disagreement about how far-reaching the rights that these considerations create should be – a point we do not pursue further but need to acknowledge.

We have so far assumed that there is an Intellectual Common much like a Global Common. By contrast, consider a characterization of intellectual products that overemphasizes the subjective aspect, mirroring how our previous characterization has overemphasized the objective aspect. So intellectual products are not discovered but invented or created. There is no Fregean or Popperian third realm, no Intellectual Common, no presumption against privatization. We cannot even state that instead we have a presumption in favor of *privatization* as there is no starting point vis-à-vis which anything could be priva*tized*. It appears that now we have a presumption in favor of private property rights, potentially much beyond what compensation or incentive-setting license.

But crucially, and perhaps surprisingly, the three Grotian considerations against privatization reenter: that ideas cannot be occupied in the same sense in which, say, land can be occupied; that gains for users of ideas do not depend on excluding others; and that leaving ideas unappropriated benefits everybody. Above, these considerations ensured that the presumption against privatization could generally not be overcome. (The exceptions were fairness-based compensation and conse-quentialist considerations in favor of incentives for invention.) They reenter by limiting the *extent* of rights for which now there is a presumption. These consider-ations again ensure we consider the standpoint of the people who are expected to comply with intellectual property law. Both above and here again, these consider-ations entail that we should limit private property rights to what we can obtain via appeals to fairness and incentive-setting, although they enter in rather different ways.

version of it. For abstract objects, see Rosen, Falguerea, and Martinez-Vidal, "Abstract Objects"; Burgess and Rosen, *A Subject with No Object*. (2) Karl Popper's theory of reality distinguishes among three worlds: World 1 is the world of physical objects and events; World 2 the world of mental objects and events; and World 3 is the world of the products of the human mind. See, for instance, Popper, *Objective Knowledge*.

We have operated with two caricature views on the ontology of the objects of intellectual property. The realist account unduly eliminates the contribution of creativity. The anti-realist account overstates the role of individual minds. But as we have seen, the same results follow for intellectual property regulation regardless of whether we have a third realm of ideas or ideas are human creations. So, we can state the main result of our discussion of the possibility of private intellectual property rights as follows: The ontological status of particular intellectual products must be characterized *to some extent* in terms of components readily placed into a third realm and *to some extent* by appealing to human creativity. (One of these extents may be vanishing in a given context.) So, *to the extent* that we must appeal to something in that third realm, the considerations used for this case apply; *to the extent* that we are talking about products of the mind, the considerations given for this case apply. Either way, the respective argument generates the same constraints on private rights. Therefore, these constraints apply to the full range of intellectual property.[40]

9.7 THE LIMITS OF PRIVATIZATION: SOCIAL FACTS

We defined collectively generated pattern as follows:

> Under social parameters $P_1, \ldots, P_n$ as they prevail in country C (or perhaps in countries $C_1, \ldots, C_n$), individuals with features $F_1, \ldots, F_n$ will with probability p do action A under circumstances $CI_1, \ldots, CI_n$.

Now that we have argued that the privatization of both water and ideas should be limited, the next step is to transfer these results to social facts. Privatization of the seas was possible only in limited ways since the collective-ownership status of the earth generated a presumption against privatization, and the three Grotian considerations showed that this presumption could not be overcome for the seas. For ideas, there was a challenge in replicating this argument, for it was harder to establish the presumption against privatization. A close parallel to the collective-ownership argument was available only for an understanding of ideas and related entities as belonging to an Intellectual Common. Assertions to that effect, however, had to be balanced against the view that there was at least a substantial amount of design and creation to the development of ideas as well. But the Grotian considerations could do their work even if we assumed a subjective nature for products of the mind.

For social facts, a difficulty is that, unlike for the Global and the Intellectual Commons, any presumption against privatization cannot come from the observation that no human activities created social facts. Social facts are human creations through and through. But there plausibly is a presumption against privatizing social

---

[40] Risse, "Is There a Human Right to Essential Pharmaceuticals?"; Risse, *On Global Justice*, chapter 12.

facts (like collectively generated patterns) because these facts have arisen through a great many contributions over time. Parameters $P_1, \ldots, P_n$ as they prevail in country C; the processes that made individuals have features $F_1, \ldots, F_n$; and the ways in which circumstances $CI_1, \ldots, CI_n$ arise all are consequences of a myriad of actions over time. There is no reason to think that each contribution to the creation of social facts mattered the same, nor does it make sense to assess what counts as individual contribution. Very different ontological considerations apply to the seas, ideas, and social facts. Still, the collective nature of endeavors that generate social facts also implies a presumption against any one person claiming proceeds from such social facts, much as related arguments are available for the seas and for ideas.[41]

Parallel to the case of ideas, individual contributions to social facts do play a role, at least in connecting to things to whose very existence nobody has a special claim. In this regard, ideas and collectively generated patterns both differ from the seas. In the case of ideas, one needs to take seriously the possibility that individuals contributed to the reality of images, names, symbols, and design patterns. To be sure, that would not be so for collectively generated patterns; after all, no one individual can generate such a pattern, but an individual can either generate or discover images, names, and so on. At the same time, it does take efforts to make such patterns visible and profitable. It is in this sense that individual contributions to social facts do play a role in ways similar to the case of ideas and dissimilar to the case of the seas.

In any event, the Grotian considerations reenter, in two ways. First of all, it is because one person's use of collectively generated patterns is consistent with everybody else's; generally, shared use would stimulate more activity and thus benefit everybody (again with the qualification that appropriate qualification would need to be put into place); and there is no actual act of appropriation one could perform to make collectively generated patterns one's own (and so the presumption against privatizing proceeds from such patterns should be upheld). Secondly, to the extent that effort is needed to make social facts plain or to put them to use, these considerations should limit the reach of privatization. Once again, it is indeed plausible to pay compensation to those whose work makes social facts visible, and fair to set incentives to that effect. But that would be the extent of the benefits anybody could reap from commercializing social facts. And what we have now summarized in this paragraph shows how Data as Social Facts delivers a principle – or in any event a broad guideline – that can govern control of data and thereby reveals how Big Data help define the nature of primary goods. As I cautioned earlier, this is not a crisp principle, but nonetheless arguably a guideline of enough substance to clarify the role of data within the Rawlsian theory of distributive justice.

---

[41] Under certain circumstances, however, such social facts might be used to fend off claims of people who had no share in creating them and no involvement with the cultural context in which that occurred; see Risse, "Humanity's Collective Ownership of the Earth and Immigration."

9.8 CONCLUDING REFLECTIONS AND OBJECTIONS

The current default is that data are controlled by whoever gathers them, normally companies that provide phones, tablets, personal computers, digital assistants, electronically linked household appliances, positioning systems, or search engines. However, the default should be that collectively generated patterns are collectively controlled, in ways that would allow for individual claims, liberties, powers, and protections to be sorted out in a next step. The kind of "collective" control I have in mind should be developed in terms of the democratic reforms discussed in Chapter 3. It is in such ways that the omnipresence of data should shape social primary goods.

Those who provide means to collect data that reveal such patterns should be fairly compensated for their services, and there should be incentives of sorts for companies and individuals to do work that makes data collection possible. What would be precluded is companies involved with data collection having unlimited and exclusive control over data that allows them to anticipate trends or even redirect behavior in ways that other actors could not do with those same data. At the same time, those people whose data are (potentially) collected are also entitled to consideration, especially to the kind captured under "privacy."

Recall the three cases from Section 9.2. Let me briefly indicate how one could think about them now that we see that the data should be collectively controlled. In Case 1, data analysis reveals that a certain pattern of typing on keyboards indicates the onset of a disease. Insurers pay for such information since it lets them assess applicants or adjust premiums. In this case, a context-specific understanding of privacy should be operative – which would overrule any considerations drawing on collective control – and lead to a prohibition of this use of data.[42] In Case 2, data analysis reveals that someone's reading tastes make it likely that she would be receptive to advertising for a new book. Internet sellers pay for such information. Owing to the trivial nature of the case, no regulation is needed, but the data should be broadly available so others can advertise this way as well. In Case 3, data analysis makes it likely that somebody is the kind of voter who can be persuaded to favor a certain candidate. Campaigns pay for such information. It would be in the interest of democratic politics if such data were spread broadly.

That collectively generated patterns should be collectively controlled would (obviously) not mean that everything is available to everybody indiscriminately. So, it is neither the case that companies that collect data remain without payoffs nor the case that individuals would be without entitlements to consideration in the form of claims, liberties, or protections. But these matters should be sorted out before the background of collective control over social facts. To make something like that a reality, we need a very different Internet. Much work remains to be done

---

[42] Nissenbaum, *Privacy in Context.*

to even figure out what this would mean. But acknowledging this by no means undermines the general gist of Data as Social Facts.

Let us consider two objections. One concern is this. The way I introduced collectively generated patterns defines them in terms of countries. However, in a world with much political and economic interconnectedness, this seems unduly restrictive. Social facts capture a complex reality in which country borders play some role, but we should hardly treat countries like silos for social facts. Conversely, many social facts are generated by subgroups of those who share a citizenship (recall Durkheim's finding that suicide rates vary across religious groups).[43] To push this concern, to the extent that social facts have a *transnational* reality, restrictions on privatization of the proceeds from them will be hard to limit to particular countries. To the extent that social facts have a *subnational* reality, the nationalization of proceeds from them will be hard to justify.

This objection is well taken. In response, let me say that my previous work offers a moderate justification of states and state power, appealing to the limitation of utopian reasoning. That line of argument would point to states as the most plausible contexts for the now-established limitation on privatizing the proceeds from social facts.[44] In addition, the frequently transnational underpinnings of social facts point to the necessity of international or possibly global coordination around control over data. Given the immense significance of control over data for the future of the world, this is a welcome and sensible conclusion.

Another worry is that my reasoning delivers too much – that is, delivers conclusions that go too far, are thus implausible and would reflect negatively on the reasoning itself. Imagine a shop owner who, based on past experiences with customers and passersby, has developed good judgment about who will be interested in buying what. She has drawn inferences about how to do displays in store windows, how to speak to people to entice them to buy, and so on. She has preserved her extensive insights in a diary in the back of the store. One day, competitors open a similar store next door. Following the reasoning here, it seems that this owner ought to share her diary with the competitors, which would be absurd. Similar examples are legion. Some social facts are more obvious than others. It is a life skill to spot the less obvious ones, a skill some people have, or chose to develop, to a larger extent than others – and nothing about this seems to require rectification.

We find the beginnings of a response in a speech that Ohio Senator John Sherman, principal author of the eponymous 1890 Sherman Antitrust Act, gave on the Senate floor in support of this Act. The Act prescribes rules of free competition in commerce, prohibiting anticompetitive agreements and unilateral conduct aimed at monopolizing markets. Addressing the concern that there have been monopolies for as long as there have been markets, Sherman reasons that

---

[43] Durkheim, *Suicide*.
[44] Risse, *On Global Justice*, part IV.

now the people ... are feeling the power and grasp of these combinations, and are demanding ... a remedy for this evil, only grown into huge proportions in recent times. They had monopolies ... of old, but never before such giants as in our day. You must heed their [the people's] appeal, or be ready for the socialist, the communist, and the nihilist. Society is now disturbed by forces never felt before.[45]

The Antitrust Act was proposed at a time when business conglomerates reached a size previously unknown. The problem was not that competition *occasionally* generated monopolies, but that some monopolies dominated society: "They had monopolies ... of old, but never before such giants as in our day." That is our situation as far as control over data is concerned. As a practical consequence of the argument in this chapter, in a next step we should formulate regulation that prevents concentration of control over data in relatively few places. Doing that much is consistent with still leaving many a life advantage in the hands of those who are good at deciphering hidden social facts (whose regulation, in any event, would do more harm than create good). As always in such cases, a line must be drawn somewhere, or it emerges somehow.

[45] Sherman, "Trusts," 15.

10

God, Golem, and Gadget Worshippers: Meaning of Life in the Digital Age

This tract is an argument for pleasure in the confusion of boundaries and for responsibility in their construction.

— Donna Haraway about her "Cyborg Manifesto"[1]

10.1 THE MEANING OF LIFE

Is there a significance to one's life as a whole? That is the question of the "meaning of life." Though some people mock it (which is perhaps a lasting effect of the eponymous 1983 Monty Python movie), that question matters to many and haunts more than a few.[2] It arises in the proximity of both psychological inquiries about happiness and philosophical ones about intrinsic value.[3] And to be sure, meaning, happiness, and value are related. Whatever else is true, however, questions about meaning are somewhat less self-centered and inward-looking than questions about happiness and value; questions about meaning ask about one's place in the world, and thus about how one fits in with *what else* exists.

Meaning of life and technology are not often discussed together. But the observation that meaning is concerned with one's place in the world creates an instant (if perhaps surprising) connection to technology. As nobody has taught more effectively than Don Ihde (among theorists who are not outright dystopians), we always relate to the world in technologically mediated ways.[4] But that also means

---

[1] Haraway, *Manifestly Haraway*, 7.
[2] *Monty Python's The Meaning of Life* is a British musical sketch comedy film by the Monty Python troupe, directed by Terry Jones. Monty Python's influence on comedy has been compared to that of the Beatles on music.
[3] On happiness, see Dalai Lama, *The Art of Happiness*; Lyubomirsky, *The How of Happiness*; Ben-Shahar, *Being Happy*. See also Kahneman, *Thinking, Fast and Slow*, Part V. On intrinsic value, see Zimmerman, *The Nature of Intrinsic Value*; Lemos, *Intrinsic Value*.
[4] Ihde, *Technology and the Lifeworld*.

technology might play *the wrong kind of role* in what meaning a person's life has, especially in digital lifeworlds with the dominant role that technology plays there. This chapter explores what it means for technology to play this wrong kind of role in our quest for significance, and how to counterbalance it.

The word "significance" draws on the Latin for "sign" and on the verb *facere*, to make. So, if asking about meaning is to inquire about personal significance, it is to ask if and how a life "makes for (or constitutes) a sign" of something larger: how it connects to what is outside of it.[5] Traditionally, many people drew answers to quests about personal significance from religions. But religions have presuppositions that have lost credibility in the eyes of quite a few. Accordingly, a number of secular approaches to meaning have received attention in recent times.[6] Some are rather deflationary: Life is suffering and then it ends;[7] life is absurd and cannot gain significance;[8] life is about creating hell for each other and leaves no escape.[9]

However, others are more uplifting. One is the scientific humanism formulated in seminal ways in Russell's "A Free Man's Worship" that we encountered in Chapter 7. Russell focuses on the brain's creative possibilities and reflects on how to direct them in a world fully described by science. As a humanist view, it makes human life and a celebratory attitude toward its possibilities central, consistent with a scientific outlook.[10] Personal significance comes from finding one's place in the intersubjectively inhabited life of the mind that our brains make possible. Another uplifting secular approach to meaning is the existentialist humanism of Jean-Paul

---

[5] Biologists inquiring about "the meaning of life" seek to characterize phenomena we intuitively recognize as "life" and explain how they are possible; see, for example, Nurse, *What Is Life?* By contrast, in the philosophical discussion asking about "the meaning of life" typically is to ask about the significance of one particular life (though one could also pose the question at the species level).

[6] For some such answers, see Klemke, *The Meaning of Life*; Benatar, *Life, Death, and Meaning.* See also Metz, *Meaning in Life*; Wolf, *Meaning in Life and Why It Matters*; Nagel, *What Does It All Mean?*; Eagleton, *The Meaning of Life.* I focus on recent discussions. One way or another, a fair amount of philosophy across cultures and ages can be interpreted to speak to the question of meaning. Let me also specifically mention an account that tends to be neglected in these debates but offers much insight, that of Lame Deer John Fire; see Lame Deer, *Lame Deer.* A Lakota (and thus Native American) holy man, Lame Deer articulates an understanding of meaning in which each thing (including humans) serves as a symbol for everything it is connected to.

[7] This view is associated with Arthur Schopenhauer; see, for example, Schopenhauer, *Parerga Und Paralipomena.* A short version was articulated by Butler Carson in the TV series "Downton Abbey": "We shout and scream and wail and cry but in the end we must all die"; Episode 4.2, 2013.

[8] See, for instance, Camus, *Myth of Sisyphus.* For Camus the absurdity of life consists in us humans having persistent questions about life to which the world provides no answers. For an alternative take, see Nagel, "The Absurd."

[9] In one way of reading it, this view is articulated in Jean-Paul Sartre's play "No Exit"; see Sartre, *No Exit and Three Other Plays.*

[10] Russell, "A Free Man's Worship." For the ("scientistic") view that such humanism is as incompatible with the scientific outlook as, say, theism, see Rosenberg, *The Atheist's Guide to Reality.*

Sartre and others; this view sees humans as designing their lifeworlds through choices, a task that cannot be delegated to philosophy or religion and does not relevantly engage science at all.[11] One might even say then that persons themselves "make for signs" of the whole tapestry of their choices.

And then there is also Robert Nozick's account in terms of "limited transcendence," which has received less discussion than those two but has much to offer. Nozick envisages human life as a sequence of stages where at each new stage persons reach beyond what connections to valuable things or themes around them they have already made (where an underlying account of what is valuable must be provided).[12] The starting point for this account is Nozick's observation that religions offer significance via opportunities to transcend the world of finite entities altogether – a world that by itself does not seem to permit any resting point for questions about meaning, which could only be provided by appeal to an infinite deity. But what if – and this is Nozick's view – this world of finite entities is indeed all there is, and in particular no infinite deities exist that could provide such a resting point for questions about meaning? Nozick asks how personal significance is possible *within* finite lives in a manner that comes as close to this religious approach as possible. What such finite lives still offer is *limited* transcendence – that is, transcendence from one life stage to another through the *choices* a person makes, and thus transcendence folded into a finite life.

To my mind, what makes Nozick's proposal the most appealing secular view of meaning on offer is how it combines (a) a basically humanist attitude, (b) a characterization of meaning in terms of life's embeddedness into things of value in the world, and (c) the perspective that choices can enhance a person's place in such a setting successively throughout her lifetime – which means that transcendence, to some extent, is not something that *happens* or is *externally available*, but something we can *do*. Like Russell, Nozick offers an account based on a scientific outlook. But he goes further in spelling out the dynamic and action-guiding dimensions of this approach. Like Sartre, Nozick designates an important role for choice, but he does not make it the all-encompassing element of his account. It is through the role that Nozick gives to the element of choice, though, that we can see how technology becomes relevant to meaning.

Section 10.2 develops Nozick's view, and Section 10.3 shows how technology connects to that account. To reveal how technology permeates action – a point that does not become clear on Nozick's high-altitude view – I enlist Don Ihde's reflections on the way human activity is always mediated by technology and then also Hannah Arendt's distinction among labor, work, and action as three kinds of activity.

---

[11] For example, Sartre, *Existentialism Is a Humanism*. I just mentioned Sartre's play "No Exit" as offering a different take on the meaning of life. The relationship between these texts does not concern us here.

[12] Nozick, *Philosophical Explanations*, chapter 6. It is an amusing fact that Nozick's book and the Monty Python movie appeared in the same year (1983).

But once we see both the role of choice in Nozick's account and then also see – with help from Ihde and Arendt – how technology enters, it becomes clear how technology can engage choice (and thus personal significance) the wrong way. This is a delicate matter to tease out since, as will become clear, choice *always* occurs in technologically mediated ways (especially in digital lifeworlds) – and so one could not simply say that making choices shaped by technology undermines a person's "authenticity" or anything like that. The remainder of this chapter nonetheless explores three ways for technology to (at least potentially) engage with choice in a problematic sense.

Section 10.4 turns to Norbert Wiener's 1964 *God & Golem*, a wide-ranging investigation of the change that intelligent machines would bring. In Jewish folklore, *golems* are animated anthropomorphic creatures from clay or mud. They are human creations but can be hard to control. Wiener's golem was the intelligent machine. To be sure, the inventor of cybernetics does not worry about such golems turning into actual general AI (the sheer possibility of which he disregards). But he does fear – and this is the first manner for technology to engage personal significance the wrong way – that, as technology advances, humans turn into *gadget worshippers* by overestimating what machines can do. Section 10.5 clarifies just how gadget worshipping engages choice the wrong way and explains what to do about it. The key to the advice one should give here ("what to do about it") turns on self-conscious interrogation of one's own choices – and it turns out to be the same advice that becomes applicable to all three ways in which technology might engage human choice the wrong way.

To be sure, whatever threat the gadgets of Wiener's time pose to the role of choice in the quest for significance, general AI poses a much larger one, or so it might seem. General AI not only ushers in novel kinds of golem; it also seems to bring back something rather close to an infinite entity, the kind of entity (deities) that religions used in order to provide answers to questions about personal significance. But if indeed there could and possibly will be such infinite entities after all, at least in due course their existence would be a threat to an understanding of meaning that draws inspiration from their perceived nonexistence. For if (or once) there are such entities, why would we not seek to find our own personal significance through a connection to them, which would downgrade the importance of choice? We discuss this concern – a second way for technology to engage choice the wrong way – in Section 10.5. We turn to novelist David Foster Wallace's powerful speech *What Is Water?* for further illumination, where again the key theme is conscious interrogation of one's choices.[13]

Finally, Section 10.6 takes up Ivan Illich and Barry Sanders's work on the ways that alphabetization has shaped the mind, including our sense of selfhood.[14] Illich

---

[13] Wallace, *This Is Water*.
[14] Sanders and Illich, *ABC*.

and Sanders offer a third way for technology to engage choice (and thus personal significance) the wrong way. Their point is that digital lifeworlds undermine our sense of self and the quest for meaning, which is after all triggered by that sense. While the advice to be given in response still remains the same, Illich and Sanders highlight how much is at stake for the quest for personal significance in the technological innovation that occurs all around us now.[15]

10.2 NOZICK ON LIMITED TRANSCENDENCE

Nozick's wide-ranging *Philosophical Explanations* culminates in an intriguing account of the meaning of life.[16] To get a grip on his questions, Nozick first explores how religion has succeeded at providing meaning. Broadly understood, a "religion" is a set of beliefs and practices that relate humanity to an order of existence, providing causes and purposes beyond scientific inquiry. Theism is a special case, revolving around the existence of at least one deity (supernatural beings with overwhelming powers as creators or interveners).

Religions can readily explain how a life "makes for a sign" of something larger. They offer narratives about the world that create roles for individuals and respond to queries such as "Why am I here?" or "Why does this happen?" beyond scientific explanations. Nozick asks what the most defensible account is that religions have offered. This most defensible account, he concludes, is one that provides meaning by connecting a person's life to something larger – a thing about which questions regarding *its* connection to another, even larger something do not arise. For all finite beings, this question does arise. It is only for beings that are in some sense infinite that it does not arise. Divinity's infiniteness enables it to provide meaning.[17]

At this stage of his discussion, Nozick has a notion of *intrinsic value* in place. He understands it as organic unity, integration within one's limits. For instance, for paintings this means different components of the design are interrelated; the eye is led from place to place by form and color before reaching the thematic center. For the natural world one might think of diversity within ecosystems. Scientific theories are valuable to the extent that they integrate different themes (e.g., Newtonian physics explaining motion of both bodies on Earth and heavenly bodies). The value of a human life draws in the first instance on how the parts of a body (especially the brain) that have evolved over time come together to enable us to act. This account

---

[15] For a discussion of meaning in virtual worlds (also considering the possibility that humans might have to "retreat" to such worlds in the not-too-distant future), see Chalmers, *Reality+*, chapter 17. For an investigation of meaning in the digital age from a virtue-ethics standpoint, see Vallor, *Technology and the Virtues*, Part III.

[16] Nozick, *Philosophical Explanations*, chapter 6.

[17] It is *only* for such beings, in the sense of "at most": infiniteness is a necessary but not sufficient condition here. After all, the natural numbers are of an infinite size but also a subset of the real numbers.

covers many but not all common uses of "intrinsic value," but we need not engage with Nozick's analysis of value in any detail. What matters – and I will assume as much – is that our world includes things that are intrinsically valuable (and thus of value in their own right), that this makes it worthwhile for us to relate to them in some way, and that humans are among the things that are intrinsically valuable, without exhausting this domain.

Based on his analysis of how divinity's infiniteness enables it to provide meaning, Nozick asks next how we must understand the notion of meaning so that *only* unlimitedness provides a secure basis and stopping place for further questions. This is so if meaning is about how something connects to what is outside of it; more specifically, meaning is the way something is placed in a larger context of things with intrinsic value. Then only an unlimited deity can be its own meaning (have *intrinsic meaning*) and secure the meaning of lesser beings. Nozick transfers these findings to the secular world he thinks we inhabit, where infinite deities do not exist. He seeks to preserve as much as possible the idea that meaning is generated through transcendence of one's present condition. *Limited* transcendence folds the idea of transcendence *of* (and thus *beyond*) the finite life *into* that finite life itself, as much as that is possible.

So according to Nozick's view, the meaning of a person's life is "the organized unity of the realm of value as centered on, as organized around, him."[18] That is, its meaning consists in a life's connection to other entities with intrinsic value (including but not limited to other humans). For the value of X, we need not look beyond X; yet for its meaning, we do. If asking about the meaning of a life is to inquire about significance (which coheres with everything Nozick says), it is to ask if and how a life "makes for (constitutes) as sign" of something larger – how it connects to what is outside of it. "This meaning will depend upon the array of external or wider values connected with it," he explains, "and upon the nature of the connections, their strength, intensity, closeness, the way [a person's] attachment unifies those values."[19] Meaning becomes "limited transcendence," the building of connections to things (and their integration into one's life) worth relating to.

Like Russell's view, Nozick's is a humanist one in virtue of making human life and a celebratory attitude toward its possibilities central, consistent with a scientific outlook. Unlike its religious foils, that process of building connections does not (and could not) aim to end with something *intrinsically* meaningful about which questions on its wider context of value do not arise. Anyone who approaches our subject with the presumption that there can be no personal significance without a connection to something infinite will be disappointed. But such a presumption is misguided.

Nozick's view of significance suggests an iterative growth process that could stretch over a lifetime. Persons would connect to entities of value in their environment,

---

[18]   Nozick, *Philosophical Explanations*, 611.
[19]   *Ibid.*

where making relevant connections would take time. One could think of acquiring skills; performing important work; building relationships; engaging with nature, art, or literature, and so on. Doing such things constitutes acts of limited transcendence. Depending on how intensively or extensively one goes about such pursuits, they can be transformative. What a person's life is a sign of, its significance, thereby also changes.

The life of the ethical person has greater meaning because engaging with ethics just is for that person to ask the right questions. Ethics is about relating to the value of something in appropriate ways. Suppose a person, a movement, or perhaps a part of nature or even a building or neighborhood stands in need of some assistance, input, or aid. Reflecting on what it means for me to relate to the value of these things in appropriate ways (how they matter by themselves, how I am related to them, etc.), I might conclude that it is *for me* to provide what is needed. I would take such insights as guidance for how to direct my energies: That is what it means to let one's quest for personal significance be guided by ethics. "In behaving ethically, we transcend our own limits and connect to another's value as value," as Nozick explains.[20]

Again, such an iterative process could extend over a lifetime. Or it could end when a person concludes that her life does not include (or she opts not to allocate) further capacities for building connections to additional things of value. She found a resting point in the midst of her wider context of value and would be beyond reproach for that. This approach allows for comparisons to the effect that one life is more meaningful than another, the kind of comparison I offered when stating that an ethical life has greater meaning. But there is no race to win. Comparisons will tend to be most illuminating for different possible trajectories of the same person, and least for people who lead very different lives.

That this is an iterative process is central to how Nozick transfers the idea of transcendence from religious frameworks to the finite context of a human life. The gist is not simply that we find meaning in connections to certain things around us (rather than to divine figures), but that we thereby obtain a certain level of control over how we perform acts of limited transcendence. In religious contexts, the transcendent relationship is understood in a range of ways. Part of the religious narrative might be that we simply have such a relationship that provides significance without further ado. Or it might be up to divine grace, interventions of priestly classes, or our actions to make it happen. But in the limited-transcendence view, meaning *always* is something a person can actively advance.

Luck has much to do with one's starting point in this regard. Some people find themselves thrown into a wide context of value. They have a certain level of significance as a matter of good fortune; an obvious example would be Prince Charles, who was slated to be the next king of England on the day of his birth

---

[20] Nozick, 612.

and thereby assumed an instant significance for all those who care about what the British monarchy stands for. It is often (though far from always) a feature of religious narratives that the way these narratives create significance through transcendental connections to a deity renders a person's circumstances distinctly unimportant. As opposed to this, a person's circumstances will always be important for the significance of her life in an account that ties meaning to what happens within a life. But anything beyond what good fortune provides only comes from active construction. And in another contrast to religious approaches, transcendence of this sort always is something we can *do*. We obtain here a sense of personal significance that leaves quite a bit to our initiative. To a large extent we can each be *poets of our lives* (to use a formulation from Nietzsche).[21]

10.3 PERSONAL SIGNIFICANCE MEDIATED THROUGH TECHNOLOGY

"We may thirst for more," Nozick muses. He does not mean to address believers who bemoan the absence of infinity in his account but rather speaks to people hoping our species as such will transcend its current limits. The future may bring

> contact with other forms of life, ... further human evolution, contributing humanity's special quality to the universe's symphony of life and culture. It is not difficult to imagine a wider scope for human adventure (and failure too), a broader context in which our limits can be transcended.[22]

Such a thirst obviously needs to be satisfied by *technology*. Technology is not a topic in Nozick's formidable tome. *Philosophical Explanations* pays no heed to the fact that acts in pursuit of our significance – long before we would ever "thirst for more" – are always *technologically mediated*. To appreciate how the element of choice in Nozick's view engages technology, I look at two rather different authors (though both in the tradition of Heideggerian phenomenology): Don Ihde and Hannah Arendt. Ihde distinguishes various technologically mediated ways for humans to encounter the world. Arendt characterizes various types of human activity – all of which in turn would be mediated as Ihde describes. Putting these themes together, we obtain a more nuanced view of the role technology plays in the creation of personal significance than Nozick's high-altitude perspective provides. This more nuanced view also lets us understand how technology can play *the wrong kind of role* in the ways people create personal significance.

In earlier chapters, we encountered several dystopian philosophers of technology, including Marcuse, Heidegger, Mumford, and Ellul. Without adopting their perspectives across the board – perspectives that would engulf and obstruct the pursuit

---

[21] Nietzsche, *The Gay Science*, section 299.
[22] Nozick, *Philosophical Explanations*, 618.

of any kind of significance – I acknowledge the warnings they issue. If any of those dystopian scenarios held up, pursuit of significance would return us to Adorno's dictum "Es gibt kein richtiges Leben im falschen" (there is no correct life in the midst of a wrong life).[23] The philosophy of technology has moved beyond such large-scale thinking (where indeed it is its very scale that makes such thinking hard to assess) to a more concrete engagement with how particular technologies shape human life. This work has been pioneered by Don Ihde.

The title of one of Ihde's major works is *Technology and the Lifeworld: From Garden to Earth*.[24] This garden is biblical Eden, the Garden of God from the Book of Genesis, where human involvement with the environment is *un*mediated: Adam and Eve move about naked, eat what they find (with restrictions), and have no need for or access to technology. Once expelled from paradise, humans establish "earth," a lifeworld mediated through technology. To say technology "mediates" means it does not simply come in between humans and an independently existing reality to enable humans to work *on* this reality. Instead, technology is constitutive of how we experience the world. Reality arises for us only (and always already) in and through technological mediation. Ihde distinguishes in particular among the following three ways in which this happens, but this is a non-exhaustive list.

First of all, technological artifacts become part of human experiencing, broadening how our bodies are sensitive to the world. One example is eyeglasses, devices through which we look at the world and that themselves withdraw from perception. Eyeglasses become incorporated into the way human bodies experience the world. Other examples include hearing aids, prosthetic devices, and also bikes and cars, phones, social media, construction tools, and weapons. Skills used in martial arts and many other contexts could also be mentioned. Devices, knowledge, and skills are firmly integrated into the way humans navigate their lifeworld. Ihde talks about *embodiment relations* to characterize how technology mediates access to the world this way.

Secondly, there are *hermeneutical relations*. Here the artifact does not withdraw from perception in our relation to the world but provides a representation of it: The artifact must be "read" or otherwise interpreted (hence talk about hermeneutics). A typical example is the reading of a thermometer and other measurement devices. Other cases include writing as technologically mediated language (a matter to which we return in Section 10.6), dashboards in cars or planes, clocks, medical charts, ultrasound, and MRIs, but also photography and video. Thirdly, there are *alterity relations*. Here humans do not relate *via* technology to the world but are related *to* or *with* a technology that might itself be connected to the rest of the world. Technology is a "quasi-other." People often approach technologies in

---

[23] Adorno, *Minima Moralia*, 42.
[24] Ihde, *Technology and the Lifeworld*.

anthropomorphic ways and project human properties into them (e.g., "smart-phones" and, of course, AI) or "care for" them (e.g., houses, pianos, cars).[25]

To turn to Arendt, consider her tripartite classification of agency into labor, work, and action (terms she uses in specific senses).[26] *Labor* includes practices necessary for maintaining life (e.g., food production, bodily maintenance, childcare). Such activities must be incessantly renewed and yet create nothing permanent. Since its results are used up (typically quickly), labor cannot furnish a common world where humans pursue anything beyond consumption. Then there is *work*, the production of things distinct from what already exists in nature. Work "fabricates the sheer unending variety of things whose sum total constitutes the human artifice."[27] *Homo faber*, the human understood as maker, looks at nature as the provider of materials to create that artifice and accordingly has a largely instrumental attitude toward nature.[28]

Finally, there is *action*, something hard to come by and easily confused with labor or work. Homo faber has limited freedom: Her output is judged by the ability of this output to sustain a world fit for human use. By contrast, action is the capacity to begin something new, including the ability to do the unexpected, in ways that disclose a person's self-understanding. *Political* action involves joint reassessments of the spectrum of human possibilities and actualizes our capacity to begin something new by making our world a certain way. Homo faber reveals about herself only that she can do certain work. But action and the speech that expresses it contain answers to questions about an agent's identity, answers that would also reveal a different attitude toward nature than homo faber typically displays.

To bring all this back to Nozick, recall that the pursuit of personal significance (or meaning) through limited transcendence involves choices. We have the option of going through life by connecting to more things of value, and do so in stages so that we can grow as persons. The choices involved might include each of these three

---

[25] The role of such objects in human relations can also be analyzed in terms of Latour's actor-network theory; see, for example, Latour, *Reassembling the Social*; Latour, *We Have Never Been Modern*.

[26] In *The Human Condition*, Arendt treats labor in chapter III (focused on the *animal laborans*, the laboring animal, since in this necessity to add to nutrition and reproduction humans operate much like other animals); work in chapter IV (focused on *homo faber*, the human as a maker); and action in chapter V. These three form the *vita activa*. All components are required for the flourishing of a common human life. Still, Arendt means for that list (labor, work, action) to express an ascending hierarchy of importance that modern life has inverted. She disagrees with Marx about giving what she considers an outsized status to labor as opposed to work and action. While concerns about how our current lives do violence to the human condition is Arendt's main theme, my interest is merely in the different kinds of agency she identifies.

[27] Arendt, *The Human Condition*, 136.

[28] On the history of the idea of *homo faber*, see Tönsing, "Homo Faber or Homo Credente?" As Arendt says, the "oldest conviction" of *homo faber* is that he is the measure of all things; see Arendt, *The Human Condition*, 306.

kinds of agency (labor, work, action), and this is how Nozick connects to Arendt. And it lies then in the nature of our labor, work, and action that they make connections to things of value around us. Such connections will be made with the goal of sustaining life, producing things, or initiating new projects in the presence of a plurality of viewpoints. In all of these activities, in turn, technology enters in the mediating ways that Ihde sketches (and this is how, via Arendt, Nozick connects to Ihde): Technology expands our reach by becoming part of our bodies, interprets the world for us, or connects to a multitude of quasi-others around us with and through which we engage.

Let me elaborate a bit. Labor sustains life and needs tools to do so, and therefore what it even means to sustain life over time is determined by available technology. Think about the preparation of food. A skilled cook uses kitchen equipment to transform raw food into meals, and thus prepares these meals with the assistance of equipment that, if used well, extends the possibilities of the human body itself. Some devices in the kitchen indicate temperatures or time passed and thus interpret the state of preparation the ingredients are currently in. It is not uncommon for people to develop a special relationship with their kitchen in the sense that its ensemble of devices and utensils suits their needs and skills, and this ensemble needs to be maintained (and in that sense, cared for). And what is found in a contemporary kitchen in, say, Sydney, Hamburg, or Oklahoma City varies dramatically from how food was prepared at other place and at other times.

Work fills our world with material objects ranging from houses, walls, and streets to the many gadgets that give us some joy or make life easier. What material objects we expect to that effect, how we think they ought to be produced, and what we think they ought to look like depends on available technology. For example, a medical doctor uses multifarious tools to assess the health of a human body and thus approaches this body in ways mediated by these tools – which, if used well, become an extension of her body. She has her lab analyze blood, urine, or tissue samples, and thereby the lab devices make this human body legible. Much like the cook in the earlier example, the doctor (or somebody on her behalf) takes care of the devices to make sure they remain functional. Also like in the earlier scenario, what it means to be a doctor in a contemporary medical facility in Sydney, Hamburg, or Oklahoma City varies dramatically from how healing was practiced at other place and at other times. Action designs human relationships to the extent that we allow for them not to be defined by the need to sustain life and the demand for certain products. What all this means concretely is driven by available technology. Specifically, as far as political action is concerned, Chapter 3 has already engaged with the materiality of democracy.

So Nozick offers us an account of the meaning of life as limited transcendence, which makes choice central; Arendt's account can be linked to Nozick's because it spells out in what kinds of activity people's choices become manifest; and each of these types of activity in turn is technologically mediated as discussed by Ihde – and it is through these connections that we can see how technology becomes relevant to meaning. Today, technology in digital lifeworlds mediates agency and thus the ways labor, work, and action advance personal significance and thus one's meaning of life. That is, the choices we make (in terms of which we progress through the stages of our life) now routinely involve how we deploy labor, work, or action *in digital lifeworlds* – and thus it is digital technology that mediates our relationship with the world around us (in particular, in terms of embodiment, hermeneutical and alterity relations).

And to be sure, digital technology mediating our relationship with the world around us brings enormous possibilities through the elaborate ways that such life-worlds connect humans, sophisticated machines, and abundant data. Technological innovation makes it possible for persons to traverse the stages of their lives in ways that increase connections to things of value. The Internet's pervasiveness and interconnectedness make it possible for us to reach others in unprecedented ways. The immersive character of augmented or virtual reality supplements and enriches the physical reality that our bodies inhabit. But technology can *also* enter our pursuits in wrong ways – which is the subject of the remainder of this chapter.

10.4 WIENER AND THE GADGET WORSHIPPERS

It was in 1964, the year of Norbert Wiener's death, that the mathematician and philosopher published *God & Golem, Inc.: A Comment on Certain Points Where Cybernetics Impinges on Religion.*[29] *God & Golem* is a wide-ranging investigation of the changes that intelligent machines might bring. Among Wiener's subjects are questions around life and creation, contrasts between creation and self-replication, and the hierarchy of God-human-machine, but also machine learning (long before that term was associated with a certain kind of mathematics), machine reproduction, and the place of machines in society. His essay also speaks to the ways that technology engages with the human quest for significance as I understand it, identifying one way for technology to do so *the wrong way*.

In Jewish folklore, golems are animated humanlike creatures from clay or mud. One especially famous narrative involves sixteenth-century rabbi Judah Loew ben Bezalel. Rabbi Loew fashioned his golem – affectionately called Yossele – to protect the Jews of Prague. As usual for such creatures (think *Frankenstein*), stories abound about how eventually Yossele became uncontrollable. Wiener's envisaged golem was the intelligent machine, which in his lifetime had become increasingly feasible

---

[29] Wiener, *God & Golem*. See also Conway, *Dark Hero of the Information Age*, chapter 15; Kline, *The Cybernetics Moment*, chapter 6. *God & Golem* appeared posthumously. On Wiener's life, see his autobiography, Wiener, *Norbert Wiener—A Life in Cybernetics*. See also Montagnini, *Harmonies of Disorder*; Heims, *John von Neumann and Norbert Wiener*; Conway, *Dark Hero of the Information Age*.

with technology. He imagined humans coexisting with both the god who made them and this new golem that they might one day create.[30]

Wiener even explores how it might be possible for machines to create other machines in *their* own image. It was also at this time that mathematician I. J. Good wrote "Speculations concerning the First Ultra-Intelligent Machine," the paper that introduced the notion of an *intelligence explosion*.[31] "Let an ultra-intelligent machine be defined as a machine that can far surpass all the intellectual activities of any man however clever," Good writes:

> Since the design of machines is one of these intellectual activities, an ultra-intelligent machine could design even better machines; there would then unquestionably be an "intelligence explosion," and the intelligence of man would be left far behind.[32]

Good – who collaborated with Turing on cryptography to support the British war effort – goes rather far by asserting that "the survival of man depends on the early construction of an ultra-intelligent machine."[33] So Wiener, in virtue of the ideas that he pursued in *God & Golem*, was part of an avant-garde optimism about the sheer possibility of machine intelligence that becomes very visible in Good's article. However, notwithstanding the fact that both Good and Wiener were part of this avant-garde optimism, Wiener never considers the possibility of an actual intelligence explosion – and thus his optimism in this regard falls far short of Good's.

Let me elaborate a bit on why Wiener did not seriously entertain the possibility of an intelligence explosion. Based on the state of engineering at the time, Wiener speculates that a computer equivalent to a brain would occupy a sphere of thirty feet in diameter. He finds it hard to believe that, compared with machines, "the brain does not have some advantages corresponding to its enormous operational size, which is incomparably greater than what we might expect of its physical size."[34] It is curious that someone who contemplated telegraphing a person did not anticipate that the speed of breakthroughs in his own lifetime would continue and overcome such limitations (especially regarding computational capacities).[35] Wiener does

---

[30] Wiener himself was an agnostic for most of his life, but increasingly embraced a universal spirituality and a generic humanitarian creed; see Conway, *Dark Hero of the Information Age*, chapter 15. On golems, see Idel, *Golem*; Rosenberg, *The Golem and the Wondrous Deeds of the Maharal of Prague*.

[31] Good, "Speculations Concerning the First Ultraintelligent Machine." This was a period of optimism about AI; see Nilsson, *Quest for Artificial Intelligence*, Part II. For more recent optimism regarding the occurrence of a singularity, see Kurzweil, *The Singularity Is Near*. For recent musings on AI by experts inspired by Wiener, see Brockman, *Possible Minds*.

[32] Good, "Speculations Concerning the First Ultraintelligent Machine," 33.

[33] Good, 31.

[34] Wiener, *God & Golem*, 72.

[35] For telegraphing humans, see Wiener, 36. For the view that Wiener was right not to worry about machines in ways other than he did and that instead we should focus on what humans do with them, see Pinker, "Tech Prophecy." See also Jones, "The Artistic Use of Cybernetic Beings."

think, however, that investigating how intelligent machines could enrich human life is legitimate and productive.

Despite his view on the brain's likely advantages, Wiener thinks that machines are superior in speed and accuracy, and that it is unproblematic to develop intelligent machines to put them to work: He proposes the motto "render unto man the things which are man's and unto the computer the things which are the computer's."[36] However, he believes that there is "a particular type of engineer and organizer of engineering which I shall designate by the name of *gadget worshiper*."[37] Gadget worshippers seek to build machines

> to avoid the personal responsibility for a dangerous or disastrous decision by placing the responsibility elsewhere: on chance, on human superiors and their policies which one cannot question, or on a mechanical device which one cannot fully understand but which has presumed objectivity.[38]

Wiener mentions Nazi logistics mastermind Adolf Eichmann as one terrible example. Wiener knows that this is an extreme case, but a more mundane worry is that the automatized world that gadget worshippers relish "will make smaller claims on human ingenuity than does the present one and will take over from us our need for difficult thinking, as a Roman slave who was also a Greek philosopher might have done for his master."[39] Machines pursue human goals only if appropriately designed and supervised, which continuously involves responsible agency.

To illustrate his worries, Wiener relates a tale about a magic monkey paw that fulfils wishes.[40] After an elderly couple wishes for a certain amount of money, a representative of the company that employs their son arrives. He conveys the devastating news that the son has perished in an accident, offering that very amount as restitution. Their wish failed to enumerate all the horrible circumstances under which they would *of course* not want to become beneficiaries. Due to the world's uncodifiable ambiguity, human pursuits involve responsible decision-making at every turn. As the tale illustrates, humans easily fail at that, and getting these things right is not just a matter of speed and accuracy. Accordingly, machines should never be trusted with decision-making. But their presence highlights human deficiencies (*especially* regarding speed and accuracy), and thus makes it ever more tempting to turn responsibilities over to machines. Wiener concludes (and this is a quote I also

---

[36] Wiener, *God & Golem*, 73.

[37] Wiener, 53. Emphasis is added. This motto places him in between gadget *worshipers* and figures one could call gadget *skeptics*, who see "only blasphemy and the degradation of man in the use of any mechanical adjuvants whatever to thoughts;" Wiener, 73.

[38] Wiener, *God & Golem*, 54.

[39] Wiener, 63. Eichmann naturally was on Wiener's mind since Eichmann's trial in Jerusalem happened in 1961/2, ending with his execution on June 1, 1962. See Arendt, *Eichmann in Jerusalem*.

[40] This tale appears in Jacobs, *The Monkey's Paw*.

use in the epigraph to the Preface) that "the world of the future will be an ever more demanding struggle against the limitations of our intelligence, not a comfortable hammock in which we can lie down to be waited upon by our robot slaves."[41]

One theme in the present book is a major insight from the philosophy of technology, that technology shapes human life and delineates what possibilities of being human are available. We have encountered that theme through dystopian writers, but also, in different ways, in Section 10.3. From Ihde we adopted the point that humans engage with reality always in technologically mediated ways. Pursuit of personal significance is no exception. It is therefore pointless to insist on anything like an "authentic" pursuit of significance if that means that technology is precluded from playing a large role. But Wiener offers a stern warning that even in a lifeworld that is (and is understood to be) technologically mediated – which "earth" is anyway, and digital lifeworlds are in extremis – integration of technology into one's life can go too far. The phrase "gadget worshipper" makes the concern vivid (and the applicability of the term is not limited to "a particular type of engineer and organizer of engineering"). If technology is not conscientiously integrated, the humanist outlook of limited transcendence is lost.

At the same time, Wiener's statement just cited reveals why it is so difficult to say anything specific about what conscientious integration means: Technology does increase our reach, AI especially will reflect our limitations back at us, and so we will want to engage ever more with technology. But we might thereby surrender rather than enhance our exercise of reason. Instead of the misguided worshipping of a divine being, we embrace the equally misguided worshipping of human designs. The only way forward for anyone concerned with significance is to interrogate one's choices to understand the extent to which gadget worshipping drives them. While no conclusive answer might be forthcoming, at some point an existentialist endorsement of certain choices – a self-aware embrace of certain courses of action that from then on make a person who they are – will be necessary and appropriate. This theme of self-interrogation in combination with an eventual existentialist endorsement is the general gist of the advice I wish to offer in response to the three concerns about how technology

---

[41] Wiener, *God & Golem*, 69. Computer science pioneer Joseph Weizenbaum – whose work echoes themes from both Wiener and Mumford – starts his seminal book *Computer Power and Human Reason* by stating that "we, all of us, have made the world too much into a computer, and that this remaking of the world in the image of the computer started long before there were any electronic computers;" Weizenbaum, *Computer Power and Human Reason*, ix. Weizenbaum argues that while AI may well be possible, computers will always lack wisdom and compassion. The capacity to choose makes us human. Choice, however, to Weizenbaum is the product of judgment, not calculation. On the theme of whether humans can flourish in a world of smart machines, see also Reich, Sahami, and Weinstein, *System Error*, chapter 6; Kissinger, Schmidt, and Huttenlocher, *The Age of AI*, chapter 7. To the extent that gadget worshipping amounts to an erosion of accountability, this topic has also been revisited in Nissenbaum, "Accountability in a Computerized Society."

might engage human choice the wrong way. Now that the first way of doing so is on the table, let me introduce the second one and then elaborate a bit on the advice.

10.5 GADGET WORSHIP AND GENERAL AI

Wiener was convinced that general AI was nothing to worry about. So to the extent that he was troubled by gadget worshipping, general AI was not the kind of gadget on his agenda. Thinking about these matters today, however, we must realize that the golems we might design are much more powerful than what Wiener envisaged. Some thinkers are optimistic about technological advances. Environmentalist James Lovelock thinks specifically cyborgs would greatly assist our efforts to confront climate change.[42] Owing to their intelligence and lack of tribal thinking, they would grasp the urgency of the task, recognize what to do, and make sure everyone stays the course. Lovelock does not fear that cyborgs will turn against us, if only because doing so would consume more energy than highly intelligent beings would expend due to climate change. He echoes Good's insistence that "the survival of man depends on the early construction of an ultra-intelligent machine."[43] But the possibility of general AI means we must reconsider Wiener's discussion of gadget worshipping for current technological possibilities. If gadget worshipping is the first manner in which technology might engage personal significance the wrong way, then a second manner comes on our horizon once we take the possibility of general AI more seriously than Wiener did.

A crucial point to recall at this stage is that, with their underlying humanism, possibilities of limited transcendence seem to depend on the *absence* of an infinite deity for their intellectual appeal. After all, the deity's infiniteness means that it at least potentially has one advantage that an account drawing on life's finiteness could never have: *Only* infinite beings could offer a resting point for further questions about significance. Let us now connect this point to general AI. General AI could potentially surpass anything humans can do. Perhaps this would be true only in ways translatable into speed and accuracy. But a whole lot of speed and accuracy just might eventually combine an approximation of human capacities with genuinely new possibilities from the sheer force of computation (see Chapter 1). Such a general AI might be a golem (a human creation) – and the closest thing to actual infiniteness that is possible. The sheer existence of such an entity might unsettle and destabilize anyone who thinks they are at ease in their thinking about personal significance.

As it turns out, however, general AI is not actually qualitatively different from Wiener's gadget worshipping as far as its ways of engaging human choice the wrong way is concerned. For one thing, such a golem would still be finite. It would just have possibilities of computing and storing that far surpass human capacities. So

---

[42] Lovelock, *Novacene*.
[43] Good, "Speculations Concerning the First Ultraintelligent Machine," 31.

questions about how it relates to things beyond itself do still arise. (In any event, infiniteness is a necessary rather than sufficient condition for questions about an entity's significance not to arise.) And not only do these questions arise about a general AI – arguably, what a general AI "is a sign of" (i.e., what its significance is) is a question to which we can offer the beginnings of a response. For one thing, and rather importantly, the data feeding into a general AI would come from the life that golems and designers share and the life the designers lived before. A person seeking to obtain personal significance connecting to a general AI would lean on an entity that brings enormous computational capacities to the bulk of shared experience of which that person is also part. This would make any general AI distinctly different from (and in important ways much more human-like than) the creating and intervening deity with which Nozick's investigation started.

Also recall at this stage what we said about the grand democratic AI utopia from Chapter 3. For a whole range of issues, it is not the case that there is a "most intelligent" solution that we have missed for whatever reasons. The issues for which this is worth pointing out would include *especially* those bearing on personal significance. Mainstream intelligence-research does not even think that there is only one kind of intelligence. Moreover, whoever got invested in building such a general AI will have inserted their own interests to a considerable degree already. There might be lots of benefits from engaging with such golems, perhaps along the lines sketched by Lovelock and perhaps even in ways that inform questions that arise in the process of forging one's meaning in life. Still, the situation is indeed after all not qualitatively different from what Wiener confronted when addressing the gadget worshipping on his scientific radar.

And since these two ways for technology to engage human choice are not qualitatively different, the advice one should give in response also remains the same. So let me elaborate a bit on the advice I formulated at the end of the last section. It is up to each person to connect to things of value around them. As we noted, that includes an existentialist endorsement of choices. One can surrender choices to powerful entities, including those that bring vastly superior analytical capacities to human experience. But anyone who does so (rather than merely taking advice from them) ceases to *make* choices in any interesting sense. One relinquishes the exercise of one's human capacities (and ceases to value them).

A famous line in Goethe's *Faust* states this: "For they whose striving never ceases are ours for their redeeming."[44] Like the ideas around transcendence, this originally religious thought transfers to finite contexts. The "redemption" then is not religious elevation, and there is no outside force that performs such elevation. Instead, the *right kind* of striving creates a stable understanding of significance that the person can (and must) attain for herself. What replaces (or now makes for) redemption is

---

[44] Goethe, *Faust*, Part II, verses 11936f. In German: "Wer immer strebend sich bemüht, den können wir erlösen."

the process of attaining and maintaining meaning. Adopting relevant choices from the outside, even and especially from a general AI, undermines this process.

Limited transcendence offers distinctive possibilities for resisting despair at the prospect that superintelligent entities might affect the human quest for personal significance. To fend off this despair, we need to work actively on seeing ourselves as embedded into a larger, value-filled world. We need to reconsider ecosystems, animals, art, and much more. We need to see value in many places and appreciate ourselves and other humans as part of a world that deserves more awe than excessively self-centered standpoints provide. To make that point, I conclude this section by drawing attention to some powerful passages from novelist David Foster Wallace's *What Is Water?*, a 2005 graduation address.[45]

To approach the topic of how important it is to appreciate the value-filled richness of one's environment, Wallace starts with some annoying people he encounters during daily errands. We can scoff at such people for impatient or overbearing behavior. But we can also reinterpret this behavior as the human-all-too-human actions of severely overburdened parents, nurses, neighbors, or friends. This might not be accurate – or it just might. Either way, we can *opt* to see situations that way:

> If you're automatically sure that you know what reality is, and who and what is really important – if you want to operate on your default setting – then you, like me, will probably not consider possibilities that aren't pointless and annoying. But if you really learned how to think, how to pay attention, then you will know you have other options. It will actually be within your power to experience a crowded, hot, slow, consumer-hell type situation as not only meaningful, but sacred, on fire with the same force that lit the stars – compassion, love, the subsurface unity of all things.[46]

We get to choose and do not have to take our cues from how others would standardly interpret such a situation. Wallace continues:

> Because here's something else that's true: in the day-to-day trenches of adult life, there is actually no such thing as atheism. There is no such thing as not worshipping. Everybody worships. The only choice we get is what to worship. . . . Worship power, you will end up feeling weak and afraid, and you will need ever more power over others to keep the fear at bay. Worship your intellect, being seen as smart – you will end up feeling stupid, a fraud, always on the verge of being found out. And so on. Look, the insidious thing about these forms of worship is not that they're evil or sinful, it is that they're *unconscious*. They are default settings. . . . The really

---

important kind of freedom involves attention, and awareness, and discipline, and being able truly to care about other people and to sacrifice for them, over and over, in myriad petty little unsexy ways, every day. That is real freedom. That is being taught how to think. The alternative is unconsciousness, the default setting, the "rat race," the constant, gnawing sense of having had and lost some infinite thing.[47]

We can read Wallace as drawing attention to the element of choice in Nozick's account. Our minds can relate to the world in ways that actively put us on the lookout for things and themes of value all around us. Exercising that capacity is up to us, regardless of the existence of any golems.

10.6 ILLICH AND SANDERS ON THE ALPHABETIZATION OF THE MIND

My response to gadget worshipping (and its threat to the quest for meaning) is to insist on self-conscious exercise of choice and active interrogation of how we incline to see our lives. This response applies both to the first way in which technology might engage the element of choice in Nozick's account of meaning of life the wrong way (Wiener's gadget worshipping) and to the second way (the possible advent of AI and a possible human inclination to defer to it). However, an assumption behind everything said so far is that there is an *underlying self* of sorts that searches for meaning. Technology mediates human activity, including that geared toward securing meaning. Today, digital technology increasingly does this work. But what if, instead of digital lifeworlds being the technology that *mediates* the relationship between self and world, they *undermine* selfhood and thus the framing of our discussion up to this point? That would be a third, and distinctly dramatic, way for technology to engage the element of choice in Nozick's account of meaning of life the wrong way, by undermining that whole account rather thoroughly.

That we should indeed be concerned along such lines has been pushed by social critic Ivan Illich and medievalist Barry Sanders (whom we briefly encountered in Chapter 6) in their 1989 book *ABC: The Alphabetization of the Popular Mind*.[48] Exploring how written language affects our perception of the world and ourselves in it, they worry about how computers change our sense of self. The modern understanding of the self, they argue, is inextricably intertwined with a culture dominated by *texts*. Technology designed by code that conveys information in novel ways changes the background before which we see ourselves and relate to each other. But if selfhood per se is intertwined with cultural dominance of texts, so is any quest

---

[47] Wallace, 97–123.
[48] Sanders and Illich, *ABC*.

for meaning such selves can pursue. ABC appeared while Bill Gates was first rolling out Windows and years before Steve Jobs succeeded in marketing Apple products widely. To the extent that Illich and Sanders's worries were valid then, they are much more so now.[49]

Illich and Sanders submit that human thought has experienced three major shifts. The first resulted from the introduction of alphabets. Oral traditions see *recollecting* as one kind of doing in the present. Prealphabetic bards drew on storehouses of memory to compose songs, poems, or stories, driven by the rhythm of the lyre or strum of the lute. But memory as modern humans understand it could only arise from use of texts. Recollecting became a generic background activity underlying everything rather than one distinctive doing.

Another shift occurred in the twelfth century, with the move from an oral public and a spoken reality to a literacy paradigm and a written reality. Novel ways of doing business, conducting prayer and life, and administering justice developed alongside an increasingly *pervasive* written preservation of the word. Only at that stage did the alphabetization of the popular mind gradually rise to new levels:

> Trust, power, possession, and everyday status were henceforth functions of the alphabet. The use of documents together with a new way of shaping the written page, turned writing, which in the Early and High Middle Ages had been extolled and honored as a mysterious embodiment of the Word of God, into a constituent element in the mediation of mundane relations.[50]

In an increasingly written culture, Illich and Sanders argue, contracts replace oaths. Even the sacrament of marriage, once an exchange of sentiments, becomes a legal commitment.

Illich and Sanders tell a largely Western story whose applicability elsewhere would have to be investigated (though this second shift occurred only centuries before Western expansionism took off, and thus whatever was true of the Western context would bear on the rest of the world). What is nonetheless striking is that Illich and Sanders see the modern self (if only within cultural limitations) as an "alphabetic construct." "The idea of a self that continues to glimmer in thought or memory, occasionally retrieved and examined in the light of day," they explain,

---

[49] In a seminal contribution to the debate Sanders and Illich participate in, media scholar Nicholas Carr argues that "with the exception of alphabets and number systems, the Net may well be the single most powerful mind-altering technology that has ever come into general use. At the very least, it's the most powerful that has come along since the book"; Carr, *The Shallows*, 116. Carr explores how tools we use to extend our mental faculties also modify the way we navigate our lifeworlds. He argues that contemplation, retention, reading, and even basic attention control are all negatively impacted through consistent interaction with the Internet. While the Internet offers much assistance, extensive use depletes the very capacities that make us human. That is also Heidegger's message, spelled out for digital lifeworlds. See also Turkle, *Alone Together*; Turkle, *Reclaiming Conversation*. For the background to these themes, also see Ong, *Orality and Literacy*.

[50] Sanders and Illich, *ABC*, 32.

"cannot exist without the text."[51] We all weave a cocoon of stories around ourselves and can do so only because of the narrative literary traditions of past centuries. Our own story can be told only as *one more story* in addition to so many that this canon has preserved. Our very image of the self, they submit, was made in the image of the text.

Our senses of memory and of biography were shaped in the manner of Rousseau's *Confessions* and other early autobiographies that set the stage for what it was to be an individual once the culture of the text had fully arrived.[52] By the time we get to the twentieth century, citizens see themselves

> through the eyes of various sciences as a layer cake of texts. From the 18th century on, the state has become a corporation of selves that letters examine. Where there is no alphabet there can neither be a memory conceived as a storehouse nor the "I" as its appointed watchman. With the alphabet both text and self became possible, but only slowly, and they became the social construct on which we found all our perceptions as literate people.[53]

As for the third shift, computers, and in particular – as seen from the standpoint of the late 1980s – word processing, create another watershed of change. Once again, human thought and perception are increasingly arranged more by the logic and efficiency of technical tools than by natural meanings embodied in live discourses of oral traditions. Mediated through text, memory was already once removed from experience. With the computer, Illich and Sanders assert, we are so distanced from oral traditions that *actually lived experience* becomes almost unrecognizable.

Much like the dystopian authors that have been with us throughout (Marcuse, Heidegger, Mumford, Ellul), Illich and Sanders offer a narrative of such sweeping scope that it is hard to know how to vindicate or refute it conclusively. But to the extent that their account is an accurate one, it is a striking illustration of how technologies interpret the world for us (Ihde's hermeneutical relations). More than that, written language does not just let us engage *with the world* in certain ways; it also furnishes an understanding of who we are to begin with, in ways we might find impossible to step back from and reflect on.

In response, I submit that once again the best available advice is to self-consciously interrogate choices to make them as much ours as they can be, without surrendering to gadget worshipping. Such interrogation will inevitably occur in a context that has already been shaped by technology, in ways that deprive us of any unmediated vantage point from which we could ponder the significance of our lives and who we are to begin with. And whatever else is true, this is a stark reminder of how much is at stake when it comes to technological innovation.

---

[51] Sanders and Illich, 72.
[52] Rousseau, *The Confessions*.
[53] Sanders and Illich, *ABC*, 72f.

10.7 CONCLUSION

Meaning of life and technology are rarely discussed together. Still, the observation that meaning is concerned with one's place in the world creates an instant connection to technology. Nozick's account in terms of "limited transcendence" offers an uplifting secular understanding of meaning that also, as it happens, illuminates the role of technology in the ways a life can be significant. It is through the important role Nozick gives to choice that we can see how technology becomes relevant to meaning. To reveal how technology permeates human choosing – a point that does not become clear on Nozick's high-altitude view – I have enlisted Ihde's reflections on the ways human activity is always mediated by technology (in terms of embodiment, hermeneutical or alterity relations) and Arendt's distinctions among labor, work, and action as three kinds of activity.

But if technology permeates human choosing and thereby becomes centrally connected to the pursuit of personal significance, it can also engage personal significance the wrong way. The bulk of this chapter has explored three ways for technology to engage with choice in problematic ways. One of them is for humans to turn into what Wiener calls *gadget worshippers*, by overestimating what machines can do. We might thereby surrender rather than enhance our exercise of reason. Instead of the misguided worshipping of a divine being, we embrace the equally misguided worshipping of human designs. The only way forward for anyone concerned with significance is to *interrogate* one's choices to understand the extent to which gadget worshipping drives them. In the digital century, self-interrogation is essential to make sure that one's own pursuit of significance does not drown in a flood of technological possibilities.

The interrogation of one's choices has assumed a pivotal role in this chapter's discussion on the connection between meaning of life and technology. In light of this role, it is worth noting that anti-colonial political philosopher Frantz Fanon finished up his 1952 book *Black Skin, White Masks* – which precedes the better-known *Wretched of the Earth* by about a decade – with a passionate recognition of the importance of self-interrogation: The very last line of his book is "O my body, make me always a man who questions!"[54] *Black Skin, White Masks* is an extensive study of racial entrapment. As a Black person (and specifically in virtue of being a Black *man*), Fanon found no way of understanding his place in the world other than by way of making sense of himself in a web of white preconceptions. Subjectivity in interrogation is his solution to racial entrapment: Only a person who *questions* can break out of that trap. The enormous differences between these two scenarios

---

[54] Fanon, *Black Skin, White Masks*, 181. The French original is "Ô mon corps, fais de moi toujours un homme qui interroge!"

notwithstanding, interrogation is also the only available answer to technological entrapment as far as the quest for personal significance is concerned. Interrogation is the key to what independence a person can preserve in the face of overwhelming pressures that seem poised to determine one's identity.

This is a perspective we have also found validated when it comes to the second way for technology to engage choice. Decades after Wiener, general AI not only ushers in novel kinds of golem; it also seems to bring back something rather close to an infinite entity, which would be a threat to an understanding of meaning (such as the one we adopted from Nozick) that draws inspiration from the perceived nonexistence of infinite beings. In this manner, a second way for technology to engage choice the wrong way did seem to present itself. But after some probing of the matter, it turns out after all that these new golems do pose the same challenges as those that Wiener already envisaged. For this reason, the advice regarding how to counterbalance this second way for technology to engage the quest for personal significance in the wrong way remains the same as the advice for gadget worshipping. Interrogation of one's own choices is essential.

Finally, we looked at how Illich and Sanders offer a third way for technology to engage personal significance the wrong way. Their point is that digital lifeworlds undermine our sense of self and the quest for meaning, which after all is triggered by that sense. While once more the advice to be given remains the same, Illich and Sanders highlight how dramatically much is at stake for the quest for personal significance in light of the technological innovation that occurs all around us now. Again we find that interrogation of one's choices is essential. And to be sure, the fact that things are changing, even when it comes to views of the self, does not mean they change (only) for the worse. In her celebrated 1985 essay "A Cyborg Manifesto," Donna Haraway uses the concept of the cyborg to reject rigid boundaries, such as those separating "human" from "animal" and "human" from "machine." She describes her essay as "an argument for *pleasure* in the confusion of boundaries and for *responsibility* in their construction."[55] That is not a bad way of thinking about the future. It is therefore not a bad way of ending a chapter exploring how one's quest for personal significance might be affected by the kind of innovation that sets the stage for the future.

One last point is worth noticing, though. Nozick's account would likely not work for the new golems themselves (i.e., superintelligences) were they to seek some such account. A superintelligence would presumably not grow in stages but would instantly connect to things around it. But that is unproblematic. We *are* finite

---

[55] Haraway, *Manifestly Haraway*, 7. Haraway also points out that the cyborg "would not recognize the Garden of Eden; it is not made of mud and cannot dream of returning to dust"; Haraway, 9. Cyborgs as golems of the future might differ dramatically from golems of the past.

beings: The meaning of our lives must be the meaning of the life of finite beings. But that also entails that there is personal significance to be had in genuine *growth* across a lifetime. Such growth presupposes a certain slowness of mind. Similarly, a superintelligence would of course not live a technologically mediated life quite the way humans do.

Moral Status and Political Membership: Toward a Political Theory for Life 3.0

Intelligence looks outward at the world, and asks and answers questions about the connections and relations we find there . . . But rationality looks inward, at the workings of our own minds, and asks and answers normative or evaluative questions about the connections and relations that we find there.

—Christine Korsgaard[1]

11.1 FERMI AND VON NEUMANN REVISITED

Recall the Fermi Paradox, the tension between the plausibly high probabilities for the existence of extraterrestrial life and the complete absence of evidence for it.[2] According to one resolution of the paradox, such lack of evidence reflects the fact that intelligent life tends to perish after a while (by cosmic standards). While this might happen accidentally (e.g., asteroids hit, the nearest sun expires), for this to resolve the paradox, perdition typically would come about as self-destruction in the exercise of intelligence. That, in turn, could be so because intelligent life tends to create technology that brings destruction before this life becomes known to life elsewhere. Von Neumann's "Can We Survive Technology?" would then be a milestone in diagnosing that it might now be our turn to enter this dangerous stage.[3]

Indeed, as we think about how technological innovation would continue and engage our political arrangements, one possibility is destruction. A technologically driven decades-long arms race might culminate in a devastating war. This could be a conflict between the United States and China (over Taiwan, say), following a

---

[1] Korsgaard, *Fellow Creatures*, 41.
[2] See Ćirković, *The Great Silence*; Forgan, *Solving Fermi's Paradox*. For accessible discussion, see Bostrom, "Where Are They?"
[3] von Neumann, "Can We Survive Technology?" For an assessment of the risks the world faces along the lines von Neumann had in mind, see Bostrom, "The Vulnerable World Hypothesis." See also Ord, *The Precipice*.

historical pattern of conflict in superpower-runner-up confrontations identified by Graham Allison.[4] Perhaps another Russian war of aggression eventually involves nuclear weapons, or such weapons are stolen by religious fanatics. Alternatively, an intelligence explosion eventually occurs, but something goes badly wrong, and we end up with a planetary collapse or anyway with the eradication of organic life. Other large-scale calamities are imaginable.

Regarding the technological dimensions of these matters, there are measures that could help us avert such a fate. The most radical would be to follow the Amish and abstain from further advances and even undo some. This is not on the radar as a practical possibility, if only because there is no globally shared sense that technology poses such a threat. Even if there were, geopolitical rivalry might drive technological progress. But one could also learn from the Amish at least to such an extent that public debate about technology and its life-shaping (rather than merely tool-providing) character becomes common, which might create a political atmosphere in which publics around the world are more self-conscious regarding decisions to advance technologies. History and philosophy of technology would appear in curricula, and systematic discussion about technology and its dystopian possibilities would be central to political debate. Such debate, in turn, would sometimes resolve not to rush or build certain things at all, to remove control from the private sector, or to impose more control mechanisms on governmental use of technology, as the case may be.

Short of ending up on the path to perdition, humanity might find ways of living with technology, and specifically AI, in roughly two ways. One possibility is that special AI advances relatively slowly into more and more general AI, and that general AI is integrated into the functioning of society in numerous ways. As Chapter 3 explores, such integration could benefit societies broadly or benefit only a few. But, at least for a long time, societies will not implode. This might be because intelligence is multidimensional after all, and there is no sequence of superintelligent entities that outdo each other in general abilities. Or perhaps humanity finds ways of keeping both technological possibilities and the arms races connected to them under control, perhaps along the lines of the Nuclear Non-Proliferation Treaty.[5] Either way, arrangements between humans and AI unfold fairly harmoniously and slowly – and humans remain in charge.

---

[4]   Allison, *Destined for War*.
[5]   The Nuclear Non-Proliferation Treaty seeks to prevent the spread of nuclear weapons technology, promote cooperation in peaceful uses of nuclear energy, and further nuclear disarmament; see Burns and Coyle, *The Challenges of Nuclear Non-Proliferation*. Not only did atomic energy also have much potential while harboring lethal dangers, but that threat had to be negotiated in contentious international arenas. Such an approach will avoid a scenario where some countries decide to terminate future development of general AI only to find that others continue to advance. On AI under the aspect of security and non-proliferation, see Kissinger, Schmidt, and Huttenlocher, *The Age of AI*, chapter 5.

The other possibility is that we get an intelligence explosion, and subsequently (possibly within hours) one or more forms of general AI take over. Perhaps they do so completely, but at least to such an extent that arrangements must be made with them. Humans would at best somehow still be involved in running things and at worst find themselves subjugated, perhaps in a manner resembling our relationship with animals. Many experts expect something like this to happen within decades.[6] But research might unfold more slowly, and this will only occur in centuries. In any event, both types of scenarios for humanity to end up living with technology come in a range of variations.

Developments in AI are not the only ones that shape our future. Not only climate change and technological responses to it, including geoengineering, but also gene-editing, human enhancement using pharmaceuticals and bioelectronics, nanotechnology, synthetic biology, and robotics: All these will come together *somehow* to shape our future. That future is obviously hard to predict. "Experience shows," von Neumann states, "that even smaller technological changes than those now in the cards profoundly transform political and social relationships" and do so in ways that "are not a priori predictable." Accordingly, "one should take neither present difficulties nor presently proposed reforms too seriously."[7]

One way of illustrating how hard it is to make such predictions (and thus also to throw light on that point about present difficulties and reforms) is to think about how the most prescient minds in 1900 would have thought about 1920, how in 1920 they would have thought about 1940, and so on across the twentieth century. We can safely guess that most of them (barring perhaps H. G. Wells) would have erred dramatically each time. The same point applies to what we can currently say about how the twenty-first century will progress even just for a twenty-year interval. Insights from history or social sciences generate predictions only to the extent that the future relevantly resembles the past. And chain reactions around technological innovation might undermine any such resemblance.[8]

To set the stage for our discussion, I adopt a distinction between "slow and relatively harmonious" and "fast and radical" as far as integration of AI into human life is concerned (disregarding the variations in which these scenarios come). Sections 11.2–11.4 explore questions from the "slow and relatively harmonious" scenario. Section 11.2 lays the groundwork for investigating the moral status of intelligent machines. Based on this framework, Section 11.3 explores questions about how it would make sense for humans to acknowledge moral status in machines. Section 11.4 asks if self-conscious AI could be *fully* morally equivalent to humans, exploring what an elevated moral status for machines means for the political

---

[6] Tegmark, *Life 3.0*, 42.
[7] von Neumann, "Can We Survive Technology?," 519.
[8] On difficulties around prediction once technology is involved, see Bostrom, "Technological Revolutions."

domain. Chapter 3 already explored how AI would affect democratic processes in the near future. Section 11.4 addresses a scenario further along, when questions around political membership of intelligent machines actually arise. Paying attention to what is appropriate to say about animals is useful in this context. Section 11.5 revisits some themes from the philosophy of technology to make sure we are not going astray by inquiring about the moral status of machines.

The remaining sections engage the "fast and radical" scenario. Again, we first deal with moral status and then with political membership, but now from a different angle. Section 11.6 discusses why we are philosophically so dramatically unprepared to deal with an intelligence explosion, with a focus on what moral status super-intelligences might grant *to us*. Section 11.7 looks at Max Tegmark's discussion of scenarios that could arise after an intelligence explosion. None of them involves *genuinely political* interaction among humans and machines. I add a public-reason scenario to Tegmark's list. Public reason offers prospects for machines and humans to be political together, in ways that continue our discussion in Chapter 7 about the human right to the exercise of distinctively human intelligence. That all of this is speculative goes without saying. But we do not want to start thinking about these matters in earnest only when they are upon us.

11.2 CONSIDER THE COMPUTER

But consider the lobster first. Giant sea insects dating from the Jurassic period and thus much more ancient than mammals, lobsters are widely appreciated as delicacies today. For freshness, lobsters are often boiled alive. While customers are waiting, the lobsters struggle to escape from the pot and exhibit other symptoms of a sensory system aiming to avoid pain. Lobsters are evidently sentient: They have perceptions and respond to them. For this reason, David Foster Wallace (whom we encountered in Chapter 10) compares the annual Maine Lobster Festival to Roman circuses and medieval torture fests in his celebrated short story "Consider the Lobster."[9] The 2004 story appeared in the *Gourmet* magazine, and its aim was to get those gourmets to at least *consider* the lobster.

I use "ethical" and "moral" synonymously. Ethics (which is the same as moral philosophy) is inquiry about (a) what it means for agents to relate to entities in ways appropriate to the nature of these entities or appropriate to the ways these entities connect to entities around them, and (b) what characteristics a person should possess to be disposed to act according to such standards of appropriateness. The entities could be humans, other animals, plants, ecosystems, or other parts of nature like rivers or mountains, works of art or other artifacts, or any object at all. By their

[9] Wallace, "Consider the Lobster." For animal consciousness, see Tye, *Tense Bees and Shell-Shocked Crabs*; Godfrey-Smith, *Other Minds*; Beshkar, "Animal Consciousness"; Seth, *Being You*, chapter 12.

"nature" I mean inherent features, and it is partly such features that generate questions about how one should relate to the entity in question. But how I should relate to something also depends on my history – and so my relationship – with it, and more generally on how it is embedded into a larger network of other entities. This is obvious for humans. But for example, what is appropriate for me to do regarding a work of art depends on its quality and then also on the fact that it belongs to a certain museum or collector (if indeed it does).

To act in ways that are "ethical" or "moral" is to act in a manner appropriate to the nature of the entities that one deals with (or to the ways they are connected to things around them), or to act in ways that sustain the characteristics of a person disposed to act in such a manner. To inquire about "moral status" is to investigate an entity's inherent features to ascertain whether there is anything about it in virtue of which it matters *for its own sake* how we act toward it: When we identify a being as having moral status, there is an adequate way of relating to the entity, and the reason is something about that entity. Wallace seeks to convince seafood connoisseurs that lobsters have moral status – one that requires at least that they not be boiled alive.[10]

This understanding of ethical action is about everything around us rather than merely humans or living things. This view makes differentiated inquiries about moral status straightforward. It creates ways of approaching the world with questions like these in mind: What kind of moral status does something have, and how should I relate to it? Obviously, these questions would not normally be asked just this way. There are multifarious ways of approaching these matters that need not avail themselves of philosophical language. Answers vary with the object of inquiry and mandate different behaviors depending on the entity in question and the various relations it stands in with others. Moral status might require a lot or relatively little. Perhaps the nature of lobsters makes no *other* demands on us. But the fact that they struggle to escape from danger does give us reason to kill them in different ("humane") ways.

This broad view of ethics also allows for answers to questions about how it is appropriate to deal with certain entities when it is neither their *own* nature nor how they connect to anything around them that is central to the inquiry. Kant thought a dog that has grown old doing good service should be cared for. But if the owner kills the dog, then this "is by no means in breach of any duty to the dog, since the latter is incapable of judgment, but the owner thereby damages the kindly and humane qualities in himself, which he ought to exercise in virtue of his duties to mankind."[11]

---

[10] For recent work on moral status, see Clarke, Zohny, and Savulescu, *Rethinking Moral Status*. See especially Sinnott-Armstrong and Conitzer, "How Much Moral Status Could Artificial Intelligence Ever Achieve?" See also Liao, "The Moral Status and Rights of Artificial Intelligence." For a discussion of moral status specifically regarding animals, see Kagan, *How to Count Animals*, chapters 1 and 5.

[11] Kant, *Lectures on Ethics*, 212 (27:459). For a take on moral obligations to animals that disagrees with Kant in Kantian spirit, see Korsgaard, *Fellow Creatures*.

What is required *regarding* the dog is not required because of anything *about* the dog but because of how it affects the owner. Callous termination of canine life erodes humaneness because humans, who do have moral status, share certain things with dogs, who, in Kant's view, do not have such status. Consider a related example. In 2007, a US colonel reportedly terminated a landmine-sweeping exercise because he regarded the operation as inhumane after robots kept crawling along losing legs one at a time.[12] Perhaps the colonel's reaction has a psychological explanation. But it could also be a decision (in Kantian spirit) to not needlessly desensitize natural aversions to inflicting pain.

Notions of consciousness matter greatly for assessing moral status. Chapter 1 notes that consciousness comes in a variety of forms, and these forms illuminate or allow for differing degrees of consciousness. To begin with, there is sentience, the capacity of sensing and responding to the world, a sense in which lobsters are conscious. A more demanding sense is wakefulness, which requires actual exercise of that capacity rather than merely having it. One counts as conscious only while *awake and normally alert*. In that sense, too, lobsters are conscious, certainly while escaping pain. Self-consciousness is a yet more demanding sense that understands conscious creatures as aware and also as aware that they are aware. If this is taken to involve explicit conceptual self-awareness, many nonhuman animals and even young children might fail to qualify. But if only rudimentary, implicit forms of self-awareness are required, a wide range of nonlinguistic creatures might count as self-conscious (and whether lobsters do is a hard question).

A common stance is that *only* conscious beings have a moral status that is not ultimately instrumental to something else.[13] Consciousness identifies a range of entities to whom it matters what happens to them. It does not matter to the stone that I kick it, or to my current smartphone that I smash it. But behavior affecting conscious beings interferes with beings concerned with what happens to them, which adds an important consideration when behavior is questioned. With *self-*consciousness comes the ability to make decisions or plans, to act reflectively rather than merely to react to stimuli. What requires justification is how it can be okay for one being's pursuits to overpower those of another if both are self-conscious.

But in my broad view, entities can have moral status even if they are not conscious: The criterion is that something about the entity makes certain ways of relating to it appropriate for its own sake. It is because of the way Da Vinci's *Mona Lisa* captures beauty that we should cherish it, and thus because of the painting's inherent features (rather than, say, in virtue of obligations to an artist who died long ago). And, again, questions about adequate behavior toward something can also arise even

---

[12] Wallach and Allen, *Moral Machines*, 55.
[13] As defended, for example, in Basl, *The Death of the Ethic of Life*. For speculation (on the other end of the spectrum) on whether plants, too, might have subjective standpoints, see Calvo, "What Is It Like to Be a Plant?"

if the entity itself has no moral status. An artistically worthless piece might require my care if it belongs to a person I love who cannot currently care for it herself.[14]

11.3 THE MORAL STATUS OF AI

With these basic points around moral status now in place, let us see how to *consider* the computer. Chapter 1 notes that there might eventually be conscious machines, though their consciousness would not be one embodied in organic matter. But that fact should not prevent us from recognizing in machines whatever moral status comes from consciousness (a refusal that would amount to a problematic sort of carbon chauvinism).[15] We are nowhere near a stage where these matters are practically relevant. But we do not know when they will be, and in due course we should be prepared to consider certain types of computers as entities with a moral status that comes from them being conscious. We will likely no longer use the term "computer" for machines composed and networked in ways that no longer permit easy switch-off. And needless to say, these machines will not look anything like the computer on which I type these words.[16]

But once we see that machines could have whatever status comes from consciousness, we should revisit the point that moral status assumes a variety of ways. Recall the lobster. In the first instance, the same questions about what we owe to lobsters – and for what reasons – arise once we get toward conscious machines. But as it also turns out, especially once we ask how to live with AI politically, a special set of issues about the status of AI arises: AI might realize agency and also make things more complicated in new ways by realizing agency very differently than we do.

To approach these matters, a set of distinctions formulated by James Moor continues to be useful.[17] To begin with, *ethical impact agents* are agents whose actions have consequences, intended or unintended, for beings with moral status. Any robot is such an agent if its actions can harm or benefit humans. But that ability

---

[14] Questions around moral status have long been controversial, especially the extent to which it would be appropriate to ascribe it to anything other than conscious beings. This section too will be controversial but also brushes over much subtlety. See also Jaworska and Tannenbaum, "The Grounds of Moral Status"; Streiffer, "At the Edge of Humanity."

[15] This term seems to have originated with Carl Sagan; see, for example, Sagan, *The Cosmic Connection*, chapter 6. But Sagan did not seem to regard carbon chauvinism as problematic. See also Bostrom and Yudkowsky, "The Ethics of Artificial Intelligence."

[16] For recent discussion of whether machines might be conscious and how we would know if nonorganic material possesses consciousness, see Schneider, *Artificial You*. See also Tye, *Tense Bees and Shell-Shocked Crabs*, chapter 10; Seth, *Being You*, chapter 13. For reflections on what "machines" are and if they can be conscious, see Harnad, "Can a Machine Be Conscious? How?" See also Kiverstein, "Could a Robot Have a Subjective Point of View?" For the argument that AI, even with efforts to build in human values, will lead to creatures very different (and ontologically disconnected) from us and that thus our standard ethical vocabulary no longer applies, see Lorenc, "Artificial Intelligence and the Ethics of Human Extinction."

[17] Moor, "Four Kinds of Ethical Robots."

would not give robots moral status. Secondly, *implicit ethical agents* are agents whose design has ethical considerations built in, such as through safety or security features. (Think of automatic teller machines checking availability or limiting the daily amount that can be withdrawn.) Again, this type of machine does not seem to have any moral status.

Thirdly, *explicit ethical agents* can secure and process ethical information about a variety of situations, make sensitive determinations about what to do, and even work out resolutions where considerations conflict. (One might think of ever more sophisticated chatbots.) Finally, *full ethical agents* are explicit ethical agents who also have metaphysical features we usually reserve for agents *like us*, such as consciousness, intentionality, or free will. At least both explicit ethical agents and full ethical agents do have moral status (the former in virtue of having certain features that could make them relevantly like pieces of art, a consideration that might conceivably also include at least some implicit ethical agents). More interestingly, in the space between explicit and full ethical agents, there could be a variety of types of moral status. Androids, say, could display hallmarks of agency, such as interactions with the environment, combined with a level of independence and adjustability.[18]

Explicit ethical agents short of full ethical agency hardly deserve *all* the consideration that full ethical agents do, but nor would they plausibly deserve *none*. One implication of this last point is that we ought not to develop general AIs that would do demeaning work *and* would be conscious (in order to be more human-like in interactions). Joanna Bryson once provocatively asserted that "robots should be slaves" and thus be treated as property.[19] But the fact that we create machines makes them property *only as long as* nothing about them gives them moral status inconsistent with being property (which might very well defeat the ownership status that comes from design). Children, too, are humanly created. But their humanity overrules any demands from the fact that they have been so created.[20] Thus there should be no legal entitlements to own them, though this does not mean that legal frameworks did not provide for that possibility (as the *patria potestas*, "the power of a father," did in Roman law). While the line is hard to draw, at some point robots with sufficiently much consciousness should not be property. In any event, the world that humans and intelligent machines share should not include any relations that meaningfully count as enslavement (as the use of *nonsentient* machines, no matter their complexity, would not).[21]

---

[18] Floridi and Sanders, "On the Morality of Artificial Agents." For an exploration of artificial morality and the agency of robots, see also Misselhorn, "Artificial Morality. Concepts, Issues and Challenges."

[19] Bryson, "Robots Should Be Slaves." See also Schwitzgebel and Gaza, "A Defense of the Rights of Artificial Intelligences."

[20] On this topic, see also Basl and Sandler, "The Good of Non-Sentient Entities."

[21] For a relational understanding of ties between human and machines, see Coeckelbergh, *Growing Moral Relations*. For a shorter treatment, see Coeckelbergh, *Introduction to Philosophy of Technology*, chapter 8.

As long as machines are merely highly complex or even recognizably intelligent, they might still have moral status of sorts (as works of art or ecosystems do), but that would imply little in terms of how they ought to be treated. It would be unproblematic to put such machines to work. But we must be careful not to create machines that possess consciousness and that, once created, have claims not defeated by the fact that we created them (for vividness, recall the golems from Chapter 10).[22] That being careful in this regard might be hard is clear from the fact that, as Anil Seth writes, "although we do not know what it would take to create a conscious machine, we also do not know what it would *not* take."[23] Once machines exist that are arguably conscious, we face moral-status problems that are familiar from our discussion about lobsters and other animals. And eventually we might confront the challenge of creating entities that have moral status where appropriate responses mean accommodating the capacity for agency – that is, we might confront vexing questions about just what moral status artificial explicit ethical agents or full ethical agents have, and just what kind of behavior toward them would be adequate in response. These questions arise outside of our experience with nervous systems that have emerged through evolution.[24]

Such issues would likely be divisive. Some people would build or acquire AI to exploit it, including for companionship ranging from caretaking to sexual services.[25] Holding conscious robots in bondage will appeal to many while clouding their judgment about whether machines deserve consideration. Others might protest on the machines' behalf, in the same spirit in which they might try to improve the lives of animals. Yet others might resent their use, fearing economic competition. In extremis, these debates resemble debates around enslavement of humans (and one especially vexing feature might be disagreement about the extent to which this is so).

11.4 REVISITING THEMES FROM THE PHILOSOPHY OF TECHNOLOGY

Inquiring about moral status of machines presupposes that we inhabit a world in which the most important fact about technology is *not* that it does overwhelming damage. For instance, it is not the case that technology deprives us of all possibilities of even reasonably independent action, nor that its effective role is to provide tools to the powerful to take advantage of everyone else. Inquiring the way that we do here

[22] See Basl, "Machines as Moral Patients We Shouldn't Care About (Yet)." See also Schwitzgebel and Gaza, "Designing AI with Rights, Consciousness, Self-Respect, and Freedom."
[23] Seth, *Being You*, 272. For the argument that for the time being there should be a moratorium on work that might lead to artificial consciousness, see Metzinger, "Artificial Suffering."
[24] For how to make progress on such matters on philosophical grounds, see Schneider, *Artificial You*, chapter 4. See also Tye, *Tense Bees and Shell-Shocked Crabs*, chapter 10.
[25] On machines as sexual companions, see Levy, *Love and Sex with Robots*; Migotti et al., *Robot Sex*; Richardson, *Sex Robots*; Devlin, "The Ethics of the Artificial Lover."

makes sense only if the dystopian scenarios we have visited periodically do not describe our reality (now or in the future).

Let us briefly recall only Heidegger and Mumford to make this point. For Heidegger, the dominance of technology shapes (*enframes*) the world. Technology turns human existence into something deficient because it compels us to relate to the world in ways that deplete the richness of human experience. In Heidegger's view, the only way out is to confine oneself to caring about one's own lifeworld, to embrace an ethics *of dwelling.*[26] Technological artifacts coming up for *consideration* in their own terms is outlandish, according to this approach.

Mumford worries that once computers take over, "Automated Man" will emerge, "he who takes all his orders from the system, and who ... cannot conceive of any departure from the system, even in the interest of efficiency, still less for the sake of creating a more intelligent, vivid, purposeful, humanly rewarding mode of life."[27] Digital technology serves the megamachine elite – Mumford talks of their "private eye," as if anticipating surveillance capitalism – who expect obedience as they rule the "megatechnical wasteland."[28] Digital technology would be the epitome of everything that Mumford traced through history demonstrating how the powerful have found ever-new ways of forcing people into conformity. Overall, dystopian authors like Heidegger and Mumford issue warnings. At the very least, we need improved democratic maturity in dealing with technology (as discussed in Chapter 3) to reassure ourselves that these dystopian versions are not clearly true and to do what we can to keep them at bay.

If dystopian depictions of humanity's technological future are inaccurate, then it might now be helpful to bring into our discussion some of the more recent thinking about how human action must always be seen as embedded into a larger context, one that is also and critically populated by material objects. Inspired by Ihde's reflections on the *alterity relations* in which humans stand with technology (as discussed in Chapter 10), as well as by Winner's take on the *politics* of artifacts (as discussed in Chapter 3), Peter-Paul Verbeek speaks of the *morality of things.*[29] There is a complex interplay between humans and technologies: Humans are products of technology, and technology is produced by humans. Artifacts shape human actions and decisions and therefore also help answer questions about how we ought to act and live. As Verbeek sees it, decisions are not made by detached autonomous subjects but co-shaped by their material environment. Moral standards

---

[26] Heidegger, "Building Dwelling Thinking."

[27] Mumford, *Pentagon of Power*, 192.

[28] Curiously, even though Mumford offers discouraging analyses about human use of technology, he tends to finish books on the subject optimistically, presumably so as not to preclude any possibilities for his analyses to function as warnings that, if heeded, could make a difference: "For those of us who have thrown off the myth of the machine, the next move is ours: for the gates of the technocratic prison will open automatically, despite their rusty ancient hinges, as soon as we choose to walk out;" Mumford, 435.

[29] Verbeek, *Moralizing Technology*.

develop in interaction with technology. Verbeek might push the point too far when talking about a specific intentionality of artifacts, their "directing" role in actions. Still, this way of thinking about the embeddedness of humans into their material surroundings prepares us well for a future in which machines just might come up for moral consideration in ways they currently do not.[30]

Among the future machines, there might be cyborgs partly composed of organic parts (machines that Lovelock thinks can help with climate change),[31] while humans are modified with nonorganic parts to enhance functionality. The distinction between humans and nonhumans could become blurry. Ideas about personhood might alter once it becomes possible to upload digitalized brains (a scenario for which, again, it matters whether the mind is more than the brain, and if not, if consciousness can survive such an operation). Such scenarios entail dangers. As Wiener warned, "the world of the future will be an ever more demanding struggle against the limitations of our intelligence, not a comfortable hammock in which we can lie down to be waited upon by our robot slaves."[32] One way for humans to resolve this struggle is to enhance themselves, which might substantially increase inequality. Maybe ever more individuals will want to adapt to technological change and perhaps deploy technology to morph into a transhuman stage.[33] In extremis, such developments might eventually put an end to the biological unity of humanity as one species.

But things might not go that way. Haraway has famously praised the *posthumanist* potential of technological advancement.[34] One theme of posthumanism is appreciation of the diversity and differentiated nature of moral status and greater care in reflection on what such a status entails in specific cases. This should already prompt us to reconsider our relationship with animals and nature – which have suffered from the fact that our intelligence has claimed the planet. AI might compel us to take *it* more seriously than we have ever taken animals and force a reconsideration of many attitudes. One wonderful thing about the advent of AI might just be that it triggers greater soul-searching about what is of value in the things around us. That, in turn, could also enable people to live more meaningful lives, as explored in Chapter 10.

---

[30] A similar point could be made appealing to Latour's Actor-Network-Theory; see, for example, Latour, *Reassembling the Social*; Latour, *We Have Never Been Modern*.

[31] Lovelock, *Novacene*.

[32] Wiener, *God & Golem*, 69.

[33] Livingstone, *Transhumanism*; More and Vita-More, *The Transhumanist Reader*; Bostrom, *Superintelligence*. On the topic of human enhancement form a virtue-ethics standpoint; see Vallor, *Technology and the Virtues*, chapter 10. On enhancement generally, see also Habermas, *The Future of Human Nature*; Sandel, *The Case against Perfection*; Buchanan, *Beyond Humanity?*

[34] Haraway, *Simians, Cyborgs, and Women*; Haraway, *Manifestly Haraway*.

11.5 MACHINE POLITICS

We must be prepared for the possibility that machines eventually obtain whatever moral status comes from consciousness. But does this mean that machines would then in all regards be morally equivalent to humans? Would it be appropriate for us to treat machines that have the same level or kind of consciousness as humans the same as we would (should) treat other humans? That depends on whether – among the entities who share a level or kind of consciousness with us – *additional* distinctions are appropriate. Let us note in passing that this question arises in the neighborhood of questions such as these: Is it appropriate to draw additional distinctions even among humans, as explored, for instance, in debates about justified partiality? Or as far as other animals are concerned, is it appropriate, for instance, to treat wolves and dogs differently despite roughly similar cognitive capacities? So far, we have not encountered other entities that, for all we know, are conscious at the level of human self-consciousness (no matter what we think about animal consciousness generally). The question of whether among such creatures (humans or others) *additional* distinctions would be appropriate has not arisen. But to see if something like that might eventually be the case, let us consider the domain of the political, in comparison with how animals fare, or should fare, in that domain.

As Chapter 2 notes, the *concept* of the political concerns ways in which order is created. In addition, we can distinguish various *conceptions* of the political. Such conceptions answer questions about what kind of agency and structures will normally or should bear on how order is created. Conceptions drawing on Aristotle look at processes of creating order by way of emphasizing human transformation through activities of ruling and being ruled, or characterize the kind of activity that becomes possible in such a setting or the features that essentially matter to the shared life in *poleis*. Among scholars who have recently worked within such an Aristotelean understanding, we find Hannah Arendt. As she writes,

> to be political, to live in a *polis*, mean[s] that everything [is] decided through words and persuasion and not through force and violence. In Greek self-understanding, to force people by violence, to command rather than to persuade, [are] prepolitical ways to deal with people characteristic of life outside the *polis*.[35]

Polis life enabled humans to get along in ways unavailable before. Prospects of solving conflicts by reasoned argument made it possible for ruling and being ruled to become temporary states.[36] Recall from Chapter 10 that, for Arendt, action is about

---

[35] Arendt, *The Human Condition*, 26f.
[36] In *On Justice*, chapter 14, I propose a different conception of the political. The *frame of human life* is the set of institutions and practices, as well as activities within them, that organize capacities for mutual aid and balance tendencies to compete and cooperate. For Aristotle, the *polis* does that job. Today, institutions and practices that do so are embedded into a human web that has coalesced into a world society. According to the frame-of-human-life conception, the

initiating something new that expresses a person's identity. Political action is the shared endeavor of maintaining or redoing the world as we jointly inhabit it. It matters greatly, then, that a shared world has been created through acts reflecting the identity of those involved. Political practices and traditions and our ways of interpreting what political action means today are shaped by how persons have acted in the past (how they have projected identities) and how they have thereby created shared understandings that include a memory culture. How then could it make sense for *artificial intelligences* – though they might be as self-conscious and more intelligent than us – to participate in political processes thus understood?

One way of expressing this doubt is that what is needed to participate in political action as Arendt understands it (something humans can in principle do) is a cognitive capacity different from intelligence and self-consciousness – something that humans possess *in addition* to those two, but that AI might not possess even if it does possess intelligence and the same level and type of consciousness. The Kantian tradition provides such a capacity: It offers an account of *rationality* (in Kant's German, *Vernunft*) as a distinct capacity. Christine Korsgaard has rearticulated that notion for use in an exploratory discussion of how humans might differ from (and what obligations they might have toward) animals.[37] She is aware that which creatures actually possess the forms of cognition she discusses, if any do, is an empirical question that philosophy alone cannot answer.

In line with how we discuss the term in Chapter 1, Korsgaard understands an *intelligent* animal in terms of its ability to learn from experiences to solve problems through deliberative processes. Intelligence increases the range of behavior available through inheritance. Rationality, Korsgaard explains, "is a normative power grounded in a certain form of self-consciousness."[38] So it is something only self-conscious beings can possess, but still a capacity beyond self-consciousness

---

political is about designing that frame at the global, or species-wide, level. This was a conception of the political designed to fit with the role of public reason as I develop it there for the global context. While this is a different conception from Arendt's, the emphasis she puts on action, speech, memory, and meaning is consistent with it. On the human web, see McNeill and McNeill, *The Human Web*. On the world society, which we encountered in previous chapters, see Meyer, *World Society*.

[37] Korsgaard, *Fellow Creatures*. For alternative takes on the status of animals, see, for example, Kagan, *How to Count Animals*; Singer, *Animal Liberation*; Donaldson and Kymlicka, *Zoopolis*. For the argument that worrying too much about consciousness takes us ever further away from coming to terms with animals, see Dawkins, *Why Animals Matter*. Dawkins thinks that animals matter because for humans to be healthy animals need to be healthy. For the argument that domestication of animals provides a good model for how to integrate AI into human life, see Müller, "Domesticating Artificial Intelligence." In recent times, human bodies and brains have been the model for Artificial Intelligence, but AI and both robotics might also benefit from drawing inspiration from how the bodies and brains of other animals operate; see Rus, "The Machines from Our Future."

[38] Korsgaard, *Fellow Creatures*, 40.

(and different from intelligence). Rational beings can reflect on what causes their beliefs and actions and decide if such causes count *as good reasons.*

"So the difference between rationality and intelligence is this," Korsgaard clarifies:

> Intelligence looks outward at the world, and asks and answers questions about the connections and relations we find there—most obviously about causal relations, but also spacial [sic] and temporal and social relations. But rationality looks inward, at the workings of our own minds, and asks and answers normative or evaluative questions about the connections and relations that we find there. In particular, practical rationality raises questions about whether the attitudes and the facts that motivate our actions give us good reasons to act.[39]

Rationality is a distinct capacity, one that humans possess and other animals, for all we know, do not. To be sure, empirical confirmation is needed: The philosophical contribution here is the delineation of the capacities and giving their existence a prima facie plausibility. Rationality bestows a specific character upon our actions. We can govern ourselves in terms of principles of our choosing, and as autonomous beings can be held responsible for what we do. Understanding rationality as a capacity separate from intelligence and consciousness also reconnects to Arendt's conception of action. Intelligence and self-consciousness are needed for successful political action. But once we understand action generally and political action specifically in terms of genuine initiation that expresses our identity, rationality likewise is required, over and above intelligence and self-consciousness.

Korsgaard's points apply to AI as well. In March 2016, one of the top Go players in the world, Lee Sedol, was defeated by AlphaGo. AlphaGo is an AI designed at DeepMind, a London lab then owned by Google. What became especially famous was AlphaGo's thirty-seventh move in the second game, a move that dumbfounded experts including Lee. DeepMind had originally trained its AI on the history of Go strategy. But AlphaGo had traversed a process of learning all its own via a machine-learning technique called Reinforcement Learning, which enables learning in an interactive environment by trial and error. AlphaGo thereby developed an innovative take on ancient human activities, learning everything there was to know only to transcend that knowledge.[40]

The expertise with which AI plays Go has rapidly advanced. But Move 37 still illuminates the possible impact of AI on human life. AI might have access to the entirety of human experience and reflection as captured digitally, including history, sciences, art, legal systems, and philosophy. It could know all digitally recorded facts and comprehend the logic of all known systems of thoughts. It could absorb all commonly used criteria to compare such systems, such as comprehensiveness,

---

[39] Korsgaard, 41.
[40] See Metz, "In Two Moves, AlphaGo and Lee Sedol Redefined the Future." See also Livingston and Risse, "On the Impact of Artificial Intelligence on Human Rights over the Next 20–30 Years."

consistency, or factual plausibility. It might eventually do all this very fast, conscious of what it is doing. But much as animals are capable of many things without rising to the level of rationality, none of what even a self-conscious AI can do might amount to exercising *rationality* as Korsgaard understands it and as Arendt thinks it is necessary for political action.

To be sure, Korsgaard insists on the separateness of rationality from intelligence and self-consciousness, but also argues (with Kant, against Kant) for the good of animals to be included in the pursuit of our own good. She proposes a combined commitment to human distinction in the domain of cognitive capacities and a substantially increased understanding of the moral status of animals (vis-à-vis both common practice and Kant's own view). The political domain must be organized within such constraints. But a further question is just what all this means for the role of animals (or the consideration they are due) in the political domain, or then also for the place of AI in this domain. That animals are incapable of rationality will have certain implications, and ditto for AI.

But these implications might ultimately not amount to much, certainly not as far as animals are concerned. Under the heading of *zoopolis*, Sue Donaldson and Will Kymlicka make far-reaching proposals for integrating animals into our cooperative relations as fellow *citizens*.[41] What underlies their proposal is a broader understanding of the domain of the political than Arendt and the Aristotelian tradition propose. For Donaldson and Kymlicka, politics is about negotiating the relationships among entities with a subjective well-being who find themselves in close proximity under human-devised structures. These relationships include ways of ruling together but also involve "assisted" and "dependent" agency.[42] Already for humans, citizenship involves support (e.g., for elderly or sick people or for the unemployed) or outright dependence (e.g., for people with severe disabilities), and so differentiated webs of relations.

Animals – with whom we have symbiotic living arrangements – could be part of such webs. Such webs would recognize animals' nature and abilities, but also the ways they stand in assistance or dependency relations with us. People can be supported by and indeed be dependent on animals in a variety of ways, from farming/herding to transportation to assistance for people who are blind. Sometimes humans act as advocates, speaking up for them in officially sanctioned ways. But that would not be because animals are not citizens or otherwise not part of the political domain. That would be because it lies in the nature of the *kind* of citizens they are that much in the exercise of citizenship as we know it in a world prejudiced against nonhuman animals must be reconsidered once we respond adequately to their moral status. The same could eventually be true for intelligent machines.

---

[41] Donaldson and Kymlicka, *Zoopolis*.
[42] Donaldson and Kymlicka, chapter 3.

One upshot is how much is open in this domain. We do not know whether machines, once they reach a level of intelligence and self-consciousness comparable to humans, will remain deficient regarding other cognitive capacities. Perhaps rationality supervenes on suitable combinations of intelligence and self-consciousness and would therefore be present in superintelligent self-conscious machines. If it is present, and if other ways of singling out humans are unavailable, intelligent machines should be full members in the domain of the political. If not, we have additional questions to discuss as to what kind of citizens machines could be, much as such questions already arise for animals.

11.6 HOW WOEFULLY UNPREPARED WE ARE

Section 11.1 distinguishes "slow and relatively harmonious" from "fast and radical" as far as the integration of AI into human life is concerned. So far, we have explored questions about the "slow and relatively harmonious" scenario. We now turn to the "fast and radical" one. To begin with, let me elaborate a bit more on how woefully unprepared we are philosophically for anticipating superintelligences. As we discussed in Chapter 1 and revisited earlier in this chapter, we do not know if machines can be conscious. So, there is a rather important aspect of the future that technological innovation is currently creating that we do not understand. Another thing we do not understand is whether superintelligences have reason to see themselves as inhabiting a moral community with us.

A community consists of entities that take each other seriously as having a moral status, instead of the strong ones considering the weaker ones mostly on instrumental terms (as we do with animals). We have investigated if in the "slow and relatively harmonious" scenario *we* might eventually have reason to live in such a community *with machines*. What about the other way round, in the "fast and radical" scenario? Do our moral theories give us reason to think *they* – machines that would arise through an intelligence explosion, rather than through gradual processes – would want to live that way *with us*? Chapter 4 started with this topic, exploring the right to the exercise of human intelligence in Life 3.0. This section continues that discussion.

Suppose an intelligence explosion delivers machines that are not only intelligent but also self-conscious and rational, regardless of whether rationality is a capacity by itself or supervenes on the others. Under this assumption it is *more likely* than in any other scenario that such machines would incline to live in moral community with humans. Such superintelligences could review human history and know both our amazing achievements and demonic inclinations.[43] These inclinations would cover not only what humans have done to each other but also what they have done to

---

[43] On this, see Wrangham and Peterson, *Demonic Males*.

other species and to the natural environment.[44] So we must ask: How confident can we be that the fact that superintelligences possess the cognitive capacities necessary to acknowledge moral status in others *actually* make them acknowledge ours and see it as something worth protecting?

One might think here of the dispute between David Hume and Kant about whether rationality fixes values. Hume famously thought that reason did nothing to fix values: Beings endowed with rationality, consciousness, and intelligence might have any goals as well as any range of attitudes, especially toward humans.[45] If so, superintelligences could have just about any value commitment, including ones that strike us as absurd (such as maximizing the number of paperclips in the universe).[46] How can we know that such plans are misguided, given that super-intelligences are massively smarter and thus *different* from us? And if we cannot know this, then maybe we should not be very confident that superintelligences that possess the requisite cognitive capacities would acknowledge our moral status.

By contrast, the Kantian view derives morality from rationality, and thus holds that acknowledging moral status in others is part of what is involved in being rational. Kant's Categorical Imperative requires of us to always act in ways that pass a generalization test. Certain actions are impermissible because they would not hold up if everybody performed them: There would be no property to begin with if everybody stole, no communication if everybody reserved the right to lie, and no type of human society at all with gratuitous violence being abundant. Kant's point is that rational beings actually *contradict themselves* by violating other rational beings. Immoral action, that is, is irrational on an agent's own terms.[47]

The argument for this last claim proceeds roughly as follows. It is only our rational choosing that gives any value to anything to begin with. This means that by valuing anything at all, we are committed to valuing our capacity to value. But wrecking other rational beings in pursuit of our interests – for instance, by stealing from them, by deceiving them, or by deploying gratuitous violence against them – wrecks *their* capacities to value. *Their* capacities to value, however, are relevantly the same

---

[44] As far as treatment of animals is concerned, they would know the kind of thing that motivated Peter Singer to become one of the thinkers behind the animal liberation movement; see, for example, Singer, *Animal Liberation*.

[45] As Hume famously claims "'Tis not contrary to reason to prefer the destruction of the whole world to the scratching of my finger. 'Tis not contrary to reason for me to chuse my total ruin, to prevent the least uneasiness of an Indian or person wholly unknown to me. 'Tis as little contrary to reason to prefer even my own acknowledg'd lesser good to my greater, and have a more ardent affection for the former than for the latter"; Hume, *A Treatise of Human Nature*, Book 2, Part 3, Section 3, paragraph 6. On Hume, see, for example, Garrett, *Hume*; Cohon, *Hume's Morality*.

[46] This example appears in Bostrom, "Ethical Issues in Advanced Artificial Intelligence." See also Bostrom, *Superintelligence*, chapters 6 and 12.

[47] The main source is Kant's 1785 *Groundwork of the Metaphysics of Morals*; see Kant, *Practical Philosophy*, 37–108. On Kantian moral thought, see, for example, Hill, *Dignity and Practical Reason in Kant's Moral Theory*; Wood, *Kant's Ethical Thought*.

capacities whose possession *we* must value in ourselves. It is for this reason that disregarding other people in such strong ways creates a contradiction in the rational agent's mind (as it would mean to disregard something that one must not disregard in oneself). In other words, anyone living up to their own rationality would also be moral, and being immoral is being irrational.

Humans will often fail in this regard since we are rather bad at living up to our rational nature. Even those of us who are trying their best to do right by people tend to be partial, favoring some people over others even to the point of willingly inflicting deeply immoral behavior on people for whom we do not care much. But that also means that, if Kant is right, superintelligences as envisaged here might be role models of ethical behavior: They would live up to their rationality, and thereby automatically always be moral agents. We cannot readily change human nature, and human nature is intensely parochial in its judgments and commitments. But AI might close the gap that opens when humans, with their enduringly small-group-oriented DNA that keeps them from living up to their rationality, operate in a global context. AI might show us what it means to live up to one's rational nature (and thus, on the Kantian view, what it means to act morally) beyond the narrow circle of people whom we treat properly because we care about them.[48]

There are doubts, however, that Kant's derivation of morality from rationality works as intended. These doubts draw especially on the claim that a *contradiction* arises from the fact that certain behaviors toward other people undermine these people's capacity to value. The point there was that by undermining this capacity (which I would do by mistreating them in certain ways) I would disregard a capacity that I am obligated to honor in myself. The worry about this argument is that it might well not be actually contradictory to act in such ways, since disregarding someone else's capacity to value simply is not the same as disregarding my own – after all, in the one case it is another person's capacity, and in the other it is mine. Instead, acting in such ways would express disregard for a fundamental similarity between two humans that it would certainly be *unreasonable* – but not contradict-ory – to disregard.

To be sure, if indeed something like this argument does work, we should not worry about superintelligences. Arguably we are rational *enough* for this kind of argument to generate protection for humble humans in an era of much smarter machines. But since a host of philosophers who are smart by contemporary standards reject the Kantian view, the matter is not settled. And we do not know what it looks like from the standpoint of a superintelligence.

Of course, some kind of morality could govern a community consisting of both humans and superintelligences with superintelligences in charge even if morality

---

[48] Petersen, "Superintelligence as Superethical"; Chalmers, "The Singularity: A Philosophical Analysis." On human morality in its evolutionary context, see, for example, Kahneman, *Thinking, Fast and Slow*; Greene, *Moral Tribes*.

cannot be derived from rationality alone. Thus there might be other ways of seeing how superintelligences might grant a certain moral status to us. There is, for instance, the Hobbesian approach of envisaging what would happen to humans aiming for self-preservation in a state of nature without shared authority.[49] (In the first instance, this argument has of course been offered *for humans.*) Hobbes argues that although these individuals would not act on shared values, just by thinking with a clear mind (as they would on a Kantian picture), they would quickly experience the nastiness of life without shared authority.

Far from being vile, they would strike against each other in anticipation of what might otherwise happen to them. Even if they would know themselves to be cooperative and give others the benefit of the doubt, they could not be sure others would do the same and might strike first given how much is at stake. This argument might also apply to superintelligences. That is, unless there is only one superintelligence, or all superintelligences are linked, such reasoning might apply to such machines as well, and they would accept a shared authority. Hobbes's state of nature would then describe the original status of superintelligences *vis-à-vis each other.* It is unclear, however, if such an authority will benefit humans, and if a situation would arise from this where superintelligences would grant a moral status to us.

Or perhaps T. M. Scanlon's ideas about appropriate responses to what is of value would help to see how morality could govern a community consisting of both humans and superintelligences with superintelligences in charge even if morality cannot be derived from rationality alone. My understanding of what it means to be "moral" or "ethical" from Section 11.2 has already drawn on this approach.[50] According to Scanlon's approach the essence of morality is neither its derivability from rationality (as it is for Kant), nor is it the insight that life is terrible without a shared authority. Instead, what morality is all about is to react in appropriate ways to something else, where what is appropriate draws especially on this other entity's nature. In this sense, a superintelligence might also be moral, by reacting appropriately toward what it observes. Perhaps we have some chance at getting protection or even some level of emancipation in mixed societies of humans and machines, given that the abilities of the human brain are astounding and arguably merit respect (as discussed in Chapter 7). That is, a certain kind of behavior toward us would be appropriate because of the amazing features of the human brain.

To be sure, the brains of animals also have amazing capacities, which has not led us to treat them in appropriately considerate ways. Instead of displaying an enlightened anthropocentrism, we have too often instrumentalized the rest of nature.[51]

---

[49] This argument appears in Hobbes, *Leviathan*. On Hobbes, see also Kavka, *Hobbesian Moral and Political Theory*. For a nonstandard interpretation of Hobbes on equality, see Hoekstra, "Hobbesian Equality."

[50] Scanlon, "What Is Morality?"

[51] On enlightened anthropocentrism, see Williams, "Must a Concern for the Environment Be Centred on Human Beings?"

But superintelligences might of course outperform us in such matters – they might do a better job at responding appropriately to an entity's nature. The distinctively human life would then receive some protection because it is worthy of respect. We cannot know for sure, but we need not be pessimistic. What is clear, however – and this the upshot of the discussion in this section of various ways in which morality might govern mixed communities of humans and superintelligences – is how woefully unprepared we are in anticipating what might come. And one important issue with regard to which we are unprepared is to have a good grasp of whether superintelligences will grant us a moral status.[52]

11.7 POLITICS IN LIFE 3.0: PUBLIC REASON

The uncertainly around what kind of moral status superintelligences that arise after an intelligence explosion would grant us also makes it hard to say anything about the domain of the political in Life 3.0. In an imaginative chapter in *Life 3.0*, Tegmark nonetheless explores multiple possibilities that might prevail after the development of general AI.[53]

To be sure, Tegmark considers scenarios under which AI would not be developed beyond a certain stage. One is what he calls *Gatekeeper*, where humanity only builds one superintelligence to make sure that no others are built. Gatekeeper polices the technology landscape with as little disruption as possible. Alternatively, in *Nineteen Eighty-Four*, a global Orwellian surveillance state bans AI research to sustain the state's power; a *Reversion* scenario inspired by Amish attitudes toward technology involves the dismantling of technological advances; or an *Egalitarian Utopia* uses technology to offer a high standard of living for everyone, which undermines any serious interest in building a superintelligence. Short of such scenarios, Tegmark submits, there will be an intelligence explosion eventually.

One class of scenarios afterwards involves superintelligences peacefully coexisting with humans. In *Enslaved God*, there would exist an almost omniscient and omnipotent entity over which nonetheless humans have control. The enslaved superintelligence provides well-being and opportunities beyond anything historic-ally possible. Alternatively, superintelligences would peacefully coexist with humans because they (the superintelligences) opt to do so. One such scenario is *Libertarian Utopia*, where around the world there are three different zones: machine-only zones, human-only ones, and mixed zones. A robust system of property rights makes such arrangements possible. Similar to Enslaved God, in *Protector God* we have an omnipotent and omnipresent superintelligence devoted to enabling humans to live

---

[52] For discussion of the morality of superintelligence, see Corabi, "Superintelligence as Moral Philosopher."

[53] Tegmark, *Life 3.0*, chapter 5. On the subject of sharing our social world with artificial minds, also see Shulman and Bostrom, "Sharing the World with Digital Minds."

meaningful lives. One variation is *Benevolent Dictator*, where again AI takes care of people but governance is less human-focused than under Protector God. Another variation is *Zookeeper*, where humans are kept around only for entertainment.

These scenarios of peaceful coexistence differ dramatically in terms of how humans fare. But we continue to be around. Alternatively, humans might go extinct in ways connected to the advent of AI. In *Conqueror*, superintelligences claim the earth and destroy us. Perhaps they pursue goals that deviate substantially from ours, such as maximizing the number of paperclips. Or they might opt to destroy us because we consume too much energy, have horrible records of dealing with each other and setting standards of interaction across species, or are bad for sustainability, or for any number of different reasons. In *Self-Destruction*, human action vanquishes us. Atomic weaponry might unfold its destructive potential, or AI weapons might. Finally, a benign counterpart to Conqueror is *Descendants*, which sees humans gracefully phased out by family policies that increasingly shrink populations. AI appreciates humans for their achievements but does not see the point of our continued presence.

Tegmark's list illustrates the open-endedness of our future with technology. Strikingly, none of the scenarios that have humans and superintelligences coexist involves a *genuinely shared political life*. Section 11.4 explored how it might make sense *for us* to build a shared political life with AI. *Pace* Tegmark, might this make sense for superintelligences as well? A public reason approach offers a tentatively affirmative answer. As discussed in Chapter 4, public reason captures the highest level of maturity that a society can reach in Life 2.0, and in the process can delineate what kind of role specialized AI could play in public discourse. Public reason also offers guidance once superintelligences enter public life.

To be sure, public reason offers a solution to a problem that arises from a distinctly human history. During that history, the only serious enduring challenge typically was how to get along with other humans. To be sure, that challenge arose *with full force* because of the inherently conflicting ways for humans to comprehend the world. Rawls proposed a way for humans to attain the highest possible degree of freedom in a society, a way that involves acceptance of the fact that interpretive diversity does not per se mean that any side to such disagreement is irrational, unreasonable, malicious, or self-centered. That is, the possibility of political *unity* requires acceptance of quite a bit of *separation* in terms of comprehensive doctrines that let people make sense of the world in their own ways.

Superintelligences would know everything there is to know about history and about the findings and methods of empirical sciences, as well as about the humanities with their (the humanities') ability to do textual work and thus to reconstruct the emergence of written traditions. Accordingly, AI can make each comprehensive doctrine measure up to the whole weight of available understanding of this doctrine's history and contents, and confront it with other ways of understanding the world in comparative perspective. Such scrutiny might find that some doctrines that hold up by human standards fail to do so by AI standards. Superintelligences might undermine the founding myths of religions, discredit the ways these religions were pushed forward, or throw doubts on the self-understanding of textual traditions. Adherents might experience a kind of doubt that skepticism of other humans never aroused. Outsiders might question why mutual respect should lead them to accept worldviews that AI finds wanting.

The effect could be like that of the arrival of extraterrestrials whose sheer presence might destabilize traditions in which humans are distinctly favored by God and in which God has found distinctive ways of communicating with them. A new class of judges on human affairs would have arrived who make up their minds independently of the need to accommodate other humans and of limitations of human cognition, while having access to all human knowledge. Some doctrines might not survive these shockwaves. Others might usher in novel ways of reading their tradition, less insistent on the truthfulness of founding myths and instead concerned with the wisdom encapsulated in these traditions. Religions might reinvent themselves. And after all, these events might unfold only after a long period of time during which humans would already be trying to adjust to technological advances and thus be reconsidering many things.

But after initial destabilization and reorientation, public reason's attempt at reconciling doctrines *to each other* might also help to include the superintelligences. Precisely because it formulates a platform on which humans can get along in abstraction from how they have so far interpreted history, public reason might include new participants. Endowed with immense intelligence, self-consciousness, and rationality, superintelligences might find a public-reason framework with a thinned-out and reformed set of doctrines worth joining. In any event, the kind of AI that has emerged from our design might do so. To be sure, we are talking about *alien* intelligence in that AI has not emerged from the evolutionary processes of organic matter. Still, this AI would not be alien at all in the sense that all it knows and can do is based on what humans know and can do. Recall again AlphaGo defeating the human champion: AI played a game devised by humans and at least initially learned from the wealth of human Go strategies.[54]

Why would superintelligences be willing to join humans under a public-reason umbrella? In a first step, recall from Chapter 7 that, to the extent that we can substantiate the meaning of human life in the godless world that science describes, we can also substantiate a right to the exercise of genuinely human intelligence vis-à-vis AI in Life 3.0. Then note again that public reason offers a considered way of living together at the highest attainable level of human freedom responsive to the variety of ways that humans interpret the world (plausibly now in somewhat

---

[54] To be sure, we would need to understand reasonably well just how AI reaches conclusions, an issue discussed under the heading of a "right to an explanation"; see, for example, Vredenburgh, "The Right to Explanation."

reformed versions). Therefore, both reasonable humans and AI that also possesses the kind of rationality needed for a shared political life would recognize that a polity guided by public reason is a suitable place for *humans* to exercise this right. If AI recognize that much, it just might also make sense for it to interact with humans as they exercise their intelligence, and do so in that public-reason forum. Again, all this is speculative, and larger questions about legitimacy among radically different beings certainly remain. But what I have said here might just be possible. And for the time being, this is not a bad place to end.

Epilogue

You can never plan the future by the past.

—Edmund Burke[1]

L'avenir est fait de la même substance que le présent.

—Simone Weil[2]

Weitermachen!

—Herbert Marcuse[3]

This book seeks to help set an agenda in a new domain of inquiry where things have been moving fast, an agenda that brings debates that have long preoccupied political thinkers into the era of AI and Big Data (and possibly the age of the singularity). Our discussions have been exploratory, rather than guided by a set of theses and the need to argue for them. Some topics we covered are genuinely new, but others continue older debates – though often in ways that call for a breaking down of boundaries as political thought has traditionally drawn them. One point I have made throughout is that the advent of AI requires that the relationship among various traditions of political thought be reassessed. All such traditions must fully integrate the philosophy of technology. Technological advancement will continue for the time being, one way or another, if only because of geopolitical rivalry. Therefore, the task for political thought is to address the topics that likely come our way and to distinguish among the various timeframes (such as Life 2.0 and Life 3.0) in which they might do so.

---

[1] Burke, "A Letter to a Member of the National Assembly (1791)," 55.
[2] Weil, *Pensées sans ordre concernant l'amour de Dieu*, 12. The English translation is "The future is made from the same stuff as the present."
[3] The English translation is "carry on!" This is the epitaph on Marcuse's tombstone at Dorotheenstadt Cemetery in Berlin.

The introductory Chapter 1 ("Digital Lifeworlds in Human History") took stock of the current situation confronting political theory, trying to make sense of digital lifeworlds in the narrative of humanity. We do not know if Life 3.0 will ever arise. But if it does, it will be from within digital lifeworlds: lifeworlds that already fundamentally change our lives and thus require intense scrutiny, even if there will never be a Life 3.0.

Chapter 2 ("Learning from the Amish: Political Philosophy as Philosophy of Technology in the Digital Century") introduced the Amish as an unusual case of a community intensely concerned with maintaining control over how technology shapes its future. In the age of AI, there are good reasons as to why technology and its regulation should be just about as central to mainstream politics as they are to the way the Amish regulate their affairs. Accordingly, in this age political philosophy must always also be philosophy of technology. I used the Marxist tradition to identify three senses in which technology is political (the foundational, enframing, and interactive senses) and argued that the Rawlsian tradition also should and can recognize versions of these senses.

Chapter 3 ("Artificial Intelligence and the Past, Present, and Future of Democracy") explored how specialized AI has changed the materiality of democracy, not just in the sense that independently given actors now deploy different tools. AI changes how collective decision-making unfolds and what its human participants are like. I investigated how to design AI to harness the public sphere, political power, and economic power for democratic purposes. Thereby, this chapter also continued the discussion from Chapter 2 by developing how technology is political in the foundational sense.

In Chapter 4 ("Truth Will Not Set You Free: Is There a Right to It Anyway? Elaborating on the Work Public Reason Does in Life 2.0"), we first explored how damaging untruth can be, especially in digital lifeworlds. But untruth plays a significant role as an enabler of valued psychological and social dynamics. There can therefore be no comprehensive right to truth. But that much is consistent with there being a right to truth *in specific contexts*. And to be sure, protecting the public sphere for the exercise of citizenship from a public-reason standpoint means that the state must protect truth telling and sanction untruth. Still, the moral concern behind truthfulness in this context is not best captured in terms of an actual right to truth but instead by a broader endorsement of the value of truth.

Chapters 5–8 explored what kind of rights are needed to protect individuals as knowers and knowns in digital lifeworlds, with their novel possibilities to advance or undermine individuals in these capacities. Chapter 5 ("Knowing and Being Known: Investigating Epistemic Entitlement in Digital Lifeworlds") introduced the notion of *epistemic actorhood* that lets us capture the place of an individual in a given episteme (drawing on ideas articulated by Foucault). Epistemic actorhood comes with the four roles of individual epistemic subject, collective epistemic subject, individual epistemic object, and collective epistemic object. Using this vocabulary, we could then also articulate the notions of an epistemic right and of epistemic justice and develop them in the context of digital lifeworlds.

Chapter 6 ("Beyond Porn and Discreditation: Epistemic Promises and Perils of Deepfake Technology") explored the many epistemic promises and perils of deepfake technology, putting to use the framework of epistemic actorhood from Chapter 5. My goal was to help set an agenda around these matters to make sure that this technology can assist with the realization of epistemic rights and epistemic justice and unleash human creativity, rather than inflict epistemic wrongs of any sort.

Chapter 7 ("The Fourth Generation of Human Rights: Epistemic Rights in Life 2.0 and Life 3.0") argued that, at this stage in history, an enhanced set of epistemic rights that strengthen existing human rights – as part of a *fourth generation* of human rights – is needed to protect epistemic actorhood in those four roles introduced in Chapter 5. Epistemic rights are already exceedingly important because of the epistemic intrusiveness of digital lifeworlds in Life 2.0, and they should also include a suitably defined right to be forgotten. If Life 3.0 does emerge, we might also need a right altogether different from what is currently acknowledged as human rights, the right to exercise human intelligence to begin with.

Chapter 8 ("On Surveillance Capitalism, Instrumentarian Power, and Social Physics: Securing the Enlightenment for Digital Lifeworlds") discussed how surveillance capitalism in digital lifeworlds threatens the Enlightenment ideal of individuality itself (as discussed by Kant and Durkheim) and what it takes to secure the Enlightenment for digital lifeworlds. I drew on democracy and epistemic rights to investigate how Enlightenment ideals can be secured in such lifeworlds. We also explored (and rejected) the position that rights, especially human rights, are enough to articulate a promising normative vision for society.

Chapter 9 ("Data as Social Facts: Distributive Justice Meets Big Data") drew on Grotius's account of the ownership of the seas to develop an account of collective ownership of collectively generated data patterns. The current default is that data are controlled by whoever gathers them. But the default should be that collectively generated patterns are collectively controlled, in ways that would allow for individual claims, liberties, powers, and protections to be sorted out in a next step. The kind of "collective" control that I have in mind should be developed in terms of the democratic reforms discussed in Chapter 3.

Chapter 10 ("God, Golem, and Gadget Worshippers: Meaning of Life in the Digital Age") used as its starting point Robert Nozick's proposal for how to think about the meaning of life. Technology might enter the human quest for meaning the wrong way. This chapter explored what this possibility amounts to and how to respond to it. To this end, we enlisted Norbert Wiener's notion of "gadget worshippers," people who surrender control over their lives to machines in ways that are not appropriate to what these machines can do. The best (and only feasible) way of making sure technology does not enter one's pursuit of meaning the wrong way is intense self-interrogation.

Finally, Chapter 11 ("Moral Status and Political Membership: Toward a Political Theory for Life 3.0") introduced a distinction between "slow and relatively harmonious" and "fast and radical" as far as the integration of AI into human life is concerned. Regarding the "slow and relatively harmonious" scenario, I explored a set of questions about how it would make sense for humans to acknowledge some such status in machines (in a variety of ways). Paying attention to what is appropriate to say about animals in that regard turned out to be useful. As far as the "fast and radical" scenario is concerned, I first explored why philosophically speaking we are so dramatically unprepared to deal with an intelligence explosion. I also articulated a public-reason scenario that, under certain circumstances, could offer a vision for a political context genuinely shared between humans and superintelligent machines.

Only time will tell how the agenda that this book seeks to contribute to will develop. We should aim to be as well prepared as possible for what might come. Von Neumann was right that we will need "patience, flexibility, intelligence" to get through.[4] Only time will tell if that is all we need and if, in some interesting sense of "we," we can even find our way to these virtues.

---

[4]   See von Neumann, "Can We Survive Technology?," 519.

Bibliography

Abbate, Janet. *Inventing the Internet.* Cambridge, MA: MIT Press, 2000.

Achen, Christopher H., and Larry M. Bartels. *Democracy for Realists: Why Elections Do Not Produce Responsive Government.* Princeton: Princeton University Press, 2017.

Adams, Frederick. "The Informational Turn in Philosophy." *Minds and Machines* 13 (4) (2003): 471–501.

Adorno, Theodor W. *Minima Moralia: Reflexionen aus dem beschädigten Leben.* Frankfurt: Suhrkamp, 1980.

Negative Dialectics. New York: Continuum, 1981.

Adriaans, Pieter. "Information." In *Stanford Encyclopedia of Philosophy*, edited by Edward N. Zalta. Palo Alto: Stanford University, 2020. https://plato.stanford.edu/entries/information/.

Adriaans, Pieter, and Johan van Benthem. "Introduction: Information Is What Information Does." In *Philosophy of Information*, edited by Pieter Adriaans and Johan van Benthem, 3–28. Amsterdam: North Holland, 2008.

eds. *Philosophy of Information.* Amsterdam: North Holland, 2008.

Agar, Jon. *The Government Machine: A Revolutionary History of the Computer.* Cambridge, MA: MIT Press, 2003.

Turing and the Universal Machine: The Making of the Modern Computer. Cambridge: Icon Books, 2017.

Agüera y Arcas, Blaise. "Do Large Language Models Understand Us?" *Daedalus* 151, no. 2 (2022): 183–97.

Albert, Mathias. *A Theory of World Politics.* Cambridge: Cambridge University Press, 2016.

Alexander, James. "Notes towards a Definition of Politics." *Philosophy* 89, no. 2 (2014): 273–300.

Alexander, Jeffrey C., and Philip Smith, eds. *The Cambridge Companion to Durkheim.* Cambridge, UK: Cambridge University Press, 2005.

Allison, Graham. *Destined for War: Can America and China Escape Thucydides's Trap?* Boston, MA: Mariner Books, 2018.

Allo, Patrick. "Putting Information First: Luciano Floridi and the Philosophy of Information." *Metaphilosophy* 41, no. 3 (2010): 247–54.

Amnesty International. "Cameroon: Credible Evidence That Army Personnel Responsible for Shocking Extrajudicial Executions Caught on Video," July 12, 2018. www.amnestyusa

.org/press-releases/cameroon-credible-evidence-that-army-personnel-responsible-for-shocking-extrajudicial-executions-caught-on-video/.

Anderson, Benedict. *Imagined Communities: Reflections on the Origin and Spread of Nationalism*. London: Verso, 1983.

Anderson, Elizabeth. *Private Government: How Employers Rule Our Lives*. Princeton: Princeton University Press, 2017.

Angwin, Julia. *Dragnet Nation: A Quest for Privacy, Security, and Freedom in a World of Relentless Surveillance*. New York: Times Books, 2014.

Angwin, Julia, Jeff Larson, Surya Mattu, and Lauren Kirchner. "Machine Bias." *ProPublica*, May 23, 2016. www.propublica.org/article/machine-bias-risk-assessments-in-criminal-sentencing.

Applebaum, Anne. *Twilight of Democracy: The Seductive Lure of Authoritarianism*. New York: Knopf Doubleday, 2021.

Arendt, Hannah. *Eichmann in Jerusalem: A Report on the Banality of Evil*. New York: Penguin, 2006.

 The Human Condition. Chicago: University of Chicago Press, 1958.

 The Origins of Totalitarianism. New York: Harcourt Brace Jovanovich, 1973.

 "Truth and Politics." In *The Portable Hannah Arendt*, edited by Peter Baehr, 545–75. London: Penguin, 2003.

Aristotle. *Politics*. Translated by C. D. C. Reeve. Indianapolis: Hackett, 1998.

Arrieta-Ibarra, Imanol, Leonard Goff, Diego Jiménez-Hernández, Jaron Lanier, and E. Glen Weyl. "Should We Treat Data as Labor? Moving beyond 'Free'." *AEA Papers and Proceedings* 108 (2018): 38–42.

Ayyub, Rana. "I Was the Victim of a Deepfake Porn Plot Intended to Silence Me." *Huffington Post*, November 21, 2018. www.huffingtonpost.co.uk/entry/deepfake-porn_uk_5bf2c126e4bof32bd58ba316.

Bacon, Francis. *Francis Bacon: The Major Works*. Edited by Brian Vickers. New York: Oxford University Press, 2008.

 Sacred Meditations. Radford: SMK Books, 2018.

Bai, Tongdong. *Against Political Equality: The Confucian Case*. Princeton: Princeton University Press, 2019.

Balkin, Jack M. "Free Speech in the Algorithmic Society: Big Data, Private Governance, and New School Speech Regulation." *UC Davis Law Review* 51 (2018): 1149–210.

Balkun, Mary McAleer, and Marta Mestrovic Deyrup, eds. *Transformative Digital Humanities: Challenges and Opportunities*. New York: Routledge, 2020.

Ball, James. *Post-Truth: How Bullshit Conquered the World*. London: Biteback, 2018.

Barocas, Solon, and Andrew D. Selbst. "Big Data's Disparate Impact." *California Law Review* 104, no. 3 (2016): 671–732.

Bartels, Larry M. *Unequal Democracy: The Political Economy of the New Gilded Age*. Princeton: Princeton University Press, 2018.

Bartlett, Jamie. *The People vs. Tech: How the Internet Is Killing Democracy (and How We Save It)*. London: Ebury Press, 2018.

Basl, John. *The Death of the Ethic of Life*. New York: Oxford University Press, 2019.

 "Machines as Moral Patients We Shouldn't Care About (Yet): The Interests and Welfare of Current Machines." *Philosophy & Technology* 27, no. 1 (2014): 79–96.

Basl, John, and Ron Sandler. "The Good of Non-Sentient Entities: Organisms, Artifacts, and Synthetic Biology." *Studies in the History and Philosophy of Biological and Biomedical Science* 44, no. 4 (2013): 697–705.

BBC News. "John F Kennedy's Lost Speech Brought to Life," March 16, 2018. www.bbc.com/news/uk-scotland-edinburgh-east-fife-43429554.

Bell, Daniel A. *The China Model: Political Meritocracy and the Limits of Democracy.* Princeton: Princeton University Press, 2016.

Ben-Itto, Hadassa. *The Lie That Wouldn't Die: The Protocols of the Elders of Zion.* Portland: Vallentine Mitchell, 2005.

Ben-Shahar, Tal. *Being Happy: You Don't Have to Be Perfect to Lead a Richer, Happier Life.* New York: McGraw-Hill Education, 2010.

Benatar, David, ed. *Life, Death, and Meaning: Key Philosophical Readings on the Big Questions.* Lanham: Rowman & Littlefield, 2016.

Benjamin, Ruha, ed. *Captivating Technology: Race, Carceral Technoscience, and Liberatory Imagination in Everyday Life.* Durham, NC: Duke University Press, 2019.

Race after Technology: Abolitionist Tools for the New Jim Code. Medford: Polity, 2019.

Benjamin, Walter. *The Arcades Project.* Translated by Howard Eiland and Kevin McLaughlin. Cambridge, MA: Harvard University Press, 1999.

The Work of Art in the Age of Its Technological Reproducibility, and Other Writings on Media. Edited by Michael W. Jennings, Brigid Doherty, and Thomas Y. Levin. Cambridge, MA: Harvard University Press, 2008.

Benkler, Yochai, Robert Faris, and Hal Roberts. *Network Propaganda: Manipulation, Disinformation, and Radicalization in American Politics.* New York: Oxford University Press, 2018.

Benkler, Yochai, Casey Tilton, Bruce Etling, Justin Clark, Robert Faris, Jonas Kaiser, and Carolyn Schmitt. "Mail-in Voter Fraud: Anatomy of a Disinformation Campaign." Berkman Klein Center for Internet & Society at Harvard University, No. 2020-6, October 2020. https://cyber.harvard.edu/publication/2020/Mail-in-Voter-Fraud-Disinformation-2020.

Benn, Claire, and Seth Lazar. "What's Wrong with Automated Influence." *Canadian Journal of Philosophy* 52, no. 1, (2022) 125–148.

Berners-Lee, Tim. *Weaving the Web: The Original Design and Ultimate Destiny of the World Wide Web.* San Francisco: Harper, 2000.

Bernhardt, Chris. *Turing's Vision: The Birth of Computer Science.* Cambridge, MA: MIT Press, 2017.

Bernholz, Lucy, Hélène Landemore, and Rob Reich, eds. *Digital Technology and Democratic Theory.* Chicago: University of Chicago Press, 2021.

Beshkar, Majid. "Animal Consciousness." *Journal of Consciousness Studies* 15, no. 3 (2008): 5–33.

Bijker, Wiebe. "Why and How Technology Matters." In *The Oxford Handbook of Contextual Political Analysis,* edited by Robert E. Goodin and Charles Tilly, 681–707. Oxford: Oxford University Press, 2006.

Bimber, Bruce. *Information and American Democracy: Technology in the Evolution of Political Power.* Cambridge: Cambridge University Press, 2003.

Binns, Reuben. "Fairness in Machine Learning: Lessons from Political Philosophy." *Proceedings of Machine Learning Research* 81 (2018): 1–11.

Bishop, J. "The Cleroterium." *The Journal of Hellenic Studies* 90 (1970): 1–14.

Blair, Ann, Paul Duguid, Anja-Silvia Goeing, and Anthony Grafton, eds. *Information: A Historical Companion.* Princeton: Princeton University Press, 2021.

Blevins, Cameron. *Paper Trails: The US Post and the Making of the American West.* New York: Oxford University Press, 2021.

Block, Ned. "Troubles with Functionalism." In *Readings in the Philosophy of Psychology*, Vols. 1 & 2, 268–305. Cambridge, MA: Harvard University Press, 1980.

Bly, Robert W. *Charles Proteus Steinmetz: The Electrical Wizard of Schenectady*. Fresno: Quill Driver Books, 2018.

Bobbio, Norberto. *The Age of Rights*. Cambridge: Polity, 1996.

Boehm, Christopher. *Hierarchy in the Forest. The Evolution of Egalitarian Behavior*. Cambridge, MA: Harvard University Press, 1999.

Boli, John. "World Polity Theory." In *Encyclopedia of Globalization*, edited by Roland Robertson and Jan Aart Scholte, 1299–302. New York: Routledge, 2006.

Boli, John, Selina Gallo-Cruz, and Matthias Matt. "World Society, World-Polity Theory, and International Relations." In *The International Studies Encyclopedia*, edited by Robert A. Denemark. Malden: Wiley-Blackwell, 2010.

Bostrom, Nick. "Ethical Issues in Advanced Artificial Intelligence." In *Cognitive, Emotive and Ethical Aspects of Decision Making in Humans and in Artificial Intelligence*, edited by Iva Smit and George E. Lasker, Vol. 2, 12–17. Tecumseh, Ontario: International Institute for Advanced Studies in Systems Research and Cybernetics, 2003.

Superintelligence: Paths, Dangers, Strategies. Oxford: Oxford University Press, 2016.

"Technological Revolutions: Ethics and Policy in the Dark." In *Nanoscale: Issues and Perspectives for the Nano Century*, edited by Nigel M. de St. Cameron and M. Ellen Mitchell, 129–52. Hoboken: Wiley, 2007.

"The Vulnerable World Hypothesis." *Global Policy* 10, no. 4 (2019): 455–76.

"Where Are They? Why I Hope the Search for Extraterrestrial Life Finds Nothing." *MIT Technology Review*, April 22, 2008. www.technologyreview.com/2008/04/22/220999/where-are-they/.

Bostrom, Nick, and Eliezer Yudkowsky. "The Ethics of Artificial Intelligence." In *The Cambridge Handbook of Artificial Intelligence*, edited by Keith Frankish and William M. Ramsey, 316–34. Cambridge: Cambridge University Press, 2014.

Böttiger, Helmut. *Konrad Zuse: Erfinder, Unternehmer, Philosoph und Künstler*. Petersberg: Imhof, 2011.

Bowker, Gordon. *Inside George Orwell: A Biography*. New York: Palgrave Macmillan, 2003.

Braddon-Mitchell, David, and Frank Jackson. *Philosophy of Mind and Cognition: An Introduction*. Malden: Wiley-Blackwell, 2006.

Braman, Sandra. "Defining Information: An Approach for Policy-Makers." *Telecommunications Policy* 13, no. 3 (1989): 233–42.

Brandt, Allan M. *The Cigarette Century: The Rise, Fall, and Deadly Persistence of the Product That Defined America*. New York: Basic Books, 2009.

Brashier, Nadia M., and Elizabeth J. Marsh. "Judging Truth." *Annual Review of Psychology* 71, no. 1 (2020): 499–515.

Brennan, Jason. *Against Democracy*. Princeton: Princeton University Press, 2017.

Bringsjord, Selmer, and Naveen Sundar Govindarajulu. "Artificial Intelligence." In *Stanford Encyclopedia of Philosophy*, edited by Edward N. Zalta, 2018. https://plato.stanford.edu/entries/artificial-intelligence/.

Brockman, John, ed. *Possible Minds: Twenty-Five Ways of Looking at AI*. New York: Penguin, 2019.

Brook, Andrew, and Don Ross, eds. *Daniel Dennett*. Cambridge: Cambridge University Press, 2002.

Brooks, David. "The Philosophy of Data." *New York Times*, February 4, 2013. www.nytimes.com/2013/02/05/opinion/brooks-the-philosophy-of-data.html.

Broussard, Meredith. *Artificial Unintelligence: How Computers Misunderstand the World.* Cambridge: MIT Press, 2019.

Browne, Simone. *Dark Matters: On the Surveillance of Blackness.* Durham: Duke University Press, 2015.

Bruderer, Herbert. *Konrad Zuse und die Schweiz: Wer hat den Computer erfunden?* München: Oldenbourg, 2012.

Brundage, Miles, Shahar Avin, Jack Clark, Helen Toner, Peter Eckersley, Ben Garfinkel, Allan Dafoe, et al. "The Malicious Use of Artificial Intelligence: Forecasting, Prevention, and Mitigation." *Future of Humanity Institute,* Oxford, February 2018. https://arxiv.org/ftp/arxiv/papers/1802/1802.07228.pdf.

Brunton, Finn, and Helen Nissenbaum. *Obfuscation: A User's Guide for Privacy and Protest.* Cambridge, MA: MIT Press, 2016.

Bruntrup, Godehard, and Ludwig Jaskolla, eds. *Panpsychism: Contemporary Perspectives.* New York: Oxford University Press, 2016.

Bryson, Joanna. "Robots Should Be Slaves." In *Close Engagements with Artificial Companions,* edited by Yorick Wilks, 63–74. Amsterdam: John Benjamins, 2010.

Buchanan, Allen E. *Beyond Humanity? The Ethics of Biomedical Enhancement.* Oxford: Oxford University Press, 2011.

"Marx as Kierkegaard: Review of Richard W. Miller, 'Analyzing Marx.'" *Philosophical Studies* 53, no. 1 (1988): 157–72.

Buchanan, Bruce G. "A (Very) Brief History of Artificial Intelligence." *AI Magazine* 26, no. 4 (2005): 53–60.

Buckle, Stephen. *Natural Law and the Theory of Property: Grotius to Hume.* Oxford: Clarendon, 1991.

Burgess, John P., and Gideon Rosen. *A Subject with No Object: Strategies for Nominalistic Interpretation of Mathematics.* Oxford: Clarendon, 1997.

Burke, Edmund. "A Letter to a Member of the National Assembly (1791)." In *The Works of the Right Honorable Edmund Burke in Twelve Volumes,* edited by Peter J. Stanlis, Vol. 4, 48–60. London: John C. Nimmo, 1887.

Burns, Richard Dean, and Philip E. Coyle. *The Challenges of Nuclear Non-Proliferation.* Lanham: Rowman & Littlefield, 2015.

Bynum, Terrell Ward. "Philosophy in the Information Age." *Metaphilosophy* 41, no. 3 (2010): 420–42.

Calvo, Paco. "What Is It Like to Be a Plant?" *Journal of Consciousness Studies* 24, no. 9–10 (2017): 205–27.

Camus, Albert. *The Myth of Sisyphus and Other Essays.* Translated by Justin O'Brien. New York: Vintage, 1991.

Caplan, Bryan. *The Myth of the Rational Voter: Why Democracies Choose Bad Policies.* Princeton: Princeton University Press, 2008.

Capurro, Rafael. *Information: Ein Beitrag zur Etymologischen und Ideengeschichtlichen Begründung des Informationsbegriffs.* München: Saur, 1978.

Capurro, Rafael, and Birger Hjørland. "The Concept of Information." Edited by B. Cronin. *Annual Review of Information Science and Technology, Information Today,* 37 (2003): 343–411.

Caro, Robert A. *The Power Broker: Robert Moses and the Fall of New York.* New York: Vintage, 1975.

Carr, Nicholas G. *The Shallows: How the Internet Is Changing the Way We Think, Read and Remember.* London: Atlantic, 2011.

Carter, Matt. *Minds and Computers: An Introduction to the Philosophy of Artificial Intelligence*. Edinburgh: Edinburgh University Press, 2007.

Cavedon-Taylor, Dan. "Photographically Based Knowledge." *Episteme* 10, no. 3 (2013): 283–97.

Cellan-Jones, Rory. "Stephen Hawking Warns Artificial Intelligence Could End Mankind." *BBC News*, December 2, 2014. www.bbc.com/news/technology-30290540.

Ceruzzi, Paul E. *A History of Modern Computing*. Edited by William Aspray. Cambridge, MA: MIT Press, 2003.

Chadwick, Ruth, Mairi Levitt, and Darren Shickle, eds. *The Right to Know and the Right Not to Know: Genetic Privacy and Responsibility*. Cambridge: Cambridge University Press, 2014.

Chakrabarti, Samidh. "Hard Questions: What Effect Does Social Media Have on Democracy?" *Meta*, January 22, 2018. https://about.fb.com/news/2018/01/effect-social-media-democracy/.

Chalmers, David J. *The Conscious Mind: In Search of a Fundamental Theory*. New York: Oxford University Press, 1996.

  Reality+: Virtual Worlds and the Problems of Philosophy. New York: Norton, 2022.

  "The Singularity: A Philosophical Analysis." *Journal of Consciousness Studies* 17, no. 9–10 (2010): 7–65.

Chan, Joseph. *Confucian Perfectionism: A Political Philosophy for Modern Times*. Princeton: Princeton University Press, 2015.

Chandler, Simon. "Why Deepfakes Are a Net Positive for Humanity." *Forbes*, May 9, 2020. www.forbes.com/sites/simonchandler/2020/03/09/why-deepfakes-are-a-net-positive-for-humanity/?sh=66ce5922f84f.

Cheney-Lippold, John. *We Are Data: Algorithms and the Making of Our Digital Selves*. New York: NYU Press, 2017.

Chojecki, Przemek. *Artificial Intelligence Business: How You Can Profit from AI*. Independently published, 2020.

Chomsky, Noam. "A Review of B. F. Skinner's 'Verbal Behavior.'" In *The Essential Chomsky*, edited by Anthony Arnove, 1–30. New York: The New Press, 2008.

Christian, David. *Maps of Time: An Introduction to Big History*. Berkeley: University of California Press, 2004.

Christiano, Thomas. "Algorithms, Manipulation, and Democracy." *Canadian Journal of Philosophy* 52, no. 1 (2022): 109–124.

Ci, Jiwei. *Democracy in China: The Coming Crisis*. Cambridge, MA: Harvard University Press, 2019.

Ćirković, Milan M. *The Great Silence: Science and Philosophy of Fermi's Paradox*. Oxford: Oxford University Press, 2018.

Claeys, Gregory. "'Individualism,' 'Socialism,' and 'Social Science': Further Notes on a Process of Conceptual Formation, 1800–1850." *Journal of the History of Ideas* 47, no. 1 (1986): 81–93.

Clark, Maudemarie, and David Dudrick. *The Soul of Nietzsche's Beyond Good and Evil*. New York: Cambridge University Press, 2012.

Clarke, Bruce. "Information." In *Critical Terms for Media Studies*, edited by W. J. T. Mitchell and Mark B. N. Hansen, 157–71. Chicago: University of Chicago Press, 2010.

Clarke, Steve, Hazem Zohny, and Julian Savulescu, eds. *Rethinking Moral Status*. New York: Oxford University Press, 2021.

Coady, C. A. J. *Testimony: A Philosophical Study*. Oxford: Clarendon, 1992.

Coady, David. "Epistemic Injustice as Distributive Injustice." In *The Routledge Handbook of Epistemic Injustice*, edited by Ian James Kidd, José Medina, and Gaile Pohlhaus Jr, 61–68. London: Routledge, 2017.

Cockburn, Cynthia, and Susan Ormrod. *Gender and Technology in the Making*. London: Sage Publications, 1993.

Coeckelbergh, Mark. *Growing Moral Relations: Critique of Moral Status Ascription*. Houndmills: Palgrave Macmillan, 2012.

Introduction to Philosophy of Technology. New York: Oxford University Press, 2019.

The Political Philosophy of AI: An Introduction. Medford: Polity, 2022.

Cohen, G. A. "Forces and Relations of Production." In *Analytical Marxism*, edited by John Roemer, 11–22. New York: Cambridge University Press, 1986.

Karl Marx's Theory of History. Princeton: Princeton University Press, 1978.

Cohen, Joshua. "Minimalism About Human Rights: The Most We Can Hope For?" *Journal of Political Philosophy* 12, no. 2 (June 1, 2004): 190–213.

"Review of 'Karl Marx's Theory of History: A Defense,' by G. A. Cohen." *Journal of Philosophy* LXXIX, no. 5 (1982): 266–68.

"Truth and Public Reason." In *Philosophy, Politics, Democracy: Selected Essays*. Cambridge, MA: Harvard University Press, 2009.

Cohen, Julie E. "Examined Lives: Informational Privacy and the Subject as Object." *Stanford Law Review* 52 (2000): 1373–1438.

Cohon, Rachel. *Hume's Morality: Feeling and Fabrication*. Oxford: Oxford University Press, 2012.

Cole, Samantha. "AI-Assisted Fake Porn Is Here and We're All Fucked." *Motherboard*, December 11, 2017. www.vice.com/en/article/gydydm/gal-gadot-fake-ai-porn.

Conway, Flo. *Dark Hero of the Information Age: In Search of Norbert Wiener, the Father of Cybernetics*. New York: Basic Books, 2006.

Cooke, Jacob E., ed. *The Federalist*. Middletown: Wesleyan University Press, 1961.

Coomaraswamy, Radhika. "Reinventing International Law: Women's Rights as Human Rights in the International Community." *Commonwealth Law Bulletin* 23, no. 3–4 (1997): 1249–62.

Corabi, Joseph. "Superintelligence as Moral Philosopher." *Journal of Consciousness Studies* 24, no. 5 (2017): 128–49.

Costandi, Moheb. *Neuroplasticity*. Cambridge, MA: MIT Press, 2016.

Costanza-Chock, Sasha. *Design Justice: Community-Led Practices to Build the Worlds We Need*. Cambridge, MA: MIT Press, 2020.

Cover, Thomas M., and Joy A. Thomas. *Elements of Information Theory*. Hoboken: Wiley-Interscience, 2006.

Crawford, Kate. *Atlas of AI: Power, Politics, and the Planetary Costs of Artificial Intelligence*. New Haven: Yale University Press, 2021.

Cuélla, Mariano-Florentino, and Aziz Z. Huq. "Economies of Surveillance." *Harvard Law Review* 133 (2020): 1280–1336.

Dahl, Robert. "The Concept of Power." *Behavioural Science* 2, no. 3 (1957): 201–15.

Dalai Lama. *The Art of Happiness: A Handbook for Living*. New York: Riverhead Books, 2020.

Dantzig, George B. "Linear Programming." *Operations Research* 50, no. 1 (2002): 42–47.

Darwall, Stephen. *The Second-Person Standpoint: Morality, Respect, and Accountability*. Cambridge, MA: Harvard University Press, 2009.

Dasgupta, Binayak. "BJP's Deepfake Videos Trigger New Worry Over AI Use in Political Campaigns." *Hindustan Times*, September 21, 2020. www.hindustantimes.com/india-news/bjp-s-deepfake-videos-trigger-new-worry-over-ai-use-in-political-campaigns/story-6WPlFtMAOaepkwdybm8b1O.html.

Davies, Guy. "David Beckham 'Speaks' 9 Languages for New Campaign to End Malaria." *ABC News*, April 9, 2019. https://abcnews.go.com/International/david-beckham-speaks-languages-campaign-end-malaria/story?id=62270227.

Dawkins, Marian Stamp. *Why Animals Matter: Animal Consciousness, Animal Welfare, and Human Well-Being*. New York: Oxford University Press, 2012.

Dean, Jeffrey. "A Golden Decade of Deep Learning: Computing Systems & Applications." *Daedalus* 151, no. 2 (2022): 58–74.

DeCrew, Judith. "Privacy." In *Stanford Encyclopedia of Philosophy*, edited by Edward N. Zalta, 2018. https://plato.stanford.edu/entries/truth/.

Deibert, Ronald J. *Black Code: Surveillance, Privacy, and the Dark Side of the Internet*. Toronto: Signal, 2013.

Reset: Reclaiming the Internet for Civil Society. Toronto: House of Anansi Press, 2020.

Deleuze, Gilles. *Difference and Repetition*. Translated by Paul Patton. New York: Columbia University Press, 1995.

DeLillo, Don. *White Noise:* New York: Penguin, 1986.

Demy, Timothy J. *Jacques Ellul on Violence, Resistance, and War*. Edited by Jeffrey M. Shaw. Eugene: Pickwick, 2016.

Dennett, Daniel C. *From Bacteria to Bach and Back: The Evolution of Minds*. New York: Norton, 2018.

Consciousness Explained. Boston: Back Bay Books, 1992.

Kinds of Minds: Toward an Understanding of Consciousness. New York: Basic Books, 1997

Derrida, Jacques. "Force of Law: The Mystical Foundation of Authority." In *Deconstruction and the Possibility of Justice*, 3–67. New York: Routledge, 1992.

Devlin, Kate. "The Ethics of the Artificial Lover." In *Ethics of Artificial Intelligence*, edited by S. Matthew Liao, 271–92. New York: Oxford University Press, 2020.

Devlin, Keith. *Logic and Information*. Cambridge: Cambridge University Press, 1991.

Dickson, Bruce. *The Party and the People: Chinese Politics in the Twenty-first Century*. Princeton: Princeton University Press, 2021.

D'Ignazio, Catherine, and Lauren F. Klein. *Data Feminism*. Cambridge, MA: MIT Press, 2020.

Dilloway, James. *Human Rights and World Order: Two Discourses to the H.G. Wells Society*. Nottingham: H. G. Wells Society, 1998.

Domingos, Pedro. *The Master Algorithm: How the Quest for the Ultimate Learning Machine Will Remake Our World*. New York: Basic Books, 2018.

Donaldson, Sue, and Will Kymlicka. *Zoopolis: A Political Theory of Animal Rights*. Oxford: Oxford University Press, 2013.

Dostoevsky, Fyodor. *Demons*. Edited by Ronald Meyer, translated by Robert A. Maguire. London: Penguin, 2008.

Dow, Sterling. "Aristotle, the Kleroteria, and the Courts." *Harvard Studies in Classical Philology* 50 (1939): 1–34.

Dowding, Keith. *Rational Choice and Political Power*. Cheltenham: Elgar, 1991.

Downing, Lisa. *The Cambridge Introduction to Michel Foucault*. Cambridge: Cambridge University Press, 2008.

Doyle, Sir Arthur Conan. *The Adventures of Sherlock Holmes, and Other Stories*. Edited by Michael A. Cramer. San Diego: Canterbury Classics, 2011.

Drahos, Peter. *A Philosophy of Intellectual Property*. Aldershot: Routledge, 1996.

Dretske, Fred I. "Entitlement: Epistemic Rights without Epistemic Duties?" *Philosophy and Phenomenological Research* LX, no. 3 (2000): 591–606.

    "Epistemology and Information." In *Philosophy of Information*, edited by Pieter Adriaans and Johan van Benthem, 29–48. Amsterdam: North Holland, 2008.

    Knowledge and the Flow of Information. Stanford: Center for the Study of Language and Information, 1999.

    "Précis of Knowledge and the Flow of Information." *The Behavioral and Brain Sciences* 6, no. 1 (1983): 55–90.

Dreyfus, George B. J. *Recognizing Reality: Dharmakirti's Philosophy and Its Tibetan Interpretations*. Albany: State University of New York Press, 1997.

Dreyfuss, Emily. "Want to Make a Lie Seem True? Say It Again. And Again. And Again." *Wired*, February 11, 2017. www.wired.com/2017/02/dont-believe-lies-just-people-repeat/.

Dubois, Elizabeth, and Grant Blank. "The Echo Chamber Is Overstated: The Moderating Effect of Political Interest and Diverse Media." *Information, Communication & Society* 21, no. 5 (2018): 729–45.

Duff, Alistair S. *A Normative Theory of the Information Society*. New York: Routledge, 2013.

Durkheim, Emile. *Suicide: A Study in Sociology*. Edited by George Simpson, translated by John A. Spaulding. New York: The Free Press, 1997.

    "What Is a Social Fact?" In *The Rules of Sociological Method: And Selected Texts on Sociology and Its Method*, edited by Steven Lukes, translated by W. D. Halls, 50–9. New York: The Free Press, 1982.

Dutant, Julien. "The Legend of the Justified True Belief Analysis." *Philosophical Perspectives* 29, no. 1 (2015): 95–145.

Dworkin, Ronald. *Life's Dominion: An Argument about Abortion, Euthanasia, and Individual Freedom*. New York: Knopf, 1993.

    Sovereign Virtue: The Theory and Practice of Equality. Cambridge, MA: Harvard University Press, 2000.

Dyson, George. *Darwin among the Machines: The Evolution of Global Intelligence*. New York: Basic Books, 2012.

    "The Third Law." In *Possible Minds: Twenty-Five Ways of Looking at AI*, edited by John Brockman, 33–40. New York: Penguin, 2019.

    Turing's Cathedral: The Origins of the Digital Universe. New York: Vintage, 2012.

Eagleton, Terry. *The Meaning of Life: A Very Short Introduction*. Oxford: Oxford University Press, 2008.

Eden, Amnon H., James H. Moor, Johnny H. Soraker, and Eric Steinhart, eds. *Singularity Hypotheses: A Scientific and Philosophical Assessment*. New York: Springer, 2013.

"Eighty Moments That Shaped the World." The British Council, June 30, 2016. www.britishcouncil.org/sites/default/files/80-moments-report.pdf.

Eisikovits, Nir, and Dan Feldman. "AI and Phronesis." *Moral Philosophy and Politics*, forthcoming.

Eliot, T. S. *The Complete Poems and Plays, 1909–1950*, New York: Harcourt Brace Jovanovich, 1971.

Ellis, Emma Grey. "People Can Put Your Face on Porn—and the Law Can't Help You." *Wired*, January 26, 2018. www.wired.com/story/face-swap-porn-legal-limbo/.

Ellul, Jacques. *The Technological Society*. Translated by John Wilkinson. New York: Vintage, 1964.

Elster, Jon. *Making Sense of Marx*. New York: Cambridge University Press, 1985.

Emerson, Ralph Waldo. *Emerson's Complete Works*. Vol. IX (Poems). New York: Houghton, 1894.

Engels, Friedrich. "On Authority." In *Marx and Engels: Basic Writings on Politics and Philosophy*, edited by Lewis S. Feuer, 502–5. Garden City: Doubleday, 1959.

Engler, Alex. "Fighting Deepfakes When Detection Fails." Brookings, November 14, 2019.

Enoch, David. "The Disorder of Public Reason." *Ethics* 124, no. 1 (2013): 141–76.

    Taking Morality Seriously: A Defense of Robust Realism. Oxford: Oxford University Press, 2011.

Eriksen, Niels Nymann. *Kierkegaard's Category of Repetition.* Berlin: De Gruyter, 2000.

Eubanks, Virginia. *Automating Inequality: How High-Tech Tools Profile, Police, and Punish the Poor.* New York: St. Martin's Press, 2018.

Faden, Ruth R., Tom L. Beauchamp, and Nancy M. P. King. *A History and Theory of Informed Consent.* New York: Oxford University Press, 1986.

Falcón y Tella, Fernando. *Challenges for Human Rights.* Leiden: Martinus Nijhoff, 2007.

Fanon, Frantz. *Black Skin, White Masks.* Translated by Charles Lam Markmann. London: Pluto Press, 1986.

Feenberg, Andrew. *Critical Theory of Technology.* Oxford: Oxford University Press, 1991.

    Heidegger and Marcuse: The Catastrophe and Redemption of History. New York: Routledge, 2004.

    Questioning Technology. London: Routledge, 1999.

    "Replies to My Critics." In *Democratizing Technology: Andrew Feenberg's Critical Theory of Technology*, edited by Tyler J. Veak, 175–210. Albany: State University of New York Press, 2006.

    Transforming Technology: A Critical Theory Revisited. New York: Oxford University Press, 2002.

Ferguson, Andrew Guthrie. *The Rise of Big Data Policing: Surveillance, Race, and the Future of Law Enforcement.* New York: NYU Press, 2019.

Fifield, Anna. *The Great Successor: The Divinely Perfect Destiny of Brilliant Comrade Kim Jong Un.* New York: PublicAffairs, 2019.

Fisher, William. "Theories of Intellectual Property." In *New Essays in the Legal and Political Theory of Property*, edited by Stephen R. Munzer, 168–200. New York: Cambridge University Press, 2001.

Floridi, Luciano. *The Ethics of Information.* Oxford: Oxford University Press, 2013.

    The Fourth Revolution: How the Infosphere Is Reshaping Human Reality. Oxford: Oxford University Press, 2014.

    Information: A Very Short Introduction. Oxford: Oxford University Press, 2010.

    The Logic of Information: A Theory of Philosophy as Conceptual Design. Oxford: Oxford University Press, 2019.

    The Philosophy of Information. Oxford: Oxford University Press, 2013.

Floridi, Luciano, and J. W. Sanders. "On the Morality of Artificial Agents." *Mind and Machine* 14, no. 3 (2004): 349–79.

Foer, Franklin. *World Without Mind: The Existential Threat of Big Tech.* New York: Penguin, 2017.

Forgan, Duncan H. *Solving Fermi's Paradox.* New York: Cambridge University Press, 2019.

Forsythe, David P. *Human Rights in International Relations.* Cambridge: Cambridge University Press, 2017.

Foucault, Michel. *The Archaeology of Knowledge: And the Discourse on Language.* New York: Vintage, 1982.

    Discipline and Punishment: The Birth of the Prison. London: Travistock, 1977.

    The History of Sexuality, Vol. 1: An Introduction. Translated by Robert Hurley. New York: Vintage, 1990.

The History of Sexuality, Vol. 2: The Use of Pleasure. Translated by Robert Hurley. New York: Vintage, 1985.

The History of Sexuality, Vol. 3: The Care of the Self. Translated by Robert Hurley. New York: Vintage, 1988.

The Order of Things: An Archaeology of the Human Sciences. New York: Vintage, 1994.

Power/Knowledge: Selected Interviews and Other Writings, 1972–1977. Edited by Colin Gordon. New York: Vintage, 1980.

Frank, Thomas. *Listen, Liberal: Or, What Ever Happened to the Party of the People?* New York: Metropolitan Books, 2016.

Frankfurt, Harry G. *On Bullshit.* Princeton: Princeton University Press, 2005.

Frege, Gottlob. "Der Gedanke. Eine Logische Untersuchung." *Beiträge zur Philosophie des Deutschen Idealismus* 1, no. 2 (1918): 58–77.

Fricker, Miranda. *Epistemic Injustice: Power and the Ethics of Knowing.* New York: Oxford University Press, 2007.

Friedman, Uri. "Defending Assad, Russia Cries 'Fake News.'" *The Atlantic*, April 11, 2018. www.theatlantic.com/international/archive/2018/04/russia-syria-fake-news/557660/.

Fukuyama, Francis. *The Origins of Political Order: From Pre-Human Times to the French Revolution.* New York: Farrar, Straus and Giroux, 2012.

Political Order and Political Decay: From the Industrial Revolution to the Globalization of Democracy. New York: Farrar, Straus and Giroux, 2014.

Fung, Archon, and Joshua Cohen. "Democracy and the Digital Public Sphere." In *Digital Technology and Democratic Theory*, edited by Lucy Bernholz, Hélène Landemore, and Rob Reich, 23–61. Chicago: University of Chicago Press, 2021.

Future Today Institute. "Tech Trends Report 2021," 2021. https://futuretodayinstitute.com/trends-stories/.

Gabriel, Iason. "Towards a Theory of Justice for Artificial Intelligence." *Daedalus* 151, no. 2 (2022): 218–31.

Galloway, Scott. *The Four: The Hidden DNA of Amazon, Apple, Facebook, and Google.* New York: Portfolio, 2017.

Gambino, Lauren. "Denying Accuracy of Access Hollywood Tape Would Be Trump's Biggest Lie." *The Guardian*, November 29, 2017. www.theguardian.com/us-news/2017/nov/29/denying-accuracy-of-access-hollywood-tape-would-be-trumps-biggest-lie.

Gardner, Howard E. *Frames of Mind: The Theory of Multiple Intelligences.* New York: Basic Books, 2011.

Intelligence Reframed: Multiple Intelligences for the Twenty-first Century. New York: Basic Books, 2000.

Multiple Intelligences: New Horizons in Theory and Practice. New York: Basic Books, 2006.

Garrett, Don. *Hume.* New York: Routledge, 2014.

Gaukroger, Stephen. *Francis Bacon and the Transformation of Early-Modern Philosophy.* New York: Cambridge University Press, 2001.

Gellman, Barton. *Dark Mirror: Edward Snowden and the American Surveillance State.* New York: Penguin, 2020.

Geras, Norman. "The Controversy about Marx and Justice." In *Marxist Theory*, edited by Alex Callinicos, 211–68. Oxford: Oxford University Press, 1989.

Gess, Nicola. *Halbwahrheiten: Zur Manipulation von Wirklichkeit.* Berlin: Matthes & Seitz, 2021.

Ghezzi, Alessa, Ángela Guimarães Pereira, and Lucia Vesnic-Alujevic, eds. *The Ethics of Memory in a Digital Age: Interrogating the Right to Be Forgotten.* Houndmills: Palgrave Macmillan, 2014.

Ghosh, Dipayan. *Terms of Disservice: How Silicon Valley Is Destructive by Design*. Washington, DC: Brookings, 2020.

Gilbert, Margaret. "Durkheim and Social Facts." In *Debating Durkheim*, edited by Herminio Martins and William Pickering, 86–109. New York: Routledge, 1994.

On *Social Facts*. Princeton: Princeton University Press, 1992.

Gilbert, Sam. *Good Data: An Optimist's Guide to Our Digital Future*. London: Welbeck, 2022.

Gilens, Martin. *Affluence and Influence: Economic Inequality and Political Power in America*. New York: Princeton University Press, 2014.

Gill, David W., and David Lovekin, eds. *Political Illusion and Reality: Engaging the Prophetic Insights of Jacques Ellul*. Eugene: Pickwick, 2018.

Glanzberg, Michael. "Truth." In *Stanford Encyclopedia of Philosophy*, edited by Edward N. Zalta, 2018. https://plato.stanford.edu/entries/truth/.

Gleick, James. *The Information: a History, a Theory, a Flood*. New York: Vintage, 2012.

Globe Newswire. "Global VFX Market Will Reach USD 19,985.64 Million by 2024: Zion Market Research," September 27, 2018. www.globenewswire.com/news-release/2018/09/27/1577156/0/en/Global-VFX-Market-Will-Reach-USD-19-985-64-Million-By-2024-Zion-Market-Research.html.

Glover, Jonathan. *Humanity: A Moral History of the Twentieth Century*. New Haven: Yale University Press, 2012.

Godfrey-Smith, Peter. *Other Minds: The Octopus, the Sea, and the Deep Origins of Consciousness*. New York: Farrar, Straus and Giroux, 2017.

Goethe, Johann Wolfgang von. *Faust: A Tragedy*. Edited by Cyrus Hamlin, translated by Walter W. Arndt. New York: Norton, 1998.

Goff, Philip. *Consciousness and Fundamental Reality*. New York: Oxford University Press, 2017.

Galileo's Error: Foundations for a New Science of Consciousness. New York: Pantheon, 2019.

Goldberg, Sanford C. *Relying on Others: An Essay in Epistemology*. Oxford: Oxford University Press, 2010.

Goldman, Alvin I., and Matthew McGrath. *Epistemology: A Contemporary Introduction*. New York: Oxford University Press, 2014.

Good, Irving John. "Speculations Concerning the First Ultraintelligent Machine." *Advances in Computers* 6, no. 99 (1965): 31–83.

Gordon, Peter E., Espen Hammer, and Max Pensky, eds. *A Companion to Adorno*. Oxford: Wiley-Blackwell, 2020.

Greene, Joshua. *Moral Tribes: Emotion, Reason and the Gap Between Us and Them*. New York: Penguin, 2014.

Greenman, Jeffrey P. *Understanding Jacques Ellul*. Eugene: Cascade Books, 2012.

Greenwald, Glenn. *No Place to Hide: Edward Snowden, the NSA, and the U.S. Surveillance State*. New York: Metropolitan Books, 2014.

Griffiths, Alison. *Wondrous Difference*. New York: Columbia University Press, 2001.

Groebner, Valentin. *Who Are You? Identification, Deception, and Surveillance in Early Modern Europe*. Translated by Mark Kyburz and John Peck. Brooklyn: Zone Books, 2007.

Grofman, Bernard, Guillermo Owen, and Scott L. Feld. "Thirteen Theorems in Search of the Truth." *Theory and Decision* 15, no. 3 (1983): 261–78.

Grosheide, F. W. "Database Protection—The European Way." *Washington University Journal of Law & Policy* 8, no. 1 (2002): 39–77.

Grotius, Hugo. *The Free Sea*. Edited by David Armitage. Indianapolis: Liberty Fund, 2004.
  The Rights Of War And Peace: Three Volume Set. Edited by Richard Tuck. Indianapolis,
  IN: Liberty Fund, 2005.
Gstrein, Oskar Josef. "Right to Be Forgotten: European Data Imperialism, National Privilege,
  or Universal Human Right?" *Review of European Administrative Law* 13, no. 1 (2020):
  125–52.
Gutmann, Amy. "Democracy." In *A Companion to Contemporary Political Philosophy*, edited
  by Robert E. Goodin, Philip Pettit, and Thomas W. Pogge, 521–31. Oxford: Wiley-
  Blackwell, 2007.
Gutting, Gary. *French Philosophy in the Twentieth Century*. Cambridge: Cambridge
  University Press, 2001.
Habermas, Jürgen. *Between Facts and Norms: Contributions to a Discourse Theory of Law and
  Democracy*. Translated by William Rehg. Cambridge, MA: MIT Press, 1996.
  The Future of Human Nature. Cambridge: Polity, 2003.
  *The Structural Transformation of the Public Sphere: An Inquiry into a Category of Bourgeois
  Society*. Cambridge, MA: MIT Press, 1991.
  "Zum Geleit." In *Antworten auf Herbert Marcuse*, edited by Jürgen Habermas, 9–16.
  Frankfurt: Suhrkamp, 1968.
Hacker, P. M. S. *Human Nature: The Categorial Framework*. Malden: Wiley-Blackwell, 2010.
Hacking, Ian. *The Taming of Chance*. Cambridge: Cambridge University Press, 1990.
Halavais, Alexander. *Search Engine Society*. Cambridge: Polity, 2017.
Halpern, Orit. *Beautiful Data: A History of Vision and Reason since 1945*. Durham: Duke
  University Press, 2015.
Hamano, Teru. "H. G. Wells, President Roosevelt, and the Universal Declaration of Human
  Rights." *Life & Human Rights* 9, Autumn Issue (1998): 6–16.
Hammer, Espen. *Adorno and the Political*. London: Routledge, 2013.
Hammond, J. W. *Charles Proteus Steinmetz: A Biography*. Breinigsville: Merchant Books,
  2008.
Han, Hélène Béatrice. *Foucault's Critical Project: Between the Transcendental and the
  Historical*. Translated by Edward Pile. Palo Alto: Stanford University Press, 2002.
Hansen, Mogens Herman. *The Athenian Democracy in the Age of Demosthenes: Structure,
  Principles, and Ideology*. Translated by J. A. Crook. Oxford: Blackwell, 1991.
Harari, Yuval Noah. *Homo Deus: A Brief History of Tomorrow*. New York: Harper, 2017.
  "Why Technology Favors Tyranny." *The Atlantic*, October 2018. www.theatlantic.com/
  magazine/archive/2018/10/yuval-noah-harari-technology-tyranny/568330/.
Haraway, Donna. *Manifestly Haraway*. Minneapolis: University of Minnesota Press, 2016.
  Simians, Cyborgs, and Women: The Reinvention of Nature. London: Routledge, 2015.
Harnad, Steve. "Can a Machine Be Conscious? How?" *Journal of Consciousness Studies* 10,
  no. 4–5 (2003): 67–75.
Hart, Roderick P. *Trump and Us: What He Says and Why People Listen*. Cambridge:
  Cambridge University Press, 2020.
Hartch, Todd. *The Prophet of Cuernavaca: Ivan Illich and the Crisis of the West*. New York:
  Oxford University Press, 2015.
Hartzog, Woodrow. *Privacy's Blueprint: The Battle to Control the Design of New Technologies*.
  Cambridge, MA: Harvard University Press, 2018.
Hasher, Lynn, David Goldstein, and Thomas Toppino. "Frequency and the Conference of
  Referential Validity." *Journal of Verbal Learning and Verbal Behavior* 16, no. 1 (1977):
  107–12.
Haugeland, John. "Analog and Analog." *Philosophical Topics* 12, no. 1 (1981): 213–25.

Hayek, F. A. *Law, Legislation, and Liberty*. Edited by Jeremy Shearmur. Chicago: University of Chicago Press, 2022.
  The Road to Serfdom. Edited by Bruce Caldwell. Chicago: University of Chicago Press, 2007.
  "The Use of Knowledge in Society." *American Economic Review*. 35, no. 4 (1945): 519–30.
Headrick, Daniel R. *When Information Came of Age: Technologies of Knowledge in the Age of Reason and Revolution 1700–1850*. New York: Oxford University Press, 2000.
Hegel, Georg Wilhelm Fredrich. *Hegel: Elements of the Philosophy of Right*. Edited by Allen W. Wood, translated by H. B. Nisbet. Cambridge: Cambridge University Press, 1991.
Heidegger, Martin. "Building Dwelling Thinking." In *Poetry, Language, Thought*, 141–60. New York: Harper, 2013.
  "Die Frage nach der Technik." In *Vorträge und Aufsätze*, 13–44. Pfüllingen: Neske, 1954.
  Holzwege. Frankfurt: Klostermann, 1950.
  The Question Concerning Technology, and Other Essays. Translated by William Lovitt. London: Garland, 1977.
Heil, John. *Philosophy of Mind: A Contemporary Introduction*. New York: Routledge, 2012.
Heilweil, Rebecca. "How Deepfakes Could Actually Do Some Good." *Vox*, June 29, 2020. www.vox.com/recode/2020/6/29/21303588/deepfakes-anonymous-artificial-intelligence-welcome-to-chechnya.
Heims, Steve Joshua. *John von Neumann and Norbert Wiener: From Mathematics to the Technologies of Life and Death*. Cambridge, MA: MIT Press, 1980.
Helbing, Dirk, Bruno S. Frey, Gerd Gigerenzer, Ernst Hafen, Michael Hagner, Yvonne Hofstetter, Jeroen van den Hoven, Roberto V. Zicari, and Andrei Zwitter. "Will Democracy Survive Big Data and Artificial Intelligence?" *Scientific American*, February 25, 2017. www.scientificamerican.com/article/will-democracy-survive-big-data-and-artificial-intelligence/.
Held, David. *Introduction to Critical Theory: Horkheimer to Habermas*. Cambridge: Polity, 1991.
Hennessy, Brittany. *Influencer: Building Your Personal Brand in the Age of Social Media*. New York: Citadel, 2018.
Henry, John. *Knowledge Is Power: How Magic, the Government and an Apocalyptic Vision Helped Francis Bacon to Create Modern Science*. Cambridge: Icon Books, 2017.
Hertwig, Ralph, Gerd Gigerenzer, and Ulrich Hoffrage. "The Reiteration Effect in Hindsight Bias." *Psychological Review* 104, no. 1 (1997): 194–202.
Higgins, Eliot. *We Are Bellingcat: Global Crime, Online Sleuths, and the Bold Future of News*. New York: Bloomsbury, 2021.
Hill, Thomas E. *Dignity and Practical Reason in Kant's Moral Theory*. Ithaca: Cornell University Press, 1992.
Hobbes, Thomas. *Leviathan*. Edited by Richard Tuck. Cambridge: Cambridge University Press, 1991.
Hochschild, Arlie Russell. *Strangers in Their Own Land: Anger and Mourning on the American Right*. New York: The New Press, 2018.
Hoekstra, Kinch. "Hobbesian Equality." In *Hobbes Today: Insights for the 21st Century*, edited by S. A. Lloyd. Cambridge: Cambridge University Press, 2013.
Hoffman, Jane S. *Your Data, Their Billions: Unraveling and Simplifying Big Tech*. New York: Post Hill Press, 2022.
Hoffmann, Anna Lauren. "Rawls, Information Technology, and the Sociotechnical Bases of Self-Respect." In *The Oxford Handbook of Philosophy of Technology*, edited by Shannon Vallor, 231–49. Oxford: Oxford University Press, 2022.

Hohfeld, Wesley. *Fundamental Legal Conceptions*. Edited by W. Cook. New Haven: Yale University Press, 1919.

Holland, Max. "The Truth Behind JFK's Assassination." *Newsweek Magazine*, November 20, 2014. www.newsweek.com/2014/11/28/truth-behind-jfks-assassination-285653.html.

Honore, A. M. "Ownership." In *Making Law Bind: Essays Legal and Philosophical*. Oxford: Oxford University Press, 1961.

Hopkins, Robert. "Factive Pictorial Experience: What's Special about Photographs?" *Nous* 46, no. 4 (2012): 709–31.

Horkheimer, Max. *Dialectic of Enlightenment*. New York: Seabury Press, 1972.

Horkheimer, Max, and Theodor W. Adorno. *Dialectic of Enlightenment*. New York: Continuum, 1999.

Horwich, Paul. *Truth*. Oxford: Clarendon, 1999.

Hugo, Victor. "Les Misérables." Translated by Lee Fahestock and Norman MacAfee. New York: Signet Classics, 2013.

Hume, David. *A Treatise of Human Nature*. CreateSpace Independent Publishing Platform, 2015.

Hunt, Earl. *Human Intelligence*. New York: Cambridge University Press, 2010.

Idel, Moshe. *Golem: Jewish Magical and Mystical Traditions on the Artificial Anthropoid*. Brooklyn: KTAV Publishing House, 2019.

Igo, Sarah E. *The Known Citizen: A History of Privacy in Modern America*. Cambridge, MA: Harvard University Press, 2018.

Ihde, Don. *Technology and the Lifeworld: From Garden to Earth*. Bloomington: Indiana University Press, 1990.

Innes, David C. *Francis Bacon*. Phillipsburg, NJ: P & R Publishing, 2019.

Ionescu, Gita, ed. *The Political Thought of Saint Simon*. Oxford: Oxford University Press, 1976.

Jacobi, Robert. *Reboot: Der Code für eine widerstandsfähige Wirtschaft, Politik und Gesellschaft*. Hamburg: Murmann, 2021.

Jacobs, W. W. *The Monkey's Paw and Other Tales of Mystery and the Macabre*. Chicago: Academy Chicago Publishers, 2005.

Jaeggi, Rahel. *Alienation*. Edited by Frederick. New York: Columbia University Press, 2014.

Janich, Peter. *What Is Information?* Translated by Eric Hayot and Lea Pao. Minneapolis: University of Minnesota Press, 2018.

Jarvis, Simon. *Adorno: A Critical Introduction*. Cambridge: Polity, 1998.

Jasanoff, Sheila, and Sang-Hyun Kim, eds. *Dreamscapes of Modernity: Sociotechnical Imaginaries and the Fabrication of Power*. Chicago: University of Chicago Press, 2015.

Jaworska, Agnieszka, and Julie Tannenbaum. "The Grounds of Moral Status." In *Stanford Encyclopedia of Philosophy*, edited by Edward N. Zalta, 2021. https://plato.stanford.edu/entries/truth/.

Jaworski, William. *Philosophy of Mind: A Comprehensive Introduction*. Malden, MA: Wiley-Blackwell, 2011.

Jemielniak, Dariusz. *Thick Big Data: Doing Digital Social Sciences*. Oxford: Oxford University Press, 2020.

Jerónimo, Helena M., José Luís Garcia, and Carl Mitcham, eds. *Jacques Ellul and the Technological Society in the 21st Century*. Dordrecht: Springer, 2013.

Jonas, Hans. *The Imperative of Responsibility: In Search of an Ethics for the Technological Age*. University of Chicago Press, 1985.

Jones, Caroline A. "The Artistic Use of Cybernetic Beings." In *Possible Minds: Twenty-Five Ways of Looking at AI*, edited by John Brockman, 254–65. New York: Penguin, 2019.

Jungherr, Andreas, Gonzalo Rivero, and Daniel Gayo-Avello. *Retooling Politics: How Digital Media Are Shaping Democracy*. Cambridge: Cambridge University Press, 2020.

Kafka, Franz. *The Trial*. Translated by David Wyllie. Mineola: Dover, 2009.

Kagan, Shelly. *How to Count Animals, More or Less*. Oxford: Oxford University Press, 2019.

Kahn, Paul W. *Political Theology: Four New Chapters on the Concept of Sovereignty*. New York: Columbia University Press, 2011.

    Putting Liberalism in Its Place. Princeton: Princeton University Press, 2008.

    "Sacrificial Nation." *Utopian*, March 29, 2010. www.the-utopian.org/post/2340099709/sacrificial-nation.

Kahneman, Daniel. *Thinking, Fast and Slow*. New York: Farrar, Straus and Giroux, 2013.

Kandiyali, Jan, ed. *Reassessing Marx's Social and Political Philosophy: Freedom, Recognition, and Human Flourishing*. London: Routledge, 2018.

Kant, Immanuel. *Lectures on Ethics*. Edited by J. B. Schneewind, translated by Peter Heath. Cambridge: Cambridge University Press, 2001.

    Practical Philosophy. Edited by Mary J. Gregor. New York: Cambridge University Press, 1996.

Kavka, Gregory. *Hobbesian Moral and Political Theory*. Princeton: Princeton University Press, 1986.

Kelly, Kevin. *What Technology Wants*. New York: Viking, 2010.

Kerner, Catherine, and Mathias Risse. "Beyond Porn and Discreditation: Promises and Perils of Deepfake Technology in Digital Lifeworlds." *Moral Philosophy and Politics* 8, no. 1 (2021): 81–108.

Keyssar, Alexander. *The Right to Vote: The Contested History of Democracy in the United States*. New York: Basic Books, 2009.

Kierkegaard, Søren. *Kierkegaard's Writings, Volume VI: Fear and Trembling/Repetition*. Translated by Edna H. Hong and Howard V. Hong. Princeton: Princeton University Press, 1983.

    Kierkegaard's Writings, Volume XIII: The Corsair Affair and Articles Related to the Writings. Translated by Edna H. Hong and Howard V. Hong. Princeton: Princeton University Press, 2009.

    Kierkegaard's Writings, Volume XIV: Two Ages - The Age of Revolution and the Present Age/ A Literary Review. Translated by Howard V. Hong and Edna H. Hong. Princeton: Princeton University Press, 2009.

King, David. *The Commissar Vanishes: The Falsification of Photographs and Art in Stalin's Russia*. London: Tate, 2014.

Kissinger, Henry A., Eric Schmidt, and Daniel Huttenlocher. *The Age of AI: And Our Human Future*. New York: Little, Brown and Company, 2021.

Kittler, Friedrich A. "The Artificial Intelligence of World War: Alan Turing." In *The Truth of the Technological World: Essays on the Genealogy of Presence*. Translated by Erik Butler, 178–94. Palo Alto: Stanford University Press, 2014.

    Gramophone, Film, Typewriter. Palo Alto: Stanford University Press, 1999.

Kiverstein, Julian. "Could a Robot Have a Subjective Point of View?" *Journal of Consciousness Studies* 14, no. 7 (2007): 127–39.

Klein, Naomi. *This Changes Everything: Capitalism vs. The Climate*. New York: Simon & Schuster, 2014.

Kleinman, Alexis. "Porn Sites Get More Visitors Each Month Than Netflix, Amazon and Twitter Combined." *Huffington Post*, December 6, 2017. www.huffpost.com/entry/internet-porn-stats_n_3187682.

Klemke, E. D., ed. *The Meaning of Life*. New York: Oxford University Press, 1999.

Kline, Ronald R. *The Cybernetics Moment: Or Why We Call Our Age the Information Age.* Baltimore: Johns Hopkins University Press, 2017.

Klinkner, Melanie, and Howard Davis. *The Right to The Truth in International Law*. London: Routledge, 2021.

Knight, Will. "The Defense Department Has Produced the First Tools for Catching Deepfakes." *MIT Technology Review*, August 7, 2018.

Koch, Christof. *Consciousness: Confessions of a Romantic Reductionist*. Cambridge, MA: MIT Press, 2012.

  The Feeling of Life Itself: Why Consciousness Is Widespread but Can't Be Computed. Cambridge, MA: MIT Press, 2020.

Kolakowski, Leszek. *Main Currents of Marxism: The Founders - The Golden Age - The Breakdown*. New York: Norton, 2008.

Koopman, Colin. *How We Became Our Data: A Genealogy of the Informational Person.* Chicago: University of Chicago Press, 2019.

Kornwachs, Klaus, and Konstantin Jacoby, eds. *Information. New Questions to a Multidisciplinary Concept*. Berlin: Akademie Verlag, 1996.

Korsgaard, Christine M. *Fellow Creatures: Our Obligations to the Other Animals*. Oxford: Oxford University Press, 2018.

Koschorke, Albrecht. *Fact and Fiction: Elements of a General Theory of Narrative*. Berlin: De Gruyter, 2018.

Kramm, Matthias. "When a River Becomes a Person." *Journal of Human Development and Capabilities* 21, no. 4 (2020): 307–19.

Kraybill, Donald B. *What the Amish Teach Us: Plain Living in a Busy World*. Baltimore: Johns Hopkins University Press, 2021.

Kraybill, Donald B., Karen M. Johnson-Weiner, and Steven M. Nolt. *The Amish*. Baltimore: Johns Hopkins University Press, 2018.

Krücken, Georg, and Gili S. Drori, eds. *World Society: The Writings of John W. Meyer*. New York: Oxford University Press, 2009.

Kuflik, Arthur. "Moral Foundations of Intellectual Property Rights." In *Owning Scientific and Technical Information: Value and Ethical Issues*, edited by Vivian Weil and John Snapper. New Brunswick: Rutgers University Press, 1989.

Kuhn, Thomas S. *The Structure of Scientific Revolutions*. Chicago: University of Chicago Press, 1970.

Kurzweil, Ray. *The Singularity Is Near: When Humans Transcend Biology*. New York: Penguin, 2006.

Lackey, Jennifer. *Learning from Words: Testimony as a Source of Knowledge*. New York: Oxford University Press, 2010.

Lame Deer, John. *Lame Deer: Seeker of Visions*. Edited by Richard Erdoes. New York: Simon & Schuster, 1972.

Landemore, Hélène. "Open Democracy and Digital Technologies." In *Digital Technology and Democratic Theory*, edited by Lucy Bernholz, Hélène Landemore, and Rob Reich, 62–89. Chicago: University of Chicago Press, 2021.

  Open Democracy: Reinventing Popular Rule for the Twenty-First Century. Princeton: Princeton University Press, 2020.

Langton, Rae. "Speech Acts and Unspeakable Acts." *Philosophy & Public Affairs* 22, no. 4 (1993): 293–330.

Langton, Rae, and Jennifer Hornsby. "Free Speech and Illocution." *Legal Theory* 4, no. 1 (1998): 21–37.

Larkin, Philip. *Collected Poems*. Edited by Anthony Thwaite. New York: Farrar, Straus and Giroux, 1989.

Larson, Erik J. *The Myth of Artificial Intelligence: Why Computers Can't Think the Way We Do*. Cambridge, MA: Harvard University Press, 2021.

Lash, Scott M. *Critique of Information*. London: Sage, 2002.

Latour, Bruno. *Reassembling the Social: An Introduction to Actor-Network-Theory*. Oxford: Oxford University Press, 2007.

We Have Never Been Modern. Translated by Catherine Porter. Cambridge, MA: Harvard University Press, 1993.

Lauren, Paul Gordon. *The Evolution of International Human Rights: Visions Seen*. Philadelphia: University of Pennsylvania Press, 2011.

Lechner, Frank, and John Boli. *World Culture: Origins and Consequences*. Oxford: Blackwell, 2005.

Lee, Dami. "Deepfake Salvador Dalí Takes Selfies with Museum Visitors." *The Verge*, May 10, 2019. www.theverge.com/2019/5/10/18540953/salvador-dali-lives-deepfake-museum.

Lee, Harper. *To Kill a Mockingbird*. New York: Lippincott, 1960.

Lemos, Noah M. *Intrinsic Value: Concept and Warrant*. Cambridge, MA: Cambridge University Press, 1994.

Lenski, Wolfgang. "Information: A Conceptual Investigation." *Information* 1, no. 2 (2010): 74–118.

Leonard, Andrew. "How Taiwan's Unlikely Digital Minister Hacked the Pandemic." *Wired*, July 23, 2020. www.wired.com/story/how-taiwans-unlikely-digital-minister-hacked-the-pandemic/.

Lepore, Jill. "Rock, Paper, Scissors: How We Used to Vote." *The New Yorker*, October 13, 2008. www.ghhsapush.com/uploads/8/0/6/2/80629020/jill_lepore_-_rock_paper_scissors. pdf.

These Truths: A History of the United States. New York: Norton, 2019.

Lesne, Annick. "The Discrete vs. Continuous Controversy in Physics." *Mathematical Structures in Computer Science* 17, no. 2 (2007): 1–39.

Levy, David. *Love and Sex with Robots: The Evolution of Human-Robot Relationships*. New York: Harper, 2007.

Levy, Neil. "The Value of Consciousness." *Journal of Consciousness Studies* 21, no. 1–2 (2014): 127–38.

Lewis, David. "Analogue and Digital." *Nous* 5, no. 3 (1971): 321–27.

Liang, Percy, and Rishi Bommasani. "On the Opportunities and Risks of Foundation Models." Stanford Institute for Human-Centered Artificial Intelligence. Stanford University, August 2021. https://fsi.stanford.edu/publication/opportunities-and-risks-foundation-models.

Liao, S. Matthew. "The Moral Status and Rights of Artificial Intelligence." In *Ethics of Artificial Intelligence*, edited by S. Matthew Liao, 271–92. New York: Oxford University Press, 2020.

List, Christian, and Philip Pettit. *Group Agency: The Possibility, Design, and Status of Corporate Agents*. Oxford: Oxford University Press, 2013.

Livingston, Steven, and Mathias Risse. "On the Impact of Artificial Intelligence on Human Rights Over the Next 20-30 Years." *Ethics and International Affairs* 33, no. 2 (2019): 141–58.

Livingstone, David. *Transhumanism: The History of a Dangerous Idea*. CreateSpace Independent Publishing Platform, 2015.

Locke, John. *Second Treatise of Government*. Edited by C. B. Macpherson. Indianapolis: Hackett, 1980.

Lohr, Steve. *Data-Ism: The Revolution Transforming Decision Making, Consumer Behavior, and Almost Everything Else*. New York: Harper, 2015.

Loiperdinger, Martin, and Bernd Elzer. "Lumiere's Arrival of the Train: Cinema's Founding Myth." *The Moving Image* 4, no. 1 (2004): 89–118.

Longino, Helen E. *Science as Social Knowledge: Values and Objectivity in Scientific Inquiry*. Princeton: Princeton University Press, 1990.

Lorenc, Theo. "Artificial Intelligence and the Ethics of Human Extinction." *Journal of Consciousness Studies* 22, no. 9–10 (2015): 194–214.

Losee, Robert M. *The Science of Information: Measurement and Applications*. San Diego: Academic Press, 1990.

Lovejoy, Arthur. *The Great Chain of Being: A Study in the History of Ideas*. Cambridge, MA: Harvard University Press, 1936.

Lovelock, James. *Novacene: The Coming Age of Hyperintelligence*. Cambridge, MA: MIT Press, 2020.

Löwenthal, Leo, and Norbert Guterman. *Prophets of Deceit: A Study of the Techniques of the American Agitator*. Edited by Alberto Toscano, Max Horkheimer, and Herbert Marcuse. New York: Verso, 2021.

Lukacs, Georg. *The Theory of the Novel*. Cambridge, MA: MIT Press, 1974.

Lukes, Steven. "Durkheim's 'Individualism and the Intellectuals.'" *Political Studies* XVII, no. 1 (1969): 14–30.

    Emile Durkheim: His Life and Work: A Historical and Critical Study. Stanford: Stanford University Press, 1985.

    Individualism. New York: Harper & Row, 1973.

    Marxism and Morality. Oxford: Oxford University Press, 1985.

    Power: A Radical View. New York: Palgrave Macmillan, 2005.

Lyon, Aidan. "Data." In *Oxford Handbook of Philosophy of Science*, edited by Paul Humphreys, 738–58. New York: Oxford University Press, 2016.

Lyubomirsky, Sonja. *The How of Happiness: A New Approach to Getting the Life You Want*. New York: Penguin, 2008.

Macaulay, Thomas. "What Is Synthetic Data and How Can It Help Protect Privacy?" *Tech Advisor*, October 1, 2019. https://www.techadvisor.com/article/738852/what-is-synthetic-data-and-how-can-it-help-protect-privacy.html.

MacKinnon, Catherine A. *Feminism Unmodified*. Cambridge, MA: Harvard University Press, 1987.

Mackintosh, Nicholas. *IQ and Human Intelligence*. Oxford: Oxford University Press, 2011.

Macrae, Norman. *John von Neumann*. New York: Pantheon, 1992.

Malanczuk, Peter. *Akehurst's Modern Introduction to International Law*. New York: Routledge, 1997.

Manning, Christopher D. "Human Language Understanding & Reasoning." *Daedalus* 151, no. 2 (2022): 127–38.

Manuel, Frank. *The New World of Henri Saint-Simon*. Cambridge, MA: Harvard University Press, 1956.

Manyika, James, ed. *AI & Society, Spring 2022 Issue of Daedalus*. Cambridge, MA: American Academy of Arts and Sciences, 2022

Marcuse, Herbert. *Heideggerian Marxism*. Edited by John Abromeit and Richard Wolin. Lincoln: University of Nebraska Press, 2005.

One-Dimensional Man: Studies in the Ideology of Advanced Industrial Society. Edited by Douglas Kellner. Boston: Beacon Press, 1991.

"Some Social Implications of Modern Technology." In *Technology, War and Fascism: Collected Papers of Herbert Marcuse.* Edited by Douglas Kellner, Vol. 1, 39–66. New York: Routledge, 1998.

Margetts, Helen. "Rethinking AI for Good Governance." *Daedalus* 151, no. 2 (2022): 360–71.

Marino, Lori. "The Landscape of Intelligence." In *The Impact of Discovering Life Beyond Earth*, edited by Steven J. Dick, 95–112. Cambridge, MA: Cambridge University Press, 2016.

Martin, Bradley K. *Under the Loving Care of the Fatherly Leader: North Korea and the Kim Dynasty.* New York: St. Martin's Griffin, 2006.

Massimini, Marcello, and Giulio Tononi. *Sizing Up Consciousness: Towards an Objective Measure of the Capacity for Experience.* Oxford: Oxford University Press, 2018.

Matheson, David. "A Duty of Ignorance." *Episteme* 10, no. 2 (2013): 193–205.

May, Todd. *Philosophy of Foucault.* New York: Routledge, 2006.

Mayer-Schönberger, Viktor. *Delete: The Virtue of Forgetting in the Digital Age.* Princeton: Princeton University Press, 2011.

Mayer-Schönberger, Viktor, and Kenneth Cukier. *Big Data: A Revolution That Will Transform How We Live, Work, and Think.* Boston: Mariner Books, 2014.

Mazower, Mark. *Governing the World: The History of an Idea, 1815 to the Present.* New York: Penguin, 2013.

McCarthy, John, Marvin L. Minsky, Nathaniel Rochester, and Claude E. Shannon. "A Proposal for the Dartmouth Summer Research Project on Artificial Intelligence." *AI Magazine* 27, no. 4 (2006): 12–14.

McLellan, David, ed. *Karl Marx: Selected Writings.* Oxford: Oxford University Press, 1977.

Marxism After Marx. Basingstoke: Palgrave Macmillan, 2007.

McLuhan, Marshall. *Counterblast.* New York: Harcourt, Brace & World, 1969.

Understanding Media: The Extensions of Man. Cambridge, MA: MIT Press, 1994.

McNamee, Roger. *Zucked: Waking Up to the Facebook Catastrophe.* New York: Penguin, 2019.

McNay, Lois. *Foucault: A Critical Introduction.* Cambridge: Polity, 1994.

McNeill, J. R., and William H. McNeill. *The Human Web: A Bird's-Eye View of World History.* New York: Norton, 2003.

Medina, José. *The Epistemology of Resistance: Gender and Racial Oppression, Epistemic Injustice, and Resistant Imaginations.* Oxford: Oxford University Press, 2012.

Mehr, Hila. "Artificial Intelligence for Citizen Services and Government." Ash Center for Democratic Governance and Innovation, Harvard University, August 2017. https://ash .harvard.edu/files/ash/files/artificial_intelligence_for_citizen_services.pdf.

Mercieca, Jennifer. *Demagogue for President: The Rhetorical Genius of Donald Trump.* College Station: Texas A&M University Press, 2020.

Merlan, Anna. *Republic of Lies: American Conspiracy Theorists and Their Surprising Rise to Power.* New York: Metropolitan Books, 2020.

Metz, Cade. "In Two Moves, AlphaGo and Lee Sedol Redefined the Future." *Wired*, March 16, 2016. www.wired.com/2016/03/two-moves-alphago-lee-sedol-redefined-future/

Metz, Thaddeus. *Meaning in Life.* Oxford: Oxford University Press, 2014.

Metzinger, Thomas. "Artificial Suffering: An Argument for a Global Moratorium on Synthetic Phenomenology." *Journal of Artificial Intelligence and Consciousness* 8, no. 1 (2021): 43–66.

Meyer, John W. *World Society: The Writings of John W. Meyer*. Edited by Georg Krücken and Gili Drori. Oxford: Oxford University Press, 2010.

Meyer, John W., and Mathias Risse. "Thinking About the World: Philosophy and Sociology." *Carr Center Discussion Paper Series* 2018-005, 2018. https://carrcenter.hks.harvard.edu/files/cchr/files/ccdp_2018_005_thinkingaboutworld.pdf.

Michaelian, Kourken, and John Sutton. "Memory." In *Stanford Encyclopedia of Philosophy*, edited by Edward N. Zalta, 2017. https://plato.stanford.edu/entries/truth/.

Migotti, Mark, Nicole Wyatt, Brian Earp, Anders Sandberg, Ezio di Nucci, Noreen Hertzfeld, Litska Strikwerda, et al. *Robot Sex: Social and Ethical Implications*. Edited by John Danaher and Neil McArthur. Cambridge, MA: MIT Press, 2017.

Miller, Eugene. "What Does 'Political' Mean?" *Review of Politics* 42, no. 1 (1980): 56–72.

Miller, Richard W. *Analyzing Marx: Morality, Power and History*. Princeton: Princeton University Press, 1984.

Mills, Charles W. *Black Rights/White Wrongs: The Critique of Racial Liberalism*. New York: Oxford University Press, 2017.

 "White Ignorance." In *Race and Epistemologies of Ignorance*, edited by Shannon Sullivan and Nancy Tuana, 13–38. Albany: State University of New York Press, 2007.

Minow, Martha. *Saving the News: Why the Constitution Calls for Government Action to Preserve Freedom of Speech*. New York: Oxford University Press, 2021.

Misselhorn, Catrin. "Artificial Morality. Concepts, Issues and Challenges." *Society* 55, no. 2 (2018): 161–69.

Mitchell, Melanie. *Artificial Intelligence: A Guide for Thinking Humans*. New York: Farrar, Straus and Giroux, 2019.

Mittelstadt, Brent Daniel, Patrick Allo, Mariarosaria Taddeo, Sandra Wachter, and Luciano Floridi. "The Ethics of Algorithms: Mapping the Debate." *Big Data & Society* 3, no. 2 (2016): 1–21

Montagnini, Leone. *Harmonies of Disorder: Norbert Wiener: A Mathematician-Philosopher of Our Time*. Berlin: Springer, 2018.

Moor, James H. "Four Kinds of Ethical Robots." *Philosophy Now* 72 (2009): 12–14.

Moore, Martin. *Democracy Hacked: How Technology Is Destabilising Global Politics*. London: Oneworld, 2020.

Moran, Dermot. *Introduction to Phenomenology*. New York: Routledge, 2000.

More, Max, and Natasha Vita-More, eds. *The Transhumanist Reader: Classical and Contemporary Essays on the Science, Technology, and Philosophy of the Human Future*. Chichester: Wiley-Blackwell, 2013.

Morozov, Evgeny. "Capitalism's New Clothes." *The Baffler*, February 4, 2019. https://thebaffler.com/latest/capitalisms-new-clothes-morozov.

Morsink, Johannes. *The Universal Declaration of Human Rights*. Philadelphia: University of Pennsylvania Press, 1999.

Mouffe, Chantal. *On the Political*. London: Routledge, 2005. https://thebaffler.com/latest/capitalisms-new-clothes-morozov.

Moyn, Samuel. *Not Enough: Human Rights in an Unequal World*. Cambridge, MA: Belknap, 2018.

Muirhead, Russell, and Nancy Rosenblum. *A Lot of People Are Saying: The New Conspiracism and the Assault on Democracy*. Princeton: Princeton University Press, 2020.

Müller, Luise. "Domesticating Artificial Intelligence." *Moral Philosophy and Politics*, forthcoming.

Mumford, Lewis. *Myth of the Machine: Technics and Human Development*. New York: Harcourt Brace Jovanovich, 1967.

Pentagon of Power: The Myth of the Machine, Vol. II. New York: Harcourt Brace Jovanovich, 1974.

Technics and Civilization. Chicago: University of Chicago Press, 2010.

Murdoch, Iris. *The Sovereignty of Good*. London: Routledge, 2014.

Nagel, Jennifer. *Knowledge: A Very Short Introduction*. Oxford: Oxford University Press, 2014.

Nagel, Thomas. "The Absurd." In *Mortal Questions*, 11–23. Cambridge: Cambridge University Press, 2012.

Equality and Partiality. New York: Oxford University Press, 1991.

Mind & Cosmos: Why the Materialist Neo-Darwinian Conception of Nature Is Almost Certainly False. New York: Oxford University Press, 2012.

What Does It All Mean? A Very Short Introduction to Philosophy. New York: Oxford University Press, 1987.

"What Is It Like to Be a Bat?" *Philosophical Review* 83, no. 4 (1974): 435–50.

Neumann, John von. "Can We Survive Technology?" In *John von Neumann: Collected Works*, edited by A. H. Taub, Vol. VI, 504–19. Oxford: Pergamon, 1961.

Niebuhr, Reinhold. *Moral Man and Immoral Society: A Study in Ethics and Politics*. Eugene: Wipf and Stock, 2010.

Nietzsche, Friedrich. *Beyond Good and Evil. Prelude to a Philosophy of the Future*. Translated by Walter Kaufmann. New York: Vintage, 1966.

The Gay Science: With a Prelude in Rhymes and an Appendix of Songs. Translated by Walter Kaufmann. New York: Vintage, 1974.

On the Genealogy of Morality. Translated by Maudemarie Clark and Alan J. Swensen. Indianapolis: Hackett, 1998.

Nietzsche: The Anti-Christ, Ecce Homo, Twilight of the Idols: And Other Writings. Edited by Aaron Ridley, translated by Judith Norman. New York: Cambridge University Press, 2005.

Nietzsche: Thus Spoke Zarathustra. Edited by Robert Pippin, translated by Adrian Del Caro. Cambridge: Cambridge University Press, 2006.

Nilsson, Nils J. *Quest for Artificial Intelligence*. New York: Cambridge University Press, 2009.

Nissenbaum, Helen. "Accountability in a Computerized Society." *Science and Engineering Ethics* 2, no. 1 (1996): 25–42.

Privacy in Context: Technology, Policy, and the Integrity of Social Life. Stanford: Stanford Law Books, 2009.

Noble, Safiya Umoja. *Algorithms of Oppression: How Search Engines Reinforce Racism*. New York: NYU Press, 2018.

Nozick, Robert. *Anarchy, State, and Utopia*. New York: Basic Books, 1974.

Philosophical Explanations. Cambridge, MA: Belknap, 1983.

Nurse, Paul. *What Is Life? Five Great Ideas in Biology*. New York: Norton, 2021.

Oakeshott, Michael. *On Human Conduct*. Oxford: Clarendon, 1975.

Ober, Josiah. *The Rise and Fall of Classical Greece*. Princeton: Princeton University Press, 2015.

O'Connor, Cailin, and James Owen Weatherall. *The Misinformation Age: How False Beliefs Spread*. New Haven: Yale University Press, 2020.

O'Neil, Cathy. *Weapons of Math Destruction: How Big Data Increases Inequality and Threatens Democracy*. New York: Broadway Books, 2017.

O'Neill, Onora. *A Philosopher Looks at Digital Communication*. Cambridge: Cambridge University Press, 2022.

Ong, Walter J., ed. *Orality and Literacy: 30th Anniversary Edition*. London: Routledge, 2012.

Ord, Toby. *The Precipice: Existential Risk and the Future of Humanity*. New York: Hachette Books, 2021.

Origgi, Gloria. *Reputation: What It Is and Why It Matters*. Translated by Stephen Holmes and Noga Arikha. Princeton: Princeton University Press, 2017.

Orwell, George. *1984*. New York: Signet Classic, 1961.

    The Collected Essays, Journalism, and Letters of George Orwell. Edited by Sonia Orwell and Ian Angus. New York: Harcourt, Brace & World, 1968.

Osoba, Osonde A., and William Welser. *An Intelligence in Our Image: The Risks of Bias and Errors in Artificial Intelligence*. Santa Monica: RAND Corporation, 2017.

Paris, Britt, and Joan Donovan. "Deepfakes and Cheap Fakes: The Manipulation of Audio and Visual Evidence." *Data and Society*, September 18, 2019. www.readkong.com/page/deepfakes-and-cheap-fakes-5950741.

Pariser, Eli, and Danielle Allen. "To Thrive Our Democracy Needs Digital Public Infrastructure." *Politico*, January 5, 2021. www.politico.com/news/agenda/2021/01/05/to-thrive-our-democracy-needs-digital-public-infrastructure-455061

Park, Y. Gloria. "Truth as Justice: Legal and Extralegal Development of the Right to Truth." *Harvard International Review* 31, no. 4 (2010): 24–27.

Partington, John S. *Building Cosmopolis: The Political Thought of H.G. Wells*. Aldershot: Routledge, 2016.

    "Human Rights and Public Accountability in H. G. Wells' Functional World State." In *Cosmopolitics and the Emergence of a Future*, edited by D. Morgan and G. Banham, 163–90. Basingstoke: Palgrave Macmillan, 2007.

Pasquale, Frank. *The Black Box Society: The Secret Algorithms That Control Money and Information*. Cambridge, MA: Harvard University Press, 2016.

Peirce, Charles S. "The Fixation of Belief." In *Philosophical Writings of Peirce*, edited by Justus Buchler, 5–22. New York: Dover, 2011.

Pentland, Alex. *Social Physics: How Social Networks Can Make Us Smarter*. New York: Penguin, 2015.

    "The Death of Individuality." *New Scientist* 222, no. 2963 (2014): 30–1.

Peterfreund, Emanuel, and Jacob T. Schwartz. "The Concept of Information." *Psychological Issues* 7 (1971): 115–25.

Peters, John Durham. "Information: Notes Toward a Critical History." *Journal of Communication Inquiry* 12, no. 2 (1988): 9–23.

    The Marvelous Clouds: Toward a Philosophy of Elemental Media. Chicago: University of Chicago Press, 2016.

Petersen, Steve. "Superintelligence as Superethical." In *Robot Ethics 2.0: From Autonomous Cars to Artificial Intelligence*, edited by Patrick Lin, Keith Abney, and Ryan Jenkins, 322–37. New York: Oxford University Press, 2017.

Pickstock, Catherine. *Repetition and Identity: The Literary Agenda*. Oxford: Oxford University Press, 2014.

Piketty, Thomas. *Capital in the Twenty - First Century*. Translated by Arthur Goldhammer. Cambridge, MA: Belknap, 2014.

Pinker, Steven. "Tech Prophecy and the Underappreciated Causal Power of Ideas." In *Possible Minds: Twenty-Five Ways of Looking at AI*, edited by John Brockman, 100–112. New York: Penguin, 2019.

Plato. *The Republic of Plato*. Translated by Allan Bloom. New York: Basic Books, 2016.

    The Theaetetus of Plato. Edited by Myles Burnyeat, translated by M. J. Levett. Indianapolis: Hackett, 1990.

Popper, Karl R. *Objective Knowledge: An Evolutionary Approach.* Oxford: Oxford University Press, 1972.

Posner, Eric A., and E. Glen Weyl. *Radical Markets: Uprooting Capitalism and Democracy for a Just Society.* Princeton: Princeton University Press, 2018.

Preville, Philip. "How Barcelona Is Leading a New Era of Digital Democracy." *Medium,* November 13, 2019. https://medium.com/sidewalk-talk/how-barcelona-is-leading-a-new-era-of-digital-democracy-4a033a98cf32.

Price, Don K. *The Scientific Estate.* Oxford: Oxford University Press, 1968.

Prior, Matthew T. *Confronting Technology: The Theology of Jacques Ellul.* London: Pickwick, 2020.

Purdon, James. *Modernist Informatics: Literature, Information, and the State.* New York: Oxford University Press, 2015.

Putnam, Hilary. "Minds and Machines." In *Mind, Language, and Reality,* 362–85. Cambridge, MA: Cambridge University Press, 1975.

Quong, Jonathan. *Liberalism Without Perfection.* Oxford: Oxford University Press, 2011.

Rachels, James. "Why Privacy Is Important." *Philosophy & Public Affairs* 4, no. 4 (1974): 323–33.

Rapoport, Anatol. "What Is Information?" *Synthese* 11, no. 3 (1953): 157–73.

Rauch, Jonathan. *The Constitution of Knowledge: A Defense of Truth.* Washington: Brookings, 2021.

Rawls, John. *Justice as Fairness: A Restatement.* Edited by Erin Kelly. Cambridge, MA: Belknap, 2001.

    The Law of Peoples, with The Idea of Public Reason Revisited. Cambridge, MA: Harvard University Press, 1999.

    Political Liberalism. New York: Columbia University Press, 1996.

    A Theory of Justice. Revised Edition. Cambridge, MA: Harvard University Press, 1999.

Raz, Joseph. *The Morality of Freedom.* Oxford: Oxford University Press, 1986.

Redding, Anna Crowley. *Google It: A History of Google.* New York: Feiwel & Friends, 2018.

Rees, Tobias. "Non-Human Words: On GPT-3 as a Philosophical Laboratory." *Daedalus* 151, no. 2 (2022): 168–82.

Reich, Rob, Mehran Sahami, and Jeremy M. Weinstein. *System Error: Where Big Tech Went Wrong and How We Can Reboot.* New York: Harper, 2021.

Reilly, Jessica, Muyao Lyu, and Megan Robertson. "China's Social Credit System: Speculation vs. Reality." *The Diplomat,* March 30, 2021. https://thediplomat.com/2021/03/chinas-social-credit-system-speculation-vs-reality/.

Richards, Neil. *Why Privacy Matters.* New York: Oxford University Press, 2021.

Richardson, John. *Heidegger.* New York: Routledge, 2012.

Richardson, Kathleen. *Sex Robots: The End of Love.* Cambridge: Polity, 2022.

Rini, Regina. "Deepfakes and the Epistemic Backstop." *Philosopher's Imprint* 20, no. 24 (2020): 1–16.

Risse, Mathias. "On American Values, Unalienable Rights, and Human Rights: Some Reflections on the Pompeo Commission." *Ethics & International Affairs* 34, no. 1 (2020): 13–31.

    "Arguing for Majority Rule." *Journal of Political Philosophy* 12, no. 1 (2004): 41–64.

    "Data as Collectively Generated Patterns: Making Sense of Data Ownership." *Carr Center Discussion Paper Series.* Cambridge, MA, April 26, 2021. https://carrcenter.hks.harvard.edu/files/cchr/files/210426-data_ownership.pdf.

    "The Fourth Generation of Human Rights: Epistemic Rights in Digital Lifeworlds." *Moral Philosophy and Politics* 8, no. 2 (2021): 351–78.

On Global Justice. Princeton: Princeton University Press, 2012.

"Human Rights as Membership Rights in World Society." In *Human Rights, Democracy, and Legitimacy in a World of Disorder*, edited by Gerald L. Neuman and Silja Vöneky, 25–50. Cambridge: Cambridge University Press, 2018.

"Humanity's Collective Ownership of the Earth and Immigration." *Journal of Practical Ethics* 4, no. 2 (2016): 87–122.

"Is There a Human Right to Essential Pharmaceuticals? The Global Common, the Intellectual Common, and the Possibility of Private Intellectual Property." In *Global Justice and Bioethics*, edited by Ezekiel Emanuel and Joseph Millum, 43–77. Oxford: Oxford University Press, 2012.

On Justice: Philosophy, History, Foundations. New York: Cambridge University Press, 2020.

"Origins of Ressentiment and Sources of Normativity." *Nietzsche Studien* 32, no. 1 (2003): 142–70.

"The Virtuous Group: Foundations for the 'Argument from the Wisdom of the Multitude.'" *Canadian Journal of Philosophy* 31, no. 1 (2001): 53–84.

Risse, Mathias, and Gabriel Wollner. *On Trade Justice: A Philosophical Plea for a New Global Deal*. Oxford: Oxford University Press, 2019.

Ritchie-Calder, Lord. *On Human Rights*. London: H. G. Wells Society, 1967.

Ritman, Alex. "James Dean Reborn in CGI for Vietnam War Action-Drama." *The Hollywood Reporter*, November 6, 2019. www.hollywoodreporter.com/movies/movie-news/afm-james-dean-reborn-cgi-vietnam-war-action-drama-1252703/.

Rojas, Raúl. *Die Rechenmaschinen von Konrad Zuse*. Berlin: Springer, 1998.

Rosen, Gideon, Jose L. Falguerea, and Concha Martinez-Vidal. "Abstract Objects." In *Stanford Encyclopedia of Philosophy*, edited by Edward N. Zalta, 2021. https://plato.stanford.edu/entries/truth/.

Rosen, Jeffrey. "The Right to Be Forgotten." *Stanford Law Review* 64 (2012): 88–92.

Rosen, Michael. *Dignity: Its History and Meaning*. Cambridge, MA: Harvard University Press, 2012.

Rosenberg, Alex. *The Atheist's Guide to Reality: Enjoying Life without Illusions*. New York: Norton, 2012.

Rosenberg, Daniel. "Data Before the Fact." In *"Raw Data" Is an Oxymoron*, edited by Lisa Gitelman, 15–40. Cambridge, MA: MIT Press, 2013.

Rosenberg, Yudl. *The Golem and the Wondrous Deeds of the Maharal of Prague*. Translated by Curt Leviant. New Haven: Yale University Press, 2007.

Rothman, Joshua. "The White House's Video of Jim Acosta Shows How Crude Political Manipulation Can Be." *The New Yorker*, November 8, 2018. www.newyorker.com/news/current/the-white-houses-video-of-jim-acosta-shows-how-crude-political-manipulation-can-be.

Rousseau, Jean-Jacques. *The Confessions*. Translated by J. M. Cohen. London: Penguin, 1953.

Runciman, David. *How Democracy Ends*. London: Profile Books, 2019.

Rus, Daniela. "The Machines from Our Future." *Daedalus* 151, no. 2 (2022): 100–113.

Russell, Bertrand. "A Free Man's Worship." In *Mysticism and Logic*, 25–30. London: Allen & Unwin, 1976.

Russell, Stuart. *Human Compatible: Artificial Intelligence and the Problem of Control*. New York: Viking, 2019.

Sagan, Carl. *The Cosmic Connection: An Extraterrestrial Perspective*. Cambridge: Cambridge University Press, 2000.

Saltman, Roy G. *The History and Politics of Voting Technology: In Quest of Integrity and Public Confidence*. New York: Palgrave Macmillan, 2006.

Sandel, Michael J. *The Case against Perfection: Ethics in the Age of Genetic Engineering.* Cambridge, MA: Belknap, 2009.

Sanders, Barry, and Ivan Illich. *ABC: Alphabetization of the Popular Mind.* New York: Vintage, 1989.

Sartre, Jean-Paul. *Existentialism Is a Humanism.* Edited by Arlette Elkaïm-Sartre and Annie Cohen-Solal, translated by Carol Macomber. New Haven: Yale University Press, 2007.

No Exit and Three Other Plays. Translated by Stuart Gilbert. New York: Vintage, 1989.

Satter, Raphael. "Experts: Spy Used AI-Generated Face to Connect with Targets." *AP News,* June 13, 2019. https://apnews.com/article/ap-top-news-artificial-intelligence-social-platforms-think-tanks-politics-bc2f19097a4c4fffaa00de6770b8a60d.

Savedoff, Barbara E. *Transforming Images: How Photography Complicates the Picture.* Ithaca: NCROL, 2000.

Scanlon, T. M. "Rights, Goals, and Fairness." In *The Difficulty of Tolerance: Essays in Political Philosophy,* by T. M. Scanlon, 26–42. Cambridge: Cambridge University Press, 2003.

"Some Main Points in Rawls' Theory of Justice." *Journal of Ethical Reflection* 1, no. 2 (2020): 35–49.

"What Is Morality?" In *The Harvard Sampler: Liberal Education for the Twenty-First Century,* edited by Jennifer M. Shephard, Stephen Michael Kosslyn, and Evelynn Maxine Hammonds, 243–266. Cambridge, MA: Harvard University Press, 2011.

Schacht, Richard. *Alienation.* New York: Allen & Unwin, 1971.

Schleifer, Ronald, and Robert Markley. *Kierkegaard and Literature: Irony, Repetition, and Criticism.* Norman: University of Oklahoma Press, 1984.

Schlesinger, Arthur M. "The Challenge of Change." *New York Times,* July 27, 1986.

Schmitt, Carl. *Der Begriff des Politischen: Text von 1932, mit einem Vorwort und drei Corollarien.* Berlin: Duncker & Humblot, 1963.

Verfassungslehre. Berlin: Duncker & Humblot, 1928.

Schneider, Susan. "Alien Minds." In *The Impact of Discovering Life Beyond Earth,* edited by Steven J. Dick, 189–206. Cambridge: Cambridge University Press, 2016.

Artificial You. Princeton: Princeton University Press, 2019.

Schneier, Bruce. *Click Here to Kill Everybody: Security and Survival in a Hyper-Connected World.* New York: Norton, 2018.

Data and Goliath: The Hidden Battles to Collect Your Data and Control Your World. New York: Norton, 2015.

Scholz, Lauren H. "Big Data Is Not Big Oil: The Role of Analogy in the Law of New Technologies." *Tennessee Law Review* 85 (2020): 63–93.

Schopenhauer, Arthur. *Parerga und Paralipomena.* Sämtliche Werke, Vol. 4. Frankfurt: Suhrkamp, 1963.

Schultz, Julianne. *Reviving the Fourth Estate: Democracy, Accountability and the Media.* New York: Cambridge University Press, 1998.

Schulz, William F., and Sushma Raman. *The Coming Good Society: Why New Realities Demand New Rights.* Cambridge, MA: Harvard University Press, 2020.

Schwandt, Silke, ed. *Digital Methods in the Humanities: Challenges, Ideas, Perspectives.* Bielefeld: Bielefeld University Press, 2021.

Schwitzgebel, Eric, and Mara Gaza. "A Defense of the Rights of Artificial Intelligences." *Midwest Studies in Philosophy* 39, no. 1 (2015): 98–119.

"Designing AI with Rights, Consciousness, Self-Respect, and Freedom." In *Ethics of Artificial Intelligence,* edited by S. Matthew Liao, 459–79. New York: Oxford University Press, 2020.

Sclove, Richard E. *Democracy and Technology*. New York: The Guilford Press, 1995.

Scott, James C. *Seeing Like a State: How Certain Schemes to Improve the Human Condition Have Failed*. New Haven: Yale University Press, 1998.

Scott, Kevin. "I Do Not Think It Means What You Think It Means: Artificial Intelligence, Cognitive Work & Scale." *Daedalus* 151, no. 2 (2022): 75–84.

Searle, John. "Minds, Brains and Programs." *Behavioral and Brain Sciences* 3, no. 3 (1980): 417–57.

Searle, John R. *The Mystery of Consciousness*. New York: The New York Review of Books, 1997.

Seiffert, Helmut. *Information über die Information*. München: Beck, 1968.

Sen, Amartya. *Development as Freedom*. New York: Anchor, 2000.

Seth, Anil. *Being You: A New Science of Consciousness*. New York: Dutton, 2021.

Shadbolt, Nigel, and Roger Hampson. *The Digital Ape: How to Live (in Peace) with Smart Machines*. Oxford: Oxford University Press, 2019.

Shannon, Claude E. "A Mathematical Theory of Communication." *Bell System Technical Journal* 27, no. 3 (1948): 379–423.

Shattuck, John, Sushma Raman, and Mathias Risse. *Holding Together: The Hijacking of Rights in America and How to Reclaim Them for Everyone*. New York: The New Press, 2022.

Shaw, William H. "'The Handmill Gives You the Feudal Lord': Marx's Technological Determinism." *History and Theory* 18, no. 2 (1979): 155–76.

Sherman, John. "Trusts: Speech of Hon. John Sherman of Ohio, Delivered in the Senate of the United States, Friday, March 21, 1890." Washington, DC: Unidentified Publisher, 1890.

Shiffrin, Seana Valentine. "Intellectual Property." In *A Companion to Contemporary Political Philosophy*, edited by Robert E. Goodin, Philip Pettit, and Thomas W. Pogge, 653–68. Oxford: Blackwell, 2007.

"Lockean Arguments for Private Intellectual Property." In *New Essays in the Legal and Political Theory of Property*, edited by Stephen R. Munzer, 138–67. New York: Cambridge University Press, 2001.

Shorey, Paul. *What Plato Said*. Chicago: University of Chicago Press, 1933.

Shulman, Carl, and Nick Bostrom. "Sharing the World with Digital Minds." In *Rethinking Moral Status*, edited by Steve Clarke, Hazem Zohny, and Julian Savulescu, 306–26. New York: Oxford University Press, 2021.

Siewert, Charles. *The Significance of Consciousness*. Princeton: Princeton University Press, 1998.

Sikkink, Kathryn. *Evidence for Hope: Making Human Rights Work in the Twenty-first Century*. Princeton: Princeton University Press, 2017.

Singer, Peter. *Animal Liberation: A New Ethics for Our Treatment of Animals*. New York: Random House, 1975.

Sinnott-Armstrong, Walter, and Vincent Conitzer. "How Much Moral Status Could Artifical Intelligence Ever Achieve?" In *Rethinking Moral Status*, edited by Steve Clarke, Hazem Zohny, and Julian Savulescu, 269–89. New York: Oxford University Press, 2021.

Skinner, B. F. *Beyond Freedom and Dignity*. New York: Bantam Books, 1971.

Walden Two. Indianapolis: Hackett, 2005.

"Smart City Observatory." IMD Business School, 2021. www.imd.org/smart-city-observatory/home/.

Smith, David C., and William F. Stone. "Peace and Human Rights: H. G. Wells and the Universal Declaration." *Canadian Journal of Peace Research* 21, no. 1 (1989): 21–6, 75–8.

Smith, David Woodruff. *Husserl*. London: Routledge, 2013.

Smith, Ian. "'Roundhay Garden Scene' Recorded in 1888, Is Believed to Be the Oldest Surviving Film in Existence." *The Vintage News*, January 10, 2016. www.thevintagen ews.com/2016/01/10/roundhay-garden-scene-is-believed-to-be-the-oldest-known-video-foot age/?firefox=1.

Snow, Jackie. "Deepfakes for Good: Why Researchers Are Using AI to Fake Health Data," *Fast Company*, September 24, 2018.

Snyder, Timothy. *The Road to Unfreedom: Russia, Europe, America*. New York: Tim Duggan Books, 2019.

    On Tyranny: Twenty Lessons from the Twentieth Century. New York: Tim Duggan Books, 2017.

Solove, Daniel J. *The Digital Person: Technology and Privacy in the Information Age*. Fredericksburg: NYU Press, 2006.

Somin, Ilya. *Democracy and Political Ignorance: Why Smaller Government Is Smarter*. Stanford: Stanford University Press, 2016.

Sosa, Ernest, Jaekwon Kim, Jeremy Fantl, and Matthew McGrath, eds. *Epistemology: An Anthology*. Malden: Wiley-Blackwell, 2008.

Sparks, Jacob, and Athmeya Jayaram. "Rule by Automation: How Automated Decision Systems Promote Freedom and Equality." *Moral Philosophy and Politics*, forthcoming.

Sreenivasan, Gopal. *The Limits of Lockean Rights in Property*. Oxford: Oxford University Press, 1995.

Starr, Paul. *The Creation of the Media: Political Origins of Modern Communications*. New York: Basic Books, 2005.

Stasavage, David. *The Decline and Rise of Democracy: A Global History from Antiquity to Today*. Princeton: Princeton University Press, 2020.

Sternberg, Robert J., and Scott Barry Kaufman, eds. *The Cambridge Handbook of Intelligence*. Cambridge: Cambridge University Press, 2011.

Stewart, Rory. "Lord of Misrule: Review of Tom Bower, Boris Johnson: *The Gambler*, W. H. Allen." *Times Literary Supplement*, November 6, 2020. https://go.gale.com/ps/i.do?id= GALE%7CA646304358&sid=googleScholar&v=2.1&it=r&linkaccess=abs&issn=030766IX& p=LitRC&sw=w&userGroupName=mlin_oweb&isGeoAuthType=true.

Strawson, Galen, Peter Carruthers, Frank Jackson, William G. Lycan, Colin McGinn, David Papineau, Georges Rey, J. J. C. Smart, and et al. *Consciousness and Its Place in Nature: Does Physicalism Entail Panpsychism?* Edited by Anthony Freeman. Exeter: Imprint Academic, 2006.

Streiffer, Robert. "At the Edge of Humanity: Human Stem Cells, Chimeras, and Moral Status." *Kennedy Institute of Ethics Journal* 15, no. 4 (2005): 347–70.

Sunny, Dhillon. "An Optimistic View of Deepfakes." *Tech Crunch*, July 4, 2019. https:// techcrunch.com/2019/07/04/an-optimistic-view-of-deepfakes/.

Sunstein, Cass R. *The Ethics of Influence: Government in the Age of Behavioral Science*. New York: Cambridge University Press, 2016.

Susskind, Daniel. *A World without Work: Technology, Automation, and How We Should Respond*. New York: Metropolitan Books, 2020.

Susskind, Jamie. *The Digital Republic: On Freedom and Democracy in the 21st Century*. New York: Pegasus, 2022.

    Future Politics: Living Together in a World Transformed by Tech. Oxford: Oxford University Press, 2018.

Taplin, Jonathan. *Move Fast and Break Things: How Facebook, Google, and Amazon Cornered Culture and Undermined Democracy*. New York: Back Bay Books, 2018.

Taulli, Tom. *Artificial Intelligence Basics: A Non-Technical Introduction.* New York: Apress, 2019.

Tegmark, Max. *Life 3.0: Being Human in the Age of Artificial Intelligence.* New York: Knopf, 2017.

Thaler, Richard H., and Cass R. Sunstein. *Nudge: Improving Decisions About Health, Wealth, and Happiness.* New York: Penguin, 2009.

Theunissen, L. Nandi. *The Value of Humanity.* Oxford: Oxford University Press, 2020.

Thompson, David L. *Daniel Dennett.* New York: Continuum, 2009.

Thomson, Judith Jarvis. "The Right to Privacy." *Philosophy & Public Affairs* 4, no. 4 (1975): 295–314.

Thorley, John. *Athenian Democracy.* New York: Routledge, 2004.

Thorp, Teresa M. *Climate Justice: A Voice for the Future.* Houndmills: Palgrave Macmillan, 2014.

Tönsing, Detlev L. "Homo Faber or Homo Credente? What Defines Humans, and What Could Homo Naledi Contribute to This Debate?" *HTS Teologiese Studies/Theological Studies* 73, no. 3 (2017): 1–4.

Toyama, Kentaro. "Technology as Amplifier in International Development." i conference 2011, February 2011. www.kentarotoyama.org/papers/Toyama%202011%20iConference%20-%20Technology%20as%20Amplifier.pdf.

Trout, J. D. *The Empathy Gap: Building Bridges to the Good Life and the Good Society.* New York: Viking Adult, 2009.

"Trump's False or Misleading Claims Total 30,573 Over 4 Years." *Washington Post*, January 24, 2021. www.washingtonpost.com/politics/2021/01/24/trumps-false-or-misleading-claims-total-30573-over-four-years/.

Tuck, Richard. *The Rights of War and Peace: Political Thought and the International Order from Grotius to Kant.* Oxford: Oxford University Press, 1999.

Turing, Alan. "Computing Machinery and Intelligence." *Mind* 59, no. 236 (1950): 433–60.

Turkle, Sherry. *Alone Together: Why We Expect More from Technology and Less from Each Other.* New York: Basic Books, 2017.

 Reclaiming Conversation: The Power of Talk in a Digital Age. New York: Penguin, 2016.

Tye, Michael. *Tense Bees and Shell-Shocked Crabs: Are Animals Conscious?* New York: Oxford University Press, 2016.

UNESCO. "World Trends in Freedom of Expression and Media Development: Global Report 2017/2018." UNESCO and University of Oxford, 2018.

Vaidhyanathan, Siva. *The Googlization of Everything*: Berkeley: University of California Press, 2012.

Vallor, Shannon. *Technology and the Virtues: A Philosophical Guide to a Future Worth Wanting.* New York: Oxford University Press, 2016.

Van Gulick, Robert. "Consciousness." In *Stanford Encyclopedia of Philosophy*, edited by Edward N. Zalta, 2014. https://plato.stanford.edu/entries/consciousness.

Vasak, Karel. "Human Rights - A Thirty-Year Struggle: The Sustained Efforts to Give Force of Law to the Universal Declaration of Human Rights." *UNESCO Courier* 30, no. 11 (1977): 29–30

Vedaschi, Arianna. "Globalization of Human Rights and Mutual Influence between Courts: The Innovative Reverse Path of the Right to the Truth." In *The Culture of Judicial Independence: Rule of Law and World Peace*, edited by Shimon Shetreet, 107–33. Leiden: Martinus Nijhoff, 2014.

Véliz, Carissa. *Privacy Is Power: Why and How You Should Take Back Control of Your Data.* London: Bantam, 2021.

Verbeek, Peter-Paul. *Moralizing Technology: Understanding and Designing the Morality of Things.* Chicago: University of Chicago Press, 2011.

Vleet, Jacob E. Van, and Jacob Marques Rollison. *Jacques Ellul: A Companion to His Major Works.* Eugene: Cascade Books, 2020.

Vredenburgh, Kate. "The Right to Explanation." *Journal of Political Philosophy* 30, no. 2 (2022): 209–29.

Wagar, W. Warren. *H. G. Wells and the World State.* New Haven: Yale University Press, 1961.

Wajcman, Judy. *Feminism Confronts Technology.* University Park: Penn State University Press, 1991.

Waldron, Jeremy. "Disagreements about Justice." *Pacific Philosophical Quarterly* 75, no. 3–4 (1994): 372–87.

  Law and Disagreement. Oxford: Oxford University Press, 1999.

  The Right to Private Property. Oxford: Clarendon, 1988.

Wall, Steven. "Is Public Justification Self-Defeating?" *American Philosophical Quarterly* 39, no. 4 (2002): 385–94.

Wallace, David Foster. "Consider the Lobster." In *Consider the Lobster and Other Essays*, 235–54. Boston: Back Bay Books, 2007.

  This Is Water: Some Thoughts, Delivered on a Significant Occasion, about Living a Compassionate Life. New York: Little, Brown and Company, 2009.

Wallach, Wendell, and Colin Allen. *Moral Machines: Teaching Robots Right from Wrong.* Oxford: Oxford University Press, 2010.

Walton, Kendell. "Transparent Pictures: On the Nature of Photographic Realism." *Nous* 18, no. 1 (1984): 67–72.

Waltz, Kenneth. *Theory of International Politics.* New York: McGraw-Hill, 1979.

Warren, Samuel, and Louis Brandeis. "The Right to Privacy." *Harvard Law Review* 4, no. 5 (1890): 193–220.

Watkin, Christopher. *Michel Foucault.* Phillipsburg, NJ: P & R Publishing, 2018.

Watson, Lani. "Systematic Epistemic Rights Violations in the Media: A Brexit Case Study." *Social Epistemology* 82, no. 2 (2018): 88–102.

Weale, Albert. *The Will of the People: A Modern Myth.* Cambridge: Polity, 2018.

Webb, Amy. *The Big Nine: How the Tech Titans and Their Thinking Machines Could Warp Humanity.* New York: PublicAffairs, 2020.

Webb, Maureen. *Coding Democracy: How Hackers Are Disrupting Power, Surveillance, and Authoritarianism.* Cambridge, MA: MIT Press, 2020.

Weber, Max. *Economy and Society.* Translated by Keith Tribe. Cambridge, MA: Harvard University Press, 2019.

Weil, Simone. *Pensées sans ordre concernant l'amour de Dieu.* Paris: Éditions Gallimard, 1962.

Weizenbaum, Joseph. *Computer Power and Human Reason: From Judgment to Calculation.* San Francisco: W. H. Freeman & Co, 1976.

Wells, H. G. *'42 to'44: A Contemporary Memoir upon Human Behaviour during the Crisis of the World Revolution.* London: Secker&Warburg, 1944.

  The Common Sense of War and Peace. London: Penguin, 1940.

  Mind at the End of Its Tether. London: Heinemann, 1945.

  The New World Order: Whether It Is Attainable, How It Can Be Attained, and What Sort of World a World at Peace Will Have to Be. London: Secker&Warburg, 1940.

  The Rights of Man. New York: Vintage, 2017.

  The Rights of Man: An Essay in Collective Definition. Brighton: Poynings, 1943.

  The Rights of Man, or What Are We Fighting For? London: Penguin, 1940.

The War in the Air. London: Penguin, 2007.

World Brain. Redditch: Read Books, 2016.

Wenar, Leif. "Epistemic Rights and Legal Rights." *Analysis* 63, no. 2 (2003): 142–46.

"Political Liberalism: An Internal Critique." *Ethics* 106, no. 1 (1995): 32–62.

"Rights." In *Stanford Encyclopedia of Philosophy*, edited by Edward N. Zalta, 2015. https://plato. stanford.edu/archives/fall2015/entries/rights/.

West, Darrell M. *The Future of Work: Robots, AI, and Automation*. Washington, DC: Brookings, 2019.

Westerlund, Mika. "The Emergence of Deepfake Technology: A Review." *Technology Innovation Management Review* 9, no. 11 (2019): 39–52.

White Jr., Lynn. *Medieval Technology and Social Change*. Oxford: Oxford University Press, 1966.

White, Nicholas P. *Plato on Knowledge and Reality*. Indianapolis: Hackett, 1976.

Wiener, Norbert. *Cybernetics or Control and Communication in the Animal and the Machine*. Cambridge, MA: MIT Press, 2019.

God & Golem, Inc.; A Comment on Certain Points Where Cybernetics Impinges on Religion. Cambridge, MA: MIT Press, 1964.

The Human Use of Human Beings: Cybernetics and Society. London: Free Association Books, 1989.

Norbert Wiener—A Life in Cybernetics. Edited by Ronald R. Kline. Cambridge, MA: MIT Press, 2018.

"A Scientist Rebels." *Bulletin of the Atomic Scientists* 3, no. 1 (1947): 31.

Wiggershaus, Rolf. *The Frankfurt School: Its History, Theories, and Political Significance*. Translated by Michael Robertson. Cambridge, MA: MIT Press, 1995.

Wiggins, David. "Claims of Need." In *Needs, Values, Truth*, 1–57. Oxford: Oxford University Press, 1987.

Williams, Bernard. "Must a Concern for the Environment Be Centred on Human Beings?" In *Making Sense of Humanity and Other Philosophical Papers*, 233–40. Cambridge, MA: Cambridge University Press, 1995.

Truth and Truthfulness: An Essay in Genealogy. Princeton: Princeton University Press, 2004.

Winner, Langdon. *Autonomous Technology: Technics-out-of-Control as a Theme in Political Thought*. Cambridge, MA: MIT Press, 1977.

"Do Artifacts Have Politics?" *Daedalus* 109, no. 1 (1980): 121–36.

The Whale and the Reactor: A Search for Limits in an Age of High Technology. Chicago: University of Chicago Press, 1986.

Wolf, Susan. *Meaning in Life and Why It Matters*. Princeton: Princeton University Press, 2012.

Wolff, Jonathan. *Why Read Marx Today?* Oxford: Oxford University Press, 2002.

Wood, Allen W. *Kant's Ethical Thought*. New York: Cambridge University Press, 1999.

Woolgar, Steve, and Geoff Cooper. "Do Artefacts Have Ambivalence? Moses' Bridges, Winner's Bridges and Other Urban Legends in S&TS." *Social Studies of Science* 29, no. 3 (1999): 433–49.

Wrangham, Richard W., and Dale Peterson. *Demonic Males: Apes and the Origins of Human Violence*. New York: Houghton Mifflin, 1996.

Wrone, David R. *The Zapruder Film: Reframing JFK's Assassination*. Lawrence: University Press of Kansas, 2003.

Wu, Tim. *The Attention Merchants: The Epic Scramble to Get inside Our Heads*. New York: Vintage, 2017.

Wuthnow, Robert. *The Left Behind: Decline and Rage in Small-Town America.* Princeton: Princeton University Press, 2019.

Young, James Sterling. *The Washington Community 1800–1828.* New York: Columbia University Press, 1966.

Young, Julian. *Heidegger's Later Philosophy.* Cambridge: Cambridge University Press, 2001.

Zimmerman, Michael E. *Heidegger's Confrontation with Modernity: Technology, Politics, and Art.* Bloomington: Indiana University Press, 1990.

Zimmerman, Michael J. *The Nature of Intrinsic Value.* Lanham: Rowman & Littlefield, 2001.

Zimmermann, Annette, and Chad Lee-Stronach. "Proceed with Caution." *Canadian Journal of Philosophy Canadian Journal of Philosophy* 52, no. 1 (2022): 6–25.

Zinn, Howard. *A People's History of the United States.* New York: Harper, 2015.

Zuboff, Shoshana. *The Age of Surveillance Capitalism: The Fight for a Human Future at the New Frontier of Power.* New York: PublicAffairs, 2019.

Zuckerman, Ethan. "The Case of Digital Public Infrastructure." Knight First Amendment Institute at Columbia University, January 17, 2020. https://knightcolumbia.org/content/the-case-for-digital-public-infrastructure.

    "What Is Digital Public Infrastructure?" Center for Journalism & Liberty, November 17, 2020. www.journalismliberty.org/publications/what-is-digital-public-infrastructure.

Index

.

For EU product safety concerns, contact us at Calle de José Abascal, 56–1°,
28003 Madrid, Spain or eugpsr@cambridge.org.

www.ingramcontent.com/pod-product-compliance
Ingram Content Group UK Ltd.
Pitfield, Milton Keynes, MK11 3LW, UK
UKHW020359140625
459647UK00020B/2562